尼山丛书

向世界讲好中国故事

第二届、第三届儒家经典跨语言诵读大会优秀作品集

国承彦◎主编

CUCP 中国传媒大學出版社
·北 京·

图书在版编目（CIP）数据

向世界讲好中国故事：第二届、第三届儒家经典跨语言诵读大会优秀作品集 / 国承彦主编.
-- 北京：中国传媒大学出版社，2025.7

ISBN 978-7-5657-3914-9

Ⅰ. B222-49

中国国家版本馆CIP数据核字第20258XN988号

向世界讲好中国故事

——第二届、第三届儒家经典跨语言诵读大会优秀作品集

XIANG SHIJIE JIANGHAO ZHONGGUO GUSHI

—— DI-ER JIE、DI-SAN JIE RUJIA JINGDIAN KUAYUYAN SONGDU DAHUI YOUXIU ZUOPINJI

主　　编　国承彦
策划编辑　赵　欣
责任编辑　张　嵘
责任印制　秦　英
封面设计　清美百川

出版发行　中国传媒大学出版社
社　　址　北京市朝阳区定福庄东街1号　　**邮　　编**　100024
电　　话　86-10-65450528　65450532　　**传　　真**　65779405
网　　址　http://cucp.cuc.edu.cn
经　　销　全国新华书店

印　　刷　唐山玺诚印务有限公司
开　　本　889mm × 1194mm　1/16
印　　张　黑白 22.5　彩插 0.25
字　　数　567千字
版　　次　2025年7月第1版
印　　次　2025年7月第1次印刷

书　　号　ISBN 978-7-5657-3914-9　　**定　　价**　98.00元

本社法律顾问：北京嘉润律师事务所　郭建平

《向世界讲好中国故事》编委会

第二届儒家经典跨语言诵读大会年度盛典精彩瞬间

▲开场舞蹈《孔子》

▲歌曲《幽兰操》

▲中外友人演绎《礼之本》

▲歌舞《让世界充满爱》

▲情景演绎《朋自远方》

▲美籍汉学家、山东大学儒学高等研究院副教授孟巍隆阐释《和之美》

▲盛典现场

第三届儒家经典跨语言诵读大会年度盛典精彩瞬间

▲开场节目《杏坛之上》

▲尼山世界儒学中心孔子研究院儒家文化传播体验中心首席讲解员、副研究馆员唐亚伟讲述《孔子家语——家风继世长》

▲情景诵读《跨越时空的对话》

▲融合节目《和鸣世界》

▲融合节目《家和美韵》

▲歌舞《Hello Kongzi》

▲盛典现场

序 言

在浩瀚的人类文明星空中，每一颗文明的星辰都以其独特的光芒点缀着夜空，交相辉映，共同绘制出一幅绚丽多彩的世界文明画卷。儒家经典，作为中华文明宝库中熠熠生辉的瑰宝，历经千年岁月的洗礼，依然以其深邃的智慧和博大的情怀，跨越时空的界限，焕发出永恒的魅力。

儒家经典所蕴含的“仁爱”“礼义”“和合”“大同”等核心理念，在不同的语言环境中得到了新的解读与阐释。这不仅丰富了儒家思想的内涵，更推动了全球文化的多样性与包容性发展。

儒家经典跨语言诵读大会面向全球中华文化爱好者，以诵读、写作等丰富多彩的形式，搭建起一座跨越语言与文化的桥梁。大会汇聚了来自世界各地的参与者，他们用各自的母语诵读儒家经典，用双语书写文化交流的华美乐章，让儒家的智慧在英语的流畅中流淌，在法语的浪漫中陶醉，在西班牙语的热情中燃烧，在德语的严谨中沉淀……这不仅是一场语言的盛宴，也是文化多样性的一次精彩演绎与呈现。每一种语言，都承载着其独特的文化背景与思维方式。它们宛如一把把神奇的钥匙，为我们打开了通往不同文明世界的大门，让我们得以领略儒家经典在不同语言与文化背景下的独特魅力。

尼山世界儒学中心、中国孔子基金会肩负着传承弘扬中华优秀传统文化、深化世界文明交流互鉴的使命，致力于通过多种语言和广泛渠道，向世界讲好中国故事，传播中国声音，以多元化的形式展现一个真实、立体、全面的中国形象。儒家经典跨语言诵读大会正是这一使命的生动实践与具体体现。

自 2021 年创办以来，儒家经典跨语言诵读大会已连续成功举办三届，累计吸引了来自全球 72 个国家和地区的近 20 万名中国文化爱好者热情参与，活动专题访问量突破 1 亿人次，海内外 100 余家媒体竞相报道，共同搭建起了一个多语种、跨文化、高水平的交流平台。这一盛会不仅促进了中外人文交流互鉴，更极大地提升了中华文化的传播力与影响力，成为国际交流传播领域的一张亮丽名片。

《向世界讲好中国故事》一书，汇集了第二届、第三届儒家经典跨语言诵读大会的获奖佳作，这些作品是文化交流的硕果，是心灵对话的印记，更是儒家文化在全球范围内的共鸣与回响。它们以文字和影像为载体，生动记录了不同文化背景下的人们对儒家经典的共同热爱与传承，展现了文化交流的无限魅力，为我们提供了宝贵的精神滋养。

让我们以儒家经典跨语言诵读大会为桥梁，持续推动文化多样性的发展与繁荣，让不同文化背景下的智慧与思想在这里交汇碰撞，共同绘制人类文明的新画卷。愿这些智慧的火花，如同繁星点点，照亮人类前行的道路，引领我们共同迈向更加和谐、包容、繁荣的未来。

本书文字内容在出版过程中进行了必要的编辑加工与内容优化，包括但不限于逻辑梳理、语句润色、专业术语校准及内容结构调整等，因此与配套视频略有出入，特此说明。

编　者

Preface

In the vast starry sky of human civilization, each cultural star adorns the night with its unique radiance, shining together to create a splendid and vibrant tapestry of world civilizations. The Confucian classics, as dazzling treasures within the treasury of Chinese civilization, have endured the trials of millennia. Yet, with their profound wisdom and boundless compassion, they transcend the boundaries of time and space, radiating an eternal charm.

The core principles embodied in the Confucian classics—such as “benevolence”, “propriety and righteousness”, “harmony and unity”, and “great unity”—have been endowed with new interpretations and meanings in different linguistic contexts. This not only enriches the connotation of Confucian thought but also fosters the diversity and inclusiveness of global culture.

The Cross-Lingual Chanting Assembly of Confucian Classics is a platform for global enthusiasts of Chinese culture, bridging languages and civilizations through diverse activities such as recitation and writing. This event brings together participants from around the world, who recite Confucian classics in their native tongues and compose bilingual masterpieces of cultural exchange. As Confucian wisdom flows eloquently in English, enchants romantically in French, burns passionately in Spanish, and settles with precision in German... this is not merely a feast of languages but also a splendid showcase of cultural diversity. Each language carries its unique cultural heritage and way of thinking, acting like a magical key that unlocks doors to different civilizations. Through them, we gain a profound appreciation for the distinctive charm of Confucian classics across various linguistic and cultural landscapes.

The Nishan World Center for Confucian Studies and the China Confucius Foundation, bearing the mission to inherit and promote China’s outstanding traditional culture while deepening mutual learning and cultural exchanges among world civilizations, are committed to narrating China’s stories and amplifying China’s voice globally. Through multilingual approaches and diverse channels, they present a truthful, multidimensional and comprehensive image of China. The Cross-Lingual Chanting Assembly of Confucian Classics stands as a vivid practice and concrete embodiment of this very mission.

Since its inception in 2021, the Cross-Lingual Chanting Assembly of Confucian Classics has been successfully held for three consecutive years, attracting nearly 200,000 enthusiastic participants from 72 countries and regions worldwide. The event’s dedicated webpage has garnered over 100 million visits, while more than 100 domestic and international media outlets have covered it extensively. Together, these efforts have established a multilingual, cross-cultural and high-level platform for exchange. This grand event has not only facilitated mutual learning and cultural exchanges between China and other countries but has also significantly enhanced the global reach and influence of Chinese culture. It has become a distinguished hallmark in the field of international communication and cultural exchange.

Telling China's Stories to the World is a collection of award-winning works from the second and third Cross-Lingual Chanting Assembly of Confucian Classics. These pieces represent the fruitful achievements of cultural exchange, the imprints of heartfelt dialogues, and the global resonance of Confucian culture. Through the mediums of text and imagery, they vividly document people from diverse cultural backgrounds sharing a common passion for and commitment to Confucian classics. These works showcase the boundless charm of cultural exchange while providing us with invaluable spiritual nourishment.

Let us take the Cross-Lingual Chanting Assembly of Confucian Classics as a bridge to continuously promote the development and prosperity of cultural diversity, and let the wisdom and thoughts from different cultural backgrounds converge and spark here, working together to paint a new panorama of human civilization. May these sparks of wisdom, like twinkling stars, illuminate the path forward for humanity, guiding us toward a more harmonious, inclusive and prosperous future.

The text of this book has undergone necessary editing and content optimization during the publishing process, including but not limited to logical organization, language refinement, terminology calibration, and content structure adjustment. Therefore, it may differ slightly from the accompanying video, and this is hereby noted.

目录

上编　第二届儒家经典跨语言诵读大会优秀作品集

中英篇

中韩篇

中俄篇

中法篇

中德篇

中日篇

中葡篇

中西篇

下编　第三届儒家经典跨语言诵读大会优秀作品集

中英篇

中韩篇

中俄篇

中法篇

中德篇

中日篇

中葡篇

中西篇

中阿篇

中意篇

中越篇

上编

第二届儒家经典跨语言诵读大会优秀作品集

中 英 篇

《诗经·关雎》诵读

《关雎》，收录在《国风·周南》，是《诗经》第一篇。人们通常认为这是一首描写男女恋爱的情诗。此诗首章根据关雎鸟相向合鸣、相依相恋的场景，兴起淑女配君子的联想。

关关雎鸠，在河之洲。
窈窕淑女，君子好逑。
参差荇菜，左右流之。
窈窕淑女，寤寐求之。
求之不得，寤寐思服。
悠哉悠哉，辗转反侧。
参差荇菜，左右采之。
窈窕淑女，琴瑟友之。
参差荇菜，左右芼之。
窈窕淑女，钟鼓乐之。

By riverside are cooing
A pair of turtledoves;
A good young man is wooing
A fair maiden he loves.
Water flows left and right
Of cresses here and there;
The youth yearns day and night
For the good maiden fair.
His yearning grows so strong,
He cannot fall asleep,
He tosses all night long,
So deep in love, so deep!
Now gather left and right

The cresses sweet and tender!
O lute, play music bright
For the bride sweet and slender!
Feast friends at left and right
With cresses cooked tender!
O bells and drums, delight
The bride so fair and slender!
(Translator: Xu Yuanchong)

作品编号：4373
姓　　名：路爱（Almoalem Loai Ammar）
　　　　　康晓微（Krainova Ekaterina）
国　　籍：也门、俄罗斯
组　　别：国际组
单位名称：山东理工大学国际教育学院

《论语》选句诵读

《论语》博大精深，我们一直在不断学习，多次研读后感受不一，不禁心生感叹和崇拜之情。

子　曰："学而时习之，不亦说乎？有朋自远方来，不亦乐乎？人不知而不愠，不亦君子乎？"

The Master (Confucius) said, "Is it not pleasant to acquire knowledge and be able to constantly apply it? Is it not delightful to receive friends coming from afar? A man who feels no resentment at being cold-shouldered by others, is he not a gentleman (man of perfect virtue)?"

子　曰："巧言令色，鲜矣仁！"

The Master said, "There is little benevolence behind a glib tongue and fine features."

曾子曰："吾日三省吾身：为人谋而不忠乎？与朋友交而不信乎？传不习乎？"

The disciple Zengzi said, "Every day I examine myself repeatedly: Have I been insincere in my dealing with others? Have I been untrustworthy in my interactions with my friends? Have I failed to put into practice what I have learnt?"

子　曰："不患人之不己知，患不知人也。"

The Master said, "It doesn't bother me that men do not know me; what bothers me is my not knowing them."

子　曰："《诗》三百，一言以蔽之，曰：'思无邪'。"

Der Meister sprach: „Das Buch der Lieder enthält dreihundert Stücke. Will mn sie in einem einzigen Satz zusammenfassen, so kann man sagen: ‚Der Gedanke ist nichts Böses.'"

子　曰："吾十有五而志于学，三十而立，四十而不惑，五十而知天命，六十而耳顺，七十而从心所欲，不逾矩。"

Der Meister sprach: „Mit fünfzehn war mein ganzes Bestreben auf das Lernen gerichtet. Mit dreissig verstand ich die Riten, weshalb ich selbstständig wurde. Mit vierzig beherrschte ich verschiedene Wissengebiete, deshalb hatte ich keine Zweifel mehr. Mit fünfzig kannte ich die Vorsehung der Himmels. Mit sechzig hatte ich ein so feines Gehöre, dass ich die Wahrheit aus allem heraushören konnte. Mit siebzig konnte ichden Wünschen meines Herzens folgen, ohne das rechte Mass yu überschreiten."

有子曰：“其为人也孝弟，而好犯上者，鲜矣；不好犯上，而好作乱者，未之有也。君子务本，本立而道生。孝弟也者，其为仁之本与！”

The disciple of Confucius Youzi said, “Few men harboring filial and fraternal reverence are also fond of offending their superiors. Moreover, there has never been a man who refused to offend his superiors and at the same time was fond of stirring up trouble. The gentleman devotes himself to cultivating the Basic; once that is established, the True Way follows. Filial and fraternal reverence—is this not the root of benevolence?”

子　曰：“视其所以，观其所由，察其所安。人焉廋哉？人焉廋哉？”

Der Meister sprach: „Überprüfer, mit wem er sich einlässt, beobachte, auf welche Weise er vorgeht, um seine Ziele zu erreichen. Erkenne, worin seine Seele Ruhe findet. Wie kann ein Mensch da noch sein Inneres verbergen? Wie kann ein Mensch da noch sein Inneres verbergen?“

子　曰：“学而不思则罔，思而不学则殆。”

Der Meister sprach: „Lernen ohne zu denken,stiftet Verwirrung; aber Denken ohne zu lernen wird arger Zweifel hervorrufen.“

子　曰：“里仁为美。择不处仁，焉得知？”

The Master said, “It is benevolence which makes a neighborhood a fine one. If a man chooses not to live in such a neighborhood, how can he be accounted wise?”

子　曰：“不仁者不可以久处约，不可以长处乐。仁者安仁，知者利仁。”

Der Meister sprach: „Wer keine Menschlichkeit innehat, kann eine Notlage nicht lange ertragen und wird auch nicht lange in Freude leben. Wer die Menschlichkeit innehat, findet darin innere Ruhe; der Weise zieht daraus Gewinn.“

子　曰：“唯仁者能好人，能恶人。”

The Master said, “Only the man of benevolence knows whom to love and whom to hate.”

子　曰：“苟志于仁矣，无恶也。”

Der Meister sprach: „Zoehlt man den Wille auf die Menschlichkeit, gibt es nichts Böses.“

子　曰：“人之过也，各于其党。观过，斯知仁矣。”

The Master said, “A man’s faults stem from his particular social situation. By observing his faults we can tell his social position.”

子　曰：“朝闻道，夕死可矣。”

Der Meister sprach: „Hätte ich morgens den rechten Weg erfahren, könnte ich abends getrost sterben.“

子　曰：“君子之于天下也，无适也，无莫也，义之与比。”

The Master said, “In his dealings with the world the gentleman has no preferences and no aversions; he simply adopts the right course of action in the circumstances.”

子　曰：“君子怀德，小人怀土；君子怀刑，小人怀惠。”

Der Meister sprach: „Der Ehrbare sehnt sich nach Tugend, der Gemeine sehnt sich nach der Heinaterde; der Ehrbare denkt an das Gesetz, der Gemeine denkt an die Vorteil.“

子　曰：“放于利而行，多怨。”

The Master said, “Acting solely in one’s own interest always incurs ill will.”

子　曰：“不患无位，患所以立；不患莫己知，求为可知也。”

Der Meister sprach: „Es sollte einen nicht bekümmern, wenn man kein Amt innehat; es sollte einen aber bekümmern, wenn man die notwendigen Fähigkeiten dazu nicht hat. Es sollte einen nicht bekümmern, wenn man nicht von anderen anerkannt wird, trachtet man nur danach, dass seine Fähigkeiten wert sind, anerkannt zu werden.“

子　曰：“君子喻于义，小人喻于利。”

The Master said, “The gentleman fixes his attention on righteousness, the petty man fixes his on gain.”

子　曰：“见贤思齐焉，见不贤而内自省也。”

Der Meister sprach: „Wenn man einen Würdigen sieht, so trachte man danach, ihm gleich yu werden. Wenn man einen Unwürdigen sieht, so prüfe man sein eigenes Inneres.“

梁启超曾说：“少年智则国智，少年富则国富，少年强则国强。”看到我们的传统文化被这么多的外国人所喜欢，作为青年一代，我们必将担负国家重任，践行文化自信，向世界讲好中国故事。

作品编号：4092

姓　　名：Sibanda Mtabisi、Saffirna Suppiah、Meraiel Andon、Moses Giwa、陈静、杨一琦、高畅、赵晓宇、陶墨寒

国　　籍：津巴布韦、马来西亚、密克罗尼西亚、中国

组　　别：国际组

单位名称：山东建筑大学

《论语·为政》品读

该作品来自聊城大学的曼尼，他是津巴布韦的学生。作品主要体现了该生品读《论语》时在学习、做人、做事方面的感悟。其中一段着重强调了学习的重要性。他对此不但理解深刻，而且也将其应用到了自己的汉语学习中，真正做到了“知行合一”。

大家好！我叫曼尼，来自津巴布韦。我是聊城大学国际教育交流学院一名大四的学生，专业是国际经济与贸易。在这几年的学习中，我逐渐认识到，中华文化博大精深、令人折服，儒家文化更是影响深远。你听：

子　曰：“学而时习之，不亦说乎？有朋自远方来，不亦乐乎？人不知而不愠，不亦君子乎？”

The Master said, “Is it not pleasant to learn with a constant perseverance and application? Is it not delightful to have friends coming from distant quarters? Is he not a man of complete virtue, who feels no discomposure though men may take no note of him?”

曾子曰：“吾日三省吾身，为人谋而不忠乎？与朋友交而不信乎？传不习乎？”

The philosopher Tsang said, “I daily examine myself on three points: whether, in transacting business for others, I may have been not faithful; whether, in intercourse with friends, I may have been not sincere; whether I may have not mastered and practised the instructions of my teacher.”

子　曰：“学而不思则罔，思而不学则殆。”

The Master said, “Learning without thought is labour lost; thought without learning is perilous.”

其中，我最喜欢的一句话是“学而不思则罔，思而不学则殆”。它告诉我们，在学习过程中要学会思考，只有这样才不会望文生义，迷惑而无所得；同时，除了学会思考，还要有恒心和毅力，努力地坚持学习，否则就会变成胡思乱想，没有收获。我把这一思想用到了学习汉语上。果然，我学习汉语越来越顺利，水平也有了明显提高。现在不仅能流利地用汉语和中国人对话，而且还能说好多像“八百标兵奔北坡，炮兵并排北边跑”这样的绕口令呢。

中国是我喜爱的国家，我喜欢中国的语言和文化。我要珍惜在这里学习的机会，好好学习中国的语言和文化，并努力把中国文化、中国故事介绍给我的国家，介绍给更多的外国人，努力当好中国文化的传播使者，为中非友谊作出力所能及的贡献。

谢谢大家！

作品编号：4039

姓　　名：曼尼（Fortune Tafadzwa Manyewe）

国　　籍：津巴布韦

组　　别：国际组

单位名称：聊城大学

《大学》智慧点亮人生明灯

《大学》原是《小戴礼记》(《礼记》)第四十二篇，相传为春秋战国时期曾子（曾参）所作，是中国古代讨论教育理论的一部重要著作。文中“大学之道，在明明德，在亲民，在止于至善”是人们在学习中不断追求的目标，“修身、齐家、治国、平天下”的思想鼓舞了千百年来的中国读书人，督促他们反躬自省。如今，《大学》中所阐述的思想超越了国界，开始在国际化教育舞台显示其影响力，成为各国青年治学过程中的指路明灯。

As a contemporary college student, what goal should we pursue? And what are the principles of higher education? Maybe we can get some inspirations from the Confucian classics—*The Great Learning*.

主题一：大学之道止于至善

Max: 大家看，我这两个字写得怎么样？

其他学生：有进步，还可以。

Max: 大学——大学之道，在明明德，在亲民，在止于至善。

Prince: “道”在这里指的是宗旨对吗？大学的宗旨在于弘扬光明正大的品德，使人弃旧图新，达到最完善的境界。

Max: 对！“止于至善”就是达到最完美的境界。“知止而后有定，定而后能静，静而后能安，安而后能虑，虑而后能得。”

Prince: 喔，那这段文字如何理解呢？

Max: 这个……你们说呢？

董昆玉：那我用英语来解释吧。It means you need to know your goal first if you want to become a knowledgeable person. Only after knowing the goal of perfection where you should dwell, can you have a definite purpose in life. After that, you can achieve calmness of mind, and then have peaceful repose. With the peaceful repose, you will begin to think. After which, you will finally achieve knowledge.

黄开贤：Definitely! *The Great Learning* also tells us that there are a foundation and a superstructure in the constitution of things, as well as a beginning and an end in the course of events. Therefore, to know the proper sequence or relative order of things is the beginning of wisdom.

Prince: 解读得真好！古代典籍的智慧是超越时空限制的，可以指导我们大学生如何成长为对社会有用的人才。

主题二：大学之道格物为先

王　兰：大学生应该以“止于至善”作为目标来要求自己，并将向世人弘扬美德作为自己的使命。“古之欲明明德于天下者，先治其国；欲治其国者，先齐其家；欲齐其家者，先修其身；欲修其身者，先正其心；欲正其心者，先诚其意；欲诚其意者，先致其知；致知在格物。”作为当代大学生，我们需要从与修身有关的小事开始做起。

李　同：“物格而后知至，知至而后意诚，意诚而后心正，心正而后身修，身修而后家齐，家齐而后国治，国治而后天下平。”大学生需要格物致知，为“修身、齐家、治国、平天下”的目标打好坚实的基础。

主题三：大学之道修齐治平

李　娜：医学生的格物致知来自日常救死扶伤的技能训练，但我们修身的关键在于心正，心正则不受情绪和个人经历的牵绊，具备一个好医生应该有的“仁心”。

昭　阳：面对广泛传播的新冠肺炎，我们附属医院的许多医生和护士义无反顾地奔赴前线抗击疫情，展现出他们英勇无畏的精神。

艾　木：医学生的“齐家、治国、平天下”在于做好示范榜样。作为未来的医生，我们需怀“仁心”展“妙术”，为国家贡献力量，在大灾大疫中冲锋陷阵、勇于奉献。一人怀仁心，则一国兴仁，君子有诸己而后求诸人。

所有学生：大学之道，在明明德，在亲民，在止于至善。君子之志，修身、齐家、治国、平天下！

作品编号：3211
姓　　名：董昆玉、Ahiafor Maxwell　等
国　　籍：中国、加纳　等
组　　别：国际组
单位名称：滨州医学院

“曾子避席”故事演绎

“曾子避席”是出自《孝经》的一个非常知名的故事，它主要讲的是孔子的弟子曾子在向老师孔子请教问题时，以一种谦卑、礼貌的态度求取知识。这里所提到的“避席”是一种非常礼貌的行为。当曾子听到老师要向他讲授知识时，他站起身来，走到席子外向老师请教，这是为了表示他对老师的尊重。曾子懂礼貌的故事被很多人赞扬，大家都在向他学习。“避席”也成了尊重师长、虚心求教的一种传统礼仪。

【开场】

马苏姆：我来自孟加拉国，我的名字叫马苏姆。

马　迪：我来自阿富汗，我的名字叫马迪。

李　毛：我来自津巴布韦，我的名字叫李毛。

合　诵：大家好，我们是山东工商学院的留学生。

【故事介绍】

马苏姆：你好，马迪。我听说你的汉语非常好。

马　迪：还好还好，因为我已经在中国3年了，我的专业是国际贸易，但是我很喜欢学习汉语。

马苏姆：嗯嗯，我也喜欢学习汉语。那我现在问你一个问题吧！

马　迪：没问题！

马苏姆：你知道中国古代的名人孔子吗？

马　迪：这个我知道，孔子是春秋时期的鲁国人，也就是我们目前所在的地方——山东省，山东是孔子的老家，因此山东被称为“孔孟之乡”。我还知道，孔子所代表的儒家思想提出了著名的“仁、义、礼、智、信、恕、孝、悌”等主张。

马苏姆：回答得很正确。看来你特别了解孔子。中国是礼仪之邦，并且自古就讲究孝道，所以我们今天要为大家介绍的故事是“曾子避席”。

马　迪：接下来请李毛来给我们讲解一下“曾子避席”的故事。

李　毛：“曾子避席”是出自《孝经》的一个非常知名的故事，它主要讲的是孔子的弟子曾子在向老师孔子请教问题时，以一种谦卑、礼貌的态度求取知识。另外，我主要想向大家介绍，这里所提到的“避席”是一种非常礼貌的行为，当曾子听到老师要向他讲授时，他站起身来，走到席子外向老师请教，表示他对老师的尊重。曾子懂礼貌的故事被很多人赞扬，大家都在向他学习。“避席”也成了尊重师长、虚心求教的一种传统礼仪。接下来我们一起来欣赏一下这个故事。

【经典诵读】

合　诵：仲尼居，曾子侍。

李　毛：子曰：“先王有志德要道，以顺天下，民用和睦，上下无怨。汝知之乎？”

马苏姆：曾子避席曰：“参不敏，何足以知之？”

马　迪：子曰：“夫孝，德之本也，教之所由生也。复坐，吾语汝。”

李　毛：“身体发肤，受之父母，不敢毁伤，孝之始也。立身行道，扬名于后世，以显父母，孝之终也。”

马　迪：“夫孝，始于事亲，中于事君，终于立身。”

合　诵：“《大雅》云：‘无念尔祖，聿修厥德。’”

李　毛：Propriety (礼) as mentioned in *The Analects of Confucius* has three layers of meanings: ceremony, etiquette and politeness. Since ancient times, China has been a country of etiquette.

The story I am telling is “Zengzi (曾子) Avoids the Mat”.

Among the disciples of Confucius was one named Zengzi. One day, Zengzi was attending Confucius, sitting beside him, when the latter remarked: “In former times, the emperors used actions of the highest morality and the purest ethics to govern the empire. They complied with the will of the people to make the relations between them harmonious, and there was no conflict between the ruler and his officials. Do you know the secret to this?”

Hearing this, Zengzi hastily vacated the mat he was sitting on, kneeled before Confucius, and bowed to him, saying with deep respect, “Master, I am too much of a dunce. Where can I learn such proper behavior? I beg you to enlighten me.” Confucius hastened to raise Zengzi to his feet, and the two men had a long discussion about this.

Propriety is one of the Chinese people’s fine traditional virtues. The promotion of propriety has encouraged harmony in society. By earnestly practicing it, Chinese people have displayed a splendid moral character, promoting Chinese civilization through the ages.

【古装表演】

李　毛：“非礼勿视，非礼勿听，非礼勿言，非礼勿动。”曾子，你明白这句话的意思吗？

马苏姆：老师，我不太明白，请老师讲解。

李　毛：这句话的意思是，所有的事情都要讲究礼貌，不符合礼的事情不能做。

马　迪：先生，有客人来啦。

李　毛：曾子，你先退下吧，我先接见客人。等我接见完客人你再出来。

马苏姆：好的，老师。

李　毛：请进。

马　迪：先生大安！

李　毛：请坐。

马　迪：谢谢先生。先生，我想向您讲一件事情！

马　迪：我今天出门的时候，因为走得太急，不小心撞到了一个人，但是当我想离开的时候，那个人抓着我的胳膊不让我离开，他觉得我不尊重他。后面我们就起了冲突，我的事情也被耽误了。先生，您认为这个事情是谁的问题？

李　毛：这个事情，我认为……

马　迪：我认为肯定是他不对，因为我向他道歉了，他还不让我走，而且我的事情也被耽误了，我非常生气。

李　毛：你仔细听我说，这个事情首先是你不对，是你撞了人家。在别人责怪你的时候，你不应该生气，你应该解释一下，你是因为有急事才不小心撞到别人的。

马　迪：先生，明白了。

（马苏姆坐在对面位置的席子上面）

李　毛：老师希望你在任何时候都要讲礼貌，不要像刚才那位客人一样鲁莽。古代的圣贤之主，有一种崇高而精妙之道。用它来治理天下，天下的人民都能够相亲相敬，这样的道理你知道吗？

马苏姆：老师我不够聪明，还望老师能把这个道理教给我。

李　毛：这就是孝，它是一切德行的根本，也是教化的根源。你回到原来的座位上，我告诉你。

（马苏姆礼貌坐下）

李　毛：人的身体四肢、毛发皮肤，都是父母赋予的，不敢予以损毁伤残，这是孝的开始。人在世上遵循仁义道德，有所建树，显扬名声于后世，从而使父母显赫荣耀，这是孝的终极目标。所谓孝，最初是从侍奉父母开始，然后效力于国君，最终建功立业，功成名就。

作品编号：1656
姓　　名：马苏姆、李毛、马迪
国　　籍：孟加拉国、津巴布韦、阿富汗
组　　别：国际组
单位名称：山东工商学院

诵读经典 国际学生传承中华文明

山东第一医科大学（山东省医学科学院）国际教育学院高度重视中国文化特别是儒家传统文化的传播和推广工作，组织国际学生积极学习《论语》，学习中国古代文化典籍中的智慧，让国际学生接受中华经典文明的浸润和滋养。

第一部分：经典诵读

Classic recitation

三十而立，四十而不惑，五十而知天命，六十而耳顺，七十而从心所欲，不逾矩。

At thirty I was firmly established. At forty I had no more doubts. At fifty I knew the rules of things in the universe. At sixty I could judge correctly whatever I had heard. At seventy I could follow my heart's desire without violating the regulations.

子曰：君子周而不比，小人比而不周。

The Master said, "A gentleman stresses unity, but he is free from collusion. The petty man does the reverse."

子曰：朝闻道，夕死可矣。

The Master said, "If I hear the truth in the morning, I may be willing to die in the evening."

子曰：人无远虑，必有近忧。

The Master said, "If a man does not give thought to problems which are still distant, he will be worried about them when they come nearer."

子曰：不愤不启，不悱不发。举一隅不以三隅反，则不复也。

The Master said, "Only when someone bursts with eagerness for learning do I instruct; only when someone bubbles to speak but fails to express himself do I enlighten. If I show one corner of a subject and he can't deduce the other three by himself, I do not continue the lesson."

子曰：益者三友，损者三友。友直，友谅，友多闻，益矣。

The Master said, "There are three types of friends that are profitable and three types that are harmful.Friendship with the upright, the devoted and the learned is profitable.

子曰：知之者不如好之者，好之者不如乐之者。

The Master said, "To prefer it is better than only to know it. To delight in it is better than merely to prefer it."

子曰：知者不惑，仁者不忧，勇者不惧。

The Master said, "He who is really wise can never be perplexed. He who is really virtuous cannot be unhappy. He who is really brave is never fearful."

子曰：学而时习之，不亦说乎？有朋自远方来，不亦乐乎？人不知而不愠 ，不亦君子乎？

The Master said, "To learn and at due times to review what one has learned, isn't that a pleasure? To have friends come to you from afar, isn't that delightful? To feel no discontent when others do not know you, isn't that what is expected of a gentleman?"

第二部分：朋辈辅导

Peer tutoring

男：所有的纸上谈兵者，都是学而不思造就的。

All those who are armchair strategist are created by learning but not thinking.

女：我知道学习之后，只有通过思考才能掌握其中精华。

I know that after studying, only through thinking can I grasp the essence of it.

男：还有，将多个知识点融会贯通，洞察事物的内在联系，形成自己的独到见解。

And we need to integrate multiple points of knowledge, gain insight into the intrinsic connections of things, and develop our own unique insights.

女：光学习不思考不好，光思考不学习也不行。

It is not good to learn without thinking, and it is not good to think without learning.

女：古之学者为已，今之学者为人。大山你可以说说吗？

In the old days men studied for the sake of self-improvement; nowadays men study in order to impress other people. Can you explain it to me?

男：意思是说：古代的学者学习是为了充实提高自已，现在的学者学习是为了装饰给别人看。每个人都不是生而知之的。古人说“活到老学到老”，是非常有道理的。让我们一起努力吧。

It means: Ancient scholars studied to enrich and improve themselves, but nowadays scholars study to decorate for others to see. Everyone is not born knowing, and the ancient saying "live and learn" is very reasonable. Let's work hard together.

第三部分：教学相长

Teaching and learning together

（场景一）

老　师：大家晚上好，你们知道孔子吗？他是中国伟大的教育家，他的教育思想影响了世界。我们今天一起来学一学他的经典话语。

Hi, everybody, Good evening. Do you know Confucius? He is a great educator in China whose educational thoughts have influenced the world. Let's learn his classic words today.

孔子说，人如果失去了信用或不讲信用，不知道他还可以做什么，

The Master said, a man who lacks reliability can be good for nothing.

就像大车没有车辕与轭相连接的木销子，小车没有车杠与横木相衔接的销钉。

He is just like a large carriage without the crossbar or a small carriage without the pin.

它靠什么行走呢？

How can they be made to go without them?

伊　思：不知命，无以为君子也；不知礼，无以立也；不知言，无以知人也。

刘　强：这个是什么意思呢？孔子说，不懂得天命，就不能做君子；不知道礼仪，就不能立身处世；不善于分辨别人的话语，就不能真正了解他。

What does this mean? The Master said, people who don't understand the view of heaven, can not be regarded as gentlemen; people who don't know rite; can not take their stands; people who don't understand words, can not understand others.

（场景二）

刘　静：敏而好学，不耻下问。

Sensitive and eager to learn, always ask questions.

艾泰睿：敏而好学，不耻下问。

Sensitive and eager to learn, always ask questions.

刘　静：嗯，你明白这句话的内容吗？

Yeah, do you know the meaning?

艾泰睿：老师，我不是很懂。

Please teacher, I don't understand well.

刘　静：是的，这是孔夫子非常有深意的一句话。孔夫子说，一个天资聪颖而又好学的人，不以向地位低于自己的人请教为耻。因为每一个人都可以教给你不同的东西，所以请接受向比你地位低的人请教这件事情，不必感到羞耻。这就是这句话的意思了。

Yeah, it is a very deep understanding sentence from Confucius. The Master said the person who was active and found of learning, was not ashamed to ask and learn from his inferiors. Because every person can teach you different things. Learning from your inferiors can be also accepted, no need to feel ashamed. This is the meaning.

艾泰睿：谢谢你，老师。

Thank you, teacher.

刘　静：我认为在将来，你也可以成为我的老师。

In the future, I think, you can also be my teacher.

（场景三）

齐　蕾：晚上好，尤苏。你最近学习《论语》吗？哪一句话给你的印象最深呢？

Good evening, Youssou. Have you been studying *The Analects of Confucius* recently? Which sentence impressed you rnost?

尤　苏：子曰："君子和而不同，小人同而不和。"

齐　蕾：你知道这是什么意思吗？

Do you know what it means?

尤　苏：我不知道。

I don't know.

齐　蕾：我来给你解释一下这句话的意思。孔子说，君子在人际交往中能够与他人保持一种和谐友善的关系，但在对具体问题的看法上却不必苟同于对方。小人习惯于在对问题的看法上迎合别人的心理、附和别人的言论，但在内心深处却并不抱有一种和谐友善的态度。

What this means is that, the Master said, a true gentleman is conciliatory but not blind-accommodating. A petty man is blind-accommodating, but not conciliatory.

齐　蕾：可以用中文跟着我念吗？子曰："人而不仁，如礼何？人而不仁，如乐何？"

Can you repeat it after me in Chinese? The Master said, "If a man does not have charity in his heart, what has he to do with rites? If a man does not have charity in his heart, what has he to do with music?"

全　体：学而不思则罔，思而不学则殆。敏而好学，不耻下问，是以谓之"文"也。温故而知新，可以为师矣。向孔子学习，温故而知新。

He who learns but does not think is lost. He who thinks but does not learn still remains puzzled. Be sensitive and eager to learn, always ask questions, that is why he was called the Cultured. If you can acquire new knowledge while reviewing the old, you may become a teacher of others. Learn from Confucius, acquiring new knowledge while reviewing the old.

作品编号：3998

姓　　名：伊思（Maminul Islam）　等

国　　籍：孟加拉国　等

组　　别：国际组

单位名称：山东第一医科大学（山东省医学科学院）

咏先贤之孝 启华夏新篇

“百善孝为先”，视频以《咏先贤之孝 启华夏新篇》为题，详细阐释了先贤孔子所论的“孝道”文化的深刻内涵，引导广大学子继承和弘扬优秀传统文化，把对父母之孝内化为爱国情怀，激励同学们为国家富强、民族振兴、人民幸福的伟大梦想而奋发图强，努力奋斗！

第一部分

“百善孝为先”，“孝”是中华文化与中华伦理的鲜明特点之一，是中国传统文化中出现最早的伦理观念，也是中国文化泛化的始发性观念和文化精神。“孝”的观念最早起源于殷商时期，最终形成于周代。中华民族文化之所以能够影响无数外来文化，在世界文化之林屹然耸立，其根本原因之一在于孝道文化；中华民族文化之所以经久不衰，成为延续至今的唯一的古文明，其根本原因之一也在于孝道文化。儒家“孝”之道在中华文化中占有举足轻重的地位。

“Filial piety is the first priority of all virtues.” “Filial piety” is one of the distinctive characteristics of Chinese culture and Chinese ethics. It is the earliest ethical concept in traditional Chinese culture, and also the initial concept and cultural spirit of Chinese culture generalization. The concept of “filial piety” first originated in the Yin and Shang Dynasties and finally formed in the Zhou Dynasty. One of the fundamental reasons why Chinese culture can influence numerous foreign cultures and stand tall in the forest of world cultures is the culture of filial piety. Filial piety is one of the fundamental reasons why Chinese culture is enduring and has become the only ancient civilization that has continued to this day. The Confucian way of “filial piety” plays a vital role in Chinese culture.

第二部分

鲁国权臣孟懿子曾向孔子请教孝道。孔子只回答了“无违”。不久后，孔子将这个道理讲给了樊迟。

Meng Yizi, a powerful minister of Lu, once asked Confucius for advice on filial duty. Confucius only answered, “don’t go against the rites.” Soon after, Confucius explained this truth to Fan Chi.

孔子："孟孙问孝于我，我对曰，'无违'。"
樊迟："弟子愚钝，不知其意。"
孔子："生，事之以礼；死，葬之以礼，祭之以礼。"

"生，事之以礼；死，葬之以礼，祭之以礼。"从孔子的回答，我们不难看出，作为子女，我们对于父母的孝要贯穿父母的一生。

"While the parents live, serve them according to the rites. When they die, bury them and make the offerings to them according to the rites." From Confucius' answer, we can easily see that as children, we should be filial to our parents throughout their lives.

孔子的弟子子夏也曾问过孔子什么是孝。

Zi Xia, a student of Confucius, also asked Confucius what filial piety was.

子夏："夫子，弟子薄闻，不知孝做何解。"
孔子："色难。有事，弟子服其劳；有酒食，先生馔，曾是以为孝乎？"
"事父母几谏。见志不从，又敬不违，劳而不怨。"
"《书》云：'孝乎惟孝，友于兄弟。施于有政。'是亦为政，奚其为为政？"

"事父母几谏。见志不从，又敬不违，劳而不怨。"孔子的这一理念并不是要儿女们愚孝，而是一种发自内心的敬，这才是儒家文化中孝的根源。

"When serving your parents, persuade them gently if they are wrong. When expressing your opinion and seeing your parents unwilling to listen, respect them but not offend them, be concerned about them, but not complain about them." This idea of Confucius is not to ask us to be blindly filial, but to respect from the deep heart, which is the root of filial duty in Confucian culture.

《孝经》曰："夫孝，始于事亲，中于事君，终于立身。"所谓孝，始于孝敬父母，而后服务社会，进而立身奉献。光耀父母、忠诚国家，忠孝两全才是终极大孝！

The traditional Chinese classics *Xiao Jing* says, "Great filial piety begins with serving parents, continues to develop in serving the country and fulfilling their duties, and ends with great achievements." It begins with honoring to parents, then serves society, and then stands up for dedication. Glory your parents, be loyal to your country. Loyalty to parents and the country are the ultimate filial piety!

跨越 2,000 年，中华孝道文化依旧熠熠生辉。"小孝"于家，"大孝"于国，新时代青年应当以孝为立身之基，以理想为马，以奋斗为刃，以实践为尺，以报国为志，践行为国奉献的大孝，捍卫吾辈之中华。

Over 2,000 years, Chinese filial piety culture still shines brightly. "Little filial piety" to the family, "great filial piety" to the country. Young people in the new era should take filial piety as the foundation, take ideals as the direction, take struggle as the weapon, take practice as the standard, take serving the country as the ambition, practice great filial piety of dedication to defend our prosperous China.

第三部分

青年愿以吾辈之微光，乘时代之东风，汇理想之星河，展强国之篇章，咏先贤之孝，启华夏新篇。

作品编号：4144
姓　　名：杨月莹　等
国　　籍：中国
组　　别：国内成人组
单位名称：山东农业工程学院

《论语》情景再现

《论语》集中体现了孔子的政治主张、伦理思想、道德观念及教育原则。我们从演练周礼、子贡拜师、探讨学问三个方面，重温孔子当年的讲学，弘扬国学的精神，传承孔子的思想。

场景一：演练周礼

旁　白：迎神，奏乐，拜——兴，拜——兴，拜——兴。

孔　子：今天，我们又把周礼演练了一遍，诸位觉得如何？

众弟子：学而时习之，不亦说乎？

孔　子：今天，还有许多朋友要到我们这里来，他们是从宋国、楚国、卫国来的，最远的是从秦国来的。他们带来了各国的最新消息，要和我们大家一起探讨学问，诸位欢迎吗？

众弟子：有朋自远方来，不亦乐乎？

颜　回：夫子，有一卫人求见。

场景二：子贡拜师

子　贡：卫人端木赐，字子贡，仰慕夫子之名，前来拜见。

孔　子：请坐。

子　贡：夫子，我想请教您一个问题。

孔　子：请讲。

子　贡：夫子，有没有一句话能奉行终身的呢？您若愿意教我，我愿拜您为师。

孔　子：其“恕”乎！己所不欲，勿施于人。

子　贡：夫子，请收下我吧。

孔　子：我愿收你为徒。

子　贡：弟子，拜见夫子。

场景三：探讨学问

孔　子：诸位到我这来学习，都有一个志向，那就是做一个谦谦君子。如何成为君子呢？君子，当以大道为志向，以德行为根基，以仁爱为依托，以六艺为修养。志于道，据于德，依于仁，游于艺。

颜　渊：夫子，何为仁？

孔　子：克己复礼为仁。一日克己复礼，天下归仁焉。

子　贡：如果有人能够对百姓广施恩惠，并且能救济大众，这样的人怎么样呢？可以称得上仁吗？

孔　子：这已经不仅是仁，而且是圣德了。夫仁者，己欲立而立人，己欲达而达人。

子　贡：夫子，如何提高自身仁德的修养？

孔　子：无非是两条：其一向贤者学习，其二以不贤的人为鉴。人家有贤德，我们自然该向人家学习。不贤的人，我们就要在心里反思自己，看自己的行为有没有违反贤德的地方。如果有，在行动上加以改进；如果没有，就要引以为戒、警惕自己。这不也是一种非常好的学习吗？这就叫作：见贤思齐焉，见不贤而内自省也。择其善者而从之，其不善者而改之。

子　贡：老师，可是自省是很难做到的啊！

孔　子：的确是这样。

曾　子：我是这样来自省的：吾日三省吾身：为人谋而不忠乎？与朋友交而不信乎？传不习乎？

孔　子：善哉！望诸位都能向曾子靠齐，切实做到自省，提高自身仁德，成为一名谦谦君子可指日而待矣，最终达到“知者不惑，仁者不忧，勇者不惧”的至高境界。

子　曰：学而时习之，不亦说乎？

Isn’t it a pleasure to study and practice what you have learned?

有朋自远方来，不亦乐乎？

Isn’t it also great when friends visit from distant places?

其“恕”乎！己所不欲，勿施于人。

What you do not want done to yourself, don’t to others.

志于道，据于德，依于仁，游于艺。

Aim at Tao, depend on De, rely on Ren, and delight in arts.

克己复礼为仁。一日克己复礼，天下归仁焉。

To subdue one’s self and return to propriety, is humaneness. If a man can for one day subdue himself and return to propriety, everyone in the world will return to humaneness.

夫仁者，己欲立而立人，己欲达而达人。

Now the man of humanity, wishing himself to be established, sees that others are established, and wishing himself to be successful, sees that others are successful.

见贤思齐焉，见不贤而内自省也。择其善者而从之，其不善者而改之。

When we see men of worth, we should think of equaling them; when we see worthless men, we should turn inwards and examine ourselves. I will select their good qualities and follow them, and find their bad qualities and avoid them.

曾子曰：吾日三省吾身：为人谋而不忠乎？与朋友交而不信乎？传不习乎？

I daily examine myself in three ways: In doing things for others, have I been disloyal? In my interactions with my friends, have I been untrustworthy? Have not practiced what I have learned?

子　曰：知者不惑，仁者不忧，勇者不惧。

The wise are not puzzled; the virtuous are not worried; and the brave are not afraid.

作品编号：3174

姓　　名：董凯烁　等

国　　籍：中国

组　　别：国内少年组

单位名称：山东省高密市高密四中文慧学校

《诗经·周南·卷耳》吟诵

《诗经·周南·卷耳》是一篇抒写怀人情感的诗作，写一位女子在野外采集苍耳的劳动过程中想起了她远行在外的丈夫，想象着他在外经历了各种艰难险阻。

【第一幕】

男：我要去服兵役了，你在家里要照顾好自己！

I'll go to serve in the military. Take care!

女：外边不比家里，别冻着，别饿着！

Ditto! Take care!

男：我走了，你快回家吧！

I'm going! Go back home!

女：我会等你回来的！

I'll be waiting for you to come back!

【第二幕】

采采卷耳，
So many gentle xanthium shoots for me to pick.
不盈顷筐。
But I can't fill my shallow basket.
嗟我怀人，
I'm missing my husband who is away from home.
置彼周行。
I put the basket by the roadside and look into the distance.

【第三幕】

陟彼崔嵬，我马虺隤。
The hill road is so steep and my horse is too tired to continue.
我姑酌彼金罍，
I may as well take out my cup and take a drink.
维以不永怀。

To drive away the endless pain.

【第四幕】

陟彼高冈，我马玄黄。

Finally I ascend the top of the hill, but my horse is too tired and haggard.

我姑酌彼兕觥，

I may as well take out my cup and take another drink.

维以不永伤。

To drive away the incessant depression!

【第五幕】

陟彼砠矣，

Finally I ascend the muddy hilltop,

我马瘏矣，我仆痡矣，

But my horse cannot go farther and my servant is whacked.

云何吁矣。

What makes me so grieved? What?

【第六幕】

女：云何吁矣？

What makes me so grieved?

嗟我怀人。

It is you far away at home that I'm missing.

男：嗟我怀人。

It is you far away at home that I'm missing.

作品编号：3725

姓　　名：黄智远　等

国　　籍：中国

组　　别：国内成人组

单位名称：东营职业学院

《中庸》之道

《中庸》是儒家经典著作，“四书”之一，宋元以后学校官定为教科书和科举的必读书。其中“博学之，审问之，慎思之，明辨之，笃行之”的学习过程和认识方法需要我们不断学习践行。作品选取《中庸》第二十章中的内容，通过情景演绎的方法向大家展示了践行《中庸》之道的重要性。

【场景一】

（学生苦恼于学习没有进展，求助老师）

T: So this term we will study this book. OK, time is up. Class is over. See you next time!
这个学期我们会学这本书，时间差不多了。下次见！

S: Miss Zhu, may I have a chat with you?
朱老师，我能跟你聊个天吗？

T: Sure, of course.
当然可以了。

S: Well, I have a physical burden for several days, and cannot find a best study condition. It seems to have a bottleneck period.
我这几天状态不太好，就是找不到最佳学习状态。好像到了一个瓶颈期。

T: Well, tell me more.
详细说说。

S: I mean my passion of learning is waning. Cause I spent hours learning everyday, but there isn't much to show all my efforts. And you know the efforts isn't proportional to the reward.
就是学习热情下降了。我感觉自己每天都在学。但努力……就是看不到效果。努力和回报不成正比。

T: I do have a suggestion for you from *The Doctrine of the Mean*. "There are requisite the extensive study of what is good, accurate inquiry about it, careful reflection on it, the clear discrimination of it, and the earnest practice of it."
我确实有一个建议给你，是《中庸》里的。“博学之，审问之，慎思之，明辨之，笃行之。”

S: But it, it’s exactly what I did!
但是，我就是这么做的呀。

T: Really? Let’s see what you have done.
哦？那我们来看看你是怎么做的吧。

【场景二】

（学生正在看书，遇到了问题，想用手机查资料，
却在打开查词软件的时候犹豫了，打开了某社交软件）

T: The superior man, while there is anything he has not studied, or while in what he has studied there is anything he cannot understand, will not intermit his labor.
有弗学，学之弗能弗措也。

【场景三】

（学生遇到了问题，去问了老师，结果没有弄明白）

S1：What does this mean?
这个是什么意思啊？

S2：I don’t know... Ask for the teacher?
我也不知道……问问老师吧？

S1：OK.
好。（问老师中）

S1：So what’s the answer?
老师怎么说？

S2：Actually... I didn’t figure it out.
其实……没听太懂……

T：While there is anything he has not inquired about, or anything in what he has inquired about which he does not know, he will not intermit his labor.
有弗问，问之弗知弗措也。
While there is anything which he has not reflected on, or anything in what he has reflected on which he does not apprehend, he will not intermit his labor.
有弗思，思之弗得弗措也。

【场景四】

（默剧：学生课后问同学课上的知识点，两个同学给了不同的答案。在两个同学辩论的时候，
学生放弃了分辨真假，甩手走人，留下后面正在辩论的两个同学）

T：While there is anything which he has not discriminated or his discrimination is not clear, he will not intermit his labor.
有弗辨，辨之弗明弗措也。

【场景五】

（学生本来在学习，另一个同学来找她逛街，她想了想，就去了）

S1：Hey, Carrie, let's go shopping!

佳丽，咱们去逛街吧！

S2：OK, let's go.

行，走吧。

T：If there be anything which he has not practiced, or his practice fails in earnestness, he will not intermit his labor.

有弗行，行之弗笃弗措也。

博学之，审问之，慎思之，明辨之，笃行之。有弗学，学之弗能弗措也；有弗问，问之弗知弗措也；有弗思，思之弗得弗措也；有弗辨，辨之弗明弗措也；有弗行，行之弗笃弗措也。人一能之，己百之；人十能之，己千之。果能此道矣，虽愚必明，虽柔必强。

There are requisite the extensive study of what is good, accurate inquiry about it, careful reflection on it, the clear discrimination of it, and the earnest practice of it. The superior man, while there is anything he has not studied, or while in what he has studied there is anything he cannot understand, will not intermit his labor. While there is anything he has not inquired about, or anything in what he has inquired about which he does not know, he will not intermit his labor. While there is anything which he has not reflected on, or anything in what he has reflected on which he does not apprehend, he will not intermit his labor. While there is anything which he has not discriminated or his discrimination is not clear, he will not intermit his labor. If there be anything which he has not practiced, or his practice fails in earnestness, he will not intermit his labor. If another man succeeds by one effort, he will use a hundred efforts. If another man succeeds by ten efforts, he will use a thousand. Let a man proceed in this way, and, though dull, he will surely become intelligent; though weak, he will surely become strong.

作品编号：1319

姓　　名：冯苗苗、付佳丽、朱峻瑶、崔丹

国　　籍：中国

组　　别：国内成人组

单位名称：烟台大学

继承华夏之礼 传承千年文明

中华文化五千年的悠久历史在人类文明的发展中独具影响力。儒家经典蕴含着中华民族的强大基因，是中华优秀传统文化的核心价值体现。中国素来有“礼仪之邦”的美誉，礼仪文化源远流长。从“不学礼，无以立”的角度，讲解礼的重要性；从“礼之用，和为贵”的角度，讲解如何用礼；最后行拜师礼，表达对孔子的尊重。我们致力于用英语讲好儒家经典，传播中国礼仪，促进人类文明交流互鉴。

【不学礼，无以立】

男：陈亢问于伯鱼曰：“子亦有异闻乎？”对曰：“未也。尝独立，鲤趋而过庭。

女：Chan Kang asked Po-yu, saying: “Have you heard any lessons from your father different from what we have all heard?” Po-yu replied: “No. He was standing alone once, when I passed below the hall with hasty steps.

男：曰：‘学《诗》乎？’对曰：‘未也。’‘不学《诗》，无以言。’鲤退而学《诗》。

女：He said to me, ‘Have you learned the *Odes*?’ On my replying ‘Not yet’, he added, ‘If you don’t learn the *Odes*, you will not be fit to converse with.’ I retired and studied the *Odes*.

男：他日，又独立，鲤趋而过庭。

女：Another day, he was in the same way standing alone, when I passed by below the hall with hasty steps.

男：曰：‘学礼乎？’对曰：‘未也。’‘不学礼，无以立！’鲤退而学礼，闻斯二者。”

女：He said to me, ‘Have you learned the rules of Propriety?’ On my replying ‘Not yet’, he added, ‘If you don’t learn the rules of Propriety, your character cannot be established.’ I retired and studied the rules of Propriety. I have heard only these two things from him.”

男：陈亢退而喜曰：“问一得三：闻《诗》，闻礼，又闻君子之远其子也。”

女：Chang Kang retired, and quite delighted, said, “I asked one thing, and I have got three things. I have heard about the *Odes*. I have heard about the rules of Propriety. I have also heard that the superior man maintains a distant reserve towards his son.”

【礼之用，和为贵】

男：有子曰：“礼之用，和为贵。”

女：The philosopher Yu said, “In practising the rules of propriety, a natural ease is to be prized.”

男：“先王之道，斯为美，小大由之。”

女：“In the ways prescribed by the ancient kings, this is the excellent quality, and in things small and great we follow them.”

男：“有所不行，知和而和，不以礼节之，亦不可行也。”

女：“Yet it is not to be observed in all cases. If one, knowing how such ease should be prized, manifests it, without regulating it by the rules of propriety, this likewise is not to be done.”

【拜师礼】

男：行，拜师礼。

女：Let’s bow to Confucius.

男：端身正仪，整肃衣冠。

女：Dress well.

男：扶手，高揖，为天地立心，拜。

女：Fold your hands and take the bow. To ordain conscience for Heaven and Earth.

男：兮！

女：At ease.

男：为生民立命，拜。

女：To secure life and fortune for the people.

男：兮！

女：At ease.

男：为往圣继绝学，拜。

女：To continue lost teachings for past sages.

男：兮！

女：At ease.

男：为万世开太平，拜。

女：To establish peace for all future generations.

男：礼成，复位。

女：After salute.

作品编号：1392
姓　　名：闫冰蕊　等
国　　籍：中国
组　　别：国内成人组
单位名称：潍坊环境工程职业学院

修身齐家治国平天下

“修身齐家治国平天下”，是儒家思想传统中知识分子尊崇的信条，也是孟子教育弟子的一句名言，意思是说，正人必先正己，治国必先治家，以自我完善为基础，治理家庭，平定天下。修身齐家治国平天下，是一句非常值得当代大学生深思的名言警句。几千年来，这句话更是广为传颂！

【独白】

儒家文化是以儒家学说为指导思想的文化流派。儒家提出的一系列道德范畴、命题、思想，丰富了中国传统道德宝库。儒家思想是中华民族千百年来不断坚持的传统。打开中国文化的历史长卷，穿越千古尘埃，扑面而来的是浓郁的儒家文化气息。

【合诵】

古之欲明明德于天下者，先治其国；欲治其国者，先齐其家；
欲齐其家者，先修其身；欲修其身者，先正其心；
欲正其心者，先诚其意；欲诚其意者，先致其知；致知在格物。
物格而后知至，知至而后意诚，意诚而后心正，
心正而后身修，身修而后家齐，家齐而后国治，国治而后天下平。

【修身】

欲诚其意者，先致其知；致知在格物。所谓诚其意者：毋自欺也。如恶恶臭，如好好色，此之谓自谦。故君子必慎其独也！

Wishing to be sincere in their thoughts, they first extended to the utmost their knowledge. Such extension of knowledge lay in the investigation of things. What is meant by “making the thoughts sincere” is allowing no self-deception; as when we hate a bad smell and when we love what is beautiful. This is called self-enjoyment. Therefore, the superior man must be careful over himself when he is alone.

【齐家】

勤俭，治家之本；和顺，齐家之本；谨慎，保家之本；诗书，起家之本；忠孝，传家之本。现在之福，积自祖宗者，不可不惜；将来之福，贻于子孙者，不可不培。

Diligence and thrift are the foundation of family governance. Harmony is the foundation of the family management. Prudence is the foundation of family preservation. Poetry is the foundation of family establishment. Loyalty and filial piety are the foundation of family succession. This blessing of the present must be cherished by those who have accumulated them from their ancestors. Those whose future blessings will be passed on to their descendants, must not fail to cultivate them.

【治国】

道之以政，齐之以刑，民免而无耻；道之以德，齐之以礼，有耻且格。故君子名之必可言也，言之必可行也。

If you guided the people by regulations and keep order among them by punishment, they may avoid doing what is wrong, but they will also lose self-respect. If you guide them by moral force and keep order among them by rites, they will keep their self-respect and come to you of their accord. Hence when a gentleman has given something a name, it may be expressed with all certainty in language; when he expressed it, it can be set in operation with certainty.

【平天下】

良禽择木而栖，贤臣择主而事。天下动之至易，安之至难。深根固本以制天下。

A fine bird chooses a tree to nestle in. And talented person chooses a master of integrity. It is easy to change the world's situation, but difficult to secure it. Deepen roots to govern the empire.

中华民族五千年的悠久文化历史，蕴含着中华民族特有的信仰追求、高尚品质、文明准则、思维方式和生活方式。这里孕育着文明，传承着经典，这是华夏儿女成长所必需的营养，是中华民族的脊梁与血脉，是中华民族的灵魂与家园。让我们传播经典，弘扬传统文化精神，促使我们通晓事理、明白处事、修身养性、健全人格，以承担起继往开来，振兴中华的历史重任！

作品编号：2418
姓　　名：许海宁　等
国　　籍：中国
组　　别：国内成人组
单位名称：齐鲁理工学院

《诗经·豳风·七月》诵读

《诗经·豳风·七月》展示了古代劳动人民一年四季的生活图景。劳作固然是辛苦的，但作者通过对农事有条不紊的叙述，也表达了古代劳动人民对生活的美好向往与祝愿。译文采用许渊冲先生的译本，期望以意传神，更好地用英文传递中国古诗之美，让外国友人领略先秦时期的风俗民情。

七月流火，九月授衣。一之日觱发，二之日栗烈。无衣无褐，何以卒岁？三之日于耜，四之日举趾。同我妇子，馌彼南亩，田畯至喜。

七月流火，九月授衣。春日载阳，有鸣仓庚。女执懿筐，遵彼微行，爰求柔桑。春日迟迟，采蘩祁祁。女心伤悲，殆及公子同归。

七月流火，八月萑苇。蚕月条桑，取彼斧斨。以伐远扬，猗彼女桑。七月鸣鵙，八月载绩。载玄载黄，我朱孔阳，为公子裳。

四月秀葽，五月鸣蜩。八月其获，十月陨萚。一之日于貉，取彼狐狸，为公子裘。二之日其同，载缵武功。言私其豵，献豜于公。

五月斯螽动股，六月莎鸡振羽。七月在野，八月在宇，九月在户，十月蟋蟀入我床下。穹窒熏鼠，塞向墐户。嗟我妇子，曰为改岁，入此室处。

六月食郁及薁，七月亨葵及菽。八月剥枣，十月获稻。为此春酒，以介眉寿。七月食瓜，八月断壶，九月叔苴。采荼薪樗。食我农夫。

九月筑场圃，十月纳禾稼。黍稷重穋，禾麻菽麦。嗟我农夫，我稼既同，上入执宫功。昼尔于茅，宵尔索绹。亟其乘屋，其始播百谷。

二之日凿冰冲冲，三之日纳于凌阴。四之日其蚤，献羔祭韭。九月肃霜，十月涤场。朋酒斯飨，曰杀羔羊。跻彼公堂，称彼兕觥，万寿无疆！

In seventh moon, Fire Star west goes; In ninth to make dress we are told. In eleventh moon the wind blows; In twelfth the weather is cold. We have no warm garments to wear. How can we get through the year? In the first moon we mend our plough with care; In the second our way afield we steer. Our wives and children take the food, to southern fields; the overseer says, “Good!”

In seventh moon, Fire Star west goes; In ninth we make dress all day long. By and by warm spring grows, And golden orioles sing their song. The lasses take their baskets deep, And go along the small pathways, To gather tender mulberry leaves in heap. When lengthen vernal days, They pile in heaps the southernwood. They are in gloomy mood. For they will say adieu to maidenhood.

In seventh moon, Fire Star west goes; In eighth we gather rush and reed. In silkworm month with axe's blow, We cut mulberry sprigs with speed. We lop off branches long and high, And bring young tender leaves in. In seventh moon we hear shrikes cry; In eighth moon we begin to spin. We use a bright red dye, And a dark yellow one, To color robes of our lord's son.

In fourth moon grass begins to seed; In fifth cicadas cry. In eighth moon to reap we proceed; In tenth down come leaves dry. In eleventh moon we go in chase, For wild cats and foxes fleet, To make furs for the sons of noble race. In the twelfth moon we meet, And manoeuvre with lance and sword. We keep the smaller boars for our reward, And offer larger ones o'er to our lord.

In fifth moon locusts move their legs; In sixth the spinner shakes its wings. In seventh the cricket lays its eggs; In eighth under the eaves it sings. In ninth it moves indoors when chilled; In tenth it enters under the bed. We clear the corners, chinks are filled. We smoke the house and rats run in dread. We plaster northern window and door, And tell our wives and lad and lass; The old year will soon be no more. Let's dwell inside, alas!

In sixth moon we've wild plums and grapes to eat; In seventh we cook beans and mallows nice. In eighth moon down we beat; In tenth we reap the rice, and brew the vernal wine, a cordial for the oldest-grown. In seventh moon we eat melon fine; In eighth moon the gourds are cut down. In ninth we gather the hemp-seed; Of fetid tree we make firewood; We gather lettuce to feed, Our husbandmen as food.

In ninth moon we repair the threshing-floor; In tenth we bring in harvest clean; The millet sown early and late are put in store, And wheat and hemp, paddy and bean. There is no rest for husbandmen: Once harvesting is done, alas! We're sent to work in lord's house then. By day for thatch we gather reed and grass; At night we twist them into ropes, Then hurry to mend the roofs again, For we should not abandon the hopes, Of sowing in time our fields with grain.

In the twelfth moon we hew out ice; In the first moon we store it deep. In the second we offer early sacrifice, Of garlic, lamb and sheep. In ninth moon frosty is the weather. In tenth we sweep and clear the threshing-floor. We drink two bottles of wine together, And kill a lamb before the door. Then we go up to the hall where, We raise our buffalo-horn cup, And wish our lord to live fore'er.

作品编号：1939
姓　　名：蒙金玲、刘畅、王文慧
国　　籍：中国
组　　别：国内成人组
单位名称：大连民族大学

朝闻道

《论语》博大精深，其中“朝闻道，夕死可矣”所表现的对真理的追求让人崇敬。阴谋欺诈不兴，盗窃祸乱不起，路不拾遗，夜不闭户，人人讲信修睦，为官选贤举能。这是传说中尧舜时代的一幅理想化的原始社会景象，也是孔子憧憬的最高理想社会。

孔子，孔氏，名丘，春秋末期鲁国陬邑人，祖籍宋国栗邑，是中国古代思想家、教育家，儒家学派创始人。孔子开创了私人讲学之风，倡导仁义礼智信。有弟子三千，其中贤人七十二。他曾带领部分弟子周游列国十三年，晚年修订六经。

Confucius, the surname of Kong, the name of Qiu, was born in the late Spring and Autumn Period in Zouyi in the state of Lu, with the ancestral home of Liyi in the state of Song. He was an ancient Chinese thinker, educator and founder of Confucianism. Confucius initiated the style of private lectures and advocated benevolence, righteousness, propriety, wisdom and trust. There are three thousand disciples, including seventy-two sages. He once led some of his disciples to travel around the world for 13 years. In his later years, he revised the six classics.

子　曰：“《诗》三百，一言以蔽之，曰：‘思无邪’。”

The Master said, “In *The Book of Poetry* are three hundred pieces, but the design of them all may be embraced in one sentence ‘Having no depraved thoughts’.”

子　曰：“吾十有五而志于学，三十而立，四十而不惑，五十而知天命，六十而耳顺，七十而从心所欲，不逾矩。”

The Master said, “At fifteen, I had my mind bent on learning. At thirty, I stood firm. At forty, I had no doubts. At fifty, I knew the decrees of Heaven. At sixty, my ear was an obedient organ for the reception of truth. At seventy, I could follow what my heart desired, without transgressing what was right.”

子　曰：“君子不器。”

The Master said, “The accomplished scholar is not a utensil.”

子　曰：“弟子入则孝，出则悌，谨而信，泛爱众，而亲仁。行有余力，则以学文。”

The Master said, “A youth, when at home, should be filial, and, abroad, respectful to his elders. He should be earnest and truthful. He should overflow in love to all, and cultivate the friendship of the good. When he has time and opportunity, after the performance of these things, he should employ them in polite studies."

子夏曰："贤贤易色 ，事父母，能竭其力；事君，能致其身；与朋友交，言而有信。虽曰未学，吾必谓之学矣。"

Tsze-hsia said, "If a man withdraws his mind from the love of beauty, and applies it as sincerely to the love of the virtuous; if, in serving his parents, he can exert his utmost strength; if, in serving his prince, he can devote his life; if, in his intercourse with his friends, his words are sincere: although men say that he has not learned, I will certainly say that he has."

曾子曰："慎终追远，民德归厚矣。"

The philosopher Tsang said, "Let there be a careful attention to perform the funeral rites to parents, and let them be followed when long gone with the ceremonies of sacrifice; then the virtue of the people will resume its proper excellence."

有子曰："信近于义，言可复也。恭近于礼，远耻辱也。因不失其亲，亦可宗也。"

The philosopher Yu said, "When agreements are made according to what is right, what is spoken can be made good. When respect is shown according to what is proper, one keeps far from shame and disgrace. When the parties upon whom a man leans are proper persons to be intimate with, he can make them his guides and masters."

子　曰"君子食无求饱，居无求安，敏于事而慎于言。"

The Master said, "He who aims to be a man of complete virtue in his food does not seek to gratify his appetite, nor in his dwelling place does he seek the appliances of ease; he is earnest in what he is doing, and careful in his speech."

子　曰："朝闻道，夕死可矣。"

The Master said, "If a man in the morning hear the right way, he may die in the evening without regret."

孔子是当时社会上最博学者之一，去世后，其弟子及再传弟子把孔子及其弟子的言行语录和思想记录下来，整理编成《论语》。该书被奉为儒家经典。孔子在世时就被尊奉为天纵之圣、天之木铎，更被后世统治者尊为孔圣人、至圣、万世师表。其思想对中国和世界都有深远的影响，其人被列为世界十大文化名人。

Confucius was one of the most erudite people in the society at that time. After his death, his disciples and retransmission disciples recorded the words, deeds, quotations and thoughts of Confucius and his disciples and compiled them into *The Analects of Confucius*. The book is regarded as a Confucian classic when Confucius was alive. He was revered as the holy man of the heaven, the wooden priest of the heaven, and also as the sage, the most holy, and the teacher of the world. His thought has a profound influence on China and the world, and he is listed as one of the top ten cultural celebrities in the world.

作品编号：344
姓　　名：李宁馨
国　　籍：中国
组　　别：国内成人组
单位名称：山东省济宁市文化传承发展中心

《论语》选读

本作品展示了当代大学生对《论语》中经典片段的中英双语诵读。小短剧的形式生动有趣，深入人心，有助于对儒家精神文化的学习和弘扬。

王：孔子仲尼，万世师表，弟子三千，有教无类。安身立命，为人处世，著为《论语》，流传于世。

尚：学而时习之，不亦说乎？有朋自远方来，不亦乐乎？人不知而不愠，不亦君子乎？

臧：To learn and at due times to repeat what one has learned, is that not after all a pleasure? That friends should come to one from afar, is this not after all delightful? To remain unsoured even though one's merits are unrecognized by others, is that not after all what is expected of a gentleman?

尚：学而不思则罔，思而不学则殆。

臧：Learning without thought is labour lost; thought without learning is perilous.

尚：吾十有五而志于学，三十而立，四十而不惑，五十而知天命，六十而耳顺，七十而从心所欲，不逾矩。

臧：At fifteen, I set my heart upon learning. At thirty, I planted my feet firm upon the ground. At forty, I no longer suffered from perplexities. At fifty, I knew what were the biddings of heaven. At sixty, I heard them with docile ear. At seventy, I could follow the dictates of my own heart, for what I desired no longer overstepped the boundaries of right.

王：君子爱财，取之有道，三省吾身，听言观行。以直报怨，以德报德，君子坦荡，小人长戚。

尚：君子无所争，必也射乎！揖让而升，下而饮，其争也君子。

臧：The student of virtue has no contentions. If it be said he cannot avoid them, shall this be in archery? But he bows complaisantly to his competitors; thus he ascends the hall, descends and exacts the forfeit of drinking. In his contention, he is still the gentleman.

尚：贤哉，回也！一箪食，一瓢饮，在陋巷，人不堪其忧，回也不改其乐。贤哉，回也！

臧：Incomparable indeed was Hui!A handful of rice to eat, a gourdful of water to drink, living in a mean street. Others would have found it unendurably depressing, but to Hui's cheerfulness it made no difference at all. Incomparable indeed was Hui!

尚：巧言令色，鲜矣仁！

臧：Fine words and an insinuating appearance are seldom associated with true virtue.

尚：志士仁人，无求生以害仁，有杀身以成仁。

臧：A man with lofty ideals or humane man never gives up humanity to save his life, but many sacrifice his life to achieve humanity.

尚：其为人也孝弟，而好犯上者，鲜矣；不好犯上，而好作乱者，未之有也。君子务本，本立而道生。孝弟也者，其为仁之本与！

臧：They are few who,being filial and fraternal, are fond of offending against their superiors. There have been none who, not liking to offend against their superiors, are fond of stirring up confusion. The superior man bends his attention to what is radical. That being established, all practical courses naturally grow up. Filial piety and fraternal submission, are they not the root of all benevolent actions?

王：不忍乱谋，时务俊杰，己所不欲，勿施于人。孔子仲尼，万世师表，著为《论语》，流传于世。

臧：We college students have learned and are learning from Confucius and his glorious thought. We should constantly practise kindness, integrity, unity of knowledge and practice. We should take the fate of the country as our primary responsibility rather than personal prosperity as the ideal of life. And we should integrate our individual ambition with the nation's, the people's and the human's.

作品编号：1390
姓　　名：臧婧宇、尚理政、王心茹
国　　籍：中国
组　　别：国内成人组
单位名称：烟台大学

Hello China

该作品以社教类广播电视节目的形式呈现，由主持人介绍、中英文诵读以及采访当代大学生三个环节串联而成。节目以《论语》中“樊迟问仁”的片段为主要内容和切入点，道出了要“善于用人”的观点。

Hello everyone! Welcome to “Hello China”, I'm Yanqi. Today we are focusing on traditional Chinese culture—the Confucianism.

The Analects of Confucius is recognized as a classics of the Confucianism, compiled by the disciples of Confucius and his descendants. *The Analects of Confucius* mainly composes of quotations and dialogues, which records the words and deeds of Confucius and his disciples, and reflects the mainly proposition of the Confucianism including political views, theoretical thoughts, moral concepts and educational principles. In modern times, studying Confucianism has become increasingly popular in education. So today we'll bring you the famous article “Fan Ch'ih Asks Benevolence” in *The Analects of Confucius*. First let's take a look at the original text.

Fan Ch'ih asked about benevolence. The Master said, “It is to love all men.” He asked about knowledge. The Master said, “It is to know all men.” Fan Ch'ih did not immediately understand these answers. The Master said, “Employ the upright and put aside all the crooked; in this way the crooked can be made to be upright.” Fan Ch'ih retired, and, seeing Tsze-hsia, he said to him, “A Little while ago, I had an interview with our Master, and asked him about knowledge. He said, ‘Employ the upright, and put aside all the crooked; in this way, the crooked will be made to be upright.’ What did he mean?” Tsze-hsia said, “Truly rich is his saying! Shun, being in possession of the kingdom, selected from among all the people, and employed Kao-yao, on which all who were devoid of virtue disappeared. Tang, being in possession of the kingdom, selected from among all the people, and employed Yi Yin, and all who were devoid of virtue disappeared.”

樊迟问仁，子曰：“爱人。”问知，子曰：“知人。”樊迟未达。子曰：“举直错诸枉，能使枉者直。”樊迟退，见子夏，曰：“乡也吾见于夫子而问知，子曰：‘举直错诸枉，能使枉者直’，何谓也？”子夏曰：“富哉言乎！舜有天下，选于众，举皋陶，不仁者远矣。汤有天下，选于众，举伊尹，不仁者远矣。”

After that part, we may get some knowledge about Confucianism. Next, follow me into our campus to hear students' views.

Wow, that's a good point!

As we know, Confucianism is the essence of our traditional Chinese culture. And if you are interested, you can get further study about *The Analects of Confucius*. That's it for today's show, see you next time, bye!

作品编号：1711
姓　　名：赵妍琦　等
国　　籍：中国
组　　别：国内成人组
单位名称：山东艺术学院戏剧学院

寻找《论语》

《论语》有着无穷无尽的生命力，值得我们每个国人去传承和发扬。《论语》不但在书本里，也在我们的日常生活中，更在我们国人的血脉和灵魂里。

大家好，我叫崇恒源，今年10岁，来自济南市历下区盛景小学。去年7月份开始，我加入了一个《论语》诵读活动，是青年儒士冷星火老师指导的。我们时而在小伙伴家里，时而在社区的凉亭下，或齐声诵读，或轮流背诵，大家沉浸在圣贤的语录中。目前我已经坚持诵读打卡360天，从“学而第一”读到了“子罕第九”，好几篇我都能背诵了，马上就读完半部《论语》了。我很高兴，可是我也有过疑惑，这些古老的话和我们现代社会有什么联系呢？于是我常常睁大眼睛在身边寻找《论语》的踪迹。

我的社区里会有《论语》吗？有！

Are there any words from Confucius in my community? Yes!

子曰：“君子喻于义，小人喻于利。”

The Master said, “The mind of the superior man is conversant with righteousness; the mind of the mean man is conversant with gain.”

学校里会有《论语》吗？有！

Are there any words from Confucius in my school? Yes!

子曰：“敏而好学，不耻下问。”

The Master said, “He was diligent and fond of learning, and he did not blush to learn from his inferiors.”

公交车上会有《论语》吗？有！

Are there any words from Confucius in a bus? Yes!

子曰：“君子怀德，小人怀土；君子怀刑，小人怀惠。”

The Master said, “A gentleman cherishes morality; a petty man, his native soil. A gentleman cherishes the rules and regulations; a petty man, small favors.”

咦，我发现地铁站也有《论语》呢！

I even find Confucian words in my subway station!

子曰：“道听而涂说，德之弃也。”

The Master said, “To gossip about what you have heard on the way is to abandon virtue.”

可是我还有一个最大的疑惑，爸爸经常鼓励我读《论语》，他公司会有吗？有，我找到了。

However, I am still just wondering, are there any words from Confucius in my Daddy's company? He always encourages me to read *The Analects from Confucius.* Yes, I've found it.

子在川上曰："逝者如斯夫！不舍昼夜。"

Standing by a stream, the Master said: "Time goes on and on like the flowing water in the river, never ceasing day or night!"

爸爸公司甚至还有一个孔子广场。

There's even a Confucius Square in my Daddy's company.

我发现家乡处处有《论语》。

So, I can find Confucius' words everywhere in my home.

原来《论语》真的与我们的现代生活息息相关啊！

It turns out that *The Analects of Confucius* is really closely related to our modern life!

作品编号：2534
姓　　名：崇恒源
国　　籍：中国
组　　别：国内少年组
单位名称：山东省济南市历下区盛景小学

《诗经·采薇》吟诵

《诗经·采薇》以一个返乡戍卒的口吻，唱出从军将士艰辛的生活和思归的情怀。这首诗运用了重叠的句式与比兴的手法，言浅意深，情景交融，集中体现了《诗经》的艺术特色，是《诗经》中广为流传的名句。在充满古韵的音乐中，济南中学学子用自己轻盈温婉的舞姿、悠扬婉转的吟唱、自信大方的双语朗诵表演，为人们诠释了这首经典作品。

采薇采薇，薇亦作止。曰归曰归，岁亦莫止。
靡室靡家，猃狁之故。不遑启居，猃狁之故。
Let us gather the thorn-ferns, let us gather the thorn-ferns;
The thorn-ferns are now springing up.
When shall we return? When shall we return?
It will be late in the (next) year.
Wife and husband will be separated,
Because of the Xian-yun.
We shall have no leisure to rest,
Because of the Xian-yun.
采薇采薇，薇亦柔止。曰归曰归，心亦忧止。
忧心烈烈，载饥载渴。我戍未定，靡使归聘。
Let us gather the thorn-ferns, let us gather the thorn-ferns;
The thorn-ferns are now tender.
When shall we return? When shall we return?
Our hearts are sorrowful.
Our hearts are sad and sorrowful;
We shall hunger, we shall thirst.
While our service on guard is not finished,
We can send no one home to enquire about our families.
采薇采薇，薇亦刚止。曰归曰归，岁亦阳止。
王事靡盬，不遑启处。忧心孔疚，我行不来！
Let us gather the thorn-ferns, let us gather the thorn-ferns;
The thorn-ferns are now hard.
When shall we return? When shall we return?

The year will be in the tenth month.
But the king's business must not be slackly performed;
We shall have no leisure to rest.
Our sorrowing hearts are in great distress;
But we shall not return from our expedition.
彼尔维何？维常之华。彼路斯何？君子之车。
戎车既驾，四牡业业。岂敢定居？一月三捷。
What is that so gorgeous? It is the flowers of the cherry tree.
What carriage is that?
It is the carriage of our general.
His war carriage is yoked;
The four steeds are strong.
Dare we remain inactive?
In one month we shall have three victories.
驾彼四牡，四牡骙骙。君子所依，小人所腓。
四牡翼翼，象弭鱼服。岂不日戒？猃狁孔棘！
The four steeds are yoked, the four steeds, eager and strong.
The confidence of the general,
The protection of the men.
The four steeds move regularly, like wings;
There are the bow with its ivory ends, and the seal-skin quiver.
Shall we not daily warn one another?
The business of the Xian-yun is very urgent.
昔我往矣，杨柳依依。今我来思，雨雪霏霏。
行道迟迟，载饥载渴。我心伤悲，莫知我哀！
At first, when we set out, the willows were fresh and green;
Now, when we shall be returning,
The snow will be falling in clouds.
Long and tedious will be our marching;
We shall hunger; we shall thirst.
Our hearts are wounded with grief,
And no one knows our sadness.

作品编号：3788
姓　　名：脱晓燕、张晨
国　　籍：中国
组　　别：国内少年组
单位名称：山东省济南中学

在水一方

此作品用中英双语介绍了《诗经》，并朗诵了其中的名篇《蒹葭》。

Born over 2,500 years ago during the Spring and Autumn Period, *The Book of Poetry* is the oldest collection of poetry in ancient China. A total of 305 poems in the collection survived to this day, thus the saying “three hundred poems”.

“By riverside a pair of turtledoves are cooing; there is a maiden fair whom a young man is wooing.” “The peach tree beams so red, how brilliant are its flowers!” “When I left here, willows shed tear. I come back now, snow bends the bough.”...The beautiful verses so familiar to our ears all come from *The Book of Poetry*.

《诗经》是中国古代第一部诗歌总集，诞生于两千五百多年前的春秋时代，目前存世三百零五篇，故有“诗三百”之说。

“关关雎鸠，在河之洲。窈窕淑女，君子好逑”“桃之夭夭，灼灼其华”“昔我往矣，杨柳依依。今我来思，雨雪霏霏”……这些我们耳熟能详的优美诗句都出自《诗经》。

其中我最喜欢的一首是《蒹葭》，今天让我们一起来诵读它。

Green, green the reed,
Frost and dew gleam.
Where’s she I need?
Beyond the stream.
Upstream I go;
The way’s so long.
And downstream, lo!
She’s thereamong.

White, white the reed,
Dew not yet dried.
Where’s she I need?
On the other side.
Upstream I go;
Hard is the way.

And downstream, lo!
She's far away.

Bright, bright the reed,
With frost dews blend.
Where's she I need?
At river's end.
Upstream I go;
The way does wind.
And downstream, lo!
She's far behind.

蒹葭苍苍，白露为霜。所谓伊人，在水一方。
溯洄从之，道阻且长。溯游从之，宛在水中央。
蒹葭萋萋，白露未晞。所谓伊人，在水之湄。
溯洄从之，道阻且跻。溯游从之，宛在水中坻。
蒹葭采采，白露未已。所谓伊人，在水之涘。
溯洄从之，道阻且右。溯游从之，宛在水中沚。

作品编号：3553
姓　　名：徐子潇
国　　籍：中国
组　　别：国内少年组
单位名称：山东省烟台市芝罘区南山路小学

《孟子》选章《鱼我所欲也》

《鱼我所欲也》是孟子以性善论为依据，对生死观进行深入讨论的文章，强调“正义”比“生命”更重要，主张舍生取义。

鱼，我所欲也；熊掌，亦我所欲也。二者不可得兼，舍鱼而取熊掌者也。生，亦我所欲也；义，亦我所欲也。二者不可得兼，舍生而取义者也。生亦我所欲，所欲有甚于生者，故不为苟得也；死亦我所恶，所恶有甚于死者，故患有所不辟也。如使人之所欲莫甚于生，则凡可以得生者，何不用也？使人之所恶莫甚于死者，则凡可以辟患者，何不为也？由是则生而有不用也，由是则可以辟患而有不为也。是故所欲有甚于生者，所恶有甚于死者。非独贤者有是心也，人皆有之，贤者能勿丧耳。一箪食，一豆羹，得之则生，弗得则死。呼尔而与之，行道之人弗受；蹴尔而与之，乞人不屑也。万钟则不辩礼义而受之。万钟于我何加焉？为宫室之美、妻妾之奉、所识穷乏者得我与？乡为身死而不受，今为宫室之美为之；乡为身死而不受，今为妻妾之奉为之；乡为身死而不受，今为所识穷乏者得我而为之，是亦不可以已乎？此之谓失其本心。

I like fish, and I also like bear's paws. If I cannot have the two together, I will let the fish go and take the bear's paws. So, I like life, and I also like righteousness. If I cannot keep the two together, I will let life go,and choose righteousness. I like life indeed, but there is that which I like more than life, and therefore, I will not seek to possess it by any improper ways. I dislike death indeed, but there is that which I dislike more than death, and therefore there are occasions when I will not avoid danger. If among the things which man likes there were nothing which he liked more than life, why should he not use every means by which he could preserve it? If among the things which man dislikes there were nothing which he disliked more than death, why should he not do everything by which he could avoid danger? There are cases when men by certain course might preserve life, and they do not employ it when by certain things they might avoid danger, and they will not do them. Therefore, men have that which they like more than life, and that which they dislike more than death. They are not men of distinguished talents and virtue only who have this mental nature. All men have it, but what belongs to such men is simply that they do not lose it. Here are small basket rice and a platter of soup, and the case is one in which the getting of them will preserve life, and the want of them will be dead. If they are offered with an insulting voice, even a tramper will not receive them, or if you first tread upon them, even a beggar will not stoop to take them. And yet a man will accept ten thousand zhong, without any consideration of propriety or righteousness. What can the ten thousand zhong add to him? When he takes them, is it not that he may obtain beautiful mansions, that he may secure the services of wives and concubines, or that the poor and needy of his acquaintance may be helped by him? In the former case the offered bounty was not received, though it would have saved from death, and now the emolument is taken for the sake of beautiful mansions. The bounty that would have preserved from death was not received and emolument is taken to get the service of wives and concubines. The bounty that would have saved from death was not received, and emolument is taken that one's poor and needy acquaintance may helped by him. Was it then not possible likewise to decline this? This is a case of what is called "losing the proper nature of one's mind".

作品编号：1507
姓　　名：王迪
国　　籍：中国
组　　别：国内少年组
单位名称：山东省日照市新营小学本部 2019 级 1 班

传承孔孟精神 胸怀家国天下

本作品结合社会主义核心价值观以及当代中职生的学习内容，通过诵读孔孟经典，提高民族自豪感，增强文化自信力。

第一部分

女 1：中华民族是一个拥有五千年悠久历史的泱泱大邦，五千年的文明孕育出灿烂辉煌的中国传统文化，使中国屹立于世界民族之林。孔孟儒家思想，自从春秋时诞生之日起，在历史的长河中愈演愈烈，成为中国传统文化中最苍劲有力的一笔。

女（合）：Without Confucius, all ages would have been like a long night.

男（合）：天不生仲尼，则万古如长夜。

女（合）：天不生仲尼，则万古如长夜。

女 1：社会主义核心价值观，它包括："倡导富强 (prosperity)、民主 (democracy)、文明（civility）、和谐（harmony），倡导自由（freedom）、平等（equality）、公正（justice）、法治（rule of law），倡导爱国（patriotism)、敬业（dedication）、诚信（integrity）、友善（friendship）。"三个倡导，十二个词的字里行间，渗透着中国传统文化的儒家思想。可以说，中国传统文化的儒家思想是社会主义核心价值观的根基，社会主义核心价值观是儒家思想精粹的继承与发扬。

女（合）：Yoo Zi said, "In carrying out the rites, it is harmony that is prized. This is what is so fine in the ways of our early kings. In all affairs, whether big or small, they followed this principle."

男（合）：有子曰："礼之用，和为贵。先王之道，斯为美，小大由之。"

女 1：孔子认为礼的运用贵在和谐，着重强调和谐的境界是人们追求的目标。

女（合）：Opportunities vouchsafed by heaven are less important than terrestrial advantages, which in turn are less important than the unity among people.

男（合）：天时不如地利，地利不如人和。

女 1：孟子也非常强调和谐的重要性，并用事例进行了证明。

男（合）：三里之城，七里之郭，环而攻之而不胜。夫环而攻之，必有得天时者矣；然而不胜者，是天时不如地利也。城非不高也，池非不深也，兵革非不坚利也，米粟非不多也；委而去之，是地利不如人和也。

女（合）：Noblemen are harmony to each other though they hold different opinions, flunkies are hostile to each other when they blindly follow the others.

男（合）：君子和而不同，小人同而不和。

第二部分

女 1： 社会主义核心价值观的第一个倡导，就有“和谐”二字，显然是儒家思想的继承与发扬，是儒家思想的现实意义与升华。

女（合）：I like life, and I also like rightness. If I cannot keep both of them, I will let life go, and choose rightness.

男（合）：生，亦我所欲也；义，亦我所欲也。二者不可得兼，舍生而取义者也。

女 1： 当生命与正义发生冲突并只能选择其一时，孟子宁愿放弃生命选择正义。平等公正，大公无私，实乃正义之举。法治，依法治国，用法律手段来不断健全和维护社会的正义，这是对儒家思想的道德理念的进一步深化与发扬。仁者爱人，这是对“仁”的最基本阐述，《论语》里面，“仁”一字总共出现了 109 次，每一次出现时的含义都不尽相同，仔细审之，它几乎涵盖了做人的全部规范，包括忠（loyalty）、孝（filial piety）、悌（fraternity）、恭（courtesy）、宽（leniency）、信（faith）。古代谈忠，现在就是爱国；孝与悌，分别是对长辈及晚辈的尊敬与友善；恭者恭敬，宽者宽容，都含友好之意；信者信义，有诚信，有信用。社会主义核心价值观中倡导的“爱国、敬业、诚信、友善”，几乎都是孔子“仁”的思想的延伸。

女（合）：Children carried in the arms all know to love their parents, and when they are grown a little, they all know to love their elder brothers.

男（合）：孩提之童，无不知爱其亲者；及其长也，无不知敬其兄也。

女（合）：Loving one’s parents is benevolent,

男（合）：亲亲，仁也；

女（合）：Respecting for elders is rightness.

男（合）：敬长，义也。

女（合）：There is no other reason—they extend love to all the people in the world.

男（合）：无他，达之天下也。

女 1： “仁”“义”是孟子“仁政”思想的核心范畴，也是儒家对人的道德水平最高的要求。孟子认为在家里如果能做到“孝悌”，走向社会就能做到“仁义”。作为当代中职生，我们不但要继承和发扬传统文化的优点，还要学习《论语》《孟子》中对我们的学习、成长、思想有启发的内容。

女（合）：To learn and at due time to review what one has learned, isn’t that a pleasure?

男（合）：学而时习之，不亦说乎？

女（合）：To have friends from afar, isn’t that delightful?

男（合）：有朋自远方来，不亦乐乎？

女（合）：To feel no discontent when others do not know you, isn’t that what is expected of a gentleman?

男（合）：人不知而不愠，不亦君子乎？

女（合）：If you can acquire new knowledge while reviewing the old, you may become a teacher of others.

男（合）：温故而知新，可以为师矣。

女（合）：One who learns but doesn't think will be lost. One who thinks but does not learn still remains puzzled.

男（合）：学而不思则罔，思而不学则殆。

女（合）：To prefer it is better than only to know it. To delight in it is better than merely to prefer it.

男（合）：知之者不如好之者，好之者不如乐之者。

女（合）：When you know a thing, say that you know it; when you don't know a thing, say that you don't know. That is true wisdom.

男（合）：知之为知之，不知为不知，是知也。

女（合）：Diligent and fond of learning, did not blush to learn from inferiors.

男（合）：敏而好学，不耻下问。

女（合）：People have this common saying, " The Kingdom, the state, the family."

男（合）：人有恒言，皆曰"天下国家"。

女（合）：The root of the Kingdom is in the state.

男（合）：天下之本在国。

女（合）：The root of the state is in the family.

男（合）：国之本在家。

女（合）：The root of the family is in the person of his head.

男（合）：家之本在身。

合：　　天下之本在国，国之本在家，家之本在身。

女 1：　孔孟儒家思想，照耀中华文明两千多年，是社会主义核心价值观的根基，必将继续指引我们民族的未来。让我们一起诵读中华经典，提高民族自豪感，增强文化自信力，扛起传承孔孟文化的大旗，让社会变得更加美好。

作品编号：1233

姓　　名：于洋　等

国　　籍：中国

组　　别：国内少年组

单位名称：山东省烟台艺术学校

我把《论语》读给你听

一部《论语》铭刻了先哲的谆谆教诲。一代师尊，为后人留下无数精神财富。用雅言传承文明，以经典浸润人生，日照市东港区第一小学的学子们吟诵《论语》经典，让千年音韵响彻幽幽校园。

千年海曲底蕴深厚，百年老校桃李芬芳。大家好，我是孙阳子，来自日照市东港区第一小学。我们的学校是一所百年老校，前身可追溯至元至正十一年（1351年）的日照儒学。学校自古就是儒家文化的传播之地。近年来，学校与时俱进，勇立潮头，在传承中华优秀传统文化的道路上走出了别样风采。

牟玉莹：我把《论语》读给你听。

团　体：我把《论语》读给你听。

全　体：我把《论语》读给你听。

全　体：子曰："学而时习之，不亦说（yuè）乎？ 有朋自远方来，不亦乐乎？人不知而不愠，不亦君子乎？"

张乐宇：The Master said, "To learn and at due times to review what one has learned, isn't that a pleasure? To have friends come to you from afar, isn't that delightful? To feel no discontent when others do not know you, isn't that what is expected of a gentleman?"

全　体：子曰："人而不仁，如礼何？人而不仁，如乐何？"

张乐宇：The Master said, "If a man does not have charity in his heart, what has he to do with rites? If a man does not have charity in his heart, what has he to do with music?"

全　体：子曰："由，诲女知之乎？知之为知之，不知为不知，是知也。"

The Master said, "Zhong Yoo, I shall teach you what wisdom is. When you know a thing, say that you know it; when you do not know a thing, admit that you do not know it. That is true wisdom."

全　体：子曰："不在其位，不谋其政。"

宋泓澄：The Master said, "He who is not in charge of some affair should not interfere in it."

全　体："席不正，不坐。"

宋泓澄："If the mat was not in the right place, he did not sit on it."

全　体：曾子曰："君子思不出其位。"

宋泓澄：Zeng Zi said, "A true gentleman never thinks of more than his own duties."

全　体：子曰：“君子成人之美，不成人之恶。小人反是。”

黄炫然：The Master said, “A gentleman enables the good wishes of others, not the bad ones. A petty man does just the reverse of this.”

全　体：子曰：“君子不器。”

黄炫然：The Master said, “A gentleman is not like an implement, which only has one specific use.”

全　体：子曰：“君子和而不同，小人同而不和。”

孙庆庆：The Master said, “A true gentleman is conciliatory but not blind–accommodating. A petty man is blind-accommodating, but not conciliatory.”

全　体：子曰：“三人行，必有我师焉！择其善者而从之，其不善者而改之。”

The Master said, “When several men are walking together, I am sure there is one I can learn from. I’d select his merits to follow, and his demerits for reference to correct my own.”

全　体：曾子曰：“士不可以不弘毅，任重而道远。仁以为己任，不亦重乎？死而后已，不亦远乎？”

牟玉莹：Zeng Zi said, “A gentleman must be broadminded and resolute, for his burden is heavy and his road is long. To practice virtue is the burden he has taken upon himself, isn’t that heavy? His journey does not end until his death, isn’t it far away?”

子曰：“温故而知新，可以为师矣。”

The Master said, “If you can acquire new knowledge while reviewing the old, you may b ecome a teacher of others.”

全　体：子曰：“学而不思则罔，思而不学则殆。”

牟玉莹：The Master said, “He who learns but does not think is lost. He who thinks but does not le arn still remains puzzled.”

牟玉莹：If goals of self and others can be unified, the world can be peaceful. Let’s be ambassadors of traditional Chinese culture, so that more people can understand traditional Chinese culture. Let’s join hands, read together, make progress together, and let excellent traditional Chinese culture go abroad.

美美与共，天下大同。让我们做中华传统文化的使者，让更多的人了解中华传统文化。让我们携起手来，一起诵读，一起进步，一起让中华优秀传统文化走出国门，走向世界。

作品编号：3436

姓　　名：孙阳子　等

国　　籍：中国

组　　别：国内少年组

单位名称：山东省日照市东港区第一小学

读《道德经》有感

老子的《道德经》，蕴含了丰富的人生哲理。千百年来，上至帝王将相，下至黎民百姓，无不从这部人类文明史上的智慧宝典中汲取治国安民、修身养性、立人处世的精髓。

大家好，我是王晨晓。今天，我与大家交流的是《道德经》。我们刚开始学习《道德经》时都会遇到的一个问题是“我该如何学习《道德经》?”我想老子可能预料到了这个问题，因为他在第十五章就给了很好的答案。

Hi, this is Wang Chenxiao. Today, What I communicate with you is the *Dao De Jing*. We all have a common question when we first start out in studying *Dao De Jing*, and that is how do I study *Dao De Jing*. I think Laozi even anticipated this question, because Chapter 15 answers it quite well.

在这里我想先讲讲《道德经》的由来。传说老子西出函谷关（函谷关在今天的河南省），关令尹喜曰：“将隐矣，强为我著书。”为何当时的人们如此希求老子的智慧？因为他曾任周朝的守藏史，可以接触到所有的历史文档，很多内容普通人都看不到。连孔子都要去找老子求道。有的人推测这 81 章就像 81 个问题的答案一样，所以第 15 个问题可能就是“我该如何学习和实践道呢？”让我们一起来看看。先一起来朗读第十五章。

And here I'd love to tell you the story of how *Dao De Jing* even came about. Well legend has it that Laozi was passing through this pass known as Hangu Pass in modern day Henan, and the guard to this pass, Yin Xi would not let him go unless he shared what he knew. And the reason why Laozi's wisdom was so sought after was he held the title of official of Royal Archives of Zhou Dynasty. So he had access to all the historical restricted documents that no one else could see. That's why even Confucius went to Laozi to seek the Dao. Now some people speculate that these 81 chapters are like answers to 81 questions, so question number 15 might have been “how do I study and practice the Dao?” Well, let us find out. So Chapter 15 reads:

古之善为道者，微妙玄通，深不可识。

夫唯不可识，故强为之容。

豫兮，若冬涉川；犹兮，若畏四邻；俨兮，其若客；涣兮，若冰之将释；敦兮，其若朴；旷兮，其若谷；混兮，其若浊。

孰能浊以静之徐清？

孰能安以动之徐生？

保此道者不欲盈，夫唯不盈，故能蔽而新成。

The ancient masters of Dao were subtle and profound with their depth unrecognizable.
Since they're unrecognizable, I'll make an effort to describe them.
Cautious as if crossing a winter stream,
Alert as if fearful of all-around danger,
Dignified as if being a guest,
Fluid as if impending melting ice,
Sincere as unaddressed wood,
Open as a valley,
And blended like muddy water.
Who can stay still in the muddy water
so as to gradually become clear?
Who can keep composure in chaos
so as to gradually develop wisdom?
Those who uphold this Dao do not seek to be over-full,
Because they do not seek to be over-full, they appear worn instead of new.

第十五章篇幅较长，老子是在描述有道者的模样。他列出了 7 种不同的品质：豫兮、犹兮、俨兮、涣兮、敦兮、旷兮、混兮。我知道你们现在可能会想："这些理解起来都非常直接对吧？"但是别忘了，老子的话从来都不仅是文字表面的意思，所以让我们试着更深入地理解其内涵。当你读到第一种品质的时候，你的脑海中可能浮现出一幅"在寒冷的冬天，一个人非常小心地穿过一条小溪"的画面，但其实，老子是在描述内心的活动，这是对于有道者的描述。他们敬畏道，敬畏宇宙的自然规律，也就是说，他们不会鲁莽或冲动地行动。第二种品质，他们保持警惕，因为他们周围都充满了危险，这种危险是什么呢？它实际上是人心的危险。因为人们会时不时地产生不好的念头，所以这些有道者不仅在保护自己的心免受这种威胁，也是在帮助人们防范自己不好的念头。第三种品质，他们很庄严，但表现得却很自然，这是因为他们尊重自己也尊重他人。第四种品质，他们谦让、温暖，随时准备着包容和化育人心，就像融化中的冰一样。第五种品质，他们就像未被雕琢过的树木一样，朴实无华且透露着深邃。第六种品质，他们像山谷一样开阔，他们对万事万物都保持开放的态度。他们有这样博大的胸怀，就没有克服不了的障碍。第七种品质，他们会走进人群与人们在一起，把人们的烦恼和问题视为自己的烦恼和问题，以最自然的方式领导和引导人们。他们不会因为觉得自己好像更好而不融入大家。这就是一位有道者的模样。

Now Chapter 15 is on the longer side and Laozi is describing how a master of Dao is like. He listed 7 different qualities. They are Cautious, Alert, Dignified, Fluid, Sincere, Open and Blended. Now I know you might think some of these are quite straight forward, right? But remember that Laozi's words are never what they seem on the surface. So let's try and dig a few layers deeper. When you read the first one, you're probably picturing someone who's, you know being very careful in crossing a stream in the icy cold winter. But here Laozi is actually talking about inner activities. This is a description of masters of Dao. They revere the Dao. They revere the natural laws of the universe. And this is to say that they would not act recklessly or wildly. And we look at the second one: they are on alert because it's full of danger around them. But what is that danger? It is actually the danger of people's hearts. Because people have unkind thoughts from time to time and so these masters of Dao are not only guarding their own hearts against this kind of danger but also helping others guard against their own unkind thoughts. And the third one, they're dignified, but in a very natural way. That's because of the respect they have for themselves and for others. And the fourth one, they're modest, and they're warm, ready to embrace and to nurture just like ice in the melting. The fifth one, they're sincere like unadorned wood, plain yet profound. The sixth one, they're open like a grand valley. They're open to all the people and possibilities. And with such a big heart there aren't any obstacles that they can't overcome. And the last one, they go in and they mix and mingle with the people. They take the people's worries and problems as their own worries and problems, they go in and they lead and they guide in the most natural way. They never separate themselves from the people as if they're better. That's the picture of a master of Dao.

我不知道你是怎么想的，但我是有些羞愧的，因为我离这模样还很远。例如，我记得有些时候，我会指出别人的错误，以一种自以为是的姿态。我也知道，有些时候我获得他人的反馈，但我不会欣然接受这些反馈，而是固执己见。甚至有时候，我完全失去了冷静，因为别人让我感到了恼怒或厌烦；也有时候，我并没有做到最真诚的自己。这样的例子不胜其数。所以你看，当我们学习《道德经》时我们并不是只学习问题、学知识。不，我们要付诸实践。我们要努力成为更好的自我，最终成为一位有道者。为了做到这一点，我们不能只模仿文本中描述的动作，因为这仍然是相当浅层的。我们要直击核心。我们要努力提升我们的知见，因为知见主宰着我们的行为。

Now I don't know about you, but I'm a little shamed, because I'm quite far from that picture. For example, I remember times when I would pick out people's mistakes but in a kind of condescending way. And I know there were times when I was receiving feedback. But I was not open to any of these feedback and I was just holding on to my own silly opinions. And there were times when I lost my composure completely because I was irritated or annoyed by someone else. And there were also times when I was just not as sincere as I could be. And the list goes on. So you see when we study *Dao De Jing*, we're not studying it like any other text, like knowledge. No, we're putting things into practice, we're trying to become better versions of ourselves and to eventually become a master of Dao. And in order to do that, we're not just mimicking the actions as described in the text because that's still quite superficial. We're getting at its core, we're trying to upgrade our believes and perceptions that lead to these actions.

现在我们回到第十五章，我们如何体现文本中描述的这七种品质？答案就在这一章的最后一部分。我们需防范自己盈，这意味着摆脱过度的欲望和贪婪，比如对金钱和名誉、爱和夸奖，甚至是舒适。因为有了这些障碍，我们心胸就不会像山谷一样开阔，也不会像融化中的冰那样温暖和滋润。不幸的是我们也将无法充分开发我们的潜力，为这个世界作出更大的一份贡献。所以在这里我也想和大家分享我自己是如何学习《道德经》的。首先，我非常认真地对待阅读原文这件事，因为这是一个穿越时空与老子链接的绝佳机会；其次，我会将我所做的与老子建议的进行比较，然后我会试图找出之间的区别和原因。好，一旦我们知道我们现在在哪里，我们要去哪里，那剩下要做的就只有出发啦。交流到此结束，谢谢大家。

So now we come back to Chapter 15. How do we embody these seven qualities as described in the text? Well, that's also written in the last part of the chapter. We need to guard ourselves against being over-full, that means getting rid of excessive desires and greed for things such as money or fame, love and compliments, or even, you know, comfort. Because with these things in the way, we're not going to be as open as a valley or as warm and nurturing as ice in the melting. And unfortunately, we won't be able to reach our full potential and do all the good that we can for this world. So here I'd also like to share with you a few tips on how I study the *Dao De Jing*. First of all, I take reading the original text very seriously because that's one great opportunity to really connect with Laozi through time and through space. And second, I compare what I do to what Laozi advises me to do and then I would try to figure out what is the difference and why. Alright, once we know where we are and where we want to go, all we need to do is to hit the road! That's all for now. Thank you.

作品编号：3723
姓　　名：王晨晓
国　　籍：中国
组　　别：国内少年组
单位名称：山东省高密市豪迈中学

中 韩 篇

诵读儒家经典 赓续中华文脉

中华民族有着源远流长的传统文化，以《论语》为代表的儒家经典便是其中的一颗璀璨明珠。本视频选取《论语》经典片段，通过诵读、情景演绎的方式进行阐释，希望能够对新时代大学生树立正确人生观、价值观起到作用。

君子怀德

镜头 1：集体合影

人物站位（韩—范—李—徐）

韩作弹古筝状，头微低；范立于身后凝神观看，然后看向镜头；李、徐摇扇子说笑，然后看镜头。

镜头 2：人物特写

韩：子曰：君子怀德，小人怀土；君子怀刑，小人怀惠。

공자께서 말씀하시기를.

군자는 큰 덕을 생각하고 소인은 안온한 삶의 터를 생각하며,

군자는 두루 적용되는 법도을 생각하고 소인은 작은 혜택을 생각한다고 하셨습니다.

君子为大德，小人为安稳之地，

君子想法度，小人想小惠。

镜头 3：徐与李

李：先天下之忧而忧，后天下之乐而乐。

徐：青山绿水，如此美景，快与我一同登高去吧！

李：如今正是埋头苦读之时，怎可耽于一时之乐。

镜头 4：范的独白

范：군자회덕 소인회토

君子怀德，小人怀土。

镜头 5：徐、李对话

徐：와，과일이 정말 먹음직스럽게 잘 익었네，우리 좀 먹어볼까？

哇，这果子真诱人，我们尝尝看吧？

李：남의 것인데 따면 안되 .

这是别人的，不能摘。

徐：왜？니가 말 안 하면 누구도 몰라 .

为什么？你不说的话，谁也不知道。

李：아무도 모른다해서 우리 맘대로 해서는 안되지 .

不能因为谁都不知道就随心所欲。

徐：와 ~ 진짜 맛있다！ 어차피 아무도 .... 아！ 근데 배가 ...

哇 ~ 真的很好吃！ 反正谁也……啊！但是……

镜头 6：范独白

范：군자회형 소인회혜

君子怀刑，小人怀惠。

镜头 7：韩独白

韩：가치있는 것을 추구하여 , 올바른 가치관을 세워 미덕과 인의를 갖춘 자만이 군자가 될 수 있습니다 .

只有追求有价值的东西，树立正确的价值观，具备美德和仁义的人才能成为君子。

父母之年

镜头 8：李独白

子　曰：父母之年，不可不知也，一则以喜，一则以惧。

공자께서 말씀하시기를 ,“부모님의 연세는 반드시 알아야 한다 , 한편으로는 부모님이 장수하심을 알게 되어서 기쁘고 다른 한편으로는 부모님의 연로하심에 더욱 정성을 기울여야 하기 때문이다 .” 라고 하셨습니다 .

孔子说：“一定要知道父母的年龄，一方面知道父母长寿很高兴，另一方面也要更加用心照顾年迈的父母。”

镜头 9：徐、范对话

范：지효야 , 부모님 올해 연세가 어떻게 되셨지 ?

致孝，令堂令尊今年贵庚?

徐：글쎄 ... 연세가 꽤 있으신데 ...

是啊……年纪不小了……

镜头 10 ：李独白

李：이것은 우리 모두가 일상에서 마주치게 되는 흔한 장면입니다 .

这是我们每个人在日常生活中遇到的常见场景。

镜头 11 ：韩人物特写

镜头 12：韩手部拿毛笔特写

사랑하는 딸 지효에게 :

그간 잘 지냈어 ?

10 월에 들어서니 날씨가 점점 싸늘해지는구나 .

밥은 잘 먹고 옷은 따뜻하게 입고 다니는지 ...

엄마는 별 탈 없이 잘 보내고 있단다 .

致亲爱的女儿致孝：

展信佳。

进入 10 月份，天气渐渐变凉了。

好好吃饭，多穿点衣服……

妈妈过得很好，没什么问题。

镜头 13：徐看信

徐看完信，望着门外自言自语：

오랜만에 엄마 편지를 받고나니 갑자기 엄마가 너무 보고 싶어지네 , 주말에 집에 한번 가봐야 겠다 !

好久没收到妈妈的信了，突然好想妈妈啊，周末得回家一趟！

镜头 14：徐室外走路

镜头 15：韩室内生病

徐：엄마 !! 엄마 왜 이러세요 ? 어디 편찮으세요 ? 왜 나한테 알리지 않으셨어요 ?
妈妈！妈妈怎么了？ 哪里不舒服吗？ 你为什么不告诉我 ?

韩：니가 걱정할 까봐 말 안 했지 , 난 괜찮으니까 너무 걱정하지마 .
怕你担心所以没说，我没事，不要太担心。

徐：엄마 ...
妈妈……

李：옛말에 "모든 선은 효에서 비롯된다" 고 하였습니다 . "父母在，不遠遊，遊必有方。" "父母之年，不可不知也。" 부모님 계실 때 먼 길을 떠나지 않으며 부득이 떠나야한다면 꼭 행방을 부모님께 알려야 합니다 .
百善孝为先。"父母在，不远游，游必有方。" "父母之年，不可不知也。" 在父母健在时不出远门，如果不得不出行的话，一定将去向告诉父母。

镜头 16：李独白

夫孝，始于事亲，中于事君，终于立身。

부모에 대한 효심을 국가에 대한 충성심으로 , 가정에 대한 책임감을 국가에 대한 책임감으로 넓혀나가는 것이 바로 유가 효도관의 핵심이라고 할 수 있습니다 . 이 또한 맹자의 "修身齐家治国平天下" 라는 치국이념과도 일맥상통합니다 .

把对父母的孝心扩大到对国家的忠诚，把对家庭的责任感扩大到对国家的责任感，这就是儒家孝道观的核心。这也与孟子"修身齐家治国平天下"的治国理念一脉相承。

见贤思齐

镜头 17：韩独白

韩：子曰："见贤思齐焉，见不贤而内自省也。"

공자께서 이르시기를 . "어진 이를 보면 그와 같아지기를 생각하고 어질지 않은 이를 보면 스스로 자신을 되돌아보라 ." 고 하셨습니다 .

镜头 18：范给徐与李两人上课

范：子曰："见贤思齐焉，见不贤而内自省也。"荀子也曾说："见善，修然必以自存也；见不善，愀然必以自省也。"与人相处，需反躬自省，有则改之，无则加勉。

镜头 19：徐与李两人对话

徐：지현아 , 우리 집 옆에 극장이 새로 생겼어 . 오후에 연극 보러 같이 갈래 ?
致贤啊，我家旁边新开了个戏院。下午要一起去看戏吗？

李：싫어 , 내일 시험 준비해야 돼서 .
不要，明天还要考试呢。

徐：같이 가자 . 진짜 재밌는 연극이래 . 내가 쏠게 .
一起去吧。听说是非常有趣的话剧。我请客。

李：書中自有黃金屋，書中自有顔如玉。 공부보다 더 재미있는 일이 어디 있겠니 ? 연극은 나중에 봐도 되잖아 . 우리 함께 시험 준비하는 건 어때 ?
哪有比学习更有趣的事？ 戏可以以后再看嘛。 我们一起准备考试怎么样？

徐：見賢思齊 , 어진 이를 보면 그와 같아지려고 애써야 한다고 공자께서 이르셨지 , 그래 , 너를 본보기로 삼아야겠어 !
孔子说过，看见贤人，就要努力跟他一样，对，我要以你为榜样！

镜头 20：韩独白

韩：젊은 시절 헛되이 보내면 늙어서 한탄할 것이니라 .
어진 사람의 장점을 배우고 늘 스스로를 되돌아본다면 현인이 될 것입니다 .
少壮不努力，老大徒伤悲。

镜头 21：集体

范：为天地立心，为生民立命。

徐：유학이 세계로 뻗어나가는 길은 멀고도 험난합니다 .
儒学"走出去"之路，道阻且长。

李：유학의 실천자로서 우리는 선조들이 물려준 유가 문명을 더욱 잘 전승하고 유학 발전을 적극 추진하여 중화민족의 위대한 부흥을 위해 끊임없이 노력해야 합니다 .
作为儒学践行者，我们要更好地传承祖先传下来的儒家文化，积极推动儒学发展，为中华民族的伟大复兴不懈努力。

韩：멀지 않은 앞날에 우리의 유가 문화가 수많은 세계문화유산 중 가장 눈부신 별이 될 것을 기원합니다 .
希望在不久的将来，我们的儒家文化将成为众多世界文化遗产中最耀眼的星星。

作品编号：3402
姓　　名：徐僮、李一凡、韩晓寒、范忠泽
国　　籍：中国
组　　别：国内成人组
单位名称：烟台大学

儒学经典诵读
《论语·述而》

“学而时习之，不亦说乎?”孔子学院的学生们在诵读《论语》，通过学习《论语》感受孔子的思想的博大精深。

场景1：学而时习之，不亦说乎?

学生甲：子曰：“学而时习之，不亦说乎?有朋自远方来，不亦乐乎?人不知而不愠，不亦君子乎?”

학생을：공자께서 말씀하시기를，“배우고 그것을 때때로 익히면 기쁘지 않겠는가? 벗이 먼 지방으로부터 찾아오면 즐겁지 않겠는가? 사람들이 알아주지 않더라도 서운해 하지 않는다면 군자가 아니겠는가?” 라고 하셨습니다.

学生乙：子曰：“学而不思则罔，思而不学则殆。”

학생정：공자께서 말씀하시기를，“배우기만 하고 생각하지 않으면 소득이 없고，생각하기만하고 배우지 아니하면 위태롭다.” 하셨습니다.

场景2：孔子学院

선생님：여러분，안녕하세요.

老师：同学们好!

학생들：안녕하세요.

学生们：老师好!

선생님：공자학원에 오신 것을 환영합니다.

老师：欢迎来到孔子学院。

선생님：여러분，올해는 한중 수교 몇주년인지 아십니까?

老师：各位知道今年是中韩建交几周年吗?

학생병：올해는 한중 수교 31 주년입니다.

学生丙：今年是中韩建交31周年。

선생님：네，맞습니다. 사실 한국과 중국은 지리적으로 인접해 있을뿐만 아니라 문화적으로도 유사성을 갖고 있으며 오랜 시간동안 긴밀한 교류를 해왔습니다. 예를 들면 지금으로부터 2 천년전에《논어》가 조선반도에 전파되어 널리 알려졌습니다. 자，오늘은 계속해서《논어》‘술이편’ 에 대해 같이 공부를 해 보겠습니다.

老师：是的，没错。韩国和中国不仅地理上相邻，在文化上也有类似性，长期以来进行了紧密的交流。例如，距今两千年前，《论语》在朝鲜半岛传播而广为人知。那么，今天我们将继续学习《论语》中的“述而”篇。

학생들：네 .

学生们：好。

학생들：공자께서 말씀하시기를 . “세 사람이 길을 가면 반드시 나의 스승이 있으니 , 그 선한 것을 택하여 따르고 그 불선한 것을 보고는 자신의 잘못을 고쳐야 한다 .”

学生们：“三人行，必有我师焉！择其善者而从之，其不善者而改之。”

학생을：선생님 , 이 말의 유래에 대해 알고 싶습니다 .

学生乙：老师，这句话有什么典故吗？

선생님：옛날에 공자는 제자들을 데리고 여러 나라를 두루 돌아다니셨습니다 .

老师：据说，孔子当年与弟子周游列国……

场景三：三人行，必有我师焉

제자：얘야 ! 수레가 지나갈 수 있도록 길을 비켜주겠니 ?

弟子：哎，小孩！能否让路？好让我们过去。

꼬마：수레가 지나가도록 성이 비켜야 합니까 ? 아니면 수레가 성을 비켜지나가야 합니까 ?

小孩：这世上只有人给城池让路的，没有城池给人让路的。

제자：요 녀석 , 어서 비켜서지 못해 ! (제자가 아이를 밀치려고 할 때)

弟子：哎！你这小孩，快让开！

공자 ：아이의 말이 맞네 , 수레가 지나가도록 성을 허무는 법이 어디 있는가 ? 우리 눈에는 장난감으로 보일지 모르겠지만 , 아이 눈에는 버젓한 성이라네 .

孔子：他说的没错，哪有拆了城池给人让路的道理呢？虽然在我们看来这只是一个玩具，但是在孩子眼里，这就是一座城池。

아이：참 이상한 어르신이네요 . 성문을 두고 왜 성을 돌아가세요 ?

小孩：您这老先生好没道理，放着城门不走，为何绕城而过？

공자：(허허 웃으며 아이가 자신을 오해할 까봐) 하하 , 아니 , 너가 잘 만들어 놓은 걸 망가뜨릴까봐 돌아가는 것이니 나한테 고마워해야 하는 거 아닌가 ?

孔子：我是看你城建得好，怕踩坏了，才绕道而过，你应该感谢我才对呀？

아이：(못마땅한 듯) 사람이 지나다닐 수 없는 성은 무슨 소용이 있겠습니까 ? 사람들이 다니라고 성을 만든 것인데 .

孩子：不是的，老先生，城若不让人过，要城有何用？我建的城就是让大家走的。

공자：성문이 이렇게 작은데 내가 어떻게 건너갈 수 있겠느냐 ?

孔子：你建的城门这么小，我如何过去呢？

아이：(머리를 굴리더니 뭔가 깨우친듯) 아참 ! 어른이니 큰 성문으로 다녀야죠 . 그럼 다시 큰 성문을 만들어 드리겠습니다 . 잠시만요 .

孩子：对，你是大人，应该走大城门，我再给您建个大的吧。请稍等。

아이：어르신，안녕히 가십시오．

小孩：老先生，请上路前行吧。

공자："세 사람이 길을 가면 그 중에 반드시 나의 스승이 있다" 고 이 아이는 비록 어리지만 예절을 잘 알고 있으니 나의 스승이 될만하네．

孔子：三人行，必有我师焉！这孩子虽小，却懂礼仪，可以做我的老师了。

场景四：择其善者而从之，其不善者而改之

노파：도와주세요．도와주세요．도와주세요．도와주세요．

老奶奶：行行好，帮帮我，行行好，帮帮我！（说着抓住了路人的衣袖）

행인갑：이 손 안 놔？

路人甲：还不放手？

노파：도와주세요．사흘 동안 아무것도 못 먹었어요．

老奶奶：行行好，我已经三天没有吃东西了！

행인갑：내 옷이 더러워지잖아．저리 꺼지지 못해！

路人甲：你弄脏了我的衣服！还不赶快滚开！

노파：아이구，아이구 ...

老奶奶：哎哟哎哟……

행인 을：어르신，괜찮으세요？무슨 일이에요？뭘 도와드릴까요？

路人乙：老人家，您没事吧？发生什么事情了？有什么可以帮到您的吗？

노파：도와주세요．사흘 동안 아무 것도 못 먹었어요．도와주세요．

老奶奶：行行好，我已经三天没吃东西了。行行好。

행인 을：할머니，많지는 않지만 받으세요．

路人乙：老奶奶，虽然不多但请收下。

노파：정말이에요？감사합니다！감사합니다！

老奶奶：真的吗？太感谢了！感谢您！

공자：이 세상에는 좋은 사람도 있고 나쁜 사람도 있으며 성품이 정직한 사람도 있고 정직하지 못한 사람도 있다．가장 중요한 것은，좋은 것을 본받고 나쁜 것을 살펴 스스로 고쳐야 하느니라．

孔子：这个世界上有好人也有坏人，有品行正直的人也有品行不正直的人，最重要的是择其善者而从之，其不善者而改之。

제자：네，명심하겠습니다．

弟子：我会铭记在心的。

场景五：再回孔子学院

선생님：이것이 바로 이 말의 유래입니다．사우학생 잘 이해하셨어요？

老师：这就是这句话的典故。思雨同学理解了吗？

학생을：네，잘 이해했습니다．선생님께서 자세히 설명해 주셔서 감사합니다．

学生乙：是的，理解了。谢谢老师的详细讲解。

학생정: 선생님 덕분에 많은 것을 배웠습니다.

学生丁：谢谢老师，今天学到了很多。

학생갑: 선생님, 저도 앞으로 반드시 공자님의 가르침을 마음속에 새길 것입니다.

学生甲：老师，今后我一定把孔子的教诲铭记在心。

학생병: 앞으로 꼭 다른 사람의 장점을 배우고, 자신의 단점을 고치도록 노력하겠습니다.

学生丙：以后一定要努力学习别人的长处，改正自己的短处。

선생님: 좋습니다. 이것이 바로 중국유가 경전의 매력입니다. 자 계속해서 오늘 배운 내용을 익혀 봅시다.

老师：很好，这就是中国儒家经典的魅力。我们今天再复习一下学过的内容吧。

학생들: 네.

学生们：好。

학생들: 세 사람이 길을 가면 반드시 나의 스승이 있으니, 그 선한 것은 택하여 따르고 그 불선한 것을 보고는 자신의 잘못을 고쳐야 한다.

学生们：三人行，必有我师焉！择其善者而从之，其不善者而改之。

作品编号：1965

姓　　名：冯一婷、殷子涵、王骋骜、张思雨、于雷

国　　籍：中国

组　　别：国内成人组

单位名称：烟台大学

《论语·学而》诵读

《论语》是儒家的一部典范之作，对后世产生了深远的影响。其中对我影响最大的是“学而”篇。值得反复研磨细读。

《论语》是记录春秋时期孔子及其弟子言行的语录文集，成书于战国前期。《论语》是儒家的一部典范之作，对后世产生了深远的影响。它较为集中地体现了孔子的政治主张、伦理思想等。《论语》的思想是中华民族精神和智慧的源泉。中国的小孩子们从很小就开始接触《论语》。其中对我影响最大的是“学而”篇。今天和大家一起学习。

《논어》는 춘추시대 공자와 제자들의 언행을 기록하기 위해 편찬한 인용문집으로 전국(戰國) 초기 (初期) 에 쓰여졌다.《논어》는 유교의 본보기로 후세에 지대한 영향을 미쳤다. 공자의 정치적 명제와 윤리사상을 집중적으로 표현하고 있다.《논어》의 사상은 중화민족의 정신과 지혜의 뿌리이다. 중국 어린이들은 어릴 때부터《논어》를 접한다. 그 중 제게 가장 큰 영향을 준 것은“學而”篇이었다. 오늘 그 내용들을 여러분들과 함께 공부해 보겠다.

子　曰：“学而时习之，不亦说乎？有朋自远方来，不亦乐乎？人不知而不愠，不亦君子乎？”

공자께서 말씀하시기를,“배우고 그것을 때때로 익히면 기쁘지 않겠는가? 벗이 먼 지방으로부터 찾아오면 즐겁지 않겠는가? 사람들이 알아주지 않더라도 서운해 하지않는다면 군자가 아니겠는가?” 하셨다.

其含义是：学习知识要经常复习它，也很愉快。有志同道合的人从远方来，也很快乐。别人不了解我，我却不生气，也是道德上有修养的人。

의미는 다음과 같다. 지식을 배우려면 자주 복습해야 하며 또한 그 과정은 매우 즐거운 것이다. 마음이 맞는 사람들이 멀리서 찾아오면 매우 기뻐한다. 다른 사람들은 나를 이해하지 못하지만 나는 화를 내지 않음으로써 도덕적으로 교양이 있는 사람이다.

曾子曰：“吾日三省吾身：为人谋而不忠乎？与朋友交而不信乎？传不习乎？”

증자께서 말씀하기를,“나는 날마다 세 가지로 스스로 반성하노니. 남을 위하여 일을 도모함에 충실하지 못한가? 벗과 더불어 사귐에 성실하지 못한가? 스승에게 전수 받은 것을 익히지 못하는가?” 하였다.

曾子说：“我每天三次反省自己：为别人做事，是否尽心、忠实？和朋友交往，是否真诚？对老师所传授的知识，是否认真复习？”

증자는 “하루에 세 번씩 스스로 반성한다. 남을 위해 일할 때 성심성의껏 충실한가? 친구와 사귈 때 진실한가? 선생님이 전수해 주신 지식에 대해 열심히 복습했는가?”

孔子的智慧过了两千年，在现代生活中依然发挥作用、启发生活，具有深刻意义。《论语》中蕴含的道理，值得我们仔细阅读并认真思考。

공자님의 지혜는 2000 년이나 지나도 현대 사회에서도 여전하 유용하고 삶을 일깨워 주고 깊은 의미가 담겨 있다.《논어》에 나타내는 도리는 정말 우리 모두가 자세히 읽고 진지하게 생각해 볼 만하다.

作品编号：194
姓　　名：滕琦
国　　籍：中国
组　　别：国内成人组
单位名称：山东青年政治学院

《论语》选章诵读

《论语》作为儒家学派最具代表性的作品，至今依旧有着极为深刻的教育意义，其中所蕴含的丰富的思想哲理和深厚的文化底蕴，博大精深，是值得我们认真研习的经典佳作。本次通过对《论语》中的两段名句进行诵读解析来深刻体会其中的智慧所在，并联系实际生活加以思考。在不断地学习中会收获不一样的心得体会，让人不禁感叹，心生崇拜。在诵读《论语》的过程中我们也应当从书面到实际，充分领会其所带来的现实指导意义，更好地领会儒家思想这一中华文明瑰宝。

原文：樊迟问仁。子曰："居处恭，执事敬，与人忠。虽之夷狄，不可弃也。"

译文：번지（樊遲）가 인（仁）에 대하여 물으니 . 공자께서 말씀하시기를 , "거처（居處）할 때에는 공손히 하며 , 일을 집행할 때에는 공경하여 하며 , 남을 대할 때에는 충실하게 할 것이니 . 이것은 비록 오랑캐 나라에 가더라도 버려서는 안 된다 ." 하셨다 .

原文：子绝四：毋意，毋必，毋固，毋我。

译文：공자께서는 네 가지의 마음이 전혀 없으셨으니 , 사사로운 뜻이 없었으며 , 기필코（期必）하는 마음이 없었으며 , 집착（執著）하는 마음이 없었으며 , 이기심（利己心）이 없으셨다 .

阐述 / 演绎内容：

우리가 모두 알고 있는 것처럼《논어》는 유교 경전 중 하나로 주로 공자와 그 제자의 언행을 모아 정치 , 경제 , 철학 , 교육 , 문학 등 여러 방면에 다양한 내용으로 유학의 가장 주요한 경전이자 오늘날 우리가 공자를 연구하는 주요 사료 중 하나입니다 . 언어가 세련되고 생동감이 있는 대화로 구성된 어록체 산문의 모범입니다 .

《논어》는 유교 사상에 무시할 수 없는 대표적인 역할을 하며《논어》를 공부하면 수천 년의 문화 역사와 민족 사상의 핵심을 더 잘 이해할 수 있습니다 .

樊迟问仁。子曰："居处恭，执事敬，与人忠。虽之夷狄，不可弃也。"

번지（樊遲）가 인（仁）에 대하여 물으니 . 공자께서 말씀하시기를 , "거처（居处）할 때에는 공손히 하며 , 일을 집행할 때에는 공경하여 하며 , 남을 대할 때에는 충실하게 할 것이니 . 이것은 비록 오랑캐 나라에 가더라도 버려서는 안 된다 ." 하셨다 .

이 장은 '인 (仁)' 의 실천 방안 중에서 '공 (恭)' , '경 (敬)' , '충 (忠) 에 대해서 일상 생활과 연관해서 설명하고 있다 . 즉 "생활 속에서 공손한 마음을 유지하고 업무 중에 성실하고 경외하며 조금도 소홀히 하지 않으며 다른 사람과 사귈 때 충성을 다하면 어디든지 통할 수 있다." 라는 의미이다.

저의 졸견에 따르면 인은 사람을 대하는 방법일 뿐만 아니라 삶의 지혜를 내포하고 있으며 삶에 임하는 태도를 대표합니다. 자기 삶에 대해 반듯하고 적극적인 자세를 갖고, 외부와 교류할 때 우호적이고 개방적인 자세이다. 태도를 바르게 해야 생활이 규칙적이고 효율적이며 친구를 사귈 때에도 올바르고 효과적입니다. 하루하루를 허비하지 말고 긍정적인 태도와 규칙적인 상태로 살아야 인생의 가치를 높일 수 있습니다.

사람 사이의 원만한 교류를 위해서는 외부 요인과 긍정적인 자세가 서로 보완하여 올바른 태도를 발전시키는 밥법으로 '공, 경, 충' 을 일상생활에서 실천하는 것입니다.

子绝四：毋意，毋必，毋固，毋我。

공자께서는 네 가지의 마음이 전혀 없으셨으니, 사사로운 뜻이 없었으며, 기필코 (期必) 하는 마음이 없었으며, 집착 (執著) 하는 마음이 없었으며, 이기심 (利己心) 이 없으셨다.

공자는 네 가지 병폐를 근절해야 한다고 하면서 주관적인 의심, 실현하려는 기대, 고집, 이기심 등 공자의 절사 (絶四) 는 인간의 도덕관념과 가치 관념에 관한 것이다. 사람은 이 몇 가지를 먼저 해야만 도덕을 보완하고 고상한 인격을 수양할 수 있다.

이 4 대 문제를 지키고 실천하는 것은 어려운 일이다.

그래서 우리가 절대 어기지 말라고 집요하게 요구하는 것도 아니고 우리 스스로 언행을 자제하고 최대한 어기지 않도록 의식적인 규범이 있거나 어기는 게 점점 줄어들고 있습니다. 이 네 문장은 공자 사상의 매우 중요한 부분인데 이것은 사실 세계관을 나타내기도 하고 자신과 세계의 관계를 인식하고 자신의 보잘 것 없음을 깨닫는 것뿐만 아니라 겸손함을 낳기도 합니다.

《논어》로 대표되는 유교 사상은 중국 문화사에서 중요한 위치를 차지할 뿐만 아니라 동아시아 각국에 광범위한 영향을 미칩니다. 한국과 일본에서는 윤리와 의례가 유교적인·의·예의 관점에 의해 영향을 받은 것이 오늘날에도 뚜렷하게 나타나고 있습니다.

"반 부의 논어가 천하를 다스리고 만세의 스승이 고금을 빛내고 있습니다."

《논어》와 공자에 대한 세간의 평가로 과거와 현재에 어떤 영향력을 행사하고 있는지 알 수 있습니다. 2000 년이 지난 오늘날에도《논어》에는 칭찬이 자자하고 그 안에 담긴 지혜에 대한 진지한 연구와 깊은 깨달음이 필요합니다.

众所周知,《论语》是儒家经典之一，集中记录了孔子及其弟子的言行，在政治、经济、哲学、教育、文学等各个方面都有所涉猎，是儒学最重要的经典作品，也是我们今天研究孔子的主要史料之一。这是一本语言干练、由生动对话构成的语录体散文典籍。

《论语》在儒教思想中具有不可忽视的代表性作用，学习《论语》可以更好地了解几千年的文化历史和民族思想的核心。

这一章就"仁"的实践方案中"恭""敬""忠"与日常生活之间的联系进行了阐释，即在生活中保持谦逊的心态，在工作中诚实敬畏，毫不疏忽，与他人交往时要尽忠职守，只要做到这些，到哪里都可以行得通。

我的拙见是，仁不仅是一种待人之道，更蕴涵着生活的智慧，它代表着一种面对生活的态度。对自己的生活持端正、积极的态度，与外部交流时持友好、开放的态度。态度放端正，生活才能有规律、有效率，交朋友时也能正确、有效。不要虚度光阴浪费任何一天，只有以积极的态度和有规律的状态生活，才能提高人生的价值。

外部因素和积极态度相辅相成时，才能实现人与人之间的更有益、有效的交流。端正生活态度才可以在日常生活中实践“恭”“敬”“忠”。

孔子认为人应当杜绝四种弊病，即主观怀疑、过分期待、固执己见、自私自利。孔子的“绝四”观念都是与人类的道德观念和价值观念息息相关的。只有做到这几点，才能完善道德，培养高尚的人格。

坚持并实践这四大信条实属难事，所以我们并不是执着地要求绝不违反，而是我们自身能有意地克制言行，最大限度地遵守这一观点，能有意识地规范自己或是能使违反的行为越来越少。这四个信条是孔子思想的重要组成部分，它既体现了一种世界观，也是对自己和世界的关系的认知，能认识到自己的微不足道，产生谦卑感。

以《论语》为代表的儒教思想不仅在中国文化史上占有重要地位，且对东亚其他国家的思想文化都具有广泛的影响。时至今日，韩国和日本的伦理礼仪中儒教“仁、义、礼”观点的影响也是显而易见的。

“半部论语治天下，万世师表耀古今。”通过这句脍炙人口的评价，便能知晓孔子及《论语》自古以来有着多么深远的影响力。时至2,000年后的今天，人们提起《论语》仍然赞不绝口。这其中蕴含的智慧需要我们认真地进行研究，深刻地体会和领悟。

作品编号：1244
姓　　名：徐婉莹
国　　籍：中国
组　　别：国内成人组
单位名称：山东青年政治学院

传儒学经典 扬古韵新声

徜徉于儒学的海洋，感受深厚的文化底蕴，学习“有朋自远方来，不亦乐乎”的交友之道、“礼之用，和为贵”的处世之道、“独学而无友”的互学发展之道。我们着眼山东，将之推至中国与世界。我们传承创新，将歌曲《朋自远方》以韩语的方式重新吟唱，旨在传儒学经典，扬古韵新声！

《论语·学而》子曰：“有朋自远方来，不亦乐乎？”

好客山东，孔圣故里。历史悠久，文化灿烂，尊尚仁义，素有“孔孟之乡，礼仪之邦”的美誉。山东子弟崇礼尚宾，纯朴厚道，热情好客。儒家文化不断发扬光大。好客山东，敞开胸怀。山东省一直在着力打造“好客山东”的品牌，“好客山东欢迎您”，山东正敞开胸怀，热情拥抱世界各地朋友，传扬优秀儒家文化。孔子研究院院长杨朝明老师解释道：“如果把中华文明比喻成一棵大树，这棵大树的主干就是儒家文化，大树的根部则是包括孔子在内的先哲们。”

《论语·学而》有子曰：“礼之用，和为贵。先王之道，斯为美，小大由之。有所不行，知和而和，不以礼节之，亦不可行也。”

21 世纪是一个多元化的世纪，但是当今世界局势仍不太平，而以孔孟为代表的儒家文化所提倡的“和而不同、和为贵”的思想，将为世界文化的多元化、取长补短、互相促进作出贡献，也将成为世界各国和平共处的准则。自改革开放以来，中国在很多领域坚持自主研发，谋求独立自强，掌握核心技术。但是中国的发展不是为了一家独大，而是为了促进全人类走向合作开放、互利共赢的大道。礼的推行和应用要以和谐为贵，但是为追求和谐而固守礼仪也是不可取的。

《礼记·学记》“独学而无友，则孤陋而寡闻。”

新型冠状病毒性肺炎疫情考验了 21 世纪世界各国的团结与互助能力。在解答这道考题的进程中，中国又一次为世界开出了药方，无偿为许多国家提供疫苗。这些做法进一步展现了 21 世纪中国的大国外交。由此可见，互学互鉴、合作共享是各国更好发展的重要前提，文化亦是如此。在历史发展的长河中，儒家文化要想保持时代性、先进性，就要取其精华，去其糟粕，既继承优秀传统文化，又要弘扬时代精神，运用大众传媒、人际传播等多种方式显示中华儒家文化的独特魅力。要致力于将儒家文化发展成为不同地域、不同国家和平交流沟通的媒介。

儒学源自中国，泽被世界。韩国成均馆大学已经成了世界上保存最完整的传统儒教高等学府，被称为“传统儒教文化的活化石”。随着时代和社会的发展，中韩之间儒学的交流一定会更加密切，共同开创更加美好的明天。

作为韩语系学子的我们，不仅要做未来两国儒学交流发展的见证者、参与者，更要做交流合作成果的共享者和未来儒学发展故事的讲述者，让儒家文化在时代潮流中焕发出新的生机与活力，让儒家文化在世界交流合作中展现出更美的风姿与韵味！

合唱:《朋自远方》

一本书 一个梦 深深种在我心中
一滴水 一捧土 灌溉青春的色彩
跨千山 踏万水 一生朋友最珍贵
我知道 是与非 未来自己去描绘

学而时习之 不亦说乎
有朋自远方来 不亦乐乎
人不知而不愠 不亦君子乎
人不知而不愠 不亦君子乎

跨千山 踏万水 一生朋友最珍贵
我知道 是与非 未来自己去描绘

学而时习之 不亦说乎
有朋自远方来 不亦乐乎
人不知而不愠 不亦君子乎
人不知而不愠 不亦君子乎

天多大 海多阔 年轻的心要远飞
我和你 你和我
相知相伴相依偎

공자께서 “벗이 멀리서 찾아주니 이 또한 즐겁지 아니한가?” 라고 말씀하셨습니다.

손님 접대를 좋아하는 산동은 공자의 고향입니다. 산동은 유구한 역사와 찬란한 문화를지녔으며 인의를 숭상하는 곳이기도 합니다. 따라서 산동은 “공자와 맹자의 고향, 예의지국” 이라는 미명을 갖고 있습니다. 산동 사람들은 예의를 중히 여기고 손님을 소중히 대하며 순박하면서도 열정적인 것이 특징입니다. 이처럼 산동 사람들은 공자의 유가문화를 끊임없이 계승하고 발전시키고 있습니다. 산동은 손님 접대를 좋아하고 포용력이 넓은 도시입니다. 산동성은 “프렌들리 산동(Friendly Shandong)” 이라는 브랜드를 만들기 위해 주력하고 있습니다. “플렌들리 산동, 여러분들을 환영합니다.” 라는 문구로 세계 각지의 친구들을 열정적으로 환영하면서 우수한 유가 문화를 끊임없이 전파하고 있습니다 . 공자연구원 원장이신 양조명 선생은 “중화 문명을 한 그루의 큰 나무에 비유한다면 , 이나무의 줄기는 유가 문화이고 , 뿌리는 공자와 공자를 비롯한 선현들이다 .” 라고 말씀하셨습니다 .

유자는 “예 (禮) 가 행해지는 것은 화 (和) 가 귀 (貴) 하니 , 선왕 (先王) 의 도 (道) 도 이것을 아름답게 여겼다 . 그러므로 작은 일과 큰 일 모두 이것을 따랐지만 , 잘 되지 않는 면도 있었다 . 조화를 알고 조화를 도모하되 예절을 함께 하지 않으면쓸모없는 일이 된다 .” 라고 말했습니다 .

21 세기는 다원화가 공존하는 세기이지만 오늘날 세계 정세는 여전히 태평하지 않습니다 . 이와 같은 국면에는 공자와 맹자를 대표로 하는 유가 문화에서 제창하는 “화이부동 , 화위귀” 의 사상을 기준으로 내세워 , 세계 문화의 다원화를 위해 단점을 보완하고 장점을 발휘하여 서로가 발전할 수 있도록 기여해야 합니다 . 이처럼 공자의 사상은 세계각국이 평화롭게 공존하는 데 준칙이 되리라 믿습니다 . 개혁개방 이후 , 중국은 여러 분야에서 독자적인 연구개발을 지속하면서 독립자강을 도모하였고 핵심적인 기술을 확보하였습니다 . 그러나 중국의 발전은 어느 한 나라의 홀로서기를 위한 것이 아니라 전인류가 협력하고 상생하는 길로 나아가기 위한 것입니다 . 공자가 제창하는 “예” 의 보급과 응용은 조화를 귀하게 여겨야 하지만 , 조화를 추구하기 위해 예의만 고수하는 것도 바람직하지 않습니다 .

벗 없이 혼자 배운 사람은 식견이 좁으며 고루하다 .

코로나 19 사태는 21 세기 세계 각국의 단합과 공조 능력을 시험하고 있습니다 . 이 문제를 해결하는 과정에서 중국은 또 한 번 세계를 위한 처방전과 여러 나라에 백신을 무상 공급함으로써 21 세기 중국의 대국 외교를 보여주게 되었습니다 . 이를 통해 서로 배우고 협력하며 공유하는 것은 각국이 더 잘 발전하기 위해 중요한 전제이며 , 문화도 그러함을 알 수 있습니다 . 역사 발전의 과정에서 유가 문화가 시대성과 선진성을 유지하려면 정수를 취하고 찌꺼기는 과감히 버려야 합니다 . 우수한 전통 문화를 계승할 뿐만 아니라 시대 정신을 고양해야 하며 , 대중매체나 대인 커뮤니케이션 등 다양한 방식을 활용하여 중국 유가 문화의 독특한 매력을 나타내야 합니다 . 유가 문화를 서로 다른 언어 , 서로 다른 지역 , 서로 다른 나라가 평화롭게 교류하고 소통하는 매개체가 되도록 힘을 기울여야 합니다 .

유학은 중국에서 유래했지만 유교 문화는 세계 각국의 문화를 윤택해 주었습니다 . 예를 들면 , 한국의 성균관대학교는 세계에서 가장 잘 보존된 전통 유교의 최고 학부로서 “전통 유교문화가 살아있는 화석” 으로 불리고 있습니다 . 시대와 사회가 발전함에 따라 중한 양국 간의 유학 교류는 더욱 긴밀해지고 , 더 나은 내일을 함께 열어가게 될 것입니다 .

우리는 한국어학과의 학생으로서 앞으로 양국 간 유학 교류와 유학 발전의목격자 , 참여자가 되고자 합니다 . 양국 협력의 성과를 교류하는 공유자인 동시에 미래의 유학 발전에 대해 이야기를 전하는 내러이터가 되고자 다짐해봅니다 . 유가 문화가 시대의 조류 속에서 새로운 생기와 활력을 불러일으킬 수 있도록 노력해 보고자 합니다 . 유가 문화가 세계 교류 협력에서 보다 아름다운 자태와 운치를 드러낼 수 있도록 노력해 보고자 합니다 .

노래 <봉자원방>

책 한권 꿈 하나 내 마음 속 깊이
물 한 방울 흙 한 줌 다채로운 내 청춘
산 넘어 물 건너 가장 소중한 친구
시비를 가리며 스스로 그린 미래

학이시습지 불역열호
유붕자원방래 불역락호
인부지이불온 불역군자호
인부지이불온 불역군자호

산 넘어 물 건너 가장 소중한 친구
시비를 가리며 스스로 그린 미래

학이시습지 불역열호
유붕자원방래 불역락호
인부지이불온 불역군자호
인부지이불온 불역군자호

하늘 높고 바다 넓어 젊은 마음은 멀리
나와너 너와나 서로 함께한 우리

作品编号：1793
姓　　名：李嘉琪、张立薇、张晓晴、赵鑫禹
国　　籍：中国
组　　别：国内成人组
单位名称：烟台大学

孔子梦游古今，《论语》周游世界

孔子在睡梦中到了现代儒家经典诵读比赛的排练现场，看了孩子们多种语言的《论语》诵读后，不由得发出《论语》周游世界的感慨。

【中文】

子曰："学而时习之，不亦说乎？有朋自远方来，不亦乐乎？人不知而不愠，不亦君子乎？"

【俄语】

子曰："温故而知新，可以为师矣。"

Учитель сказал:

— Тот, кто, повторяя старое, узнает новое, может быть наставником людей.

【法语】

子曰："学而不思则罔，思而不学则殆。"

Le Maître dit : « Étudier sans réfléchir est une occupation vaine; réfléchir sans étudier est dangereux. »

【西班牙语】

子曰："三人行，必有我师焉！择其善者而从之，其不善者而改之。"

Confucio dijo: "entre 3 caminantes, debe haber alguien que pueda ser mi maestro. Aprendo sus cualidades y guardarme de sus defectos."

【日语】

子曰："岁寒，然后知松柏之后凋也。"

曰く、くして、るに柏のむにるることをる。

【德语】

子夏曰："与朋友交，言而有信。"

Wer im Umgang mit Freunden immer zu seinem Wort steht.

【韩语】

子曰："有教无类。"

공자께서 말씀하시기를, "가르침이 있음에 그 배우는 사람의 차별은 없다." 하셨다.

子曰："性相近也，习相远也。"

공자께서 말씀하시기를, "천성은 서로 비슷하나 습관에 따라 큰 차이가 생긴다." 하셨다.

子曰：“君子不器。”

공자께서 말씀하시기를, “군자는 그릇으로 국한되지 않는다.” 하셨다.

子曰：“君子求诸己，小人求诸人。”

공자께서 말씀하시기를, “군자는 자신에게서 잘못을찾고 소인은 남에게서 문제를 찾는다.” 하셨다.

子曰：“人无远虑，必有近忧。”

공자께서 말씀하시기를, “사람이 원대한 사려가 없으면, 반드시 가까운 우환이 생긴다.” 하셨다.

子曰：“过而不改，是谓过矣。”

공자께서 말씀하시기를, “허물이 있는데도 고치지 않는 것을 진짜 허물이라 한다.” 하셨다.

作品编号：933
姓　　名：孙菁宸、宋沂璇、宋之希、赵子悦、张志泽、梁翰森、丁若寒、贾博源、李伟晨、王泽轩
国　　籍：中国
组　　别：国内少年组
单位名称：山东省济南市济阳区济南天山实验学校

《论语·里仁》诵读

情景剧通过学生诵读《论语》“里仁”篇第六节的内容，在古琴伴奏下，以舞台剧小故事的形式，解释孔子提倡的“仁”的含义。

中文诵读

子曰：“我未见好仁者、恶不仁者。好仁者，无以尚之；恶不仁者，其为仁矣，不使不仁者加乎其身。有能一日用其力于仁矣乎？我未见力不足者。盖有之矣，我未之见也。”

情景剧

金泰宇：공자께서 말씀하시기를，“나는 인을 좋아하는 사람이나，불인을 미워하는 사람을 보지 못하였다．인을 좋아하는 사람은 ...”

子　曰：我未见好仁者、恶不仁者。好仁者……

金浩阳：“태우 씨，무엇을 그렇게 열심히 읽고 있나요？”
泰宇，你在读什么，那么认真？

金泰宇：《논어》‘이인편’ 읽고 있어요．
我在读《论语》的“里仁”篇。

金浩阳：그래요？방금 읽었던 내용은 무슨 뜻이죠？
是吗，那你刚才读的是什么意思呀？

金泰宇：공자께서 인을 좋아하는 사람이나，불인을 미워하는 사람을 보지 못하였다고 말씀하셨다．인을 좋아하는 사람은 그보다 더 할 것이 없고，불인을 싫어하는 사람은 그가 인을 할 때에 불인한 것으로 하여금 그의 몸에 가까이 하지 못하게 한다．하루라도 그 힘을 인에 쓰는 이가 있는가？힘이 부족한 사람을 아직 보지 못하였고 아마도 그런 사람이 있을 것이나 아직 보지 못하였다고 하셨다．

孔　子：我没有见过爱好仁德的人，也没有见过厌恶不仁的人。爱好仁德的人，是不能再好的了；厌恶不仁的人，在实行仁德的时候，不让不仁德的人影响自己。有人能一天把自己的力量用在实行仁德上吗？我还没有看见力量不够的。这种人可能还是有的，但我没见过。

金浩阳：네 ~ 근데 그 안에 나온 인은 데체 무슨 뜻이죠？너무 어려운데요．
嗯，可是你说的“仁”到底是什么意思呢？太难了。

金泰宇：그럼 옛날이야기 하나 해 볼까요?
那我们来看个小故事吧。

金浩阳：네 ~ 좋아요 ~

好啊。

金浩明：孔子提倡“仁”这个状态，真的是非常的重要。他觉得“仁”这个状态可不只是一种道德要求，它实际上是指一个人的整体素养。

张广增：快来看看我，浑身上下都透着“仁”。

金浩明：既然是整体素养，那谦虚肯定是很重要的。你那么爱吹牛，你怎么可能符合“仁”的要求呢。总而言之，有了仁，才是人。没有仁，呃，他也还是人。但就不是一个高尚的人一个纯粹的人一个有道德的人一个脱离了低级趣味的人。“仁”不仅是一种道德要求，还是一种审美要求。孔子认为最好的人，是符合“仁”这个要求的人，也就是仁者。

张广增：“仁者”？

金浩明：哎呀，还是让孔夫子告诉你什么叫“仁者”吧。

刘培生：君子当以大道为志，以德行为根基，以仁爱为依托，以六艺为修养。爱人、孝悌、忠恕、博施济众、己所不欲勿施于人。三人行，必有我师焉！人人学为君子，实现天下归仁，以求天下大同。君子固穷，小人穷斯滥矣。岁寒，然后知松柏之后凋也。朝闻道，夕死可矣。教更多的人学为君子，实现天下归仁！

金泰宇：이제 인은 무엇인지 알게 됐나요?
你现在知道什么是“仁”了吗？

金浩阳：네 ~ 알게 됐어요 ~ 그럼 우리 같이 읽어 볼까요？
嗯，知道了。那我们一起读吧！

金泰宇：네 ~
好啊。

공자께서 말씀하시기를，“나는 인을 좋아하는 사람이나，불인을 미워하는 사람을 보지 못하였다．인을 좋아하는 사람은 그보다 더 할 것이 없고，불인을 싫어하는 사람은 그가 인을 할 때에 불인한 것으로 하여금 그의 몸에 가까이 하지 못하게 한다．하루라도 그 힘을 인에 쓰는 이가 있는가？나는 힘이 부족한 사람을 아직 보지 못하였다．아마도 그런 사람이 있을 것이나 아직 보지 못하였다．”하셨다．

作品编号：1398
姓　　名：刘伟　等
国　　籍：中国
组　　别：国内少年组
单位名称：山东省烟台艺术学校

中 俄 篇

生于忧患而死于安乐

“生于忧患而死于安乐”，出自战国时期孟子及其弟子的著作《孟子·告子下》，意思是忧患使人发愤图强，因而得生；安逸使人好逸怠惰，因而致死。这个成语包含着深刻的哲理，体现了中国人的人生智慧。一方面，它引导人们把困难和逆境看作激励自己奋进的动力，自觉地在困难和逆境中磨炼自己，不屈不挠地争取胜利，这也造就了中华民族不畏艰险、自强不息的精神；另一方面，它告诉人们，在生活中要具有忧患意识，未雨绸缪、居安思危、防患于未然。

舜发于畎亩之中，傅说举于版筑之间，胶鬲举于鱼盐之中，管夷吾举于士，孙叔敖举于海，百里奚举于市。故天将降大任于是人也，必先苦其心志，劳其筋骨，饿其体肤，空乏其身，行拂乱其所为，所以动心忍性，曾益其所不能。

人恒过，然后能改；困于心，衡于虑，而后作；征于色，发于声，而后喻。入则无法家拂士，出则无敌国外患者，国恒亡。然后知生于忧患而死于安乐也。

Мэн-цзы говорил:Шунь выявил себя среди полевых канав, когда был землепашцем; Фу Юэ выдвинули на высокую должность, когда он, находясь между досками и бревнами для трамбовки, работал на стронтельстве; Цзяо Гэ выдвинули, когда он был среди корзин с рыбой и солью, занимаясь продажей этих продуктов; Гуань И-у был выдвинут из служилых людей-ши; Сунь-Шу Ао выдвинулся, живя в уединении на берегу моря; Бо-ли Си был выдвинут на городском базаре. Следовательно, перед тем как ниспослать великое назначение таким людям, Небо обязательно испытывает их сердца и волю в горестях нужды, изнуряет их жилы и кости в труде, морит их тела и кожу голодом, опустошает их в лишениях, идет наперекор им, спутывает все, что они делают. Небо тем самым еще больше увеличивает в них то, в чем они неспособны, подвигая сердца их к терпеливости.

Постоянно ошибаясь, тогда только человек может исправиться. Испытывая стеснение в сердце и преграды в размышлениях, человек тогда возбуждается и совершает ошибку; человек познает ошибку только после того, как найдет ее подтверждение в изменении окраски лица, в звучании голоса собеседников. Владение того правителя, который, входя в свои чертоги, не находит в них ни образцовых наставников, ни смышленых помощников среди служилых-ши, а выходя из них, не предается заботам ни о внешних напастях, ни о вражеских владениях, обычно подвергается гибели. Тогда только эти правители познают, что их жизнь заключается в заботах и печалях, а смерть — в покое и радостях.

作品编号：4369
姓　　名：杰米德（Sharifullin Demid）
国　　籍：俄罗斯
组　　别：国际组
单位名称：山东理工大学国际教育学院

从儒家思想看“仁”的内在意蕴

儒家文化是以儒家学说为指导思想的文化流派，儒家文化中的“仁”，是儒家学派道德规范的最高原则，是孔子思想体系的理论核心。“仁”最初是指人与人的一种亲善关系。孔子把“仁”定义为“爱人”。

颜渊问仁。子曰：“克己复礼为仁。一日克己复礼，天下归仁焉。为仁由己，而由人乎哉？”颜渊曰：“请问其目。”子曰：“非礼勿视，非礼勿听，非礼勿言，非礼勿动。”颜渊曰：“回虽不敏，请事斯语矣！”

Янь Юань спросил о человеколюбии. Учитель ответил:

— Сдерживать себя, с тем чтобы во всем соответствовать требованиям ритуала, — это и есть человеколюбие. Если кто-либо в течение одного дня будет сдерживать себя, с тем чтобы во всем соответствовать требованиям ритуала, все в Поднебесной назовут его человеколюбивым. Осуществление человеколюбия зависит от самого человека, разве оно зависит от других людей?

Янь Юань сказал:

— Я прошу рассказать о правилах (осуществления человеколюбия).

Учитель ответил:

— На то, что не соответствует ритуалу, нельзя смотреть; то, что не соответствует ритуалу, нельзя слушать; то, что не соответствует ритуалу, нельзя говорить; то, что не соответствует ритуалу, нельзя делать.

Янь Юань сказал:

— Хотя я и не достаточно сообразителен, буду поступать в соответствии с этими словами.

颜渊问如何行仁？孔子说：“约束自己以符合礼制就是仁。有一日能做到这样，天下就称其仁。这样做全靠自己，还能靠别人吗？”颜回说：“请问具体的要点。”孔子说：“不符合礼制的事不看，不符合礼制的事不听，不符合礼制的事不说，不符合礼制的事不做。”颜回说：“我虽然不聪敏，但一定依据这些话做。”

仲弓问仁。子曰：“出门如见大宾，使民如承大祭。己所不欲，勿施于人。在邦无怨，在家无怨。”仲弓曰：“雍虽不敏，请事斯语矣！”

Чжун-гун спросил о человеколюбии.

Учитель ответил:

— Вне своего дома относись к людям так, словно принимаешь дорогих гостей. Используй народ так, словно совершаешь важное жертвоприношение. Не делай людям того, чего не желаешь себе, и тогда и в государстве и в семье к тебе не будут чувствовать вражды.

Чжун-гун сказал:

— Хотя я недостаточно сообразителен, но буду поступать в соответствии с этими словами.

仲弓问怎样才算仁？孔子说："出去工作如同会见重要外宾，治理百姓好像承担重大祭典。自己所不想要的，便不要强加于人。在国家工作中没有怨恨，在家族生活中没有怨恨。"仲弓说："我虽然不够聪敏，但一定照这话去做。"

作品编号：1550
姓　　名：王喀秋莎、王雨函、许洁、赵春意
国　　籍：中国、俄罗斯
组　　别：国内成人组
单位名称：青岛滨海学院

《论语》中的仁、学、孝、信

《论语》博大精深，在中国文化中具有不可替代的作用。纵观整个中国的历史，可以毫不夸张地说，是《论语》奠定了中华文化的格局，塑造了中华民族的性格。它值得我们反复研读。

"君子喻于义，小人喻于利。"

«Благородный муж знает только долг, низкий человек знает только выгоду.»

"The gentleman understands what is moral, the small man understands what is profitable."

首先，孔子重仁。

子曰："巧言令色，鲜矣仁！"

The Master said, "Clever talk and a pretentious manner have little to do with benevolence."

"己所不欲，勿施于人。"

«Не делай другим того, чего не желаешь себе.»

其次，孔子尚学。

子曰："温故而知新，可以为师矣。"

The Master said, "If you can acquire new knowledge while reviewing the old, you may become a teacher of others."

"敏而好学，不耻下问。"

«Он был мудр, любил учиться и не стыдился обращаться за советами к нижестоящим.»

再次，孔子重孝。

"父母在，不远游，游必有方。"

«Пока родители живы, не уезжай далеко, а если уехал, обязательно живи в определенном месте.»

有子曰："其为人也孝弟，而好犯上者，鲜矣；不好犯上，而好作乱者，未之有也。君子务本，本立而道生。孝弟也者，其为仁之本与！"

Yoo Zi said, "If people behave well towards their parents and elder brothers, few will show a disposition to resist their superiors. And as for such men starting a revolution, no instance of it has ever occurred. It is upon the fundamental that a gentleman works. When the fundamentals are firmly set up, rules and virtues come into being. Filial piety and fraternal love are certainly the root of benevolence."

最后，孔子尚信。

子曰："人而无信，不知其可也。"

The Master said, "People who have no faith do not know what they can do."

"知之为知之，不知为不知，是知也。"

«Если знаешь что-либо считай, что знаешь; а если не знаешь что-либо считай, что не знаешь, — это и есть правильное отношение к знанию.»

中华优秀传统文化是中华民族的突出优势，也是我们在世界激荡中站稳脚跟的根基。作为大学生，我们更应该向世界讲好中国故事，传播好中国声音，促进人类文明交流互鉴，提高国家文化软实力和中华文化的影响力。以上就是我们带给大家的《论语》双语诵读的全部内容。

作品编号：1301
姓　　名：赵子涵、刘林青
国　　籍：中国
组　　别：国内成人组
单位名称：齐鲁理工学院

《论语》中的求学之道

身处知识快速迭代的社会，青年学生应如何面对日复一日的学习生活？孔夫子教导我们要学思相结合，温故而知新。学习是辛苦的，但是颜回“不改其乐”的精神却可以如明灯一样照亮青年学习的前行之路。那怎样才算好学呢？《论语》告诉我们——敏于事而慎于言。走近先贤，汲取智慧。青年学生要弘扬传统文化精髓，创造民族美好未来。

孔子是中华民族历史上第一个伟大的教育家，孔子首创平民教育，继承、发展和传播了古代文化。孔子在一生的教学实践活动中，积累了一套极有价值的教学理论，在许多方面反映了朴素的辩证法和唯物主义观点。他的教育思想、教学方法、治学态度，以及所倡导的互敬互爱的师生关系，直到今天仍然值得我们学习和借鉴。

Конфуций был первым великим просветителем в истории китайской нации. Он стал пионером образования для простого народа, унаследовал, развил и распространил древнюю культуру. На протяжении всей своей педагогической практики Конфуций накопил набор ценных педагогических теорий, во многом отражающих простую диалектику и материалистическую точку зрения. Его педагогическое мышление, методы преподавания, отношение к обучению, уважительные и любящие отношения между учителями и учащимися, которые он пропагандировал, и сегодня достойны нашего изучения и обращения.

在科学技术高速发展、社会日新月异的今天，知识迭代的速度也随之加快，这就要求我们要不断地去学习，其中包含着两个方面的内容：一是学习知识要学思结合，二是对于所学知识要温故知新。

В условиях быстрого развития науки и техники, общество сегодня быстро меняется, скорость итерации знаний также ускоряется, что требует от нас продолжения обучения, которое содержит два аспекта, первое - учиться, сочетая знание и размышление; второе — повторять усвоенное, чтобы познавать новое.

这正是《论语》中孔子所说的“学而不思则罔，思而不学则殆”。

Учитель сказал «Учиться и не размышлять — бесполезно размышлять и не учиться — подвергать себя опасности» .

学习的过程是枯燥的，但，梅花香自苦寒来，对此，颜回正是我们的榜样。子曰：“贤哉，回也！一箪食，一瓢饮，在陋巷，人不堪其忧，回也不改其乐。贤哉，回也！”

Процесс обучения утомителен, но корень учения горек, да плод его сладок. В этом отношении Янь Хуэй служит для нас образцом для подражания. Учитель сказал: «О, как мудр Хуэй! Он довольствуется одной чашкой риса и утоляет жажду ковшом из тыквенной коры, живет в ветхой лачуге. Другие не вынесли бы таких лишений, а он всегда доволен. О, как мудр Хуэй!»

其实，颜回不是甘于贫穷、认同贫穷，而是不惧贫穷。为了摆脱贫穷，颜回这种苦中作乐的精神如一盏灯，可以照亮我们那段枯燥的路。

На самом деле Янь Хуэй не хочет быть бедным или отождествлять себя с бедностью, но не боится бедности. Чтобы избавиться от бедности, дух Янь Хуэй, который находит радость в страданиях, как лампа, может осветить наш участок, скучный путь.

那怎样才算是好学呢？子曰："君子食无求饱，居无求安，敏于事而慎于言，就有道而正焉，可谓好学也已。"

Что же делает человека хорошим учеником? Учитель сказал: «Если благородный муж не думает о насыщении в еде, не заботится об удобном жилье, в делах усерден, в речах осторожен, способен сам ради исправления сблизиться с теми, кто обладает Путем, про такого можно сказать, что он любит учиться.»

学习是一个循序渐进的过程，从挖地基做起，才能矗立起一幢幢的高楼大厦、成就一片又一片的风景。努力吧！未来正等着年轻的我们去建设！

Обучение — это поэтапное строительство. Только выкопав фундамент, можно возвести здание и создать ландшафт. Трудитесь! Будущее ждет, когда мы, молодые, построим его!

作品编号：143
姓　　名：石凯旋
国　　籍：中国
组　　别：国内成人组
单位名称：山东交通职业学院

中 法 篇

《论语·学而》选句诵读

“学而”是《论语》第一篇的篇名。该篇提出以学习为乐事，做到人不知而不愠，反映出孔子学而不厌、诲人不倦、注重修养、严格要求自己的主张。

子曰：“学而时习之，不亦说乎？有朋自远方来，不亦乐乎？人不知而不愠，不亦君子乎？”

Le Maitre dit : « Réviser et pratiquer à temps ce qu’on a appris, n’est-ce pas un plaisir ? Il y a des amis qui viennent de loin chez toi, n’est-ce pas un délice ? Ne pas se sentir dépité quand les autres ne me savent pas, ne suis-je pas un homme cultivé ? »

有子曰：“其为人也孝弟，而好犯上者，鲜矣；不好犯上，而好作乱者，未之有也。君子务本，本立而道生。孝弟也者，其为仁之本与！”

You Zi dit : « S’il se comporte bien envers ses parents et respecte des aînés, il est certainement rare qu’il ait les intentions d’offenser son supérieur. L’homme qui aime fomenter des troubles et n’offensent pas son supérieur n’existe jamais. Un homme de biens’applique à l’essentiel du travail. Quand la fondation a été fermement établie, les règles et les vertus y sont nées. La Piété filiale et le respect envers des ainés sont réellement les racines de L’humanité ! »

曾子曰：“吾日三省吾身：为人谋而不忠乎？与朋友交而不信乎？传不习乎？”

Zeng Zi dit : « Je fais moi-même mon examen de conscience trois fois par jour: ai-je fait le travail de tout mon coeur et de toutes mes forces pour les autres ? Ai-je eu des relations fidèles avec mes amis ? Ai-je mis personnellement en pratique les connaissances qu’on m’a enseignées ? »

子夏曰：“贤贤易色，事父母，能竭其力；事君，能致其身；与朋友交，言而有信。虽曰未学，吾必谓之学矣。”

Zi Xia dit : « Quelqu’un qui préférerait l’homme d’une haute moralité et de grand savoir que la beauté des femmes, qui s’occuperait de ses parents sans ménager ses efforts, qui servirait son souverain en risquant sa vie, qui tiendrait sincèrement ses promesses envers ses amis, pour ainsi dire il aurait du prestige. Même s’il se dit qu’il n’a pas reçu l’éducation, je dirai certainement qu’il a déjà bien étudié et qu’il a été bien éduqué. »

子贡曰：“夫子温、良、恭、俭、让以得之。”

Zi Gong répondit : « Il les a obtenues par sa gentillesse, sa bienveillance, sa courtoisie, sa fnugalite et sa modestie. Son moyen de découverte est tout à fait different de celui des autres, N'est-ce pas ? »

有子曰："礼之用，和为贵。先王之道，斯为美，小大由之。"

You Zi dit : « Le rôle important des rites, en fin de compte, c'est l'harmonie. C'est le moyen le plus précieux que les anciens souverains sages emploient pour gouverner leur pays. C'est cela qui inspire toutes les affaires, grandes ou petites. »

子曰："君子食无求饱，居无求安，敏于事而慎于言，就有道而正焉，可谓好学也已。"

Le Maître dit : « L'homme de bien mange sans rechercher le rassasiement et habite sans rechercher le confort. Il est diligent dans le travail et prudent à ses paroles. Il demande conseil aux hommes moraux et ainsi corrige ses propres fautes. On peut dire que cet Homme est avide de connaissance. »

子贡曰："贫而无谄，富而无骄，何如?"子曰："可也。未若贫而乐，富而好礼者也。"子贡曰："《诗》云：'如切如磋，如琢如磨'，其斯之谓与?"子曰："赐也，始可与言《诗》已矣！告诸往而知来者。"

Zi Gong dit : « L'homme,malgré pauvre, ne flagorne pas; l'autre, bien qu'il soit riche, n'est pas orgueilleux, qu'en pensez-vous ? » « Ils sont assez bons » répondit le Maitre, « mais il vaut mieux que le pauvre soit gai et le riche ait un penchant aux rites. » Zi Gong dit : « Dans les *Poèmes*, il est écrit: "Traiter quelque chose comme corne qu'on coupe, comme ivoire qu'on sculpte, comme jade qu'on cisèle, comme pierre qu'on polit." N'est-ce pas la même signification ? » Le Maitre répondit: « Oh! Maintenant je peux discuter les *Poèmes* avec toi, je te dis précédemment un fait, tu sais déduire plusieurs choses de ce seul fait. »

作品编号：4370
姓　　名：马坚（Al Yousefi Abdulanser Ahmed Mohammed Abdullah）
国　　籍：也门
组　　别：国际组
单位名称：山东理工大学国际教育学院

传仁爱之心，品孔子之乐

《论语》是中国儒学的代表性著作，其在海外的译介沿着世界的东方和西方展开。本作品中，来自中国、乌克兰、马里、韩国、日本等国家的中华文化爱好者用日、英、法、韩几种语言，通过几个小场景共同演绎了对《论语》中友情、亲情、学习、为人等教诲的理解。

一、开场朗诵

尤金：

推崇仁爱仁义，以仁爱化解万物的力量。

Il a considéré la bonté et la justice comme l'article de foi, en l'appliquant pour tout résoudre.

它推动着历史的车轮带吾华夏走过沧桑，

Il a poussé la roue de l'histoire pour nous faire traverser les vicissitudes de l'histoire chinoise,

历练出无数流传至今的中华美德。

affinant d'innombrables vertus chinoises qui ont été transmises jusqu'aujourd'hui.

易布尔：

高山仰止，景行行止。

Les montagnes sont hautes, le paysage est magnifique.

虽不能至，然心向往之。

Bien que je ne puisse pas l'atteindre, j'y aspire.

余读孔子书，则愈想见其为人。

Plus je lis les livres de Confucius, plus j'ai envie de le voir dans ses comportements.

孔子，一身布衣，成就人生传奇；

Confucius, vêtu de tissu toile, a fait de sa vie une légende;

儒家经典，流芳百世。

les classiques du confucianisme ont été transmis pendant des siècles.

郑真真：

他携飞沙尘土上路，

Il a voyagé avec le sable et la poussière,

披微雨落花同行。

et avec la pluie légère et les fleurs qui tombent.

一生风尘仆仆、自强不息。

Sa vie est faite de poussière et d'amélioration de soi.

开中国教育之先河，

Il a été un pionnier de l'éducation chinoise,

诲人不倦，留万世文化，

enseignant aux gens et laissant derrière lui une culture pour toutes les générations,

造就泱泱中华"礼仪之邦"的美誉。

créant la réputation de la Chine en tant que «nation des bonnes étiquettes» .

王夯：

孔子一身布衣，铸就亮丽人生！

Confucius, vêtu de tissu toile, s'est forgé une vie brillante!

七十二贤，演绎千古佳话。

Les 72 sages, ont interprété 1 000 ans d'histoire de bons moeurs.

以博化物，以爱化人。

Éduquer les gens avec amour.

以博爱感天地，以仁爱待他人。

Toucher le ciel et la terre avec un amour universel, traiter les autres avec bienveillance.

孔子将做人的真谛装载进《论语》，

Confucius a changé le véritable sens de l'être humain dans les *Entretiens de Confucius*,

其肉身虽早已化作灰烬，

Bien que son corps soit depuis longtemps réduit en cendres,

其思想却已穿越了千年时空，

ses pensées ont traversé des millénaires de temps et d'espace,

如山中树木，生长不息。

comme les arbres dans les montagnes qui poussent sans fin.

一句"逝者如斯"的感唱，

Ses mots, «Le temps passe ainsi, s'écoulant jour et nuit»,

更是令千古智者为之共鸣。

ont trouvé écho auprès des sages de tous les temps.

Regardons, tout le monde est en train d'apprende les *Entretiens de Confucius*. Les Français, les Japonnais, les Américains et les Coréens...

看！全世界都在学习《论语》，包括法国人、日本人、美国人还有韩国人。

二、诚信——韩语组

"人而无信，不知其可也。大车无輗，小车无軏，其何以行之哉？"

"사람이 신의가 없으면 어디에 써야할지 모르겠다. 우차牛車에 수레끌채가 없고, 마차馬車에 수레끌채 못이 없다면 어떻게 수레를 움직일 수 있겠는가?"

“人如果失去了信用或不讲信用，不知道他还可以做什么。就像大车没有车辕与轭相连接的木销子，小车没有车杠与横木相衔接的销钉，它靠什么行走呢？”

韩钟镇：“人而无信，不知其可也。大车无輗，小车无軏，其何以行之哉？”老师，您好。我是从韩国过来专门学习孔子思想的韩国学生。这句话到底是什么意思？

“인이무신，부지기가야．대거무예，소거무월，기하이행지재？”선생님，안녕하세요？저는 한국에서 공자 사상을 배우기 위해서 온 한국 학생입니다．이 구절이 도대체 어떤 뜻입니까？

史向前：이 말은“사람이 신의가 없으면 어디에 써야할지 모르겠다．우차牛車에 수레끌채가 없고，마차馬車에 수레끌채 못이 없다면 어떻게 수레를 움직일 수 있겠는가？”라는 뜻입니다．

这句话的意思是：“人如果失去了信用或不讲信用，不知道他还可以做什么。就像大车没有车辕与轭相连接的木销子，小车没有车杠与横木相衔接的销钉，它靠什么行走呢？”

韩钟镇：선생님．이 수레끌채와 수레끌체 못이라는 게 도대체 무슨 뜻입니까？

这个木销子和销钉是什么意思呢？

史向前：이 그림을 보시면 이것이 바로 수레끌체와 수레끌체 못입니다．이것들이 없으면 수레를 움직일 수 없겠죠？신의가 없는 사람은 이 수레끌채와 끌채 못이 없는 수레처럼 아무 곳에도 쓸 수 없다는 뜻입니다．

请看这幅画。这里就是木销子和销钉。如果没有这些，车就不能行走了吧？不讲信用的人，就像是没有木销子和销钉的车子一样，放在哪里都毫无用处。明白了吧？

韩钟镇：아！잘 알겠습니다．선생님．저도 공자님 발자취를 따라 신의있는 사람이 될 수 있도록 노력하겠습니다！

老师，明白了。我们也要追随孔子的脚步，努力做一个讲信用的人。

三、“孝道”——“父母在，不远游，游必有方”

“父母在，不远游，游必有方。”

陈高峰：“子曰：‘父母在，不远游，游必有方。’”

父母在せば、远く游ばず。游ばば必ず方有り。

张新莹：您好！您这是在读《论语》吗？这句话是什么意思呀？

こんにちは！論語を詠っているんですか。この論語はどういう意味ですか。

陈高峰：这句话是说，孔子认为“父母在的时候，不要去远处旅行，如果非要去远处旅行的话，也要告诉父母去哪里”。

この言葉はつまり、両亲が存命の时は、远くに旅行しない。心配をかけぬよう、旅行するなら行き先を必ず告げるものだ。

张新莹：谢谢！我明白了。

ありがとうございます。わかりました。

陈高峰：《论语》在日本的传播广泛吗？

日本では、論語は広く伝わっていますか。

张新莹：是啊。
そうですね～。
张新莹：先生。
～老师。
苏伦高娃：あ～、张さん。
嗨！小张！
张新莹：こんにちは！ちょっと質問があります。
您好！想请教您一个问题。
日本では孔子の教えが日本人の思想や生活に影響していますか。
在日本，孔子的教诲影响着日本人的思想以及生活吗？
苏伦高娃：もちろんですよ。日本では、古くから 人々が「心のよりどころ」にしてきました。
当然啦。孔子的思想从古时候起就成了日本人的精神依托。
张新莹：そうですか。勉強になりました。では、先生、この教えは日本語ではどのように 教えられていますか。
是吗！明白了。老师，这句话用日语如何表达呢？
苏伦高娃："父母がおられる間は、遠くに旅に出てはいけない。旅立つ時は必ず、連絡先を父母に教えなさい。"とのことですね。
父母在时尽力不要远游，如非要远游，务必要告知去处。
张新莹：そうですか。では、先生、日本では論語はいつから読み継がれてきましたか。
哦。那么，老师，日本是从什么时候开始传诵《论语》的呢？
苏伦高娃：記述によっては、『古事記』には、すでに『論語』が 伝わっていたということなので、およそ1500年ほど読み続けられていますよ。
研究表明，《古事记》中已有了《论语》传入的记载，迄今为止已有1,500余年的传诵历史。
张新莹：そうですか。勉強になりました。ありがとうございました。
这样啊，我学到了，非常感谢。

四、"学业"——英语组情景剧

"温故而知新，可以为师矣。"
"学而不思则罔，思而不学则殆。"

尤金：Hey, Celine!
你好，赛琳！
赛琳：Hey, Eugene!
你好，尤金！
尤金：Wow, you've read this book so many times. Can you get anything new from it?
哇！你已经读过这本书很多遍了，你还能从中获得新的知识吗？

赛琳：Of course! Don't you know the famous words by Confucius“温故而知新，可以为师矣”？
当然！你不知道孔子的名言吗？“温故而知新，可以为师矣。”

尤金：What does that mean?
这句话是什么意思？

赛琳：It means if you can acquire new knowledge while reviewing the old, you may become a teacher of others.
意思是：如果你能复习已经学过的知识，而且从中获得新知识，那你就能成为别人的老师。

尤金：Reasonable. Are there any other famous sayings on learning by Confucius?
原来如此！那孔子还有其他关于学习的名言吗？

赛琳：Oh, let me think. Learning without thought is labor lost; thought without learning is perilous.
嗯，让我想想。学而不思则罔，思而不学则殆。学习但是不思考会让人迷惘，思考但是不学习则会一无所得。

尤金：Confucius is really a great philosopher!
孔子真是个了不起的哲学家！

赛琳：温故而知新，可以为师矣。

尤金：温故而知新，可以为师矣。

赛琳：学而不思则罔，思而不学则殆。

尤金：学而不思则罔，思而不学则殆。

赛琳：Very good!
非常棒！

尤金：Thank you!
谢谢！

五、友情——法语组情景剧

“有朋自远方来，不亦乐乎？”

Wang: Je suis fatigué. Maman, qu'est-ce que vous faites ?
哎呀，我累了。妈妈，你在做什么？

Zhen: Je suis en train de préparer un dîner pour ce soir, parce que nous avons un invité chez nous.
今晚我们有客人来，我在准备晚餐。

Wang: Mais pourquoi préparez-vous un repas si spécial, maman ?
但是妈妈，你为什么准备这么特别的晚餐呢？

Zhen: Parce que Confucius nous dit : « Il y a des amis qui viennent de loin chez toi, n'est-ce pas un délice ? » Viens me donner un coup de main, chéri.
因为孔子告诉我们：“有朋自远方来，不亦乐乎？”过来帮我一下吧。

Wang: J'arrive.

我来了。

留学生：Zhenzhen, je suis là.

真真，我来啦！

Zhen:（起身相迎）Salut, entrez, je vous en prie.

你好啊，快请进。

Wang: Est-ce que vous avez faim? Maman nous a préparé un très bon dîner, je suis impatient.

你饿了吗？妈妈做了好多好吃的，我等不及了！

留学生：Je suis impatient, aussi.

我也是。

Wang: Bon, viens.

太好了，快来吧！

留学生：Nous avons appris une phrase hier, qui dit « il y a des amis qui viennent de loin chez toi, n'est-ce pas un délice? » En chinois, vous dites《有朋自远方来，不亦乐乎?》C'est bien ça?

昨天我们学了一句话，如果有朋友从远方来，会很开心。用汉语说是不是“有朋自远方来，不亦乐乎”呢？

Zhen & Wang: C'est vrai, et la phrase vient des *Entretiens de Confucius*.

非常对，这是出自《论语》的一句话。

Zhen: Viens manger.

来，过来吃饭吧。（将非洲友人引至桌前，落座，在欢声笑语中吃饭）

六、结尾——全体成员

全体成员：弟子入则孝，出则悌，

Le jeune homme doit se conduire respectueusement, chez lui envers ses parents, en société envers ses aînés.

谨而信，泛爱众，而亲仁。

Il doit être précautionneux et de bonne foi, fraterniser avec les masses populaires, ne vivre dans l'intimité qu'avec les hommes vertueux.

行有余力，则以学文。

Après que tout cela a été pratiqué, il a encore de l'énergie excédente, il va se dévouer à la littérature.

让我们传唱经典《论语》，将儒家思想世代永相传！

Chantons les classiques *Entretiens de Confucius* et transmettons notre Confucianisme aux générations à venir!

作品编号：4200

姓　　名：苏伦高娃　等

国　　籍：中国　等

组　　别：国际组

单位名称：潍坊学院

《诗经》选篇诵读

《诗经》是中国最早的一部诗歌总集，是中华文化的古老源头和中国文学的光辉起点。作为中华民族的“魂与根”，它也是世界了解中国文化、聆听中国故事的窗口。本作品用法语诵读《关雎》《无衣》，跨越语言、文化等藩篱，用国际语言演绎与阐释中国故事，向世界展现中华文明的独特魅力。

它，是我国第一部诗歌总集，百姓间生活日常、大自然生命百态、人世间万般情愫，都在其中一一展现；它，是开在纸上的花，是中国人骨子里的含蓄与浪漫。它，就是《诗经》。今天，让我们一起走进《诗经》，品味国学经典之美。

Comme le premier recueil majeur de poésies chinoises, le *Shi Jing* est une fleur sur papier, qui nous montre la vie quoditienne des gens, les états de vie et les sentiments du monde. Savourons la beauté des classiques chinois.

水岛之上，河水微澜，雎鸠和鸣。一名男子徘徊其上，不停地向对岸望去……

Sur une île, l’eau est douce et les oiseaux chantent. Un homme s’y attarde, regardant de l’autre côté...

La Belle Amie

Au bord de l’eau,
Crient deux oiseaux;
L’homme a envie,
De belle amie.
Le cresson roule,
Dans l’eau qui coule;
On fait la cour,
De nuit et jour.
L’amie refuse,
L’homme s’accuse.

Il tourne au lit,
De-là, de-ci.
Que l’amant cueille,
Les longues feuilles !
Qu’il joue la lyre !
L’amie l’admire.
Qu’on mange longs
Ou courts cressons !
La cloche sonne,
L’amie s’en donne.

大敌当前，兵临城下，将士们同仇敌忾，舞戈挥戟，协作并行，奔赴前线……

En ce moment, l’ennemi est sur le point d’attaquer la ville. Les soldats sont unis par la haine. Ils brandissent les armes et se dirigent ensemble vers le front.

La Camaraderie

Qui dit que je n'ai pas d'habit de guerre ?
Je porte le même habit que vous.
Le roi va lever une armée,
Faisons nos lances acérées.
Nous avons une haine partagée !
Qui dit que je n'ai pas d'habit de guerre ?
Je porte la même chemise que vous.
Le roi va lever une armée,
Faisons nos hallebardes acérées.
Nous allons à la bataille rangée !
Qui dit que je n'ai pas d'habit de guerre ?
Je porte la même armure que vous.
Le roi va lever une armée,
Battons-nous à la pointe de l'épée.
Marchons à la bataille rangée !

中华传统文化源远流长，是五千年中华文明生生不息、发展壮大的精神命脉与思想沃土。弘扬中华传统文化，让世界聆听中国声音。美美与共，天下大同。

Avec une longue histoire, la culture traditionnelle chinoise nourrit le sang spirituel et le sol fertile à la civilisation chinoise de 5 000 ans. Promouvons la culture traditionnelle chinoise et faisons entendre la voix de la Chine dans le monde entier. Si la beauté se manifeste par la diversité et l'intégrité, le monde sera plein d'harmonie et d'unité.

作品编号：137
姓　　名：李晓翠、潘英、李鑫、栾琦
国　　籍：中国
组　　别：国内成人组
单位名称：山东畜牧兽医职业学院

《诗经·氓》选章

《氓》是《诗经》中的一篇叙事抒情长诗，叙述一个女子从恋爱到被弃的过程。本作品展现的内容是青春期的少女起初对不成熟的感情执迷不悟，父母利用《氓》的故事对其进行规劝。

女儿："爸爸妈妈，一个男生给我写了一封信，讲了一个故事，我读给你们听！"

Papa et maman, un garçon m'a écrit une lettre. Il a raconté une histoire que je vais vous lire.

氓之蚩蚩，	Paysan, qui semblais tout candide,
抱布贸丝。	troque des toiles pour du fil.
匪来贸丝，	Le commerce n'est pas son intention réelle.
来即我谋。	Tu venais vers moi pour me parler du mariage.
送子涉淇，	J'ai traversé la rivère Qi,
至于顿丘。	jusqu'à la colline Dun pour t'accompagner.
匪我愆期，	Je ne veux traîner,
子无良媒。	Toi, tu viens sans entremetteuse honorable !
将子无怒，	Je t'en prie, ne te fâche pas !
秋以为期。	Que l'automne soit notre heure.
乘彼垝垣，	je suis montée sur ce mur croulant,
以望复关。	Pour regarder vers Fuguan !
不见复关，	Si je ne te vois pas à Fuguan,
泣涕涟涟。	Je pleure à chaudes larmes.
既见复关，	Quand je te vois à Fuguan,
载笑载言。	Je ne cesse de rire et de parler.
尔卜尔筮，	Ni la tortue, ni l'achillée,
体无咎言。	Ne m'ont rien prédit de mauvais.
以尔车来，	Viens avec ta voiture,
以我贿迁。	Qu'on y emporte ma dot !

女儿："这也太美好了吧！"

C'est tellement beau !

爸爸："孩子，这个故事的结局不是这样的。"

Chérie, ce n'est pas la fin de l'histoire.

妈妈："让我们把后面的故事讲给你听。"

Nous t'en racontons la suite.

桑之未落， Quand le mûrier garde ses feuilles,
其叶沃若。 ses feuilles sont douces au toucher.
于嗟鸠兮！ Hélas! Hélas! Ô tourterelle.
无食桑椹。 Ne t'en va pas manger les mûres.
吁嗟女兮！ Hélas! Hélas ! Ô jeune fille,
无与士耽。 Ne cherche pas à plaire aux garçons.
士之耽兮， Si un garçon tombe amoureux de toi,
犹可说也。 Il peut te quitter aussi facilement.
女之耽兮， Si une fille tombe amoureuse,
不可说也。 Elle ne pourra jamais s'en sortir.

古代女子：
桑之落矣， Lorsque le mûrier perd ses feuilles,
其黄而陨。 Celles-ci tombent, déjà jaunies.
自我徂尔， Depuis que je me suis installée chez toi,
三岁食贫。 Trois ans j'ai vécu de misère.
淇水汤汤， Comme la rivière Qi qui s'en venait haute,
渐车帷裳。 Mouillant les tentures du char!
女也不爽， Je suis toujours honnête,
士贰其行。 C'est toi qui es perfide.
士也罔极， Tu n'as pas de morale,
二三其德。 et ne sais pas être fidèle.
三岁为妇， Je sais être une femme de bonne conduite,
靡室劳矣。 et ai fait tout le ménage.
夙兴夜寐， Matin levée et tard couchée,
靡有朝矣。 pendant plusieurs années.
言既遂矣， Et...autant que cela dura,
至于暴矣。 Gruellement tu m'as maltraitée.
兄弟不知， Mes frères ne le sauront pas,
咥其笑矣。 Il s'en riraient et moqueraient,
静言思之， Quand j'y songe,
躬自悼矣。 Je me mets à pleurer.

"及尔偕老"，« Avec toi je voulais vieillir »,
老使我怨。 Et, vieilli, tu m'as fait souffrir.
淇则有岸， Et pourtant la rivière Qi a ses bords,
隰则有泮。 Et pourtant le val a des digues.
总角之宴， Coiffée en fille, je ressentais ta douceur.
言笑晏晏。 Ta voix, ton rire me fêtaient.
信誓旦旦， Ton serment fut clair telle l'aurore,
不思其反。 Je ne pensais pas que tu changerais.
反是不思， Je ne pense plus à ta trahison.
亦已焉哉！ Maintenant, c'est fini ! Hélas !

爸爸："孩子，不要轻易相信承诺。真正的感情不能只挂在嘴边。"
Chérie, ne crois pas en promesses à la légère. Les vrais amours ne peuvent pas être simplement dits.
妈妈："还有点滴的行动和长久的陪伴。"
La chose la plus importante est l'action et la compagnie.
女儿："好的，我明白了！"
D'accord, je comprends !

作品编号：2913
姓　　名：张悦、单小腾　等
国　　籍：中国
组　　别：国内成人组
单位名称：滨州学院外国语学院

《论语·学而》选读

《论语》被视为伟大的儒家经典，对中国文化影响深远。其内容反映了孔子的政治、美学和伦理思想，涉及政治、教育、文学、哲学和人生真理。它也成为中华民族重要的精神力量。今天，我们用中文和法文来解读《论语》，希望能给大家带来一些思考。

《论语》作为一部伟大的经典，承载着一位伟大哲学家的思考，对中国文化产生了深远影响。其中的内容反映了孔子的政治、美学和伦理思想，涉及政治、教育、文学、哲学以及立身处世的道理等诸多方面的内容，也成为中国人学习成长的重要精神力量。今天，我们将用中法双语朗读《论语》，希望能给大家带来一些思考。

Les Analectes de Confucius, qui véhiculent la pensée d'un grand philosophe, sont considérés comme un grand classique confucéen et ont une profonde influence sur la culture chinoise. Le contenu du livre reflète l'esthétique politique, les pensées éthiques de Confucius, et concerne la politique, l'éducation, la littérature, la philosophie et la vérité de la vie. Il est également devenu une force mentale importante pour le peuple chinois. Aujourd'hui, nous allons lire *Les Analectes de Confucius* en chinois et en français, en espérant vous apporter quelques réflexions

子曰："学而时习之，不亦说乎？有朋自远方来，不亦乐乎？人不知而不愠，不亦君子乎？"

Le Maître dit : « Réviser et pratiquer à temps ce qu'on a appris, N'est-ce pas un plaisir ? Il y a des amis qui viennent de loin chez toi, n'est-ce pas un délice ? Ne pas se sentir dépité quand les autres ne me savent pas, ne suis-je pas un homme cultivé ? »

有子曰："其为人也孝弟，而好犯上者，鲜矣；不好犯上，而好作乱者，未之有也。君子务本，本立而道生。孝弟也者，其为仁之本与！"

You Zi dit : « S'il se comporte bien envers ses parents et respecte des aînés, il est certainement rare qu'il ait les intentions d'offenser son supérieur. L'homme qui aime fomenter des troubles et n'offensent pas son supérieur n'existe jamais. Un homme de bien s'applique à l'essentiel du travail. Quand la fondation a été fermement établie, les règles et les vertus y sont nées. La Piété filiale et le respect envers des aînés sont réellement les racines de l'humainité ! »

子曰："巧言令色，鲜矣仁！"

Le Maître dit : « Celui qui a l'air hypocrite et débite des paroles mielleuses a peu de bienveillance. »

曾子曰："吾日三省吾身：为人谋而不忠乎？与朋友交而不信乎？传不习乎？"

Zeng Zi dit : « Je fais moi-même mon examen de conscience trois fois par jour: ai-je fait le travail de tout mon coeur et de toutes mes forces pour les autres ? Ai-je eu des relations fidèles avec mes amis ? Ai-je mis personnellement en pratique les connaissances qu'on m'a enseignées ? »

子曰："道千乘之国，敬事而信，节用而爱人，使民以时。"

Le Maître dit : « Pour diriger un pays de mille chars de combat, il faut suivre les principes élémentaires ci-dessous: agir avec précaution et constance, mettre l'accent sur la loyauté, économiser les frais en fonction des intérêts vitaux du peuple et faire travailler les paysans pendant la morte saison de l'année. »

子曰："弟子入则孝，出则悌，谨而信，泛爱众，而亲仁。行有余力，则以学文。"

Le Maître dit : « Le jeune homme doit se conduire respectueusement, chez lui envers ses parents, en société envers ses aînés. Il doit être précautionneux et de bonne foi, fraterniser avec les masses populaires, ne vivre dans l'intimité qu'avec les hommes vertueux. Après que tout cela a été pratiqué, il a encore de l'énergie excédente, il va se dévouer à la littérature. »

习近平主席曾说："不忘历史才能开辟未来，善于继承才能善于创新。只有坚持从历史走向未来，从延续民族文化血脉中开拓前进，我们才能做好今天的事业。"希望我们都能常读《论语》等中华经典著作，传承中华民族的精神基因！

Le Président Xi Jinping a dit : « Ce n'est qu'en n'oubliant pas l'histoire que nous pouvons ouvrir l'avenir, et ce n'est qu'en étant bons dans l'héritage que nous pouvons être bons dans l'innovation. Ce n'est qu'en insistant pour passer de l'histoire à l'avenir et en allant de l'avant à partir de la continuation du lignage culturel national que nous pouvons réussir dans ce que nous faisons aujourd'hui. » Espérons que nous lisions tous continuellement *Les Analectes de Confucius* et d'autres écrits classiques chinois pour transmettre l'esprit de la nation chinoise !

作品编号：1743
姓　　名：刘樱艺、余楚楠
国　　籍：中国
组　　别：国内成人组
单位名称：山东大学外国语学院

子路、曾皙、冉有、公西华侍坐

《论语》是我国重要的文化遗产，是打开中国传统文化的一把钥匙。本篇选自《论语·先进》第二十六章“子路、曾皙、冉有、公西华侍坐”。

子路、曾皙、冉有、公西华侍坐。

Une fois que Zi Lu, Zeng Xi, Ran You et Gongxi Hua étaient assis à côté du Maître.

子曰：“以吾一日长乎尔，毋吾以也！居则曰：‘不吾知也！’如或知尔，则何以哉？”

Le Maitre dit : « Bien que je sois plus âgé que vous, vous ne prenez pas ce point à coeur. D’ordinaire vous vous dites toujours: “Personne ne me connaît !” Si vous manifestiez vos talents à l’occasion, que voudriez-vous faire ? »

子路率尔而对曰：“千乘之国，摄乎大国之间，加之以师旅，因之以饥馑，由也为之，比及三年，可使有勇，且知方也。”

Zi Lu répondit sans hésitation : « Donne-moi un Etat de mille chars de guerre, coincé entre des voisins puissants, envahi souvent par les armées étrangères et ravagé depuis plusieurs années par la famine. Si on m’a chargé de le gouverner, en trois ans, je pourrais faire prendre le courage au peuple et lui faire savoir la morale. »

夫子哂之。

Le Maître sourit.

“求，尔何如？”

« Que voudrais-tu faire, Ran You ? » demanda-t-il.

对曰：“方六七十，如五六十，求也为之，比及三年，可使足民。如其礼乐，以俟君子。”

Ran You répondit : « Donne-moi un petit pays de soixante ou soixante-dix Li (1 Li égale 0.5 kilometre) ou plutôt de cinquante ou soixante Li, si je prenais le pouvoir, en trois ans, le peuple vivra dans l’abondance. Pour ce qui concerne les rites et la musique, il faudrait attendre l’intervention d’un vrai sage. »

“赤，尔何如？”

« Et toi, Gongxi Hua ? »

对曰：“非曰能之，愿学焉！宗庙之事，如会同，端章甫，愿为小相焉。”

L’autre répondit : « Je n’ose pas dire que j’en serais capable, mais je désirerais apprendre: dans les cérémonies du temple ancestral et dans la rencontre des grands vassaux, portant une tenue de cérémonie et un chapeau, je voudrais jouer le rôle d'un modeste acolyte. »

"点，尔何如？"

"Et toi, Dian ?"

鼓瑟希，铿尔，舍瑟而作。对曰："异乎三子者之撰！"

Zeng Xi qui avait continué à jouer de la cithare dans le temps en sourdine, à l'appel, il déposa son instrument et se leva. Il dit : « Je crains que mon choix ne soit différent des trois autres disciples. »

子曰："何伤乎？亦各言其志也。"

Le Maître dit : « Ça ne fait rien! Il s'agit tout simplement pour chacun d'exprimer sa propre aspiration. »

曰："莫春者，春服既成，冠者五六人，童子六七人，浴乎沂，风乎舞雩，咏而归。"

Zeng Xi dit : « À la fin du printemps, en tenue printanière, j'aimerais me baigner dans la rivière Yi en compagnie de cinq ou six majeurs et de six ou sept jeunes garçons. Puis on irait respirer la brise sur la terrasse des Danses de la Pluie, enfin on rentrerait en chantant. »

夫子喟然叹曰："吾与点也。"

Le Maître poussa un profond soupir et dit : « Je suis pour Dian. »

三子者出，曾皙后。曾皙曰："夫三子者之言何如？"

Quand les trois autres disciples sont sortis, Zeng Xi était en retard sur ses collégues et demanda : « Que pensez-vous de la volonté des trois autres ? »

子曰："亦各言其志也已矣！"

Le Maître dit : « Chacun a tout simplement exprimé son aspiration. »

曰："夫子何哂由也？"

Zeng Xi reprit : « Maître, pourquoi avez-vous souri à Zhong You ? »

曰："为国以礼，其言不让，是故哂之。"

Le Maître répondit : « Il a de nobles aspirations pour la patrie, il doit savoir gouverner par les rites, mais il parlait sans modestie. C'est pourquoi j'ai ri. »

"唯求则非邦也与？"

« Serait-il possible que Ran You n' ait pas de nobles aspiration pour la patrie ? » dit Zeng Xi.

"安见方六七十如五六十而非邦也者？"

Le Maître dit : « Où aurait-on jamais vu un pays de soixante ou soixante-dix Li, ou voire de cinquante ou soixante Li qui ne soit un véritable pays ? »

"唯赤则非邦也与？"

« Gongxi Hua aspirait-il noblement au gouvernement d'un pays, lui aussi ? »

"宗庙会同，非诸侯而何？赤也为之小，孰能为之大？"

« La cérémonie du temple ancestral et la rencontre des vassaux, de quoi s'agit-il, sinon d'une affaire d'un pays ? Et si Gongxi Hua ne jouait qu'un rôle de modeste acolyte, qui pourrait y assumer le premier rôle ? »

作品编号：3738
姓　　名：赵昊君　等
国　　籍：中国
组　　别：国内成人组
单位名称：山西大学

中 德 篇

《诗经》漫读

《郑风·野有蔓草》是中国古代第一部诗歌总集《诗经》中的一首诗，也是时至今日我们依旧喜爱的歌曲。这是一首恋歌，写一个露珠未干的早上，一对青年男女在田间路上不期而遇，相互倾心，欣喜之情难以抑制。

野有蔓草，零露漙兮。
有美一人，清扬婉兮。
邂逅相遇，适我愿兮。
野有蔓草，零露瀼瀼。
有美一人，婉如清扬。
邂逅相遇，与子偕臧。

《郑风·野有蔓草》是中国古代第一部诗歌总集《诗经》中的一首诗，也是时至今日我们依旧喜爱的歌曲。这是一首恋歌，写一个露珠未干的早上，一对青年男女在田间路上不期而遇，相互倾心，欣喜之情难以抑制。

Als Hymne auf die heilige und freie Ehe und Liebe der chinesischen Vorfahren, hat dieses Gedicht sowohl poetische Imagination als auch wahre Darstellung die ursprüngliche Einfachheit und Geradlinigkeit, die sich von den späteren Generationen unterscheidet. *Das Buch der Lieder* kann als der freiste Klassik seit Tausenden Jahren bezeichnet werden.

一语天然万古新，豪华落尽见真淳。《诗经》是中国第一部诗歌总集，最早的记录为西周初年，最迟产生的作品为春秋时期，上下跨度约五六百年。产生地域以黄河流域为中心，南到长江北岸，分布在现今陕西、甘肃、山西、山东、河北、河南、安徽、湖北等地。

Das Buch der Lieder spiegelt das wahre antike Leben und rührende Geschichten über Liebe und Ehe wider. Lassen Sie uns als Nächstes das Buch der Lieder eintauchen.

南有乔木，Im Siden wachsen hohe Bäume,
不可休思。Sie bieten keine Rast.
汉有游女，Am Han wohnt eine hibsche Maid,
不可求思。Sie kann nicht meine werden.
汉之广矣，Breit ist der Han Fluss, ah,

不可泳思。Kann nicht hinüberschwimmen.
江之永矣，Der Fluss ist unermesslich weit,
不可方思。Kann nicht hinüberstaken.

关关雎鸠，Ein Taubenpärchen turtelt,
在河之洲。Auf seiner Insel im Fluss.
窈窕淑女，Holdes, schönes Kind,
君子好逑。Werde meine Braut.
参差荇菜，Schilfgras hoch und tief,
左右流之。Schaukelt hier und dort.
窈窕淑女，Holdes, schönes Kind,
寤寐求之。Schlafend und wachend verlang ich nach dir.

桃之夭夭，Der Pfirsichbaum steht gesund und stark,
灼灼其华。Die Blüten sind aufgeknospet.
之子于归，Das Mädchen verlässt das Elternhaus,
宜其室家。Wird folgsam zur Schwiegermutter gebracht.
桃之夭夭，Der Pfirsichbaum steht gesund und stark,
有蕡其实。Die Früchte hängen schwer.
之子于归，Das Mädchen verlässt das Elternhaus,
宜其家室。Wird folgsam zur Schwiegermutter gebracht.

《诗经》不仅是我国最早的诗歌总集，也是一部对中国政治、社会生活产生过深远影响的经典。《诗经》的诸多篇章都具有很强的艺术性，其四言体式，其重章复沓，其声律之美，其素朴情感，其反映社会之全面，其施之教化之广大，都令人对这部经典肃然起敬。

“《诗》，可以兴，可以观，可以群，可以怨。迩之事父，远之事君。多识于鸟兽草木之名。”对我们来说，依然需要领会孔子这段话所包含的古典诗教深意，理解《诗经》在古代中国的实际面目及实际用途，通过传统经典认识古代中国。

Ich hoffe, dass Sie das Buch der Lieder lesen und die Kraft der traditionellen Kultur spüren!

作品编号：3409
姓　　名：李欣馨、杨萌、康启月、李汝鹏
国　　籍：中国
组　　别：国内成人组
单位名称：山东艺术学院

《大学》节选

将儒家经典与德语相结合，通过诵读、讲解、书写语言文字等形式，弘扬中华优秀语言文化，从中华经典中汲取智慧力量、坚定理想信念、彰显时代精神，展现社会大众尤其是青少年对中华经典的传承与创新。

大学之道，在明明德，在亲民，在止于至善。知止而后有定，定而后能静，静而后能安，安而后能虑，虑而后能得。物有本末，事有终始。知所先后，则近道矣。

Der Zweck der Universität ist es, die Helligkeit und Aufrichtigkeit der großartigen Tugend weiterzutragen, die Menschen beibringen, das Alte aufzugeben und dann nach dem Neuen zu streben, und die Menschen dazu zu bringen, sich die perfektesten Zustand zu erreichen. Kennen Sie den Zustand, was Sie erreichen sollten, festigen Sie Ihre Ehrgeiz dann; Mitnehmen Sie die fester Ehrgeiz, gehen alle Zappelig zur Ruhigkeit ein. Bewahren Sie Ihre Ruhe, dann werden Sie sich wohlfühlen und nichts bereuen; Nur wenn der Geist sich wohl fühlt, kann er dann nachdenklich sein; Nachdenkliches Ergebnis lassen Sie dann fruchtbar. Eigentlich hat jede Subjekt seinen Wurzel und Anfang, und jede Sache hat seinen Anfang und sein Ende. Nur wenn Sie die Wahrheit behersschen, dass alle seinen Quelle und End hat, bedeutet es, dass Sie schon das Ziel der Universität fest erreichen konnten.

古之欲明明德于天下者，先治其国；欲治其国者，先齐其家；欲齐其家者，先修其身；欲修其身者，先正其心；欲正其心者，先诚其意；欲诚其意者，先致其知；致知在格物。物格而后知至，知至而后意诚，意诚而后心正，心正而后身修，身修而后家齐，家齐而后国治，国治而后天下平。

Die Menschen, die solche in der Antike helle und aufrechte Tugend auf die Welt herausbringen wollte, mussten vor allem ihr eignen Land reinigen. Um ihr Land zu reinigen, mussten sie zuerst ihre Familie und Haushalte gut führen. Um ihre Familie und Haushalte gut zu führen, mussten sie zuerst auf jeden Fall ihren eignen Charakter ernsthaft kultivieren. Um ihr Charakter ernsthaft kultievieren, mussten sie zuerst ihren Geist korrigieren. Um ihren Geist zu korriegieren, mussten sie zuerst ihre Absichten aufrichtig machen. Um ihre Absichten aufrichtig zu machen, mussten sie zuerst die Kenntnisse erhalten. Um die notwendige Kenntnisse zu erhalten. Der Weg zum Kenntnissenerhalten berucht sich auf das Wissen und die Forschung jeder Sache. Nur wenn sie Wissen erhalten, könnten ihr Abschichten aufrichtig sein. Nur wenn sie Abschichten aufrichtig sein könnten, könnten sie ihren Geißt korrigieren. Nur wenn ihr Gest korrigiert wird, könnten sie ihr Charakter ernsthaft kultievieren. Nur wenn sie ihre Charakter ernsthaft kultievieren, könnten sie dann ihre Familie und Haushalte gut führen. Und nur wenn sie ihre Familie und Haushalte gut führen, könnten sie ihr eignen Land richtig herrschen. Und nur wenn sie ihr eignen Land richtig herrschen, könnten sie endlich helle und aufrechte Tugend auf die Welt herausbringen wollten und die Welt wird am Ende zum Frieden zurückgehen.

自天子以至于庶人，一是皆以修身为本。其本乱而末治者，否矣。其所厚者薄，而其所薄者厚，未之有也。此谓知本，此谓知之至也。

Von dem Behersscher bis hinten zur seinen Bürgern sollen alle ihre eignen moralischen Charakter als Grundlage kultivieren. Es ist unmöglich, dass die Menschen gerade ihren Ergibnisse erfolgreich erreicht aber gleichzeitig die wichtige Grundlage ignoriert. Bei den alten Weisen ist nicht zu finden, dass die wichtigen Grundlagen heruntergespielt werden, während die Ergibnisse geschätzt werden. Dies bezeichnet man als das Wissen um die Grundlagen, und das ist die höchste Weisheit.

所谓诚其意者：毋自欺也。如恶恶臭，如好好色，此之谓自谦。故君子必慎其独也！小人闲居为不善，无所不至，见君子而后厌然，掩其不善，而著其善。人之视己，如见其肺肝然，则何益矣。此谓诚于中，形于外，故君子必慎其独也。曾子曰："十目所视，十手所指，其严乎！"富润屋，德润身，心广体胖，故君子必诚其意。

In unseren Abschichten aufrichtig zu sein, bedeutet, dass wir sich nicht selbst betrügen. Die Ehrlichkeit soll darauf gezogen werden, zum Beispiel wenn wir nach unangenehme Grüche riechtet oder die Schönheit anschaut, sollen wir direkt unsere Meinung ausspreichen, damit wir uns unsere eignen Geist befrieden könnten. Aus diesem Grund muss ein Gentleman sehr vorsichtig sein, wenn er allein ist. Aber ein Schurke kann alles (inklusive etwas Gutes oder Schlechtes) tun, wenn er zu Hause bleibt. Nur wenn aber er einen Gentelman trifft, versteckt und verbergt er seine Taten und gibt vor, freundlich und gehorsam zum Vorschein zu sein. Tatsächlich ist es, dass er bereits durchgeschaut wird. Es ist ganz so gleich zu einem Beispiel, dass sie Ihre inneren Organe sehen können, was bringt es eigentlich also, sich zu verstecken? Das ist die so genannte innere Wahrheit, die sich mit Sicherheit auch im Äußeren zeigen wird. Deshalb muss ein Gentleman sehr vorsichtig und zurückhaltend sein, wenn er allein ist. Zengzi sagte: „Wie einschüchternd ist es für einen Mann, von allen beobachtet und von allen beschuldigt zu werden!" Reichtum kann ein Haus schmücken, Tugend kann eine Person von hohem moralischen Charakter machen, und ein breiter Geist kann zu einem friedlichen Körper führen, also muss ein Gentleman aufrichtig in seinen Absichten sein.

作品编号：1624
姓　　名：闵令雪、张舒、魏雨欣、刘奥奇、孙嘉薪
国　　籍：中国
组　　别：国内成人组
单位名称：山东农业大学

《大学》与新民学会

一、导入：

Dies ist der ehemalige Standort der Xinmin-Gesellschaft. Am 14. April 1918 versammelte sich hier die fortschrittliche Jugend unter der Leitung von Mao Zedong und Cai Hesen, um die Einweihungszeremonie der Xinmin-Gesellschaft abzuhalten. Das Wort „Xin Min“ ist dem Anfang des Klassikers *Daxue* entnommen.

这里是新民学会旧址。1918 年 4 月 14 日，以毛泽东、蔡和森为首的进步青年聚集于此，举办了新民学会成立仪式。“新民”正是取自《大学》的开篇，“大学之道，在明明德，在新民，在止于至善”。（编者注：“新民”，又作“亲民”。）

二、中文诵读：

《礼记・大学》：

大学之道，在明明德，在新民，在止于至善。

知止而后有定，
定而后能静，
静而后能安，
安而后能虑，
虑而后能得。

物有本末，事有终始。知所先后，则近道矣。

古之欲明明德于天下者，先治其国；
欲治其国者，先齐其家；
欲齐其家者，先修其身；
欲修其身者，先正其心；
欲正其心者，先诚其意；
欲诚其意者，先致其知；
致知在格物。

物格而后知至，
知至而后意诚，
意诚而后心正，
心正而后身修，
身修而后家齐，
家齐而后国治，
国治而后天下平。

三、背景介绍：

20世纪初，蔡和森的母亲葛健豪带着她的儿女们租住在四周都是坟墓的简陋墓庐里。作为一个旧时代的妇女，葛健豪冲破封建思想的束缚，带领儿女摆脱封建家庭的桎梏，举家移居长沙，投入轰轰烈烈的革命事业。

新民学会以“改造中国与世界”为宗旨，志在救国救民，其许多会员后来加入了中国社会主义青年团和共产主义小组，为中国共产党的创建做了多方面的准备，被誉为“建党先声”。

无论是葛健豪开启新生活的壮举，还是中国共产党开创的中国历史的新篇章，都是“新民”二字的经典实践！

张：Im frühen 20. Jahrhundert mieteten Cai's Mutter, Ge Jianhao, und ihre Kinder eine einfache Ruhestätte, die von Gräbern umgeben war. Als Dame der alten Ära brach Ge Jianhao mit den feudalen Konventionen und brachte auch ihre Söhne und Töchter dazu, sich zu befreien. Sie zogen gemeinsam nach Changsha und stürzten sich energisch in die revolutionäre Sache.

李：Mit dem Ziel, „China und die Welt zu verändern“, um das Land und die Menschen zu retten, schlossen sich viele ihrer Mitstreiter später der Chinesischen Sozialistischen Jugendliga und der Kommunistischen Gruppe an. Sie bereiteten die Gründung der Kommunistischen Partei Chinas vor und wurden als „Pioniere des Parteiaufbaus“ geehrt.

张：Ob man nun Ge Jianhao's Kunststück betrachtet, ein neues Leben aufzubauen,

李：oder auf das von der Kommunistischen Partei Chinas geschaffene neue Kapitel der chinesischen Geschichte blickt –

张：dies entspricht auf jeden Fall der klassischen Bedeutung des Wortes,

二人齐：das Volk zu erneuern!

四、德文诵读：

Die große Wissenschaft

Der Weg der großen Wissenschaft bringt die Klarheit der Tugend zum Leuchten, erneuert das Volk und stellt uns auf das Beste ein.

Versteht man die Basis,ergibt sich daraus eine Bestimmtheit.

Bestimmtheit bereitet uns vor, offen Acht zu geben.

Achtsamkeit macht uns gefasst.

Gefasst können wir erwägen.

Erwägend streben wir zum Erfolg.

Die Dinge erscheinen als Wurzel und Wipfel.

Die Angelegenheiten zeigen Ende und Anfang.

Versteht man die richtige Reihenfolge,dann ist man schon auf dem Weg...

Durch das Befragen der Dinge erreicht man Wissen.

Dem weiteren Wissen folgt Integrität des Sinnes.

Der integre Sinn bewirkt ein aufrechtes Herz.

Ein aufrechtes Herz bildet den Leib.
Ein gebildeter Mensch kann seine Familie arrangieren
und dadurch sein Land in Ordnung bringen.
Sind die Länder wohlgeordnet, kann die Welt in Frieden kommen.
Sind die Länder wohlgeordnet, kann die Welt in Frieden kommen.
Sind die Länder wohlgeordnet, kann die Welt in Frieden kommen.

作品编号：3200
姓　　名：崔璨、曹淑娴、陈衣卉、丰文晶、郭辉、黄静
韩硕、何嘉欣、贺扬凡、姜皓、金姝贝、刘硕
鲁姝茜、李德泽、刘怡彤、门秀珂、肖家玉
谢芹芹、向宇涵、肖佳欣、赵通、赵向、赵思雅、张迅
国　　籍：中国
组　　别：国内成人组
单位名称：湖南师范大学

中 日 篇

《论语》奇遇记

大家好，我今天为大家带来的经典诵读的作品选自儒家经典《论语》的“雍也”篇，“贤哉，回也！一箪食，一瓢饮，在陋巷，人不堪其忧，回也不改其乐。贤哉，回也！”它诠释了人生快乐的最高境界。无论外部的条件有多么艰苦，内心依旧坚不可摧，不为物所役，不为外在所困扰。一个人在道德上的高度自信才是他在这世界上无忧无惧的底气。

正所谓“斯是陋室，惟吾德馨”。快乐也是一种特殊的能力。本次表演的故事发生在日本的儒家讲堂里，我将以对《论语》一窍不通的日本小女孩小樱的身份登场。她在梦中奇幻般地穿越到了中国古代，在那里一位贵人解答了她的疑惑。

那就让我们一起开启探索之旅吧！

（大和時代にある儒教の学童で、先生が話している）

先生：子曰けんなるかなかいや！いっだんのし、いっぴょうのいん、ろうこうにあり人はその憂いに堪えず、回やその楽しみを改めず。けんなるかなかいや！

桜さん：もう一何だこれ？私全然理解できないよ！一箪の食っ、ありえない。米だけで食べて美味しいか？まあいいや一私と関係ないし…

（中国のある場所）

桜さん：えっ！ここはどこ?!

中国少女：ここは中国だよ。大丈夫ですか？

桜さん：（中国…）まさか孔子のこと、知っている？『論語』とか、そして顔回という人のこと?

中国少女：もちろん！子曰 ：けんなるかなかいや！いっだんのし、いっぴょうのいん、ろうこうにあり、人はその憂いに堪えず、回やその楽しみを改めず。けんなるかなかいや！

桜さん：回って、先生が何度も教えてくれたんだけど、どうしてもわからないんだよ…ね、颜回って、どんな人なの？

中国少女：そうですね。孔子が最も愛でっている弟子は二、三人いて、そのうちの1人は顔回であったよ。路地裏に住み、草を編んで器を作ってご飯を食べ、瓢箪で水を飲むといった素朴な人だった！他の人なら、そのつらさに耐えきれないところだが、顔回はそれを自ら楽しんでいるんだ。それはどれほどの修養を積んだことだろう！

お金も物も、ただ虚無である。それより、1杯の空茶や、野菜のほうが真実ではないか？生活はどんなに辛くても、顔回は相変わらず楽しんでいるんだ。

孔子は颜回をそれほど賞美するというのは、顔回は今の窮乏に耐えてより大きい家に引っ越すつもりはない、「回やその楽しみを改めず」というように、路地裏に住んでいたとしても、相変わらず生き生きとするからだ。

人間の喜びは三層あり。他人と比較して得た喜びは第1層である。例えば、自分の家は他人のより大きいとか。そして、以前の自分と比べて、成長したと感じる喜びは第2層。例えば。弱かった自分は今、どんな困難にあっても、負けないとか。無条件の快楽は第三層、最高の境界。人生は山あり、谷ありだ。最後まで自分のそばにいるのは自分以外の何ものでもない。目当ての物事を心から感じる、それは人の特別な能力だと思う。孔子から見て、運命を呟くのではなく、自らの志を抱いている。それは「為せば成る」というものではないか？

こういうなら、少しだけ理解しやすくなったかなあ？

（大和時代に戻った）

桜さん：そういう意味ですか、やっと分かった！いい夢だったらよね！

人の強い自信は外的からではなく、知識を高め、品性を磨き、いろんな修養をするという内的なものです。道徳の上に自信を高めるからこそ、世の中に迷わず、恐れず強くなるかもしれません。

人の心が充実しているなら、この世界は必ず心どおりにうまく行きます。私もそういう能力を探したいと思います

以上です。ご静聴どうもありがとうございます！

今天呢，我想分享《论语》当中一直激励着我前行的一句话。

子曰："贤哉，回也！一箪食，一瓢饮，在陋巷，人不堪其忧，回也不改其乐。贤哉，回也！"

场景一

时间：日本大和时代

地点：《论语》学堂

人物：主人公小樱和老师

内容：小樱在听老师讲《论语》

老师：子曰："贤哉，回也！一箪食，一瓢饮，在陋巷，人不堪其忧，回也不改其乐。贤哉，回也！"

小樱："哎呀，这都是什么呀，我完全听不懂！一箪食？怎么可能啊？如果光吃大米的话那能好吃吗？算了算了，反正和我也没什么关系……"

场景二

时间：中国古代

地点：某个庭院内

人物：主人公小樱和中国少女

内容：小樱向中国少女询问有关颜回和《论语》的事情

小樱：哎呀！这里是哪儿啊？

中国少女：这里是中国哦。你没事吧？

小樱：（中国啊……）你是不是知道孔子？比如《论语》之类的，还有一个叫颜回的人，这些你都了解吗？

中国少女：那是当然啦！子曰："贤哉，回也！一箪食，一瓢饮，在陋巷，人不堪其忧，回也不改其乐。贤哉，回也！"

小樱：说到颜回，无论老师怎么教我，我都没办法理解这个人……你说颜回他究竟是个怎样的人啊？

中国少女：孔子有两三个最喜爱的弟子，颜回就是其中之一。他真的是一个很质朴的人，一个人住在简陋的小巷子里，用干草做成容器用来吃饭，用水瓢来喝水。别人完全忍受不了的事情，颜回却可以乐在其中，这是修炼了多少年才可以达到的高度呀！

无论是荣华富贵，还是锦衣玉食，对于颜回而言都是虚的，相比之下，一杯清新的茶水和一些新鲜的蔬菜才更真实、实在。

孔子如此赞赏颜回，并不是因为他承受现在的苦难是为了未来搬到大房子里生活，而是像"回也不改其乐"这句话说的那样，他虽然住在简陋的小巷子里，但依旧可以非常快乐、自在。

人类的快乐一共有三层。第一层是与他人攀比而产生的快乐。比如你的房子比别人的大一些，你就会感到快乐。第二层是感受到自我成长的快乐。比如曾经你是一个很懦弱的人，但现在的你却能够独当一面。第三层则是无条件的快乐，也是最高层次的快乐。人生本就是起起落落，能够一直陪伴着自己走到生命尽头的人也只有自己了。所以，你要用心去感受眼下的每一个瞬间，我想那就是感受幸福的能力。在孔子看来，不对命运充满抱怨，有着自己的志向，这不正是"有志者事竟成"吗？

这样讲的话，你或许可以更好理解一些。

场景三

时间：大和时代

场地：《论语》学堂

人物：主人公小樱

内容：从梦中醒来，终于明白了这句话，并且有了自己的感触

小樱：原来是这样，我终于理解了这句话！

一个人强大的自信并不是来自外在的，而是通过提高认知、磨炼品性以及修炼自己从而让内心稳定下来。只有做到在道德上高度自信，才不会被这世间的未知和诱惑所左右。

如果你的心足够稳定，那么未来的一切都将会如你心意、顺顺利利。

我也想拥有像颜回那样喜悦的心，还有随时随地可以让自己幸福的能力。

作品编号：3582
姓　　名：洪阳媛
国　　籍：中国
组　　别：国内成人组
单位名称：青岛滨海学院

《诗经·木瓜》吟诵

先秦时期卫国的一首描述爱情的民歌，是通过赠送木瓜表达深厚情意的诗作，传诵极广。它是中华民族礼尚往来的美好写照，是中华礼仪的典范之作。

“滴水之恩，当涌泉相报。”你赠我一个木瓜，我却以价值连城的美玉回赠。不是为了回报，而是为了我们可以永远相好。在这世间，其实人与人之间的珍贵情谊是无法用金钱来衡量的。因真心无价，爱亦无价。唯有圣洁无私的爱能打破“木瓜与美玉”的天平，唤醒人与人之间那份童年时的纯真。这种高尚的情谊正是我们华夏儿女应当持守的“礼”之精髓。

唱：

投我以木瓜，报之以琼琚。
匪报也 匪报也，永以为好也！
投我以木桃，报之以琼瑶。
匪报也 匪报也，永以为好也！
投我以木李，报之以琼玖。
匪报也 匪报也，永以为好也！
投我以木李，报之以琼玖。
匪报也 匪报也，永以为好也 为好也！

诵读：

貴女は、私に花梨を贈ってくれました。
お返しに、私は美しい宝石を贈ります。
これは、お礼ではなく、永遠の愛の印です。
投我以木瓜，报之以琼琚。
匪报也 匪报也，永以为好也！
貴女は、私に桃を贈ってくれました。
お返しに、私は赤くて、美しい宝石を贈ります。
これは、お礼ではなく、永遠の愛の印です。
投我以木桃，报之以琼瑶。
匪报也 匪报也，永以为好也！
貴女は、私に李を贈ってくれました。

お返しに、私は黒くて、美しい宝石を贈ります。
これは、お礼ではなく、永遠の愛の印です。
投我以木李，报之以琼玖。
匪报也 匪报也，永以为好也！

作品编号：2539
姓　　名：孙笑莹、方汇
国　　籍：中国
组　　别：国内成人组
单位名称：山东省交通职业学院

中葡篇

诵读儒家经典，弘扬中华美德

广东外语外贸大学葡萄牙语专业的三位学生，用中文与葡语两种语言诵读《论语》中与“美德”相关的经典章节。在作品中，她们通过展示毛笔书法等个人特长，向观众展示了中国文化的独特魅力；通过阐述经典章节背后的故事，来抒发她们的所思所感；在总结时，亦抒发了《论语》在当今时代给予人们新启发的期盼。她们相信，《论语》的智慧能引领同学们以道为方向，以德为立脚点，提高同学们的道德水平，促进全面发展。与此同时，她们也表达了对中西方文化在未来能够更加深入地相互交流借鉴的期待，希望彼此在源远流长的文明长河中绽放出更加璀璨的光芒！

子曰：“天生德于予，桓魋其如予何？”

Confúcio disse: “O céu criou a virtude que existe em mim. O que Huan Tui poderá fazer comigo?”

这句话的背后有这样一个故事：公元前 492 年，孔子从卫国去陈国时经过宋国。桓魋听说以后，带兵去害孔子。幸运的是，孔子在学生的保护下，离开了宋国。在逃跑途中，他说了这句话。他认为，自己是有仁德的人，而且是上天把仁德赋予了他，所以桓魋对他是无可奈何的。在这句话里，我们可以看到孔子对于推广圣贤德行的坚持，以及面对一切艰难险阻，仍然肩负这一伟大使命的精神。而在《论语》一书中，道德，是最为重要的主题之一。

Há uma história antiga por detrás desta afirmação: Há muito tempo, por volta do ano de 492 a.c, Confúcio passou pelo estado de Song quando ia de Wei para Chen. Quando Huan soube disso, decidiu ia ter com ele com os seus guerreiros para o assasinar. Felizmente, Confúcio fugiu de Song sob a proteção dos seus discípulos, e durante a fuga proferiu estas palavras. Ele acreditava que era um homem de virtude e benevolência, e que o céu lhe tinha dado virtude, de modo que não havia nada que Huan lhe pudesse fazer. Na história, nós podemos ver a insistência de Confúcio em promover as virtudes dos sábios e o espírito de assumir esta grande missão perante todas as dificuldades. Em *Os Analectos* a virtude também é um dos temas de maior relevo.

君子如竹，竹色君子德。竹如谦谦君子，君子之姿，亦是竹之姿也。

As pessoas virtuosas são como o bambu. A postura de um homem nobre é como a postura do bambu.

君子如兰，空谷幽香。

As pessoas de caráter elevado são como orquídeas, possuem excelentes virtudes.

子曰："志于道，据于德，依于仁，游于艺。"

Confúcio disse: "Ter o espírito orientado pelo Caminho, fundamentar-se na Virtude, apoiar-se na Benevolência e cultivar-se nas Artes."

思想的高度决定人生的高度。一个人的思想品德决定了他的人生追求。忧国忧民者，不可能追名逐利。相反，一个见利忘义的人也不可能心忧天下。孔子深刻地明白这个道理，所以，在这句话中表达了他的思想。这句话是关于进德修业的秩序和方法，表现了在教育过程中，道、德、仁和艺的重要性。以道为方向，以德为立脚点，以仁为根本。仁与艺是道与德的外化表现。这四个要素对于学生的全面发展是不可或缺的。

A elevação do pensamento determina a altura da vida de uma pessoa. O carácter e os valores de uma pessoa derminam a sua ambição de vida. Uma pessoa que se preocupe com o país e o povo, é pouco provável que procure a fama e o dinheiro. Ao contrário, uma pessoa que só vê o dinheiro e esquece a justiça também é pouco provável que se preocupe com o povo. Confúcio entendeu isso profundamente, por isso ele expressa o seu pensamento nesta afirmação, a qual refere a ordem e o método (do avanço) da virtude, indica o processo de aprendizagem, a importância do Caminho, da Virtude, da Benevolência, e das Artes. O Caminho é a direção, a Virtude é a base, a Benevolência é a raiz. A benevolência e as artes são as expressões exteriores do Caminho e da virtude. Estes quatro fatores são indispensáveis para o desenvolvimento abrangente dos estudantes.

子以四教：文，行，忠，信。

Confúcio baseava o seu ensino em quatro aspetos: letra, comportamento, devoção e veracidade.

孔子以四项内容来教导学生：文化知识、（履行所学之道的）行动、忠诚、守信。

Confúcio ensinou aos seus discípulos quatro elementos: conhecimento cultural, ação (para cumprir a forma como tinham aprendido), lealdade e cumprimento da sua palavra.

在他看来，文化知识固然重要，但是道德修养也必不可少。

Na opinião do Confúcio, embora o conhecimento cultural seja importante, o cultivo moral também é essencial.

孔子在过去对于德行的推广，至今有着深刻的影响。

A propagação da virtude de Confúcio no passado tem tido um impacto profundo até aos dias de hoje.

作为学生，我们要以道为方向，以德为立脚点，以仁为根本，提高我们自身的道德水平，促进我们的全面发展。

Como estudantes precisamos de seguir o caminho baseado em sua direção, sendo a virtude a nossa base e a benevolência a nossa raiz, para melhorar os nossos próprios critérios morais e promover o nosso desenvolvimento abrangente.

我们相信，《论语》的智慧在当今时代定会绽放出更加精彩的光芒！

Acreditamos que a sabedoria de *Os Analectos* florescerá ainda mais brilhante nos dias de hoje!

作品编号：1665

姓　　名：颜露华、余俊一、杨珍琴

国　　籍：巴西、中国

组　　别：国际组

单位名称：广东外语外贸大学

循圣人足迹 弘善人之道

本作品展现了孔子与他的弟子之间的对话，对话内容强调了人们该如何做个善人。

子张问善人之道。子曰："不践迹，亦不入于室。"

Zizhang perguntou sobre as características de um homem bom, e o Confúcio disse: "ELe não pisa os passos dos outros, além disso, não entra nos quartos internos."

大家好！我是卫宇达，来自安哥拉，是华侨大学的一名留学生。我很高兴能够在这里为大家分享孔子的这一段话。

子张是孔子的弟子，他在这里向孔子请教做善人之道。也就是，做善人的方法或者什么样的人才能称为善人。

孔子说："不践迹，亦不入于室。"

孔子的答复简短但完整。我们来看他的意思。

这里的"不践迹"，"践"指的是"实践"，"迹"指的是"足迹"。谁的足迹呢？孔子在这里指的是贤人的足迹。

那我们现在把这两个概念结合起来。

孔子对弟子的答复是，如果你想做善人，那你应该学习贤人和圣人的行为，并且呢，按照他们的足迹来走。

总而言之，跟随贤人的脚步，是我们做善人的前提条件。

以上是我对这段话的理解和分享，感谢大家的倾听。

作品编号：332
姓　　名：卫宇达
国　　籍：安哥拉
组　　别：国际组
单位名称：华侨大学文学院

中 西 篇

读《论语·里仁》有感

《论语·里仁》第五章强调了"仁"的重要性，认为人们应该时刻坚守仁德，不论是在富贵还是贫贱的情况下。同时，孔子也提到了"君子"应该如何行事，认为君子不会因为追求富贵而背离仁德，也不会因为厌恶贫贱而放弃追求仁德。

子曰："富与贵，是人之所欲也；不以其道得之，不处也。贫与贱，是人之所恶也；不以其道得之，不去也。君子去仁，恶乎成名？君子无终食之间违仁，造次必于是，颠沛必于是。"

Confucio dijo: "Las riquezas y los honores son lo que los hombres desean. Si no se puede obtener en la debida manera, no podrán ser retenidos. La pobreza y la mezquindad son lo que les desagrada a los hombres. Si no se puede evitar de la manera adecuada, no deben ser evitados." Si un caballero abandona la benevolencia, ¿cómo puede alcanzar la reputación de caballero? Un caballero no abandona la benevolencia ni siquiera al comer, con prisas o en una situación difícil.

《论语·里仁》

子曰："里仁为美。择不处仁，焉得知？"

子曰："不仁者不可以久处约，不可以长处乐。仁者安仁，知者利仁。"

子曰："唯仁者能好人，能恶人。"

子曰："苟志于仁矣，无恶也。"

子曰："富与贵，是人之所欲也；不以其道得之，不处也。贫与贱，是人之所恶也；不以其道得之，不去也。君子去仁，恶乎成名？君子无终食之间违仁，造次必于是，颠沛必于是。"

得到富贵，去掉贫贱，是人们的本能欲望，只不过要通过正当的手段和途径去满足这些欲望，不能违背道义。

君子与小人的区别，就在于是否"以其道得之"。真正的君子，在面对富贵与贫贱时坚守道义，在任何时刻都不放弃对仁德的坚持，不降低对自我的要求。即使是一顿饭的工夫，或在颠沛流离之时，都应该如此。

这句名言主要涉及义与利的关系问题、个人的道德修养问题，以及君子与小人的区别。

富与贵不仅仅是物质上的体现，更重要的是精神上的体现。大多数人都想通过各种各样的办法来过上富有的日子，但是用不正当的手段来达到目的，会持续多久呢？对我影响最深刻的是一对夫妇。他们结婚时一无所有，靠自己的双手来种地、做买卖，努力工作。他们的艰辛和困难是我今天无法想象的。但是现在，他们已有车有房，生活富足。谁家有困难，他们都会热心地提供帮助。可见种什么因就会收到什么果。富贵是人们所希望的，贫贱是人们所厌恶的，此乃人之常情，无可厚非。然而，当人们处于贫困之中时，以善良、勤奋、努力获得财富、快乐和幸福，是我认为最佳的福报。所以我愿所有人，靠知识来改变命运，靠劳动来创造美好的生活。

《论语》不仅带给了我智慧和启迪，更让我感受到了爱和宁静，使我理解在生活中，所有渴望提高自己道德境界的人，都需要严格要求自己，使自己拥有一种对道德修养的执着精神。我希望它能带给大家同样的感受，所以，我们一起来读《论语》吧。

Confucio tiene un dicho muy famoso:

Las riquezas y los honores son lo que los hombres desean. Si no se puede obtener en la debida manera, no podrán ser retenidos. La pobreza y la mezquindad son lo que les desagrada a los hombres. Si no se puede evitar de la manera adecuada, no deben ser evitados. Si un hombre superior abandona la virtud, ¿cómo puede mantener su reputación?

Incluso en tan poco tiempo como es comer una comida, el hombre superior no dejará de practicar la benevolencia, ni siquiera con prisa, incluso a la deriva se aferrará a la virtud.

Yo pienso que, hacerse rico y noble y deshacerse de la pobreza y la mezquindad, es lo que todos anhelan. La diferencia entre un caballero y un villano radica en si actúa o no “según su moral”. Un verdadero caballero no solo se apega a la moralidad frente a la riqueza y la pobreza, sino que en cualquier momento de su vida, nunca debe renunciar a su insistencia en la benevolencia y reducir sus requisitos para sí mismo. Incluso si es un momento molesto, o incluso en tiempos de deriva, debería ser así.

El contenido principal de este dicho involucra la relación entre la justicia y la ganancia, el cultivo de la moral personal y la diferencia entre un caballero y un villano.

La riqueza y el prestigio no son sólo manifestaciones materiales, sino también hacen referencia a algo más importante, las experiencias morales y espirituales. La mayoría de las personas quieren vivir una vida rica a través de varios métodos, ¿pero cuánto tiempo puede durar una vida de riqueza obtenida por medios indebidos? La historia que más me impactó es la de una pareja. Cuando se casaron, no tenían nada. Dependían de sus propias manos para cultivar, hacer negocios y trabajar duro. Sus dificultades y penurias hoy superan mi comprensión. Pero ahora tienen auto y casa, y viven una vida plena. Siempre que alguien está en apuros, ayudan con entusiasmo. Esto demuestra que cosechas lo que siembras. La gente anhela la riqueza y odia la pobreza. Es parte de la naturaleza humana y no tiene nada de malo.

Cuando la gente vive en la pobreza, ser amable, diligente, trabajador y soñar con ser rico, alegre y feliz es la mejor bendición en mi opinión, y uno puede salir de la pobreza y volverse rico. Por lo tanto, deseo que todos apunten a la riqueza y al honor, cambien su destino mediante el conocimiento y creen una vida mejor mediante el esfuerzo.

"Las Analectas" no solo me trajeron sabiduría e iluminación, sino que también me hicieron sentir amor y tranquilidad. Entiendo que en la vida, todos aquellos que están ansiosos por mejorar su ámbito moral necesitan ser estrictos consigo mismos, y son ellos los que tienen un espíritu de dedicación al cultivo moral. Espero que pueda traerles el mismo sentimiento, así que leamos juntos "Las Analectas".

作品编号：3648
姓　　名：覃月（Nancy Ebong Monsuy Ning）
国　　籍：赤道几内亚
组　　别：国际组
单位名称：青岛大学

子路、曾皙、冉有、公西华侍坐

《子路、曾皙、冉有、公西华侍坐》是《论语》中篇幅最长、记述最详尽的一章。在这一章中，主人公通过对话表明了各自的不同志向，其中蕴含着深层的教育观念和社会愿景。我们对其进行了情景演绎，希望讲好中国故事，传播好中国声音，弘扬中华优秀传统文化，促进中外文明交流互鉴。

《论语》，是春秋时期思想家、教育家孔子的弟子及再传弟子记录孔子及其弟子言行的语录文集，书中较为集中地体现了孔子及儒家学派的政治主张、伦理思想、道德观念、教育原则等。也正因为这一历史原典的存在，后世之人能够追溯并找到儒家文化的根茎与起源，能够让它生生不息地繁衍壮大，并源远流长。其中篇幅最长、记述最详尽的一章是《子路、曾皙、冉有、公西华侍坐》，它详细地记述了四子陪坐、孔子问志、四子述志、孔子评志的过程。

"Las Analectas de Confucio" es una colección de charlas compiladas por los discípulos de Confucio, un pensador y educator, durante el período de las Primaveras y Otoños para registrar las palabras y acciones de Confucio y sus discípulos. El libro refleja las propuestas políticas, los pensamientos éticos, los conceptos morales y los principios educativos de Confucio y la escuela confuciana de forma relativamente concentrada. También debido a la existencia de este documento histórico, las generaciones futuras pueden encontrar el origen y la raíz de la cultura confuciana, para que se florezca y se desarrolle para siempre. El capítulo más largo y detallado es "Zi Lu, Zeng Xi, Ran You y Gongxi Hua sentados en compañía" y describe el proceso de que los cuatros, sentados, cuentan las voluntades y Confucio las evalúa.

（孔子落座写字，子路、冉有、公西华入场）

三　位：Buenos días, maestro.（作揖）

孔　子：Buenos días, siéntense.（示意三位入座）

孔　子：¿Cómo están todos? ¿Qué habéis hechos estos días?

子　路：Estoy practicando la espada y me va mejorando.

公西华：Hablando con algunos buenos amigos míos, he aprendido mucho.

冉　有：He leído ciertos libros y pienso profundamente.

曾　皙：（入场作揖）Siento llegar tarde, maestro.

孔　子：No se preocupe, siéntese.（曾皙坐）Hoy es precioso sentarnos juntos, beber té y charlar. Podrían hablar de sus propias aspiraciones libremente, si hay algo que no entienden, intercambiemos de opiniones.（看向诸位，运筹帷幄）

众　人：Vale. Entendemos.

曾　皙：Déjame servir té para ustedes.

孔　子：A menudo dicen que nadie me entiende. Si alguien les entendiera, ¿qué harían?

子　路：Si voy a gobernar un país con mil coches y soldados, que se sitúa entre grandes países sufriendo invasiones y también la hambre, siempre que me den tres años, harán a todos valientes en batallas y sensatos en la vida.

孔　子：Ran You, ¿qué harás?

冉　有：Si me deja gobernar un país que mide unos treinta kilómetros a lo ancho y largo, dentro de tres años, dejaré a los habitantes felices y a las familias, prósperas. Pero en cuanto al rito y a la música, hace falta esperar a los capaces.

孔　子：Gongxi Hua, ¿y tú?

公西华：Ni me atrevo a decir qué puedo conseguir, pero tengo ganas de aprender. O sea en las ceremonias de sacrificio en templo, o sea en las reuniones con otros países, quería vestirme con traje y sombrero, y servir de un presentador.

孔　子：Zeng Xi, y tú?

曾　皙：Lo mío es diferente de lo que han dicho ellos.

孔　子：No pasa nada. Solo se esperan tus propias voluntades.

曾　皙：Cuando llegaba la primevera, nos vestíamos con ropas del tiempo. Espero hallarme en el río de Yi, disfrutar el viento en Wuyutai, y volver a casa con un par de adultos y jóvenes.

孔　子：Admiro mucho estas ideas. Hasta aquí, todos pueden irse si no hay ningún problema.

子　路：Gracias por su atención, nos fuimos. Adiós, maestro.

曾　皙：¿Qué le parecen sus palabras?

孔　子：Son meramente algunas voluntades.

曾　皙：¿Por qué rió con las de Zhongyou?

孔　子：Se debe a la falta de modestia, es que deben administrar el país con cortesía.

曾　皙：Las palabras de Ran You no trata de acontecimintos nacionales?

孔　子：¿Por qué un lugar tan grande no puede ser un país?

曾　皙：Gongxi Hua no menciona sobre la gobernación del pais?

孔　子：¿Los sacrificios y reuniones con los otros no tienen que ver con el país? Pero si las personas como Hua solo pueden ser ministros insignificante, ¿quién puede ser el que haga cosas de gran importancia?

在本章中，主人公通过对话表达了各自不同的意趣、性格和志向。孔子业已不再年少，面对行事直率鲁莽而颇为自信的子路，他指出那些不合于礼的地方，和蔼地教育一番；面对行事谦退的冉有，他暗含鼓励与支持；面对少年成才又谦恭好学的公西华，他在鼓励之余还夹杂着一点无奈。而面对深刻明白自己心境的、同样有积极进取之志、认清时代背景的曾皙，他更是直白地表示了赞赏。此段对话语言自然，蕴含着深层的成长逻辑、教育观念和社会愿景，耐人寻味。

En este capítulo, los personajes expresan sus diferentes intereses, personalidades y ambiciones. Confucio ya no era un joven, frente a Zi Lu, una persona imprudente y bastante confiado en su aspiración, señaló la rudez con palabras simpáticas; Ante Ran You, que es modesto y cortés, implícitamente alentó y apoyó; Con Gongxi Hua, que se lleva la juventud y la humildad, además del estímulo, también siente cierta frustración. Y al dirigirse a Zeng Xi, que lo entiende y comparte con él mismo la ambición positiva y emprendedora y la comprensión de los antecedentes de los tiempos, expresó su admiración de manera directa. Es un diálogo cortidiano, pero también contiene una profunda lógica de crecimiento, conceptos educativos y visión social, lo que es digno de ser reflexionado por nosotros.

作品编号：1718
姓　　名：靳叶、王雅倩、陈天骏、颜玉玉、王成龙
国　　籍：中国
组　　别：国内成人组
单位名称：山东青年政治学院

因材施教，勤学善思——《论语》中的教育智慧

本作品由山东青年政治学院西班牙语专业教师和学生共同完成。作品聚焦《论语》中体现孔子教育思想的经典片段，采用西语诵读与情景演绎相结合的方式，生动演绎了《论语》中“为政”“先进”等篇目中的故事，以方便不同文化背景的观众感受其教育智慧，进而更好地促进儒家思想在世界范围内的传播。

子　路：“子曰：‘学而不思则罔，思而不学则殆。’”

“El Maestro dijo: ‘Quien sólo lee y estudia y no piensa la realidad puede perder el rumbo. Quien sólo reflexiona y no estudia se le agotan las ideas.’”

冉　有：“由，你在读什么书？”

“You, ¿qué está leyendo?”

子　路：“求、赤，我正在复习孔夫子讲的内容，他要求我们在学习中要善于思考，乐于求知。就像今天在课上所说的‘学而不思则罔，思而不学则殆’。”

“Qiu, Chi, estoy repasando lo que dictó el maestro Confucio. Nos pidió que en nuestros estudios seamos buenos para pensar y que estemos dispuestos a aprender. Como el maestro nos ha dictado: Quien sólo lee y estudia y no piensa la realidad puede perder el rumbo. Quien sólo reflexiona y no estudia se le agotan las ideas.”

公西华：“是的，这不正是夫子曾经告诫我们的‘不愤不启，不悱不发。举一隅不以三隅反，则不复也’吗？学习和思考是不可分割的整体。”

“Eso es. El maestro nos dijo que: ‘No llegues a ilustrar a los discípulos hasta el punto en que éstos no puedan obtener la solución después de todo esfuerzo, ni les inspires hasta que no puedan explicar lo que piensan. Si les has enseñado el este y ellos no puede deducir las otras tres direcciones, no les enseñes más.’ El aprendizaje y el pensamiento son un todo inseparable.”

冉　有：“太对了，太对了！夫子快到了，我们去吧。”

“Estoy completamente de acuerdo. El maestro debe estar a punto de llegar. Venga, vámonos.”

孔　子：“君子耻其言而过其行。评判一个人的标准不在于他说了什么，而在于他做了什么。”

“Un caballero se avergüenza de que sus palabras se excedan en sus actos. Un hombre no es juzgado por lo que dice, sino por lo que hace.”

子　路：“闻斯行诸？”（其余人都看子路）

“Maestro, ¿debo llevar inmediatamente a la práctica lo oído?”

孔　子：“有父兄在，如之何其闻斯行之？”

“Si tu padre y tu hermano mayor aún viven, ¿Cómo puedes ponerte en acción una vez oído algo?”

冉　有：“闻斯行诸？”（其余人都看冉有）

“¿Debe llevar inmediatamente a la práctica lo oído?”

孔　子：“闻斯行之。”

“Sí, lleva a la práctica lo oído sin demora.”

公西华：“由也问：‘闻斯行诸？’子曰：‘有父兄在。’求也问：‘闻斯行诸？’子曰：‘闻斯行之。’赤也惑，敢问。”

“Maestro, cuando Zi Lu le preguntó si debía ponerse en acción tan pronto como oía algo, le contestasteis que no podía hacerlo si vivían su padre y su hermano mayor. Pero cuando Qiu os hizo la misma pregunta le dijisteis que sí podía hacerlo. No lo comprendo, ¿Puedo pediros una explicación?”

孔　子：“求也退，故进之；由也兼人，故退之。”

“Ran You es tímido, por eso lo hago avanzar. Pero Zi Lu tiene arrojo por dos, por eso lo freno un poco.”

孔子在教育中，针对学生不同的特点实施不同的教学方法，并且鼓励学生独立思考，主动求知，这一教育思想在当今仍有广泛的借鉴意义。

La filosofía educativa de Confucio, que consistía en aplicar diferentes métodos de enseñanza para adaptarse a las distintas características de sus alumnos y en animarles a pensar de forma independiente y a tomar la iniciativa en la búsqueda del conocimiento, sigue teniendo una gran vigencia en la actualidad.

作品编号：1997
姓　　名：周书博、訾月琳、赵舒仪、邵涵、张原赫
国　　籍：中国
组　　别：国内成人组
单位名称：山东青年政治学院

学习《论语》经典，汲取治国智慧

周恩来是中华人民共和国的开国总理，他终其一生都在为国家与人民而奋斗。他的治国智慧，与自幼学习《论语》的经历是分不开的。《论语》中关于治国理政的思想，为他日后治理国家奠定了坚实的基础。让我们回顾《论语》中有关治国理政的经典篇章，体会其中所蕴含的深厚哲理吧！

曾子曰：“慎终追远，民德归厚矣。”

Zengzi dijo: “Cuando el monarca honra a sus antepasados con reverencia, el pueblo podrá ser honesto.”

子　曰：“为政以德，譬如北辰，居其所而众星共之。”

Confucio dijo: “Si el monarca puede gobernar un país con moralidad, será como la estrella Polar, que está en su posición, rodeada por todas las otras estrellas.”

子　曰：“能以礼让为国乎，何有？不能以礼让为国，如礼何？”

Confucio dijo: “Si el monarca es capaz de gobernar un estado observando rituales y mostrando deferencia, ¿Qué otras dificultades existen? Si no logra esto, ¿de qué le sirve el ritual?”

子　曰：“道千乘之国，敬事而信，节用而爱人，使民以时。”

Confucio dijo: “Para gobernar un gran país, el monarca tiene que tener los asuntos nacionales en serio, actuar con honradez, ser económico, amar al pueblo, reclutar a los agricultores a tenor de la temporada de labranza, para que no se retrasen el cultivo y la cosecha.”

子　曰：“道之以政，齐之以刑，民免而无耻；道之以德，齐之以礼，有耻且格。”

Confucio dijo: “Si el monarca recurre a la ley penal para gobernar al pueblo, la gente solo intentará liberarse de los castigos, pero no tendrá la vergüenza. Si dirige al pueblo con moralidad y ajusta sus palabras y actos con el ritual, la gente no solo será cortés, sino que también cumplirá las reglas.”

季康子问政于孔子。孔子对曰：“政者，正也。子帅以正，孰敢不正？”

Ji Kangzi le preguntó a Confucio cómo liderar un país. Confucio respondió: “La política significa la justicia. Si tomas un camino correcto y justo, ¿quién se atreverá a actuar al revés?”

作品编号：3206
姓　　名：吴诗宇、柳佩轩
国　　籍：中国
组　　别：国内成人组
单位名称：南开大学

中华魂，西语诵

《论语》博大精深，可以称为中华民族的精魂。西班牙语作为一门外语，被全世界很多人使用。用西班牙语朗读《论语》，可以让更多的人了解《论语》，感受《论语》的魅力。

大家好，我是山东大学外国语学院的张文玥，很高兴能够参加2022儒家经典跨语言诵读大会。今天，我节选了《论语·学而》《论语·为政》中比较经典的语段来和大家分享。

Hola, todos. Me llamo Zhang Wenyue. Y mi nombre en español es Olivia. Tengo 19 años. Soy de la Universidad de Shandong. Me gustan los clásicos confucianos y el español, hoy voy a recitar “Las Analectas”.

子　曰：“学而时习之，不亦说乎？有朋自远方来，不亦乐乎？人不知而不愠，不亦君子乎？”

Confucio dijo: “¿No es un placer aprender, repasar y practicar con frecuencia? ¿No es un placer tener gente afín que viene de lejos? ¿No es también una persona con buena moral no enojarse cuando otros no me entienden?”

子　曰：“巧言令色，鲜矣仁！”

Confucio dijo: “¡Los que tienden a usar palabras zalameras y fingir ser agradables no suelen ser personas piadosas!”

曾子曰：“吾日三省吾身：为人谋而不忠乎？与朋友交而不信乎？传不习乎？”

Zengzi dijo: “Reflexiono sobre mí mismo muchas veces al día: ¿He hecho lo mejor que pude al servir a los demás? ¿He sido poco sincero en mis interacciones con mis amigos? ¿He repasado los conocimientos que me enseñó el maestro?”

曾子曰：“慎终追远，民德归厚矣。”

Zengzi dijo: “Cuando honras a tus antepasados con reverencia, el pueblo podrá ser honesto.”

子　曰：“君子食无求饱，居无求安，敏于事而慎于言，就有道而正焉，可谓好学也已。”

Confucio dijo: “No comas para estar lleno, no vivas deseando comodidad. Trabaja mucho y habla con cautela. Codéate con personas de carácter noble. Si haces todo esto podrás llamarte estudioso.”

子　曰：“不患人之不己知，患不知人也。”

Confucio dijo: “Lo preocupante no consiste en que los demás no te entienden, sino en que no conoces a los demás.”

子　曰：“为政以德，譬如北辰，居其所而众星共之。”

Confucio dijo: “Si el monarca puede gobernar un país con moralidad, será como la estrella Polar. Todas las otras estrellas están en su torno.”

子　曰：“道之以政，齐之以刑，民免而无耻；道之以德，齐之以礼，有耻且格。”

Confucio dijo: “Si el monarca recurre a la ley penal para gobernar, las personas sólo intentarán librarse de los castigos pero perderán la integridad. Si dirige la gente con moralidad y armoniza suspalabras y actos con moralidad, ellas no sólo sabrán cortesía, sino que también cumplirán las reglas.”

子　曰：“吾十有五而志于学，三十而立，四十而不惑，五十而知天命，六十而耳顺，七十而从心所欲，不逾矩。”

Confucio dijo: “Yo decidí aprender cuandotenía quince años, y pude mantenerme a mí mismo cuando tenía treinta. Cuando tenía cuarenta, no había nada que pudiera confundirme. Y aprendí lo que significaba el destino cuando tenía cincuenta. Y podía tratar todas las ideas correctamente cuando tenía sesenta. Y cuando tenía setenta podía hacer todo lo que quería dentro del marco justificado.”

子　曰：“温故而知新，可以为师矣。”

Confucio dijo: “Si puedes sacar inspiración repasándolo estudiado, puedrás ser maestro.”

子　曰：“学而不思则罔，思而不学则殆。”

Confucio dijo: “Si sólo aprendes pero no reflexionas, te quedas perplejo. Y si sólo piensas pero no aprendes, te quedas perplejo.”

作品编号：1145
姓　　名：张文玥
国　　籍：中国
组　　别：国内成人组
单位名称：山东大学

古今演绎四子侍坐，畅谈中国梦

作品取材于《子路、曾皙、冉有、公西华侍坐》，选自《论语·先进》。作品从古代与现代角度演绎孔子和子路、曾皙、冉有、公西华这四个弟子“言志”的场景，生动再现了孔子和学生一起畅谈理想的情形。

（Los estudiantes hablan sobre el sueño chino con la profesora en la universidad moderna）
（现代大学课堂上，同学就中国梦发言）

老师：

Como los antiguos dicen: “Cuando el Gran Camino prevalece, el mundo es compartido por todos.” Así , nuestro sueño chino es heredado por generaciones de descendientes de Yan y Huang, pues, ¿Cuál es el sueño de vosotros?

古语有云：“大道之行也，天下为公。”我们的中国梦就是这样一条阳光大道，由一代代炎黄子孙传承而来。同学们的梦想又是什么呢？

学生 1：

Ser una maestra gloriosa del pueblo, como tú, enseñar y educar a estudiantes.

像老师一样成为光荣的人民教师，教书育人。

学生 2：

Quiero alistarme en el ejercito y defender las fronteras de nuestra patria.

投笔从戎，成为一名光荣的戍边战士。

学生 3：

Quiero convertirme en una doctora para salvar vidas.

我想成为一名医生，救死扶伤。

学生 4：

Me gustaría ser una traductora y una divulgadora de la cultura China.

成为一名翻译，做中国文化的传播者。

老师：

Que guay, me alegro mucho, aplaudan por ti mismo por favor y les deseo a todos que vuestros sueños se hagan realidad!

同学们志存高远，请为自己鼓掌，祝福大家梦想成真！

(Zi Lu, Zeng Xi, Ran You y Gongxij Hua se sentaron con Confucio)

(子路、曾皙、冉有、公西华陪孔子坐着)

孔子:

Porque soy mayor que vosotros, (los hombres) no me necesitan. No dejes que esto te impida decir algo. Ustedes solían decir: "Nadie me conoce. " Si alguien te conoce, ¿qué vas a hacer?

因为我年纪比你们大些,(人家)不用我了。不要因为我这一点就有话不说了。你们平时就常说:"没有人了解我呀!"假如有人了解你们,那么你们打算做些什么事情呢?

子路:

Un país de tamaño mediano con mil carros, atrapado entre grandes países, invadido por tropas extranjeras y luego enfrentó la hambruna.

一个拥有千乘兵车的中等国家,夹在大国之间,加上外国军队的侵犯,接着又遇上饥荒。

Si me permitieran gobernar este país, dentro de tres años podría darle a la gente el coraje para defender su país y también ayudarlos a entender cómo ser buenos seres humanos.

如果让我治理这个国家,三年之后,就可以使人有保卫国家的勇气,而且还懂得做人的道理。

孔子:

¿Y tú, Ran You?

冉有,你怎么样?

冉有:

Un país de sesenta o setenta kilómetros cuadrados, y cincuenta o sesenta kilómetros cuadrados, si yo lo gobierno hasta tres años, enriqueceré a la gente común.

一个六七十里或者五六十里见方的国家,如果让我去治理,三年之后,就可以使老百姓富足起来。

En cuanto a la revitalización de la doctrina músical y ritual sólo hay que esperar a que los sabios la lleven a cabo.

至于振兴礼乐教化,那就只有等待贤人君子来推行了。

孔子:

¿Gongxi Hua, qué opinas?

公西华,你怎么样?

公西华:

No me atrevo a decir lo que puedo hacer, pero estoy dispuesto a aprender a hacer algo.

我不敢说能做到什么,但愿意学着做些事情。

En el trabajo de los sacrificios en el templo, o en las reuniones de los príncipes feudales y en las comparecencias ante el emperador, me gustaría ser un pequeño maestro de ceremonias con un vestido y un sombrero de copa .

宗庙祭祀的工作,或者是诸侯会盟及朝见天子的时候,我愿意穿着礼服,戴着礼帽,做一个小小的司仪。

孔子：

Zeng Xi, ¿Qué consideras?

曾晳，你怎么样？

曾晳：

Yo no tengo el mismo talento político que los tres.

我和他们三人为政的才能不一样。

孔子：

¿Qué importa? Pero cada uno habla de sus aspiraciones.

那有什么关系呢？不过是各自谈谈自己的志向。

曾晳：

En el crepúsculo se acabó la labranza.

暮春时节(天气和暖)，春耕之事完毕。

(Yo y) cinco o seis adultos y seis o siete adolescentes fuimos a nadar en el río Yishui, disfrutamos de la brisa en la Terraza Wuyu y regresamos a casa cantando.

(我和)五六个成年人、六七个少年，到沂水里游泳，在舞雩台上吹风，唱着歌回家。

孔子：

¡Estoy de acuerdo con la idea de Zeng Xi!

我赞同曾晳的想法呀！

曾晳：

¿Qué tal las palabras de los tres?

他们三个人的话怎么样？

孔子：

¡No es más que hablar de sus propias aspiraciones!

也不过是各自谈谈自己的志向罢了！

曾晳：

¿Por qué te ríes?

您为什么笑仲由呢？

孔子：

El país se gobierna con cortesía, pero las palabras de Zi Lu no son modestas, así que me reí de él.

治国要用礼，可是他(子路)的话毫不谦让，所以我笑他。

¿No es un asunto nacional lo que Ran You está diciendo?

难道冉有讲的不是国家大事吗？

¿Cómo se puede decir que las sesenta o setenta kilométros cuadrados, y cincuenta o sesenta kilométros de cuadrados (los asuntos de los países pequeños) no son asuntos de estado?

怎么见得纵横六七十里或五六十里(的小国的事)不是国家大事呢？

¿Acaso Gongxi Hua no habla de grandes asuntos de príncipes?

难道公西华讲的不是诸侯的大事吗？

¿Qué son los sacrificios de los templos, la espera de las alianzas y las reuniones con los emperadores, si no los eventos grandes que son?

宗庙祭祀、诸侯会盟和朝见天子，不是诸侯的大事又是什么呢？

Gongxi Hua sólo puede hacer una pequeña faceta para los príncipes feudales; entonces, ¿Quién puede hacer una gran faceta para los príncipes feudales?

公西华只能替诸侯做小相，那么，谁又能给诸侯做大相呢？

作品编号：2002
姓　　名：姜兴兴、左梅、王亦飞扬、杨雅芳
国　　籍：中国
组　　别：国内成人组
单位名称：贵州财经大学

下编

第三届儒家经典跨语言诵读大会优秀作品集

中 英 篇

孔子的哲学：我启蒙之旅中的明亮光芒

孔子的哲学是中国古代伟大思想家孔子提出的一套道德伦理和政治理论。他强调了人的修养和道德行为的重要性，主张以仁爱为核心，追求和谐与和平。他提出了“己所不欲，勿施于人”的道德原则，强调了人与人之间的互动和关爱。孔子的哲学思想对中国的社会发展和人们的行为规范产生了深远的影响，成为中国传统文化的重要组成部分。

“知之为知之”这句话意味着认识和承认自己理解或掌握的东西。这部分强调了对自己知识的意识和承认的重要性。

“To know is to know that you know” implies recognizing and acknowledging what you understand or have knowledge of. This part emphasizes the importance of awareness and acknowledgment of one’s own knowledge.

“不知为不知，是知也”这句话暗示了意识到自己不知道的东西也是一种知识。它强调了谦逊和承认自己缺乏知识是通向真正智慧的一步。

“To not know is to know that you do not know. That is true knowledge.” This part suggests that being aware of what you don’t know is also a form of knowledge. It emphasizes that humility and acknowledging one’s lack of knowledge is a step toward true wisdom.

纵观历史，世界上有许多学者和哲学家的智慧和有力的话语都给予了我们祝福。其中，有一位哲学家以他那迷人的话语在几代人的心中留下了深刻印象——孔子。

Throughout history, the world has been blessed with the wisdom and powerful words of numerous scholars and philosophers. Among them, one philosopher stands out with his captivating words that have captured the minds of generations—Confucius.

作为一名在巴基斯坦探索人生复杂性的少年，我常常感到迷失在一个迷宫中，努力理解成功、爱情、领导和导师精神的基本要素。这些概念看起来像是谜团，令人困惑。成功似乎是难以捉摸的，爱情是一个神秘的谜题，领导和导师精神则似乎是遥不可及的渴望。

As a teenager navigating the complexities of life in Pakistan, I often felt lost in a labyrinth, struggling to understand the fundamental aspects of success, love, leadership, and mentorship. These concepts seemed like enigmatic puzzles, confounding my understanding. Success appeared elusive, love was a mysterious riddle, and leadership and mentorship seemed distant aspirations.

就在我读高中的时候，我第一次接触了孔子的话“知之为知之，不知为不知，是知也”。他对勤奋、努力工作和追求成功的教导深深地触动了我。

It was when I was in high school that I first encountered the words of Confucius “To know is to know that you know. To not know is to know that you don’t know. That is true knowledge”. His teachings on diligence, hard work and the pursuit of success touched me deeply.

在那些时刻，他的智慧似乎拨开了不确定性的迷雾，为我追求理想提供了明晰的方向。他的话语让我意识到即使我不知道一切，也不意味着我不能努力工作。它给了我发展自己技能、成为一个学习者的机会。孔子的教导点燃了我内心的火焰，激发出我对儒家哲学深入探究的渴望。

In those moments, his wisdom seemed to cut through the fog of uncertainty and provide clear direction for me to pursue my ideals. His words made me realize that even if I don’t know everything, it doesn’t mean I can’t work hard. It gave me the opportunity to develop my skills and become a learner. The teachings of Confucius lit a fire within me and sparked a desire to explore Confucian philosophy more deeply.

有传说称当孔子访问魏国时，他遇到了一个年轻人，这个年轻人在练习射箭。年轻人的箭一次又一次地偏离目标，但他拒绝放弃。孔子赞赏这个年轻人的毅力，走近他说：“凭着这样的决心和奉献精神，你怎么会不进步呢？继续练习吧，你一定会命中目标。”这些话激励了年轻的弓箭手。他再度努力，几个月后，成了一位技艺精湛的射手，再也不会偏离目标。

Legend says that when Confucius visited the state of Wei, he met a young man practicing archery. The young man’s arrows missed their target again and again, but he refused to give up. Confucius admired the young man’s perseverance and approached him and said, “With such determination and dedication, how can you not make progress? Keep practicing and you’ll hit your target.” These words inspired the young archer to renew his efforts, and in a few months he became such a skilled archer that he never missed his target again.

几年后，命运将我带到中国攻读本科学位，让我惊喜的是，我来到了孔子的故乡山东省。这感觉就像进入了孔子的心灵之地。空气中弥漫着他的教导精髓，景色也反映了他的精神遗产。当我探索这个地区时，我参观了祭拜他的寺庙和纪念碑，以及他的出生地曲阜。沉浸在这样的环境中，我更深入地了解了孔子的生活和思想。我了解到他对道德修养的强调，孝道的重要性，以及仁爱和正直的美德。

A few years later, fate brought me to China to pursue my undergraduate degree, and to my surprise, I found myself in Shandong Province, the home of Confucius. It was like entering the heart of Confucius. The essence of his teachings is in the air, and the landscape reflects his spiritual legacy. As I explore the area, I encounter temples and monuments, and Qufu, his birthplace. Immersed in such an environment, I gained a deeper understanding of Confucius’ life and thoughts. I learned of his emphasis on moral cultivation, the importance of filial piety, and the virtues of benevolence and integrity.

儒家思想不仅仅是一种哲学，它融入了日常生活之中，反映在当地人的友善和尊重之中。我开始欣赏孔子原则对社会规范、治理和人际关系的深远影响。在孔子的故乡以及在滨州医学院学习期间，我积极参与各种文化活动，如书法和茶道。这些实践使我对儒家传统中的细致和正念有了深入了解。书法所需的纪律反映了孔子所倡导的勤奋，强调了每一笔准确的重要性。

Confucianism is not just a philosophy, it is woven into the fabric of daily life and reflected in the friendliness and respect of the locals. I came to appreciate the profound impact of Confucius principles on social norms, governance, and human relations. While studying in the hometown of Confucius and at Binzhou Medical University, I actively participated in various cultural activities, such as calligraphy and tea ceremony. These practices have given me an insight into meticulousness and mindfulness in the Confucian tradition. The discipline required for calligraphy reflects the diligence advocated by Confucius, emphasizing the importance of accuracy in each stroke.

同样，茶道的优雅和正念反映了尊重、和谐和细节关注的价值观——儒家理想的体现。此外，这些文化活动将理论与实践之间的距离拉近，让我以实际方式体现了儒家价值观。从这些活动中获得的见解成了我日常生活的一部分，影响了我的互动、决策和对个人成长的态度。这些活动不仅仅是对文化的探索，也是一个塑造性的旅程，塑造了我的性格、观点和学术努力。

Similarly, the elegance and mindfulness of the tea ceremony reflect the values of respect, harmony and attention to details—the embodiment of Confucian ideals. Moreover, these cultural engagements have narrowed the gap between theory and practice, allowing me to embody Confucian values in a practical way. The insights gained from these immersions became part of my daily life, influencing my interactions, decision-making, and attitude toward personal growth. Participating in these activities is not just an exploration of culture, but also a formative journey that has shaped my character, perspective, and academic endeavors.

孔子对中国日常生活的影响仍然深远，成为一个持久的文化基石。他的教导塑造了社会规范，强调对长辈的尊重、孝道和道德行为，影响着人际互动、传统习俗，甚至是治理。对于像我这样在中国学习的国际年轻学生来说，孔子的哲学在伦理、道德修养和和谐生活方面提供了宝贵的经验。它为个人发展提供了一个框架，培养了勤奋、尊重和平衡生活的特质，是跨越国界和文化的宝贵指南，丰富着那些拥抱它智慧的人的生活。

Confucius' influcnce on daily life in China remains profound, becoming an enduring cultural cornerstone. His teachings shaped social norms, emphasizing respect for elders, filial piety, and ethical behavior, influencing human interactions, traditional customs, and even governance. For young international students like me studying in China, the philosophy of Confucius offers valuable experience in ethics, moral cultivation and harmonious living. It provides a framework for personal development and fosters the traits of hard work, respect and a balanced life. It is a valuable guide across borders and cultures, enriching the lives of those who embrace its wisdom.

传闻有一次，一个学生问孔子："老师，怎样获得智慧？"孔子回答道："有三种方法：第一，反思是最高尚的；第二，模仿是最容易的；第三，经验是最痛苦的。"这个故事提醒我们智慧可以通过反思、向他人学习以及从自己的经历中得出的经验来获得。孔子认为只有通过良好的治理才能实现公正和和谐的社会。他强调了以身作则的善良领导者的作用，激励他人追随他们的脚步。

According to a legend, once, a student asked Confucius, “Teacher, how to obtain wisdom?” Confucius replied, “There are three ways: First, reflection is the noblest; Second, imitation is the easiest; Third, experience is the most painful.” This story reminds us that wisdom can be gained through reflection, learning from others, and learning from our own experiences. Confucius believed that a just and harmonious society could only be achieved through good governance. He emphasized the role of good leaders who lead by example, inspiring others to follow in their footsteps.

我在中国接触儒家思想后渴望成为其深邃智慧的倡导者，在我的家乡巴基斯坦甚至在全球范围内分享这个宝贵的哲学。观察到儒家原则对日常生活产生的变革性影响，我感到有义务和使命与社区分享这种宝贵的思想。孔子的教导能激励个人发挥他们的全部潜力，建立和谐的人际关系，并积极地为社会做出贡献。

My exposure to Confucianism in China sparked a desire in me to become an advocate of its profound wisdom and to share this valuable philosophy both in my home country of Pakistan and globally. Having observed the transformational impact that Confucian principles have on everyday life, I feel an obligation and a mission to share this precious thought with the community. The teachings of Confucius have the power to inspire individuals to reach their full potential, build harmonious interpersonal relationships, and actively contribute to society.

总之，孔子的哲学为寻求智慧和个人成长的人提供了指引之光。从认识我们自己的知识到承认我们的无知，儒家的教导为成功的追求和德行的培养提供了宝贵的见解。当我们接纳这些教导，并将其融入我们的生活中时，我们可以用优雅、可理解和深邃的智慧来应对现代世界的复杂性。

In conclusion, Confucius’ philosophy is a guiding light for those seeking wisdom and personal growth. From recognizing our own knowledge to acknowledging our lack of it, Confucian teachings provide valuable insights into the pursuit of success and the cultivation of virtue. As we embrace these teachings and incorporate them into our lives, we can navigate the complexities of the modern world with grace, understanding, and profound wisdom.

作品编号：3984
姓　　名：Najibullah Khan
国　　籍：巴基斯坦
组　　别：征文类国际组
单位名称：滨州医学院

探索孔子的古老智慧：在辉煌和智慧的话语中揭示美德与和谐的深度

孔子是中国古代伟大的思想家和教育家，他的言行充满智慧。孔子倡导的美德与和谐观念是其思想的核心。他强调修身、齐家、治国、平天下，注重道德修养和人际关系，提倡仁爱、忠诚、孝道等美德。孔子的智慧启示人们如何追求内心的高尚境界，建立和谐社会与人际关系，体现了中华传统文化中美德与和谐的深刻内涵，对后世产生了深远影响。

"君子和而不同，小人同而不和。"

"A gentleman is in harmony but not in conformity; a villain is in conformity but not in harmony."

这句话阐明了人类美德和邪恶的鲜明对比。君子寻求和谐，是经过深思熟虑的协调和理解。小人则被自身利益所蒙蔽，盲目地坚持一致性，无法志同道合。这句话与中国所体现的与世界各国和谐共处的包容精神产生共鸣。

This statement illustrates the stark contrast between human virtue and evil. The gentleman seeks harmony and is well thought-out in harmony and understanding. The villain is blinded by his own interests, blindly insisting on conformity, unable to share the same interests. This phrase resonates with the spirit of inclusiveness that China embodies to live in harmony with other countries.

我的中国之旅
My Trip to China

2023 年 3 月，我从巴基斯坦一路来到山东烟台，逐步揭开了东方仙境神秘的面纱。

In March 2023, I came all the way from Pakistan to Yantai, Shandong Province, and gradually unveiled the mysterious veil of the Oriental wonderland.

山东是孔子的诞生地，也是儒家学派的一座灯塔，它的文化氛围让我对中国传统有了更深入的理解。儒家有一句经典名言是："博学之，审问之，慎思之，明辨之，笃行之。"这句话鼓励我们进行广泛的研究，谨慎地处理问题，批判性地思考，理性地辨别，真诚地行动。它是我生活中的指导准则，塑造了我对待学术和个人成长的方式。

Shandong is the birthplace of Confucius and a beacon of Confucianism, and its cultural atmosphere has given me a deeper understanding of Chinese tradition. There is a famous Confucian saying: "To learn well, to interrogate, to think carefully, to distinguish clearly, and to act earnestly." It encourages us to study extensively, approach problems prudently, think critically, discern rationally, and act sincerely. It has been a guiding principle in my life and has shaped my approach to academic and personal growth.

我在中国与孔子文化互动的经历
My Experience Interacting with Confucius Culture in China

在中国学习让我有机会探索并深入研究儒家学说。领悟儒家精神让留学生们能够更深入地了解弥漫着儒家文化的社会。在儒家文化里徜徉，加深了我对知识和美学关系的理解。我常常让自己沉浸在中国文化中。去年我参加了孔子经典朗诵比赛，这是我第一次接触儒家思想。后来我也经常参加与中国传统文化节日有关的活动，比如端午节。它是纪念爱国诗人屈原的一个节日。他主张"善政"，与孔子的"德治"思想有着密切联系。端午节能流传至今，不仅与屈原文学造诣之伟大有关，还与儒家文化所推崇的思想有着本质的联系。最近我还参加了普通话大赛，了解了剪纸这一古老的中国传统文化技艺。现在我对中国文化有了更深入的理解。

Studying in China gave me the opportunity to explore and study Confucianism in depth. Understanding the Confucian spirit enables international students to have a deeper understanding of the society which is filled with Confucian culture. Being immersed in Confucian culture has deepened my understanding of the relationship between knowledge and aesthetics. I often immerse myself in Chinese culture. Last year I participated in the Confucius Classics recitation competition, which was my first exposure to Confucianism. Later, I often participated in activities related to Chinese traditional cultural festivals, such as Dragon Boat Festival. It is a festival in memory of the patriotic poet Qu Yuan. He advocated "good governance", which was closely related to Confucius' thought of "rule by virtue". The fact that the Dragon Boat Festival can be passed down to the present day is not only related to Qu Yuan's great literary attainments, but also has an essential connection with the ideas advocated by Confucian culture. Recently, I took part in a Mandarin contest and learned about paper-cutting, an ancient Chinese traditional cultural skill. Now I have a deeper understanding of Chinese culture.

我对儒家思想的理解
My Understanding of Confucianism

孔子的另一则名言也给我留下了深刻的印象。

Another famous remark by Confucius also left a deep impression on me.

"学而不思则罔，思而不学则殆。"

"Learning without thinking is lost; thinking without learning is perilous."

这句话告诉我们学习和思考要结合起来。许多儒家经典，如《论语》《大学》和《中庸》，都包含着儒家思想，并为人们在道德修养、哲学反思和政治伦理方面提供了宝贵的指导。这些经典对中国文化的继承和发展产生了深远的影响。

It tells us that learning and thinking should be combined. Many Confucian classics, such as *The Analects of Confucius*, *The Great University* and *The Doctrine of the Mean*, contain Confucianism and provide valuable guidance for people's moral cultivation, philosophical reflection and political ethics. These classics have had a profound influence on the inheritance and development of Chinese culture.

儒家文化跨越了中国的边界，影响世界。海外华人坚持不懈地传播并发扬光大中华优秀传统文化。“士不可以不弘毅，任重而道远。”这句话警醒我们坚持对追求事物的重要性。当我踏上了解中国文化和促进中巴文化交流的旅程时，便致力于终身学习博大精深的中华文化。此外，我认为这种努力是加强中国和巴基斯坦之间友好关系的一种方式，为更光明的未来铺平了道路。

Confucian culture transcends China's borders and influences the world. Overseas Chinese have made unremitting efforts to spread and carry forward the fine traditional Chinese culture. “A scholar cannot afford not to be bold and resolute. There is a long way to go.” This sentence reminds us of the importance of persistence in pursuing things. When I embarked on my journey to understand Chinese culture and promote cultural exchanges between China and Pakistan, I committed myself to lifelong learning of the profound Chinese culture. Moreover, I see such efforts as a way to strengthen friendly relations between China and Pakistan, paving the way for a brighter future.

作品编号：4058
姓　　名：Muhammad Naveed
国　　籍：巴基斯坦
组　　别：征文类国际组
单位名称：滨州医学院

儒家思想对东亚国家的影响

儒家思想对东亚国家的历史文化产生了深远影响，被认为是世界上最重要的哲学传统之一。自其创立以来一直对中国和东亚其他国家的文化、社会关系和生活方式产生着深远的影响。即便在现代，儒家思想仍在塑造价值观和行为规范方面扮演着重要的角色。

儒家思想的一个主要原则是强调和谐社会关系的重要性。孔子的教义支持对家庭、长辈的忠诚，以及对规则和传统的尊重。这些价值观在现代社会仍然存在，体现为对长辈的尊重、对传统行为的遵循和对家庭的重视。

One of the main principles of Confucianism is to emphasize the importance of harmonious social relations. The teachings of Confucius support loyalty to family, elders, and respect for rules and traditions. These values are still present in modern society, embodied in respect for elders, adherence to traditional behavior and the importance of family.

教育是儒家思想的另一个重要方面，其影响延续至今。孔子极为重视教育和学习，认为通过深入了解世界、不断自我提升，人才能获得智慧和和谐。在中国，这一理念在现代生活中得到了持续的体现。成为儒家文化一部分的国家拥有许多注重个人发展的教育机构和知名教师。

Education is another important aspect of Confucianism, and its influence continues to this day. Confucius attached great importance to education and learning, believing that through in-depth understanding of the world and continuous self-improvement, people can gain wisdom and harmony. In China, this idea continues to find expression in modern life. Countries that have become part of Confucian culture have many educational institutions and renowned teachers that focus on personal development.

儒家思想对俄罗斯的发展产生了深刻的影响，涵盖了社会和谐、教育以及建筑等多个方面。尽管俄罗斯和中国拥有不同的历史和传统，但儒家思想的理念在俄罗斯文化中得以体现。在俄罗斯社会中，这种影响体现在家庭价值观的发展、对长辈的尊重以及对互助和社会互动的支持。儒家思想的原则为俄罗斯文化中的一个重要价值观——家庭（作为社会和可持续发展的基石）提供了支持。

Confucianism had a profound influence on the development of Russia, covering social harmony, education, and architecture. Although Russia and China have different histories and traditions, the ideas of Confucianism are embodied in Russian culture. In Russian society, this influence is reflected in the development of family values, respect for elders, and support for mutual assistance and social interaction. The principles of Confucianism provide support for an important value in Russian culture, the family, as the cornerstone of social and sustainable development.

教育是儒家思想在俄罗斯产生显著影响的另一个领域。儒家理念中关于对知识的敬畏、对教师的尊重以及知识代代相传的理念对俄罗斯的教育体系产生了深远影响。这在道德价值观的形成、对决心的重视以及对学生的高要求等方面得到了体现。俄罗斯的教育体系强调对知识和自我发展的渴望，可以追溯到儒家思想的影响。

Education is another area where Confucianism has had a significant influence in Russia. The Confucian values of reverence for knowledge, respect for teachers, and the transmission of knowledge from generation to generation have had a profound impact on the Russian education system. This is reflected in the formation of moral values, the emphasis on determination and the high demands placed on students. The emphasis in the Russian education system on the desire for knowledge and self-development can be traced back to the influence of Confucianism.

此外，儒家思想也影响了俄罗斯的建筑和景观设计。在中国，建筑和景观通常与和谐、平衡的概念相联系。俄罗斯建筑师吸收并应用了这些原则，特别是在创建花园综合体和公园区时，力图营造一种和平和谐的氛围。尽管俄罗斯和中国有着截然不同的文化传统，但儒家思想在俄罗斯的建筑中留下了痕迹。这体现了儒家思想作为宝贵遗产和哲学原则对俄罗斯社会多个领域的深刻影响。

In addition, Confucianism has influenced Russian architecture and landscape design. In China, architecture and landscape are often associated with the concept of harmony and balance. Russian architects have absorbed and applied these principles, especially when creating garden complexes and park areas, in an effort to create an atmosphere of peace and harmony. Although Russia and China have very different cultural traditions, Confucianism has left its mark on Russian architecture. This reflects the profound influence of Confucianism as a valuable heritage and philosophical principle on multiple areas of Russian society.

总体而言，儒家思想在俄罗斯的传播和融合过程中经历了一些与俄罗斯文化特色相适应的变化。然而，孔子关于家庭、教育和领导的价值观和教义仍然为中国社会内外的道德和社会行为提供了基础。儒家思想的影响不仅是文化传统的一部分，更是一种智慧与和谐基础上的生活方式，对现代社会产生了深远的影响。

In general, Confucianism has undergone some changes in the process of spreading and integrating in Russia, which is in line with the characteristics of Russian culture. However, Confucius' values and teachings on family, education, and leadership still provide a foundation for moral and social behavior within and outside Chinese society. The influence of Confucianism is not only a part of the cultural tradition, but also a way of life based on wisdom and harmony, which has had a profound impact on modern society.

作品编号：5053
姓　　名：Anam Hamid
国　　籍：俄罗斯
组　　别：征文类国际组
单位名称：滨州医学院

儒家思想，文化之桥

儒家思想是连接中国与世界其他国家和地区的文化之桥。作为一名在中国学习的非洲学生，我想分享我的故事。

想象一下，一位年轻的非洲学生沉浸在中国文化丰富多彩的景象中，在中国的核心地带进行了十年的学习，领略着儒家思想的繁复微妙之处。这段旅程不是简单的学术探索，而是一场深刻的文化奥德赛，不仅塑造了智慧，也深刻地影响了个体存在的本质。而这就是我的故事。我已经在孔子的故乡生活了十多年。

Imagine a young African student, immersed in the vibrant landscape of Chinese culture, navigating the intricate nuances of Confucianism during a decade of study in the heart of China. This journey transcends mere academic exploration; it is a profound cultural odyssey that shapes not only the intellect but also the essence of one's being. And this is my story. I have been lived on the land of the Confucius for more than ten years.

儒家思想植根于中国古代的哲学土壤，对于一位非洲学生而言，最初或许会感觉像是一片陌生的领域。然而，随着岁月的推移，这个丰富传统的层次渐次展现，让我们看到了哲学、伦理和社会和谐交织的世界。

Confucianism, with its roots deeply embedded in the philosophical soil of ancient China, may initially seem like an unfamiliar terrain for an African student. Yet, as the years unfold, the layers of this rich tradition begin to reveal themselves, offering a glimpse into a world where philosophy, ethics, and social harmony intertwine.

孔子是中国历史上备受尊崇的人物，儒家思想的核心是他的教导。对我而言，这些教导成为一枚哲学指南针，引领我穿越文化差异和语言纷繁复杂的迷宫。强调孝道、家庭的重要性以及追求道德卓越的理念深深地共鸣着，超越了文化的界限。在拥抱这些原则的过程中，我发现了一根贯穿于人类丰富经验多样性之中的通用之线。

At the core of Confucianism lies the teachings of Confucius, a revered figure in Chinese history. For me, these teachings become a philosophical compass, guiding me through the maze of cultural differences and linguistic intricacies. The emphasis on filial piety, the importance of family, and the pursuit of moral excellence resonate deeply, transcending cultural boundaries. In embracing these principles, I find a universal thread that weaves through the diverse fabric of human experience.

对儒家思想的探索并不仅仅局限于教科书的一页页，它还是一种身临其境的体验。中国城市繁忙的街道、古老寺庙宁静的庭院，以及与中国同龄人的生动对话都成为沉浸式课堂的一部分。儒家价值观渗透到日常生活中，塑造了社会互动、家庭动态，甚至是对教育的态度。我曾经是个外来者，但现在我逐渐成为这场文化交响曲中的一位参与者，为跨文化交流的旋律贡献着我独特的音符。

The journey into Confucian thought is not confined to the pages of textbooks; it is also a live experience. The bustling streets of Chinese cities, the tranquil courtyards of ancient temples, and the lively conversations with Chinese peers all become part of the immersive classroom. Confucian values permeate daily life, shaping social interactions, family dynamics, and even the approach to education. I was once a newcomer, but now I gradually become a participant in this cultural symphony, contributing my own unique notes to the melody of cross-cultural exchange.

在这文化探险中，语言成了一座桥梁，也是一道屏障。中文，作为教学语言，不仅仅是一种交流手段，也是理解儒家思想微妙差异的入口。当我首次尝试解读这些看似复杂艺术品的汉字时，我不仅仅是在解码文字，还在揭示其中蕴含的文化内涵。然而，随着每一次语言挑战的克服，儒家智慧的新层面也展现了出来。

Language becomes both a bridge and a barrier in this cultural exploration. Chinese, the language of instruction, is not just a means of communication; it is a gateway to understanding the nuances of Confucian thought. When I first tried to know these characters that seem like intricate artwork, I'm decoding not just words but the cultural connotations embedded within them. Yet, with each linguistic challenge being overcome, a new layer of Confucian wisdom unfolds.

课堂成为文化融合的微观世界。在这里，我参与超越国家界限的讨论。孔子的教导成为来自不同背景的学生的交汇点，促进对人类价值的共同理解。我作为一个外国人，现在在儒家哲学的知识讨论中找到了归属感。

Classes become a microcosm of cultural convergence. Here, I engage in discussions that transcend national origins. The teachings of Confucius become a meeting point for students from diverse backgrounds, fostering a shared understanding of human values. I, as a foreigner, now find a sense of belonging in the intellectual discourse of Confucian philosophy.

随着岁月的流逝，中国古典文化越发吸引我。《论语》《中庸》和《礼记》这些书本一开始令人望而却步，但现在变成了了解中国古代思想的窗口。我发现这些经典作品洞悉治理、社会关系和道德行为。孔子的智慧超越了时间和文化的边界，与一种证明人类共同愿望的普遍性产生了共鸣。

As years pass by, the Chinese classics have more and more attractions on me. *The Analects, The Doctrine of the Mean* and *The Book of Rites*, these texts were initially daunting, but now become windows into the intellectual landscape of ancient China. I discover the profound insights these classics offer into governance, social relationships and ethical conduct. The wisdom of Confucius transcends both time and cultural boundaries, resonating with a universality that speaks to the shared aspirations of humanity.

在学术领域之外，儒家思想的影响延伸到了日常实践和仪式的领域。传统的中国节日，带有深厚的儒家意义，成为我庆祝和反思的时刻。儒家思想中的仪式和礼节的重要性不仅仅是一个抽象的概念，更是文化表达的有形部分。参与这些文化实践，成为我文化互通不可分割的一部分。

Beyond the academic realm, Confucianism extends its influence into the realm of daily practices and rituals. Traditional Chinese festivals, with their deep-rooted Confucian significance, become moments of celebration and reflection for me. The importance of rituals and propriety in Confucian thought, is not just an abstract concept but a tangible part of cultural expression. Participating in these cultural practices becomes a living testament to the interconnectedness of cultures for me.

儒家思想对家庭动态的影响尤为显著。对长辈的尊重和家庭纽带的重要性与非洲文化精髓相契合。在接受这些价值观的同时，我发现了与我自己文化传统的共鸣，为儒家理念和我的祖国传统之间搭建了一座桥梁。

The impact of Confucianism on family dynamics is particularly pronounced. The emphasis on respect for elders and the significance of familial bonds align with the African cultural ethos. Embracing these values, I discover a resonance with my own cultural heritage, creating a bridge between Confucian ideals and the traditions of my homeland.

我不能忽视在中国作为非洲学生的更广泛背景。这个经历不仅仅是关于儒家思想的，还涉及身份和文化多样性的交叉。随着非洲学生成为中国国际社会的一部分，我们为国际视角的拼图做出贡献，挑战着刻板印象，促进相互理解。

I cannot ignore the broader context of being an African student in China. The experience is not only about Confucianism, but also about navigating the intersections of identity and cultural diversity. As the African students become part of a global community within China, we contribute to the mosaic of international perspectives, challenging stereotypes, and fostering mutual understanding.

十年的旅程达到了深刻的转变。我作为一个充满好奇的外来者来到这里，如今我成了文化大使。儒家思想，曾经是遥远的哲学，如今已经成为我智力和文化储备的一部分。我对非洲根源和儒家传统有了细微的理解，成为两个世界之间的桥梁。

The journey of a decade culminates in a profound transformation. I, who once arrived as a curious outsider, now become a cultural ambassador. Confucianism, once was a distant philosophy, is now an integral part of my intellectual and cultural repertoire. I am equipped with a nuanced understanding of both my African roots and the Confucian traditions, and emerge as a bridge between the two worlds.

总的来说，我在中国学习的故事，不仅仅关乎对儒家思想的学术追求。这是一篇关于文化沉浸、智力探索和个人成长的叙事。儒家思想成为我在跨文化交流复杂性中导航的指南。这段旅程是对教育和跨文化理解力量的真实见证，塑造出能够架起分歧、拥抱全球多样性的个体。

In conclusion, the story of my study in China, is not just about the academic pursuit of Confucianism. It is a narrative of cultural immersion, intellectual exploration and personal growth. Confucianism offers a compass for navigating the complexities of cultural exchange. The journey is a testament to the power of education and cross-cultural understanding in shaping individuals who can bridge divides and embrace global diversity.

作品编号：1797
姓　　名：乐乐（Robert Oduro）
国　　籍：加纳
组　　别：征文类国际组
单位名称：东营英华园学校

浅谈《论语》中的“孝道”

《论语》是一部记录了中国古代伟大思想家孔子及其弟子的言论和行为的经典著作。《论语》以言论简短而精炼闻名，包含了丰富的道德、政治、教育等方面的思想，对中国古代和现代社会都有重要的影响。

大家好，我是来自约旦的法丽，现在在中国聊城大学读书。来到中国后，我有幸在《论语》中读到一些关于孝顺父母的名言，这些名言谈论了孩子与父母关系中的一些情感。

“子夏问孝。子曰：‘色难。有事，弟子服其劳；有酒食，先生馔，曾是以为孝乎？’”

在这段对话中，孔夫子指出，对父母来说，最难的是让子女与他们同乐。子女为父母做事、为父母准备饮食，这些都不能算是真正的孝顺。可见，如果没有内心真挚的孝心，就不可能使父母感到幸福。

父母与孩子相伴，孩子何尝感受不到其中深情？孩子时常自顾自，而父母却时刻牵挂。细细品味，我心生感动，回忆起父母曾赋予我的恩惠。在诸多层面，我深感责任重大，因为他们期许我成为卓越之人，为构建更和谐的社会贡献一己之力。他们为我无私付出，让我的梦想得以成真，助我追求抱负。

“孟武伯问孝。子曰：‘父母唯其疾之忧。’”

孔夫子这句话的精髓在于：对于父母来说，子女应该特别关心他们的健康状况，这比担心其他方面更为重要。从孔子的谈论中，我们领悟到，我们应该留意父母的年事，一方面为他们的长寿而感到欣慰，另一方面则应该为他们的身体日渐虚弱而担忧。身体健康是人生的根基和资本。父母若患病，必然会在物质生活、情感和思想方面带来诸多问题和困扰。这也导致一些所谓的孝顺子女在长期看护父母的过程中失去了热情和耐心，正如俗话所说的“久病床前无孝子”，这样的例子还有很多。因此，相较于其他孝道要求，关心父母的健康是孝顺的基本前提。

“子曰：‘父母在，不远游，游必有方。’”

父母年事已高，子女应尽量避免长时间离家。若必须外出，应当告知父母前往何处、出行目的、预计归期，并妥善安排他们的生活。在这一点上，孔夫子强调了子女应怀有感恩之心，这也成为中国古代孝道文化的传统。

《论语》告诫我们：一定要照顾父母的感受，不要做任何让他们担心的事情。首先，我们应该体察父母的情感。我们的一言一行都应该考虑到父母的快乐与舒适。其次，要时常与父母保持联系，不让他们为我们牵挂。在古代，“父母在，不远游”是孝道的一种表现，但如今现代人难以“行不远”，因此我们不得不在这古训中再加一句“行必好”。你可以外出工作，但务必告知父母你的去向。子女们即使身在千里之外也要牵挂父母，应当定期写信、通话、视频，以免让父母为他们担忧。

身为外国人，我从《论语》中汲取营养，以更为谨慎的态度来处理与父母的关系，走向更加美好的亲子关系。

Hello everyone, I am Farah from Jordan, currently studying at Liaocheng University in China. Since coming to China, I have had the privilege of reading some quotes about filial piety in *The Analects*, discussing the emotions involved in the relationship between children and parents.

"Zixia asked about filial piety. Confucius said, 'It is difficult to be filial. If there is labor to be performed, the younger generation should bear it; if there is food and drink, the elders should be served first. Is this not a demonstration of filial piety?'"

In this dialogue, Confucius points out that for parents, the most difficult thing is to share joy with their children. Doing things for parents or preparing food and drink for them cannot be considered genuine filial piety. It is clear that without sincere filial piety from the heart, it is impossible to make parents feel happy.

Parents and children are companions, and how can children not feel the deep affection in this companionship? While children often go about their own business, parents are always concerned. Upon careful consideration, I am deeply moved, recalling the kindness my parents have bestowed upon me. In many respects, I feel a great sense of responsibility, as they expect me to become an outstanding person and contribute to building a more harmonious society. They selflessly support me, enabling my dreams to come true and helping me pursue my ambitions.

"Meng Wubo asked about filial piety. Confucius said, 'Parents' only concern is for their children's health.'"

The essence of Confucius' statement lies in the fact that children should be particularly concerned about their parents' health, which is more important than worrying about other aspects. From Confucius' discussion, we understand that we should pay attention to our parents' age, feeling both gratified for their longevity and concerned about their gradually weakening health. Physical health is the foundation and capital of life. If parents fall ill, it will inevitably bring many problems and troubles in terms of material life, emotions, and thoughts. This also leads to some so-called filial children losing their passion and patience in the long-term process of caring for their parents, as the saying goes, "There are no filial children in front of a long-term illness." There are many such examples. Therefore, compared to other requirements of filial piety, caring for parents' health is the basic premise of filial piety.

"Confucius said, 'When parents are alive, do not travel to distant places. If you must travel, there should be a clear purpose.'"

When parents are elderly, children should try to avoid being away from home for long periods. If it is necessary to go out, parents should be informed of the destination, purpose of the trip, and expected return date, and their care should be properly arranged. In this regard, Confucius emphasizes that children should have a grateful heart, which has also become a tradition in ancient

Chinese filial piety culture.

The Analects admonishes us: we must take care of our parents' feelings and not do anything to make them worry. First, we should be sensitive to our parents' emotions. Our every word and action should take into account our parents' happiness and comfort. Second, we should keep in touch with our parents regularly, not letting them worry about us. In ancient times, "when parents are alive, do not travel to distant places" was a manifestation of filial piety, but in modern times, it's difficult for people to "not travel far", so we have to add another phrase to this ancient teaching, that is "travel with a clear purpose". You can go out to work, but be sure to inform your parents of your whereabouts. Even if children are thousands of miles away, they should still care for their parents, and should regularly write letters, make calls, and have video chats, in order to prevent their parents from worrying about them.

As a foreigner, I draw nourishment from *The Analects*, which allows us to handle our relationships with our parents with a more cautious attitude, leading us towards a better parent-child relationship.

作品编号：13134
姓　　名：法丽〔Farah Tawfiq（Moh'd Adel）Hamdan〕
国　　籍：约旦
组　　别：征文类国际组
单位名称：聊城大学

我的《论语》故事

儒家思想是由孔子创立的，其核心围绕着伦理道德、自我实现以及社会价值展开。让我们继续追随孔子的教诲，汲取儒家思想的精髓，共同构筑一个更加美好的世界吧！

若要谈及与中国文化相关的名字，那必定是孔子。中国人尊称他为“先师”。孔子更是中国文化中的圣人。儒家思想是由孔子创立的一种信仰和原则，其核心围绕着伦理道德、自我实现以及社会价值展开。

儒家学说根植于对人性的热爱。其强调对长者的崇敬，家庭的神圣地位，年轻一辈对长者的顺从以及妇女对丈夫的尊重。同时，它对暴政持反对态度，认为政府的目的在于为人民服务，统治者必须具备高尚的品德和理想。儒家思想认为仁和义是至关重要的美德，“仁”代表着对人类同胞的关爱和亲密情谊，“义”则涵盖了道德、仪式、传统、智慧等。

在儒家思想中，“仁”具有非常重要的地位，也成了儒家思想的核心之一。孔子经常强调“仁”，并将其视为人类应该追求的最高道德境界。他认为，一个人应该以“仁”来对待他人，包括尊敬长辈、关爱子女、友善待人等。孔子认为，通过修养自己的“仁”，可以实现个人的完善和社会的和谐。比如“己所不欲，勿施于人”“君子喻于义，小人喻于利”等。孔子的这些话融合了他至高无上的人的特质。他与伟大的思想家亚里士多德非常相似。总之，“仁”是一种高尚的品德，是人们应该追求的道德境界，也是实现个人和社会和谐的关键。

在儒家思想中，“水”具有重要的象征意义。孔夫子经常用“水”来比喻君子的品德。他认为君子应该像水一样，能够包容他人的缺点，保持内心的平静，与他人和谐相处。在中国的婚礼上，水也常被用来象征新婚夫妇之间的和谐与平静。

中国的伟大思想家孔子，他的眼睛渴望洞察一切，他的言辞真诚而动人。在工作中，他期望展现出关怀，激发他人的尊重。面对疑惑，他热衷向他人请教。若生气，他深知愤怒会误人；若有所收获，他会思索正义和公正。

让我们继续追随孔子的教诲，汲取儒家思想的精髓，共同构筑一个更加美好的世界吧！

When it comes to names associated with Chinese culture, it must be Confucius. Chinese people respectfully refer to him as “Master” and Confucius is considered a saint in Chinese culture. Confucianism is a belief system and a set of principles established by Confucius, revolving around ethical values, self-realization, and social values.

Confucianism is rooted in love for humanity. It emphasizes respect for elders, the sacred status of the family, the obedience of the younger generation to their elders, and the respect of women for their husbands. At the same time, it opposes tyranny, believing that the purpose of government is to serve the people, and that rulers must possess noble character and ideals. Confucianism regards benevolence and righteousness as crucial virtues, where "benevolence" represents love and intimate friendship towards fellow human beings, and "righteousness" encompasses moral, ritual, tradition, and wisdom, etc.

In Confucian thought, "benevolence" holds a very important position and has become one of its core principles. Confucius often emphasized "benevolence" and regarded it as the highest moral state that humans should strive for. He believed that one should treat others with "benevolence", including respecting elders, caring for children, and being kind to others. Confucius believed that by cultivating "benevolence" in oneself, personal perfection and social harmony could be achieved. For example, "Do not do to others what you do not want done to yourself" and "A noble person values righteousness, while a petty person values profit". These statements by Confucius integrate his supreme qualities as a human being, making him very similar to the great thinker Aristotle. In conclusion, "benevolence" is a noble virtue that people should strive for, and it is also the key to achieving personal and social harmony.

In Confucian thought, "water" holds important symbolic significance. Confucius often used "water" to metaphorically describe the character of a noble person, believing that a noble person should be like water, able to accommodate the shortcomings of others, maintain inner calm, and harmoniously interact with others. In Chinese weddings, water is also often used to symbolize the harmony and tranquility between newlyweds.

The great Chinese philosopher Confucius, his eyes were eager to perceive everything, and his words were sincere and moving. In his work, he aimed to show care and inspire respect in others. Faced with doubts, he was eager to seek advice from others. If angered, he deeply understood that anger could lead to mistakes; if he gained something, he would contemplate justice and fairness.

Let us continue to follow the teachings of Confucius, draw on the essence of Confucianism, and together build a better world!

作品编号：13135
姓　　名：布达（Abdeljawad Nabil Abdeljawad Alnatsheh）
国　　籍：约旦
组　　别：征文类国际组
单位名称：聊城大学

跨越国界的儒家智慧

儒家文化不仅是中华文明的瑰宝，更是人类文明的共同财富。我热爱儒家文化，它让我领略了人类文明的璀璨之光。我希望将儒家智慧传播到更多地方，为文化交流和世界和平贡献一分力量。让我们共同珍惜和传承这份宝贵的文化财富。

大家好！很荣幸有机会参加第三届儒家经典跨语言诵读大会，并借此机会向大家分享我对儒家文化的理解和感悟。

Hello everyone! I am honored to have the opportunity to participate in the 3rd Confucian Classics Cross-Language Recitation Conference, and I would like to take this opportunity to share with you my understanding and perception of Confucian culture.

首先，我想谈谈儒家思想在巴基斯坦的传播和影响。巴基斯坦的文化传统与中国的儒家文化有着很大的差异。然而，随着全球化的推进和中巴文化交流的加深，儒家思想在巴基斯坦逐渐受到了关注和传播。

First of all, I would like to talk about the spread and influence of Confucianism in Pakistan. Pakistan's cultural traditions are very different from China's Confucian culture. However, with the advancement of globalization and the deepening of cultural exchanges between China and Pakistan, Confucianism has gradually attracted attention and spread in Pakistan.

在巴基斯坦，儒家思想的传播主要依靠学术交流和翻译工作。一些巴基斯坦学者通过对儒家经典的翻译和研究，将儒家思想引入巴基斯坦的学术界。这些学者认为，儒家思想强调人与人之间的和谐、尊重和责任，与巴基斯坦的价值观有很大的相似之处。因此，儒家思想在巴基斯坦的传播不仅有助于加深中巴文化交流，也有助于促进巴基斯坦社会的和谐发展。

In Pakistan, the spread of Confucianism relied mainly on academic exchanges and translation work. Some Pakistani scholars introduced Confucianism to Pakistani academia through the translation and study of Confucian classics. These scholars believe that Confucianism, with its emphasis on harmony, respect, and responsibility among people, bears a strong resemblance to Pakistani values. Therefore, the spread of Confucianism in Pakistan not only helps to deepen cultural exchanges between China and Pakistan, but also helps to promote the harmonious development of Pakistani society.

除了学术界，儒家思想在巴基斯坦的普通民众中也逐渐受到了关注。一些巴基斯坦人对中国的传统文化和哲学思想非常感兴趣，他们通过阅读儒家经典和参加相关的文化活动，了解和体验儒家文化的内涵和魅力。这些人对儒家思想认同和接受，不仅是因为儒家思想本身的智慧和价值，也是因为儒家文化与巴基斯坦的传统文化有着相似之处，例如尊重长辈、注重家庭和社会的和谐等。

In addition to academics, Confucianism is also gaining traction among the general population of Pakistan. Some Pakistanis are very interested in traditional Chinese culture and philosophical thoughts, and they understand and experience the connotation and charm of Confucian culture by reading Confucian classics and participating in related cultural activities. These people identify and accept Confucianism not only because of its wisdom and value, but also because of the similarities between Confucian culture and Pakistan's traditional culture, such as respect for elders and emphasis on family and social harmony.

通过这些传播和交流，儒家思想在巴基斯坦的影响力逐渐增强。一些巴基斯坦人开始将儒家思想融入自己的生活和工作中，用儒家的智慧和理念来解决问题和处理人际关系。同时，儒家思想也为巴基斯坦的社会和文化发展提供了一些新的思路和方向。

Through these spreads and exchanges, the influence of Confucianism in Pakistan gradually increased. Some Pakistanis have begun to integrate Confucianism into their lives and work, using Confucian wisdom and ideas to solve problems and manage interpersonal relationships. At the same time, Confucianism has also provided some new ideas and directions for Pakistan's social and cultural development.

其次，作为一个在山东省学习和生活多年的留学生，我深刻体会到了儒家文化在中国的影响和魅力。山东省作为儒家文化的发源地，有着丰富的儒家文化遗产和传统。在山东省，我参加了很多与儒家文化相关的活动，例如儒家经典诵读、孔子文化节等。这些活动让我更加深入地了解了儒家文化的内涵和价值观，也让我感受到了儒家文化在中国社会中的重要地位和影响。

Secondly, as an international student who has studied and lived in Shandong Province for many years, I have deeply experienced the influence and charm of Confucian culture in China. As the birthplace of Confucian culture, Shandong Province has a rich cultural heritage and traditions. In Shandong Province, I participated in many activities related to Confucian culture, such as the recitation of Confucian classics and the Confucius Cultural Festival. These activities gave me a deeper understanding of the connotation and values of Confucian culture, and also made me feel the important position and influence of Confucian culture in Chinese society.

通过这些体验和感悟，我深深地爱上了儒家文化。我认为，儒家文化是人类文明的瑰宝，它不仅对中国有着深远的影响，也对世界其他地方的文化和社会发展有着重要的借鉴作用。我希望通过自己的努力和学习，将儒家文化的智慧和价值观传播到更多的国家和地区，为促进文化交流和世界和平做出自己的贡献。

Through these experiences and insights, I fell in love with Confucian culture. I believe that Confucian culture is a treasure of human civilization, which not only has a profound impact on China, but also has an important role in the cultural and social development of other parts of the world. I hope that through my own efforts and learning, I can spread the wisdom and values of

Confucian culture to more countries and regions, and make my own contribution to promoting cultural exchanges and world peace.

最后，我想用一句话来表达我对儒家文化的敬畏和热爱："儒家文化，让我明白了人生的意义和价值，让我感受到了中华优秀传统文化的魅力和力量。"我希望借此机会，与更多的朋友们分享我对儒家文化的理解和感悟，共同探索儒家文化的奥秘和智慧。

Finally, I would like to express my awe and love for Confucian culture in one sentence: "Confucian culture has made me understand the meaning and value of life, and made me feel the charm and power of China's excellent traditional culture." I hope that through this opportunity, I can share my understanding and perception of Confucian culture with more friends, and explore the mysteries and wisdom of Confucian culture together.

作品编号：5164
姓　　名：Muhammad Atayyab Amer
国　　籍：巴基斯坦
组　　别：征文类国际组
单位名称：滨州医学院

儒家文化的海外传播与个人践行

儒家文化在海外的影响力不断扩大。作为加纳留学生，我也从中汲取了丰富的智慧与力量。我将继续努力学习儒家文化，努力成为一个有道德、有修养、有责任感的人，为推动中非文化交流与非洲和谐发展贡献自己的力量。

我是一名来自加纳的留学生，在中国山东学习了近两年的儒家文化。这段时间里，我深入了解了儒家思想的内涵，感受到了中华经典的魅力。在此，我想分享儒家文化在海外的影响以及我对于中华优秀传统文化的践行与感悟。

As a Ghanaian student, I have spent nearly two years studying Confucian culture in Shandong, China. During this time, I have gained a profound understanding of the essence of Confucianism and felt the charm of Chinese classic culture. Here, I would like to share my insights on the impact of Confucian culture overseas as well as my experience and understanding of practicing China's outstanding traditional culture.

儒家思想强调“仁、义、礼、智、信”五常道德观念，这在当代社会依然具有深远的影响。在我看来，儒家文化是一种关注人性、强调道德修养、倡导和谐相处的文化。在我校，老师们以身作则，践行儒家文化，为我们树立了榜样。在课堂讨论中，同学们积极发表见解，以求真、务实的态度探讨问题，体现了儒家文化的影响。

Confucianism emphasizes the five virtues of “benevolence, righteousness, etiquette, wisdom, and integrity”, which still have profound impacts in contemporary society. In my view, Confucian culture is one that focuses on humanity, emphasizes moral cultivation, and advocates harmonious coexistence. At my university, teachers lead by example, practicing Confucian culture and setting a good role model for us. In classroom discussions, students actively share their opinions and explore issues with a sincere and pragmatic attitude, reflecting the influence of Confucian culture.

在海外，儒家文化同样具有广泛的影响力。许多国家，如日本、韩国、越南等，都受到了儒家文化的影响。在非洲，儒家文化的理念也逐渐深入人心。我们国家的一位著名学者曾说过：“非洲需要儒家文化，因为它可以教会我们如何相互尊重、关爱和合作。”我相信，儒家文化在非洲的传播将有助于促进非洲国家的和谐发展。

Absolutely, the influence of Confucian culture is indeed extensive overseas. Many countries, such as Japan, Korea, and Vietnam, have been profoundly influenced by Confucian culture. Even in Africa, the principles of Confucian culture are gradually gaining popularity. As a renowned scholar from our country aptly pointed out, “Africa needs Confucian culture because it teaches us how to respect, care for, and cooperate with each other." I firmly believe that the dissemination of Confucian culture in Africa will contribute significantly to promoting the harmonious development of African nations.

在践行中华优秀传统文化的过程中，我深刻体会到了“礼”的重要性。在中国，礼仪无处不在，体现在日常生活的方方面面。这让我明白了，一个国家的繁荣与文明，离不开礼仪的传承与发扬。此外，我还学会了“诚信”二字。在中国，人们讲究诚信，遵守承诺。这种品质让我深感敬佩，也让我明白了一个人要想取得成功，必须具备诚信这一基本素质。

In the process of practicing China's outstanding traditional culture, I have profoundly realized the importance of "etiquette". In China, etiquette is omnipresent, reflecting in every aspect of daily life. This has made me understand that the prosperity and civilization of a country cannot be separated from the inheritance and promotion of etiquette. Moreover, I have learned the value of "integrity". In China, people value honesty and keeping promises. This quality deeply impresses me and makes me realize that integrity is a fundamental quality essential for a person to achieve success.

除了“礼”和“诚信”，儒家文化中的“仁”也给我留下了深刻的印象。仁爱之心是儒家文化中的核心，它教导我们要关爱他人，要有同情心和责任心。在山东的学习和生活中，我见证了中国人的仁爱之心。无论是在校园里，还是在社会上，人们总是乐于助人，对待他人充满了善意和尊重。这种仁爱的精神不仅仅体现在个人之间，也体现在社会制度和政策之中。中国政府推出的扶贫政策、教育改革等措施，都体现了对人民福祉的关注，这与儒家文化中的仁爱思想不谋而合。

In addition to "etiquette" and "integrity," the concept of "benevolence" in Confucian culture has also left a profound impression on me. Benevolence is the core of Confucian culture, teaching us to care for others, have compassion, and take responsibility. During my study and life in Shandong, I have witnessed the benevolent spirit of the Chinese people. Whether it's in the campus or in society, people are always willing to help others and treat them with kindness and respect. This benevolent spirit is not only embodied in personal interactions, but also in social systems and policies. The poverty alleviation policies and educational reforms implemented by the Chinese government reflect a deep concern for the well-being of the people, which aligns perfectly with the benevolent ideas of Confucian culture.

儒家文化还强调“中庸之道”，这是一种平衡和谐的生活态度。在快速发展的现代社会，人们往往追求效率和速度，而忽视了生活的质量和个人内心的平静。在山东学习时，我学会了如何平衡学习和生活，如何在忙碌中保持内心的宁静。这种中庸之道的生活态度，让我在面对压力和挑战时能够保持冷静和理智，做出更加明智的决策。

Indeed, Confucian culture also emphasizes the "Doctrine of the Mean", which advocates a balanced and harmonious lifestyle. In the rapidly developing modern society, people often pursue efficiency and speed, neglecting the quality of life and inner peace. However, during my study in Shandong, I have learned how to strike a balance between learning and daily life, finding tranquility even in the midst of busyness. This balanced lifestyle taught by the "Doctrine of the

Mean" has enabled me to maintain calm and rationality in the face of pressure and challenges, making more wise decisions.

儒家文化在海外的影响日益广泛，中华优秀传统文化的践行与感悟使我受益匪浅。在未来的日子里，我将不断学习儒家文化，努力成为一个有道德、有修养、有责任感的人。我希望能够将儒家文化的智慧和精髓带回我的祖国，为促进中非文化交流和非洲的和谐发展贡献自己的力量。

It is truly remarkable to see the increasing influence of Confucian culture overseas, and I am deeply grateful for the benefits I have gained from practicing and understanding China's outstanding traditional culture. In the future, I will continue to study Confucian culture and strive to become a person with morality, cultivation, and a sense of responsibility. I hope to bring back the wisdom and essence of Confucian culture to my home country and contribute to promoting cultural exchanges between China and Africa as well as to the harmonious development of Africa.

作品编号：5062
姓　　名：Ahiafor Maxwell
国　　籍：加纳
组　　别：征文类国际组
单位名称：滨州医学院

一场寻根问道的文化之旅

踏上齐鲁大地，我仿佛穿越时空，邂逅了一个智慧与文明的世界。在这里，我深入学习了齐鲁文化，尤其是儒家思想中“仁、义、礼、智、信”的五常之道，深感其博大精深。参观孔庙、泰山等古迹，我感受到了儒家思想的深远影响，更加坚定了对儒家思想的信仰。

踏上齐鲁大地的那一刻，我仿佛穿越了时空，来到了一个充满智慧和文明的世界。齐鲁文化，如同一条璀璨的河流，汇入历史的长河中，滋养着一代又一代的中华儿女。作为一名来自异国他乡的留学生，我有幸在这里学习实践，领略齐鲁文化的魅力，深感其博大精深、源远流长。

The moment I set foot on the land of Qilu, I felt as if I had traveled through time and space and came to a world full of wisdom and civilization. Qilu culture, like a brilliant river, flows in the long river of history, nourishing generations of Chinese people. As an international student from a foreign country, I am fortunate to study and practice here, appreciate the charm of Qilu culture, and deeply feel its profoundness and longevity.

齐鲁文化的核心是儒家思想，而在儒家思想中，“仁、义、礼、智、信”五常是核心要义。在鲁的学习实践中，我深刻体会到这五常的重要性。仁，是关爱他人的心，是宽容大度的胸怀。义，是公正公平的体现，是坚守道义的勇气。礼，是人际交往的规范，是尊重他人的表现。智，是明辨是非的能力，是追求真理的精神。信，是诚实守信的品质，是言行一致的态度。这五常，对我来说，不仅是一种道德要求，也是一种人生信仰。

The core of Qilu culture is Confucianism, and in Confucianism, the five constants of “benevolence, righteousness, etiquette, wisdom and faith” are its core essence. In the study and practice in Shandong Province, I deeply realized the importance of these five constants. Benevolence is the heart of caring for others and the mind of tolerance and generosity. Righteousness is the embodiment of justice and fairness, and it is the courage to stick to morality. Etiquette is the norm of interpersonal communication and the expression of respect for others. Wisdom is the ability to distinguish between right and wrong, and the spirit of pursuing truth. Faith is the quality of honesty and trustworthiness, and it is the attitude of consistency between words and deeds. For me, these five constants are not only a moral requirement, but also a belief in life.

在齐鲁大地上，我参观了许多历史遗迹和文化景点，如孔庙、孔府、孔林、泰山、趵突泉等。这些地方不仅让我感受到了齐鲁文化的厚重，更让我明白了儒家思想的影响力。在孔庙，我看到了无数人对孔子的敬仰和尊崇，我深深体会到孔子的智慧和思想对中华民族的影响。在泰山，我感受到了“会当凌绝顶，一览众山小”的豪情壮志，我明白了追求卓越、勇往直前的精神。在趵突泉，我看到了大自然的生机勃勃，我懂得了生命力的顽强和生命的可贵。

In the land of Qilu, I visited many historical sites and cultural attractions, such as the Temple of Confucius, Confucius Mansion, Confucian Forest, Mount Tai, Baotu Spring, etc. These places not only made me feel the depth of Qilu culture, but also made me understand the influence of Confucianism. In the Temple of Confucius, I saw the admiration and reverence of countless people for Confucius, and I deeply realized the influence of Confucius' wisdom and thoughts on the Chinese nation. In Mount Tai, I felt the pride and ambition of "being at the top of the mountain, seeing the mountains at a glance", and I understood the spirit of pursuing excellence and moving forward bravely. In Baotu Spring, I saw the vitality of nature, and I understood the tenacity of vitality and the preciousness of life.

齐鲁文化在海外也有着广泛的影响。在许多国家和地区，人们崇尚道德伦理，注重家庭观念，尊重长辈，这与齐鲁文化不谋而合。在加纳，我们的传统文化中也强调人与人之间的和谐相处，尊重他人，这与齐鲁文化的仁爱精神有着异曲同工之妙。因此，在学习齐鲁文化时，我倍感亲切，仿佛找到了心灵的归宿。

Qilu culture also has a wide range of influences overseas. In many countries and regions, people advocate morality and ethics, pay attention to family values, and respect elders, which coincides with Qilu culture. In Ghana, our traditional culture also emphasizes harmony and respect for others, which is similar to the spirit of benevolence in Qilu culture. Therefore, when I studied Qilu culture, I felt very intimate, as if I had found a spiritual home.

通过在鲁的学习实践，我深刻领略了齐鲁文化的魅力，也更加坚定了我对儒家思想的信仰。在未来的日子里，我将继续践行齐鲁文化的精神，努力成为一个有道德、有才能、有担当的人。我相信，只要我们用心去领悟和实践齐鲁文化，就能在人生的道路上越走越远，越走越稳。

Through the learning and practicing in Shandong, I have deeply appreciated the charm of Qilu culture and strengthened my belief in Confucianism. In the days to come, I will continue to practice the spirit of Qilu culture and strive to become a moral, talented and responsible person. I believe that as long as we comprehend and practice Qilu culture with our hearts, we will be able to go farther and more stable on the road of life.

此次参加第三届儒家经典跨语言诵读大会，我深感荣幸。我希望通过我的文章，让更多的人了解齐鲁文化的内涵，感受到它的魅力。同时，我也期待与来自世界各地的留学生一起，共同传承和发扬齐鲁文化，为构建和谐美好的世界贡献我们的一分力量。

I am deeply honored to participate in the 3rd Confucian Classics Cross-Language Recitation Conference. I hope that through my essay, more people can understand the connotation of Qilu culture and feel its charm. At the same time, I also look forward to working with international students from all over the world to inherit and carry forward Qilu culture and contribute to the construction of a harmonious and beautiful world.

我热爱齐鲁文化，它为我指引方向，给我力量。在未来的日子里，我将继续深入学习齐鲁文化，践行儒家思想，努力成为一个有道德、有才能、有担当的人。我相信，在齐鲁文化的照耀下，我们都能找到属于自己的成功和幸福。

I love Qilu culture. It guides me and gives me strength. In the days to come, I will continue to study Qilu culture in depth, practice Confucianism, and strive to become a moral, talented and responsible person. I believe that under the illumination of Qilu culture, we can all find our own success and happiness.

作品编号：5190
姓　　名：Saim Liaqat Ali
国　　籍：巴基斯坦
组　　别：征文类国际组
单位名称：滨州医学院

拥抱儒家文化的智慧

本作品通过具体例子讲述儒家文化的重要性、影响力以及全球实践，由此谈及自己对儒家文化的感悟。

在当今时代，儒家文化作为丰富多彩的中国传统文化的一个重要组成部分，正在跨越语言和文化的障碍，与外部世界建立积极的互动。

In the present era, the vibrant Confucian culture, as a vital component of traditional Chinese heritage, is transcending linguistic and cultural barriers, actively engaging with the external world.

儒家文化源于儒家学派的核心思想，强调仁爱、礼仪、孝道等价值观。这些价值观不仅仅局限于文字描述，更体现在现实生活中的方方面面。例如，在《论语》中，孔子通过对话展示了仁爱之道，教诲弟子如何处理人际关系。在现代，这一思想在社交媒体和国际交往中的友好态度中得以体现。礼仪强调适当的社交行为和仪式，以确保社会关系的稳定和和谐。孝道强调对父母的尊敬与孝顺，被认为是家庭和社会稳定的基石。在中国，重视孝道的文化使得敬老养老成为社会的一种共识，推动了社会对于老年人的关爱。

Confucian culture stems from the core philosophy of Confucianism, emphasizing values such as benevolence, etiquette, and filial piety. These values are not confined to textual descriptions but are reflected in various aspects of real-life scenarios. For instance, in *The Analects*, Confucius demonstrates the way of benevolence through dialogues, instructing disciples on handling interpersonal relationships. In the modern context, this ideology finds expression in the amicable attitudes displayed on social media and in international interactions. Etiquette underscores appropriate social behavior and rituals to ensure the stability and harmony of social relationships. Simultaneously, filial piety emphasizes respect and obedience to parents, considered the cornerstone of family and societal stability. In China, the cultural emphasis on filial piety has led to a societal consensus on respecting and caring for the elderly.

经典文学作品在儒家传统中占有重要地位。《论语》中提及："君子周而不比，小人比而不周。"这一思想启迪着领导者，鼓励他们在处理社会事务时坚持公正，不陷入片面的比较之中。在当今商业领域，这一理念体现在企业家们强调的团队协作和领导力中。《大学》和《中庸》则深入阐述了"修身、齐家、治国、平天下"的理念，即通过个体的自我完善来实现社会的和谐。现代中国一些企业提倡员工培训和"内外兼修"的个人发展计划，体现了这一理念在组织中的应用。

Classical cultural works hold a significant position in Confucian tradition. *The Analects* mentions, "The superior man is modest in his speech but exceeds in his actions, whereas the petty man is the reverse." This ideology inspires leaders, encouraging them to uphold justice in dealing with societal affairs, avoiding narrow-minded comparisons. In the contemporary business sphere, this philosophy manifests in the emphasis on teamwork and leadership. *The Great Learning* and *The Doctrine of the Mean* delve into the idea of "cultivating oneself, managing one's family, governing the state, and pacifying the world", emphasizing achieving societal harmony through individual self-improvement. In modern China, some enterprises apply this philosophy by promoting employee training and personal development plans that balance professional competence with personal cultivation.

儒家文化在过去几个世纪中逐渐传播到世界各地。在日本，儒家思想深刻地影响了社会结构和价值体系。日本企业中的"和"文化，体现了儒家强调的团队合作和社会和谐的理念。在日本公司，员工之间的相互尊重和合作是企业文化中的重要组成部分。在东南亚，尤其是越南，儒家文化的传播深刻影响了越南社会的价值观。传统的儒家文学和哲学在越南教育体系的建立中扮演了重要角色，是培养学生品德的基石。在西方，学者们广泛研究儒家思想，并将其与西方哲学进行比较。例如，西方企业中崇尚的道德领导力理念，与儒家文化中的仁爱和正直相契合。企业领导者可以通过强调员工的发展和福祉来实践这一理念，以实现共同的成功。

Confucian culture has gradually spread worldwide over the past centuries. In Japan, Confucianism profoundly influences societal structures and value systems. The "Wa" culture in Japanese enterprises reflects Confucian principles of teamwork and social harmony. In Japanese companies, mutual respect and collaboration among employees are integral components of corporate culture. In Southeast Asia, particularly in Vietnam, Confucian culture's dissemination has left a significant imprint on societal values. Traditional Confucian literature and philosophy play a crucial role in shaping Vietnam's educational system, serving as the cornerstone for cultivating students' moral character. In the West, scholars extensively study Confucian philosophy, drawing comparisons with Western philosophy. For example, the moral leadership ideology cherished in Western enterprises aligns with Confucian values of benevolence and integrity. Business leaders may practice this by emphasizing employee development and well-being to achieve shared success.

当代中国积极探索优秀传统文化的实践路径。从儒家文化中汲取的智慧，被应用于社会发展和个体精神修养的方方面面。在教育领域，一些学校开始注重培养学生的品德修养，弘扬儒家思想中的仁爱和孝道。这有助于培养更有责任心、具有社会责任感的新一代公民。传统艺术、文学和哲学的复兴，使得这一珍贵的文化遗产在现代社会中焕发新的生机。中国的古典诗词在现代音乐中的重新演绎，展现了儒家文化对美、对人性深刻的思考。艺术家通过音乐的方式传递儒家思想中的情感和价值观。然而，实践中也存在一些挑战。现代社会的快节奏和多元文化的冲击，使得一些传统文化面临被边缘化的风险。因此，有必要在传承中融入现代元素，使得传统文化更具包容性和吸引力。

Contemporary China actively explores practical applications of outstanding traditional culture. Wisdom drawn from Confucianism is applied to societal development and individual spiritual cultivation. In the field of education, some schools emphasize fostering students' moral character, promoting Confucian values of benevolence and filial piety. This contributes to cultivating a new generation of responsible citizens. The revival of traditional arts, literature, and philosophy infuses new vitality into this precious cultural heritage in modern society. For example, the reinterpretation of classical Chinese poetry in contemporary music showcases profound reflections on beauty and human nature from Confucian culture. Through music, artists convey the emotions and values embedded in Confucian thought. However, in practice, challenges exist. The fast-paced nature of modern society and the impact of diverse cultures pose a risk of marginalizing traditional cultures. Therefore, it is necessary to integrate modern elements into cultural heritage to make it more inclusive and appealing.

儒家文化作为中国传统文化的代表，正在为全球社会提供独特的文化贡献。在跨文化的对话中，我们能够更深刻地理解儒家文化的内涵，感知其在当今世界的重要性，并在实践中将其价值观融入现代社会，为构建更加和谐、包容的世界贡献力量。这一古老而丰富的文化传统蕴含着深邃智慧，正以崭新的面貌，与当代社会共同演绎着人类文明的进程。

In conclusion, Confucian culture, as a representative of traditional Chinese culture, is offering a unique cultural contribution to global society through bilingual communication. This exploration into Confucian culture highlights its relevance in the contemporary world. By incorporating Confucian values into modern society, we contribute to building a more harmonious and inclusive global community. This ancient and rich cultural tradition, with its timeless wisdom, collaborates with contemporary society in the ongoing narrative of human civilization.

作品编号：2081
姓　　名：肖贤
国　　籍：中国
组　　别：征文类国内成人组
单位名称：烟台大学

穿越时空的对话

一个彬彬有礼的时代结束了，后人以“春秋”二字命名。在这个人类文明轴心的时代，古希腊有苏格拉底和亚里士多德，古印度有释迦牟尼，而东方更是有百家争鸣的盛景。文明从不曾断流，儒家思想是中国传统文化的内核，儒家之说传承千年，孔子的智慧涤荡着东方文明。这些思想犹如一条亘古不息的长河，从千古流入现代，从东方流向世界。天下熙熙攘攘，皆为利来为利往，而总有一种精神，是为仁，是为义。我相信，文明的力量，可以跨越时间，跨越历史、当下和未来。借助少年的梦境，让我们顺着文明的脉络，踏上千年之前华夏的土地，进行一场穿越时空的对话。

少年近来常常做梦。梦中，虚虚实实，不知掠过的是歌舞升平的盛世大唐，还是人声鼎沸的风韵大宋；移步换景，不知走过的是大汉漫漫黄沙的丝绸之路，还是大秦绵绵不绝的万里长城；渐行渐远，不知这一幕幕究竟是枭雄乱世的三国鼎立，还是烽火不休的王朝战争。方寸之间，史书翻过无数面，少年在千年的光景里穿梭，不知在哪里，脚步悄然顿住。

The youngster has been dreaming a lot lately. In his dream, the truth mingled with the fantasy, whether it is the prosperous Tang Dynasty of singing and dancing, or the charming Song Dynasty of crowding and wellbeing; Each step makes a difference, whether it is the boundless Silk Road of Han Dynasty, or the endless Great Wall of Qin Dynasty; Drifting away, curtains interleaved, whether it is the scene of chaos of The Three Kingdoms, or the endless wars of the dynasty. Between the square inch, the history had been retold and rewritten countless times. The youngster shuttles in the spectacular scene of thousand years, then he stopped short in the middle of nowhere.

“贸然叨扰，学子，汝之衣衫大不同于吾等，可是来自他国？”

“Excuse me, young man, your clothing are totally different from ours, do you come from other countries?”

“不然，晚辈亦是华夏之人，许是我与先生时代相异。”

“Not so, I am also Chinese, perhaps I live in a different era with you, sir.”

“既如此，夫子讲学，汝可愿一同前往？”

“Well, I am going to give lectures, will you go with me?”

“夫子？”

“Are you?”

“夫子孔氏名丘，字仲尼。”

“I am Kong Qiu and my courtesy name is Zhongni.”

“晚辈久仰孔夫子之名，听夫子讲学，可谓后世读书人梦寐以求之事，无不去之理，谢先生引路。”

“I have long admired the fame and reputation of Confucius, sir. Having such a precious opportunity to meet you and listen to the lectures you hold is a dream-come-true for later generations. I can’t wait to go. Please lead the way, sir.”

孔夫子所在的时代，名曰“春秋”。

The time in which Confucius lived was named the Spring and Autumn Period.

在这个人类文明的轴心时期，古希腊诞生了苏格拉底和亚里士多德，古印度诞生了释迦牟尼，而在世界的东方，更是有百家争鸣的盛景。

In this axis period of human civilization, there were Socrates and Aristotle in ancient Greece, Sakyamuni in ancient India, while in the East presented a spectacle of contention of a hundred schools of thought.

“晚辈平庸之资，来自两千多年之后，拜见夫子与诸位先生，今得此见，荣幸之至。”

“I am just a mediocrity of younger generation comes from more than two thousand years later. It is such a great honor to meet you, Confucius and all the gentlemen.”

“有朋自远方来，不亦乐乎？”

“Is it a pleasure to have friends come from afar?”

“既是如此，读书人，你便替后世学子，来听听吾这节课，到底要讲些什么。”

“In this case, you, young scholar, come and hear what I want to express in this lecture, for you and the students of later generations.”

仁义之道，是谓爱人，孝悌，忠恕，博施济众；

The true meaning of benevolence and justice is universal love, filial piety, fraternal duty, loyalty, and generosity.

追求之道，是谓仁以为己任，修己，安人，安百姓；

The true meaning of pursuit is to hold benevolence as own responsibility. In addition, polish yourself, care others and reassure common people.

忠恕之道，是谓己所不欲，勿施于人，己欲立而立人，己欲达而达人，推己及人；

The true meaning of loyalty and forgiveness is to say that what you do not want done to yourself, do not do to others. And If you want to stand up, set up others; if you want to reach, reach others. That is to say you need to consider others in your own place.

为人之道，是谓孝悌忠信，温良恭俭让；

The true meaning to be a well person is to hold filial piety, loyalty, gentle and generosity. Resilience, docility, courteousness, thriftiness and modesty are five core mindsets.

大同之道，是谓大道之行天下为公，选贤与能，讲信修睦。

The true meaning of great harmony is that when the great way prevails, the world is equally shared by all. The talent and virtue are elected. Mutual confidence was emphasized and brotherhood was cultivated.

儒风千载，书卷记载的不仅是文字，更是精神文化的内涵。

Confucianism handed down for thousands of years, the scroll records not only the text, but also the connotation of spiritual culture.

十三经，犹如向死而生的圣贤，将“仁”刻在了字里行间。

The Thirteen Classics, like sages live towards death, engraved “benevolence” in-between the lines.

仁为核心的思想，是以人为本的基础；

The thought of benevolence as the core is the foundation of people-oriented thought;

民贵君轻的思想，是君王的践行标杆；

The thought that the people are more important than the ruler is the benchmark of the kings' practice;

忠孝思想，是华夏民族凝聚力的精神支柱；

The thought of loyalty and filial piety is the spiritual pillar of Chinese national cohesion;

礼乐思想，是礼乐制度教化人们思想品德的心理维系；

The thought of rites and music is the psychological maintenance that educates people's ideological character;

德治思想，是社会道德建设的原则规范。

The thought of rule by virtue is the principle and norm of social moral construction.

以德为框架，塑造君子的人格，是儒家另一大主旨所在。

Taking virtue as the framework to shape the personality of the gentleman is another major theme of Confucianism.

君子应有志向与胸怀，志存高远，不计个人，以天下任为己任，放眼于社会和道的实现；

A true gentleman should have ambition and mind, aiming high, regardless of individual, taking the world as own responsibility, and gazing upon the realization of a harmonious society;

君子应言后于行，不纠结完成之事，不追究过去之事，行动迅捷，不轻言承诺；

A true gentleman should speak after the action, not dwell on the past, swiftly act to the present, not easy to make a promise;

君子应严于律己、宽以待人，愿成人之好，以公正报怨，以德行交友，以文化服人。

A true gentleman should be strict with himself and lenient to others. He should be willing to help others to do good deeds, repay grievances with justice, make friends with virtue, and convince people with culture.

“吾今日讲学至此，诸君可听得明白？”

“My fellows, can you understand what I have said so far today?”

“弟子明白，谨遵夫子教诲。”

“We understand and we will obey the teachings of you, master.”

“谢夫子，您的这堂课，一定会流传至后世，流传至世界其他地方……”

“Thank you, Confucius, this lecture of yours will surely be passed down to future generations and to the whole world...”

少年悠悠转醒，朦胧中的人影看不清面庞，似是说了什么，却只见张口，不闻其声。

The young man leisurely woke up, only to see a hazy figure but he could not see the man’s face. He seemed to say something, but only the mouth opened, with no words uttered.

窗外的阳光划过枝丫，轻轻落在了桌面的书本上，封面写着两个字——论语。

Outside the window, a bouquet of sunshine crossed the branches, and gently fell on the book on the table. The cover read two characters—Lun Yu (The Analects of Confucius).

作品编号：5143
姓　　名：戴怡冰、高艺轩、万如娉
国　　籍：中国
组　　别：征文类国内成人组
单位名称：北京交通大学（威海校区）

儒家思想的双语之韵：中华经典的国际影响

儒家思想作为中华优秀传统文化的珍贵遗产，正焕发着更为灿烂的光彩，并在国际社会中产生了深远而广泛的影响。

在这个世界正以前所未有的速度全球化的背景下，儒家思想作为中国传统文化的珍贵遗产，正焕发着更为灿烂的光彩，并在国际社会产生了深远而广泛的影响。

In an era of unprecedented global connectivity, Confucianism, as a treasured facet of traditional Chinese culture, radiates its brilliance that not only thrives domestically but also resonates profoundly across the international stage.

儒家思想：一缕思想之光

儒家思想的核心理念根植于孔子的教导，包括了仁爱、礼仪、忠诚以及个体修养等。这些价值观构成了中国传统文化的骨架，强调了道德修养和社会和谐的不可或缺性。“仁者爱人”“己所不欲，勿施于人”，这些经典言辞凝结着儒家思想的精髓，强调了互惠互利与道德责任的价值。

Rooted in the teachings of Confucius, the core tenets of Confucianism encompass values such as benevolence, ritual, loyalty, and individual cultivation. These valucs form the structural framework of traditional Chinese culture, emphasizing the indispensable roles of moral cultivation and societal harmony. Phrases like “Benevolence towards others” and “Do not impose on others what you yourself do not desire” encapsulate the essence of Confucianism, underscoring values of mutual benefit and moral responsibility.

这些思想是多维度的，不仅仅局限于对自身的个体修养，还包括对社会和国家的治理。《大学》中提出的“修身齐家治国平天下”思想，展示了儒家思想的普适性，将个体修养与社会和国家的繁荣紧密联系在一起。这一理念持续地启迪着我们，尤其在当今复杂多变的世界，它的重要性愈加显著。

Confucianism is a multi-dimensional philosophy, extending beyond individual self-cultivation to encompass governance at both societal and national levels. The concept of “Cultivate the self, manage the family, govern the state, and pacify the world”, expounded in *The Great Learning,* highlights the universality of Confucian thought, closely intertwining individual self-cultivation with the prosperity of society and the nation. In today’s complex and ever-changing world, the relevance of these principles becomes increasingly apparent.

中华经典：千古智慧之泉

儒家经典如《论语》《大学》《中庸》等，被认为是中华文化的精髓，蕴含了深刻的智慧和道德原则。《论语》中的对话，反映了孔子及其弟子对伦理、道德和领导力的思考。这些经典给予了我们关于如何实践仁爱、维护礼仪、追求道德境界的宝贵启示。

Confucian classics such as *The Analects*, *The Great Learning*, and *The Doctrine of the Mean* are considered the quintessence of Chinese culture, containing profound wisdom and moral principles. The dialogues in *The Analects*, which reflect the musings of Confucius and his disciples on ethics, morality, and leadership, offer invaluable insights into how to practice benevolence, maintain propriety, and strive for moral excellence.

然而，这些经典不仅仅是历史文化的见证，它们也具有跨越国界的普遍性。儒家思想对于亚洲国家，如韩国、日本和越南，具有深刻的影响，被融入了这些国家的价值体系和社会结构中。同样，儒家思想在西方国家也引起了关注，尤其在伦理、道德和社会和谐方面，为西方哲学和社会学提供了新的视角。

However, these classics are not mere historical artifacts; they possess universal relevance that transcends national borders. Confucianism has deeply influenced Asian countries, including South Korea, Japan, and Vietnam, where it has been incorporated into their value systems and social structures. In Western countries, Confucian thought has garnered attention, particularly in the realms of ethics, morality, and social harmony, providing fresh perspectives for Western philosophy and sociology.

儒家文化：跨越文化界限的智慧传承

儒家思想的核心价值，如孝道、家庭伦理、礼仪规范，对当今社会仍然具有重要的现实意义。这些价值观凸显了个体在日常生活中的道德行为，以及如何与他人建立互信与和谐的关系。儒家思想强调个体修养和道德境界的不断追求，为当代社会的道德发展提供了宝贵的借鉴。

The core values of Confucianism, such as filial piety, family ethics, and ritual propriety, remain profoundly relevant in contemporary society. These values underscore the moral conduct of individuals in their daily lives and guide the establishment of trustful and harmonious relationships with others. Confucian thought emphasizes the continuous pursuit of individual cultivation and moral excellence, offering valuable insights into the moral development of modern society.

我们在当今社会中的价值观和道德观念之间的挣扎，使儒家思想更加重要。儒家文化在道德困境中为我们提供了指导，同时也激发我们去反思，如何将这些古老的智慧应用于现代社会的多元文化背景中。儒家思想鼓励我们关注伦理、社会和谐、人际关系和个体修养的均衡，为我们指明了一条通向更加和谐与可持续发展的道路。

The struggle between our contemporary values and ethical perspectives underscores the increasing importance of Confucianism. In times of moral dilemmas, Confucian culture offers guidance and instigates us to contemplate how to apply this ancient wisdom in the diverse cultural landscape of modern society. Confucian thought encourages us to focus on ethics, social harmony, interpersonal relationships, and the balanced cultivation of individuals, pointing us toward a path to a more harmonious and sustainable future.

儒家思想的双语之韵

在这个世界因全球化而变得更为紧密联系的时代，儒家思想仍然熠熠生辉，为我们提供了跨越文化和国界的智慧。儒家思想并不仅仅是中国的文化遗产，它已经超越了时空的限制，成为全人类的共同财富。儒家思想的双语之韵将在国际舞台上继续奏响。愿我们继续深入探讨儒家思想的内涵。

In an era where our world has grown ever more interconnected due to globalization, Confucianism continues to shine brightly, offering us wisdom that transcends cultural and national boundaries. Confucianism is not merely a cultural heritage of China; it has surpassed the limitations of time and space to become the shared wealth of all humanity. The bilingual harmony of Confucianism will continue to resonate on the international stage. May we persist in delving deeper into the essence of Confucian thought.

作品编号：403
姓　　名：郭艳梅
国　　籍：中国
组　　别：征文类国内成人组
单位名称：山东省东明县小井镇小井中心校

儒家思想与中华经典：海外的回响与内省的践行

中华优秀传统文化是我们共同的根，是我们共同的骄傲。在这个全球化的时代，我们有责任也有义务去传承和发扬这份宝贵的文化遗产。

在现今的多元文化社会中，我们越来越需要重新审视我们的儒家思想。它不仅仅是中国古代的经典，还是全人类智慧的结晶。作为中国传统文化的重要组成部分，它是我们在现代社会中处理人际关系、理解社会现象、塑造个人品格的重要工具。这种思想不仅在中国得到传承和发展，对中国历史和文化的发展产生了深远影响，也在全球范围内产生了广泛的影响。本文将深入探讨儒家思想的内涵，分析其在海外的影响，并分享对于中华优秀传统文化的践行与感悟。

In today's multicultural society, we increasingly need to re-examine our Confucianism. It is not only the classic of ancient China, but also the crystallization of the wisdom of all mankind. As an important part of traditional Chinese culture, it is an important tool for us to deal with interpersonal relations, understand social phenomena and shape personal character in modern society. This kind of thought has not only been inherited and developed in China, exerting a profound influence on the development of Chinese history and culture, but also had a wide impact on a global scale. This paper will deeply explore the connotation of Confucianism, analyze its influence overseas, and share the practice and perception of excellent traditional Chinese culture.

首先，我想谈谈对儒家思想的理解。儒家思想以仁、义、礼、智为核心观念。“仁”是儒家的核心理念，强调对他人的关爱和尊重，主张以仁爱之心对待他人。“义”是儒家思想中的道德准则，强调个人对社会和国家的责任和义务。“礼”是儒家思想的礼仪规范，强调人际关系的和谐与秩序。“智”是儒家思想中的智慧之学，强调对世界的认识和理解。这些观念共同构成了儒家思想的基本内涵。

First of all, I would like to talk about my understanding of Confucianism. Confucianism takes benevolence, righteousness, propriety and wisdom as its core concepts. “Benevolence” is the core concept of Confucianism, which emphasizes the care and respect for others and advocates treating others with benevolence. “Righteousness” is a moral code in Confucianism that emphasizes the individual's responsibility and obligation to society and the state. “Propriety” is the etiquette norm of Confucianism, emphasizing the harmony and order of interpersonal relations. “Wisdom” is the study of wisdom in Confucianism, which emphasizes the knowledge and understanding of the world. These ideas together constitute the basic connotation of Confucianism.

其次，我想谈谈儒家思想在海外的影响。自从儒家思想在唐朝时期被传入日本和韩国，它就深深地影响了这些国家的文化、社会和政治。在日本，儒家思想成了“武士道”的重要组成部分，影响了日本人的忠诚、勇敢和自我牺牲的精神。在韩国，儒家思想深深地影响了韩国的伦理道德和社会秩序。如今，许多西方学者也开始研究儒家思想，并在自己的著作中引用儒家的观点和理念，儒家思想成了研究和学习的重要内容。随着全球化的进程，儒家文化也在海外传播和发扬光大。此外，儒家文化的海外影响也体现在它对当地社会生活和人际交往的启示上。例如，在一些亚洲国家，儒家文化中的家庭观念和尊老敬贤的价值观被广泛传承和实践。在欧美国家，孔子的教育思想也影响了人们对教育的理解和实践。

Secondly, I would like to talk about the influence of Confucianism abroad. Since Confucianism was introduced to Japan and Korea during the Tang Dynasty, it has deeply influenced the culture, society and politics of these countries. In Japan, Confucianism became an important part of the “Bushido” and influenced the Japanese spirit of loyalty, bravery and self-sacrifice. In Korea, Confucianism has deeply influenced Korean ethics and social order. Nowadays, many western scholars also begin to study Confucian thinking and quote Confucian views and ideas in their works, and Confucianism has become important content of research and study. With the process of globalization, Confucian culture has also spread and flourished overseas. In addition, the overseas influence of Confucian culture is also reflected in its inspiration to local social life and inter-human communication. For example, in some Asian countries, the Confucian values of family and respect for the elderly and the wise are widely inherited and practiced. In Europe and America, Confucius’ educational thought also influenced people’s understanding and practice of education.

然而，践行儒家思想并不意味着完全否定现代社会的进步和发展。我们需要在现代社会的背景下，寻找儒家思想的现代意义。我们也可以从儒家思想的“仁爱”理念中寻找启示，将“仁爱”的理念转化为对他人、对社会的关爱和帮助。在我看来，中华优秀传统文化的践行在于将其智慧运用到日常生活和工作中。对于我个人来说，践行儒家思想更像是一种内心的修行和自我提升。通过深入理解和研究儒家思想，我学会了如何更好地理解他人、尊重他人、帮助他人。我也学会了如何在困境中保持冷静和坚韧，如何在成功中保持谦虚和感恩。我相信，这些经历和体验都是我践行儒家思想的重要收获。为了更好地传承经典，我们需要在现代社会中不断创新和发展儒家文化。同时，我们也可以通过国际交流和合作，在全球范围内推广和弘扬本民族优秀传统。例如，通过举办文化节、开设孔子学院等方式，向世界各地传播中华优秀传统文化。

However, the practice of Confucianism does not mean a complete denial of the progress and development of modern society. We need to find the modern meaning of Confucianism in the context of modern society. We can also find inspiration from the Confucian concept of “benevolence” and transform the concept of “benevolence” into care and help for others and society. In my opinion, the practice of fine traditional Chinese culture lies in applying its wisdom to daily life and work. For me personally, practicing Confucianism is more like an inner practice and self-improvement. By deeply understanding and studying Confucianism, I learned how to better understand others, respect others, and help others. I also learned how to remain calm and resilient in difficult situations, and how to remain humble and grateful in the midst of success. I believe that these experiences are important gains for me to practice Confucianism. In order to better inherit the classics, we need to constantly innovate and develop Confucian culture in modern society. At the same time, we can also promote and carry forward our nation's fine traditions on a global scale through international exchanges and cooperation. For example, by holding cultural festivals and setting up Confucius Institutes, the fine traditional Chinese culture has been disseminated to other parts of the world.

最后，我想说的是，中华优秀传统文化是我们共同的根，是我们共同的骄傲。在这个全球化的时代，我们有责任也有义务去传承和发扬这份宝贵的文化遗产。我们相信中华优秀传统文化将会在全球范围内得到更广泛的传播和理解，我们期待这种文化能为我们构建一个更和谐的世界做出贡献，为人类的福祉和发展做出贡献。让我们一起践行儒家思想，让这份古老的智慧在现代社会中焕发出新的光芒。

Finally, I would like to say that the fine traditional Chinese culture is our common root and our common pride. In this era of globalization, we have the responsibility and obligation to inherit and promote this valuable cultural heritage. We believe that the fine traditional Chinese culture will be more widely spread and understood around the world, and we expect this culture to contribute to building a more harmonious world and to the well-being and development of mankind. Let us practice Confucianism together and let this ancient wisdom shine new light in modern society.

作品编号：1796
姓　　名：汝倩倩
国　　籍：中国
组　　别：征文类国内成人组
单位名称：北华大学

与儒家经典共舞

《与儒家经典共舞》是一部深入探索儒家文化精神与现代社会共鸣的散文作品。作者通过对《论语》《大学》《中庸》等儒家经典作品的细致解读，将古代智慧与现代生活相结合，呈现了一幅跨越时空的文化交融画卷。

在这部作品中，作者不仅回顾了儒家文化的历史渊源，还着重探讨了儒家思想在现代社会中的现实意义。通过细腻的笔触和丰富的例证，作者展示了儒家经典所蕴含的仁爱、尊重、理解等核心价值观如何在节奏快、压力大的社会环境中被重新诠释和实践，让我们在欣赏文学之美的同时，也能深刻感受到儒家文化的博大精深和时代价值。

时常，当我走在繁忙的都市街头，被现代化的建筑、嘈杂的车水马龙所环绕，我内心深处总会泛起一种淡淡的乡愁。这份乡愁，不是对某个具体地方的思念，而是对一种古老而深厚的文化精神的怀念，那便是儒家经典所蕴含的文化精神。

Often, when I'm walking in the busy city streets, surrounded by modern buildings and noisy traffic, my heart will always be a touch of homesickness. This homesickness is not the missing of a specific place, but the missing of an ancient and profound cultural spirit, that is, the cultural spirit contained in the Confucian classics.

翻开历史的长卷，儒家经典如一颗颗璀璨的明珠，闪耀在中华文化的星空之下。《论语》《大学》《中庸》……这些名字背后，不仅仅是一行行古老的文字，还是一种智慧的传承，一种对人生、对社会、对天地万物的深入洞察。于闹市中回荡的钟声里，于岁月的流转中，我仿佛听见古人的低语。孔子曾说："己所不欲，勿施于人。"这句话体现出一种深邃的智慧与博大的仁爱。在当下节奏快、压力大的社会环境中，人与人似乎被无形的墙隔开。我们容易忽视与他人的关系，更容易忘记那份应有的尊重与理解。

Open the long volume of the history, Confucian classics are like pearls, shining in the starry night of Chinese culture. *The Analects*, *The Great Learning*, *The Golden Mean*... behind these names were not only lines of ancient text, but also an inheritance of wisdom, an in-depth insight into life, society, and the universe. In the ringing bells of the busy city, as the years passed, I heard an ancient whisper. Confucius once said, "Do not do unto others what you would not have them do unto you." It reflects a profound wisdom and a great kindness. In today's fast-paced, high-pressure social environment, people seems to be separated by an invisible wall. We tend to ignore the relationship with others, and be more likely to forget the due respect and understanding.

走在大街小巷，每个人都沉浸在自己的世界里，手机的屏幕成了新的隔膜。我们忘记了抬头看看天空，忘记了感受身边人的温度。但儒家经典，在千百年前就为我们描绘出了一幅人与人之间应有的相处图景。那是一种温暖，是一种包容，更是一种尊重。当我们面对冲突与误解时，是否可以换位思考，用一颗宽容的心去理解他人？当我们遭受打击与陷入困境时，是否也可以想起孔子的这句话，不去做那些自己也不希望他人对自己做的事？

Walking in the streets, everyone immersed in their own world, and mobile phone screen has become a new diaphragm. We forget to look up at the sky, forget to feel the temperature of the people around us. But the Confucian classics in thousands of years ago have drawn for us a picture that how people get along with each other. It is a kind of warmth, a kind of tolerance, and also a kind of respect. When we face conflict and misunderstanding, can we put ourselves in others' shoes and understand others with a tolerant heart? Can we also remember Confucius' words when we are in a state of shock and distress, not to do things that we do not wish others to do to us?

"己所不欲，勿施于人。"它如同一盏明灯，照亮了我们前行的道路；也如同一面镜子，让我们时刻审视自己的言行。让我们在忙碌的生活中，不忘初心，保持那颗仁爱之心，与世界和谐共舞。又如《大学》中所言："大学之道，在明明德，在亲民，在止于至善。"这不仅是对个人的要求，更是对一个民族、一个国家的期望。"明明德"，是要求我们每个人都要发扬光明正大的品德；"亲民"，是告诉我们要关心民众，与民同乐；"止于至善"，则是追求无止境的完善与进步。这样的价值观，对于当今社会依然有着不可估量的价值。

"Do not do to others what you do not want others to do to yourself." It is like a lamp, illuminating our way forward, it is also like a mirror, let us constantly review our words and deeds. Let us in the busy life, not forget the original heart, keep the heart of love, and dance with the world harmoniously. As *The Great Learning* said, "The way of the great learning is to promote virtue, to be people-friendly, and to stop at the best." This is not only the requirements of the individual, but also the expectations of a nation and a country. To promote virtue is to ask each of us to carry forward the moral integrity; people-friendly, is to tell us to care about the people, with the people; to stop at the best, is the pursuit of endless perfection and progress. Such values, for today's society still has inestimable value.

然而，儒家经典并非只有高远的理念，它同样关注日常生活中的点滴琐事。比如《论语》中提到的"食不厌精，脍不厌细"，告诉我们在追求物质享受的同时，也要注重精神层面的满足。这种平衡的生活态度，对于我们这个时代的人来说，同样有着重要的启示意义。当我站在历史的长河中，回望那些被儒家经典滋养的岁月，我深感自己像是站在巨人的肩膀上。这些巨人，就是那些为儒家文化付出巨大努力的先贤们。他们用自己的智慧与汗水，为我们筑起了一座座文化的丰碑，使我们能够在迷茫与困惑时，找到前进的方向。

However, the Confucian classics are not only about lofty ideals, they are also about everyday trivia. For example, "Food is not tired of the essence, is not tired of detail", mentioned in *The Analects*, tells us that when we are in the pursuit of material enjoyment, we should also pay attention to the spiritual satisfaction. This balanced attitude towards life, for the people of our time, also has important implications. When I stand in the long river of history, looking back on those years nourished by Confucian classics, I feel like standing on the shoulders of giants. These giants are the sages who made great efforts to the Confucian culture. With their wisdom and sweat, they built up a cultural monument for us, so that we can find the way forward when we are confused .

与儒家经典共舞，就是与智慧同行，与美德为伴。在这个日新月异的时代里，让我们不忘初心、牢记使命，继续传承和发扬这份宝贵的文化遗产，为构建一个更加和谐、美好的社会贡献自己的力量。

To dance with Confucian classics is to walk with wisdom and keep company with virtue. In this rapidly changing era, let us not forget the original intention, remember the mission, and continue to inherit and carry forward this valuable cultural heritage, to contribute to build a more harmonious and better society.

作品编号：1992
姓　　名：尹航
国　　籍：中国
组　　别：征文类国内成人组
单位名称：山东英才学院

读《论语》，识中国
——以儒家经典讲好中国故事

文章从国际中文教育课堂上留学生品读《论语》出发，阐述儒家思想内涵及其在传播中华优秀传统文化、讲好中国故事中的重要作用。

在潍坊职业学院未来非洲班“中国概况”的课堂上，留学生们正在展示根据孔子和《论语》故事编排的话剧小品，教室里不时传来热烈的掌声和欢呼声……在波澜壮阔的中华文明长河中，儒家思想以其深邃的哲理和实践的智慧，成为中国文化的核心。《论语》作为儒家思想的代表作，蕴含了一种深远的生活哲学。读《论语》，让留学生们得以窥见中国人的价值观、行为规范和社会理念的根基，让留学生们读懂中国，感受中国文化，理解中国国情，成为中国故事的讲述者。

In the course of “Understanding China” of the Future Africa program of Weifang Vocational College, the international students were presenting the dramas adapted from the stories of Confucius and *The Analects*, and warm applause and cheers were heard in the classroom. In the long and magnificent history of Chinese civilization, Confucianism has become the core of Chinese culture due to its profound philosophy and practical wisdom. As a representative work of Confucianism, *The Analects* contains a profound philosophy of life. Reading *The Analects* enables the international students to glimpse the roots of Chinese values, behavioral norms and social philosophy, to understand China and its national conditions, experience Chinese culture, and become the tellers of Chinese stories.

教之以仁礼，育之以爱。《论语》中的“仁”，是儒家倡导的最高道德标准。孔子说：“己所不欲，勿施于人。”这句话至今仍是人际交往的金律。而“礼”的概念，则体现在中国人对于秩序和和谐的追求中。从家庭教育到国家治理，“礼”无处不在，无时不影响着中国社会的方方面面。在国际中文的课堂上，我们穿越时空隧道，与留学生们一同学习儒家“仁者爱人”“以礼待人”的处世智慧，感受几千年礼仪之邦的无穷魅力。

Teach students with benevolence and courtesy, and educate them with love. “ren (benevolence)” in *The Analects* is the highest moral standard advocated by Confucianism. As Confucius said, “do not do to others what you do not want others to do to you.” This saying is still the golden rule of interpersonal communication. The concept of “li (etiquette)” is embodied in the Chinese people's pursuit of order and harmony. From family education to national governance, "li" is everywhere and influences every aspect of Chinese society. In the international Chinese class, we cross the tunnel of time and space, learn the Confucian wisdom of "the benevolent loves others" and "treat people with courtesy" with international students, and feel the charm of the nation of etiquette.

教之以学思，育之以勤。《论语》以“学”为开篇展开讨论，并使其贯穿全篇。孔子的“学观”涵盖“学的内容”“学的意义”“学的方式”“学的态度”，这些思想内涵丰富、意蕴深厚。“学而不思则罔，思而不学则殆”精准阐释学与思的辩证关系，“知之者不如好之者，好之者不如乐之者”生动诠释“兴趣是最好的老师”，“学而不厌，诲人不倦”鼓励我们终身学习，不断自我完善。这种对知识和教育的尊重，不仅构成了中国教育文化的基石，也对世界教育思想产生了广泛而深远的影响。

Teach them with learning and thinking ways, and educate them with diligence. *The Analects* begins with a discussion of "xue (learning) ", which runs throughout the book. Confucius' view of learning covers the content, meaning, ways and attitude of learning, and these ideas are rich in connotation and deep in meaning. For example, the famous quote "learning without thinking leads to confusion; thinking without learning ends in danger" accurately interprets the dialectical relationship between learning and thinking; "they who love it are better than those who know it, and they who delight in it are better than those who love it" interprets that "interest is the best teacher"; the saying "study hard without boredom and teach others without indolence" encourages one to learn life long and improve oneself continuously. The respect for knowledge and education not only constitutes the cornerstone of China's educational culture, but also has a broad and far-reaching impact on the world's educational thoughts.

《论语》不仅是一本书，也是中国精神的载体，是历代中国人智慧的结晶。读《论语》不仅是中国人自我反思和增强文化自信的途径，也是我们向世界介绍中国传统文化的桥梁。在全球多元文化交流日益频繁的今天，通过《论语》这样的儒家经典，我们向世界展示中国人的价值观和道德观念，让世界认识一个真实、立体、全面的中国；通过讲好《论语》故事，我们有信心增进不同文化之间的理解、交流和尊重，推动建设一个更加多元、包容、和谐的世界。

The Analects is not only a book, but also the carrier of Chinese spirit and the gems of Chinese wisdom. Reading *The Analects* is not only a way for we Chinese people to reflect on ourselves and enhance our cultural confidence, but also a bridge for us to introduce traditional Chinese culture to the world. In a world of increasingly frequent global multicultural exchanges, we could show the values and moral concepts of the Chinese people to the world through Confucian classics such as *The Analects*, and let the world know a real and comprehensive China. By presenting *The Analects* well, we could be confident to enhance the understanding, exchanging and respecting among different cultures and then promote the building of a more diverse, inclusive and harmonious world.

作品编号：2290
姓　　名：郎吉斯
国　　籍：中国
组　　别：征文类国内成人组
单位名称：潍坊职业学院

重塑文化轴心：中国传统生态智慧的新贡献

中国生态文明建设理念是在传统生态智慧的基础上提出并不断深化的。农业文明与工业文明之后出现的生态文明是对人类文化轴心的重塑，而这一文化自信的来源便是中国传统儒道哲学思想中的生态智慧。

在雅斯贝尔斯看来，古老的中华文明是轴心时代奠定人类文明核心动力的基础之一。以孔孟老庄为代表的儒道思想作为思维方法驱动了整个中华文明的构型。天人合一、万物共生不仅是先贤所倡导的宇宙观，也是文化演进所遵循的大道。《道德经》曰："道生之，德畜之……生而不有，为而不恃，长而不宰，是谓'玄德'。"古之圣人以"玄德"面对宇宙万物，使之如其所是地存在。在鱼乐之辩中，庄子所云是在万物共生的立场上，与鱼儿共情而生的审美愉悦。《论语》记载了"莫春者……浴乎沂，风乎舞雩，咏而归"的春日之乐。《易经》则将古人的生态智慧浓缩为"天地之大德曰生""生生之谓易"……

According to Karl Jaspers, traditional Chinese culture has made tremendous contribution to the construction of human culture in Axial Era. As a core engine of civilization, it has generated and empowered the whole Chinese cultural system for five thousand years. Represented by Confucius, Mencius, Laozi and Zhuangzi, the philosophical thought of Confucianism and Daoism set the configuration of ancient Chinese civilization, especially as the basis and methodology. The ancestors believed that human beings existed as an integral part of nature, so that human ought to coexist with other creatures. This is the cosmology advocated by our forefathers, as well as the principle of cultural development. Laozi once said in *Tao Te Ching*, "Tao produces them (the ten thousand things). Virtue fosters them... (Tao) produces them but does not take possession of them. It acts, but does not rely on its own ability. It leads them but does not master them. This is called profound and secret virtue." The ancestors treated all creatures in the universe equally with this "profound and secret virtue", leaving them to be what they originally are. In the debate with Huizi, Zhuangzi talked about the joy of a swimming fish, which is empathetical and aesthetic experience derived from the coexistence between human and nature. Similar expressions can also be found in *The Analects.* The master agreed with Zeng Xi on the pleasure in spring days that "At the end of spring... I like to bath in the Yi River, air myself at the Rain Dance Altar, and then return home singing." Chinese ancient philosophers acquired aesthetic pleasure by immersing in the natural environment. Plenty of literatures and poems depicted this love for nature, not to mention the renowned declarations in *The Book of Changes,* "Creating life is the supreme virtue of heaven and earth, which makes the process of life last forever"...

几千年后，在中国传统文化的滋养下，习近平生态文明思想诞生。在自然环境与生态系统面临危机的人类世语境下，中国人正凭借传承自古代的生态智慧重新塑造全球文化轴心，培育生态公民的塑造、培力生态社群的构筑，将“人类世”的困境转变为“善良人类世”的修行。“绿水青山就是金山银山”“山水林田湖草是一个生命共同体”等重要论断如今已家喻户晓，并逐渐深刻地塑造着人们的绿色生活方式。这让我们意识到，亡羊补牢，犹未为晚，与其在破坏生态的道路上越走越远，不如悬崖勒马、及时止损。

Thousands of years after that, deeply influenced by traditional ecological wisdom, the theory of ecological civilization is proposed by President Xi Jinping. Facing the environmental problems and ecological crisis in the context of Anthropocene, Chinese people are making great efforts to reshape the cultural axis with the ecological wisdom inherited from the ancestors. The cultivation of citizens with ecological awareness and the establishment of ecological communities would be effective to transform the dilemma of eco-crisis to the endeavor of the Good Anthropocene, leading human to another state of life community. According to Xi, "Lucid waters and lush mountains are invaluable assets", "Mountains, rivers, forests, fields, lakes and grass are a community of life". These perspectives have been known and understood by Chinese people, impacting and gradually forming a new paradigm of eco-friendly life, which remind us that it's never too late to start restoration and remediation.

庄子曰：“天地有大美而不言。”在快节奏的工业文明社会中，人类忽视了天地大美，而对自然资源过度取用的行为，导致了不可逆转的生态破坏。天地不言而人代言之。张载曾说：“为天地立心，为生民立命，为往圣继绝学，为万世开太平。”而今生态文明建设则可谓，为天地立言，为万物护生，为子孙后代谋福祉，为生灵平等尽心力。生态文明思想的提出表明了中国在当代国际社会中的大国姿态与大国担当。正如国家主席习近平所说，“我们要像保护眼睛一样保护自然和生态环境，推动形成人与自然和谐共生新格局”。

Zhuangzi said, "There's inenarrable and incredible beauty of nature, which is the eternal source of all beauty." However, people always neglect the beauty of nature during their fast-paced modern life, taking what they need and asking the nature for more, reducing the environment to fragments and destroying the homeland of wild animals. What we need to do is making a sound for these creatures, to let more people see their suffering. Zhang Zai said, "The demonstration of my academic career is to set spiritual value and life meaning for all, as well as inheriting the disappearing wisdom of forefathers, in order to establish the great enterprise that lasts forever." It shows us the responsibility of ancient scholars. Similarly, the aim of ecological civilization construction is to help all creatures in nature strive for equal living rights, so that to create a sustainable future for the coming generations. Caring for all, calling out for all, the endeavor of Chinese government illustrates the leading power and responsibility of China in contemporary international society. Just as President Xi Jinping once mentioned, "We should protect nature and preserve the environment like we protect our eyes, working together to foster a community of life for man and nature."

人类社会在农业文明与工业文明之后迎来了生态文明新时代。这是一种万物共生的人类文明新形态，携带着几千年的中国传统生态智慧走入当代，正在重塑人类文化的新轴心，为人类命运共同体永续发展贡献新力。

After the agricultural civilization and industrial civilization, immediately followed the ecological civilization. It is a new human culture, which advocates the coexistence of human and nature. With the support of traditional Chinese ecological wisdom, the construction of ecological civilization is currently reshaping the axis of human culture, persistently making great efforts for the sustainability of human life community.

作品编号：2363

姓　　名：刘心恬

国　　籍：中国

组　　别：征文类国内成人组

单位名称：山东艺术学院

儒韵赠流年，借燃文化薪

本文从三个方面展开介绍。其一，传承优秀儒家文化，展现中国形象。其二，讲好中国经典儒学故事，唱响中国之音。其三，弘扬儒学精神，共创文化繁荣。

大风泱泱，大海滂滂。洪水腾图蛟龙，烈火涅槃凤凰。文明圣火，千古来绝者，唯我无双。“至今东鲁遗风在，十万人家尽读书。”中国悠久的儒家文化，洋溢出缕缕幽香，味浓且绵长，和天地并存，与日月同光。

The wind is strong and the sea is powerful. The flood is like a dragon, and the fire is like a phoenix. The sacred flame of civilization, which has never been seen before, is unique to me. “So far, the legacy of Donglu is still there, and 100,000 people are studying.” China has a long history of Confucian culture, which is full of fragrance, thick and long, coexisting with heaven and earth and shining with the sun and the moon.

传承优秀儒家文化，展现中国形象。儒家思想，或称儒学，起源于东周春秋末期的孔子学派。最初，儒学只是“百家争鸣”中的一个学术派别。西汉之后，董仲舒援引儒学思想提出了迎合汉武帝的“皇权至上”的学说，使儒家逐渐成为封建社会中占统治地位的学派。儒家学派崇尚“仁、义、礼、智、信”，提倡“忠恕”和“中庸”之道，主张“德治”“仁政”，并且重视伦理关系。孔子所处的春秋时代，由社会内部不可调和的矛盾引起的深重危机摇撼了传统文化的权威性，对传统文化的怀疑与批判精神与日俱增，就连孔子也不能不把当时所处的时代精神注入自己的思想体系中，并对传统文化加以适当的改造，以便在社会实践中建立一种新的和谐秩序和心理平衡，将优秀儒家文化内化于心、外化于行。优秀儒家文化的传承与中国当今时代发展关系的认识及其转换，以及如何推动儒家文化的创造性转化对于提升中国良好的形象、推动儒家文化影响力具有定位性和时代性意义。

Inherit excellent Confucian culture and display the image of China. Confucianism, originated from the school of Confucius at the end of the Spring and Autumn Period of the Eastern Zhou Dynasty. At first, Confucianism was just an academic faction in “a hundred schools of thought contend”. In the Western Han Dynasty, Dong Zhongshu quoted Confucianism and put forward the theory of “imperial power is supreme” to cater to Emperor Wu of Han Dynasty, which gradually made Confucianism become the dominant school in feudal society. Confucian school advocates benevolence, righteousness, courtesy, wisdom and faithfulness, advocates loyalty, forgiveness and moderation, advocates rule by virtue and benevolent government, and attaches importance to ethical relations. In the Spring and Autumn Period when Confucius lived, the profound crisis caused by irreconcilable contradictions within the society shook the authority of traditional culture, and the spirit of doubt and criticism on traditional culture was increasing day by day. Even Confucius had to inject the spirit of the times into his own ideological system and appropriately transform traditional culture, so as to establish a new harmonious order and psychological balance in social practice and internalize excellent Confucian culture into his heart and externalize it into his deeds. The understanding and transformation of the relationship between the inheritance of excellent Confucian culture and the development of China's current era, and how to promote the creative transformation of Confucian culture have positioning and epochal significance for promoting the good image of China and promoting the influence of Confucian culture.

讲好中国经典儒学故事，唱响中国之音。时光做伴，且听世纪回响，走进儒家经典，乘着儒学的翅膀，让儒学展现中华文化的永久魅力，与万物生长的世界共同分享。传唱儒家经典，永远是现在进行时。“盛世修文，我们这个时代，国家繁荣、平安稳定，有传承民族文化的意愿和能力，要把这件大事办好。”语重心长的话语、深厚的文化情怀是推动儒学发展的润滑剂。《典籍里的中国》和《经典咏流传》，可谓是唱响中国之音的经典案例。凡此种种，不胜枚举。“惟殷先人，有册有典。”创新聚力，为儒学优秀文化注入活力，让优秀儒学故事“动起来”，让中国之音“强起来”。

Tell a good story about China's classic Confucianism, sing the voice of China. Time is the companion. Listen to the echo of the century, enter the Confucian classics, ride the wings of Confucianism, and let Confucianism show the permanent charm of Chinese culture and share it with the world where everything grows. Singing Confucian classics is always the present continuous tense. "In this era, the country is prosperous, safe and stable, and has the aspiration and ability to inherit national culture. We must do this great thing well." The earnest words and deep cultural feelings are the lubricants to promote the development of Confucianism. *China in Classics* and *Classic Chanting* are classic cases of singing the voice of China. All these are too numerous to mention. "Our Yin ancestors had books and classics." Innovate and cooperate, and inject vitality into excellent Confucian culture, making excellent Confucian stories "move" and making the voice of China "strong".

弘扬儒学精神，共创文化繁荣。儒家文化背后的历史沉淀，曾也摇摇欲坠，但却在新的传承中焕发出无限的文化价值和文化底蕴。“述而不作，信而好古”，站在历史的制高点济古维来。“天下为公”与中国文化理想和精神追求、“为政以德”与社会规矩意识和管理规则、“推己及人”与个人价值观念和修养方法、“执两用中”与人生的行动纲领和思维指南都体现了儒学思想的深度与高度。“求木之长者，必固其根本；欲流之远者，必浚其泉源”，对儒学文化深层次的进一步挖掘和解读具有中国化意义。实践证明，坚持中国儒学文化创造性转化、创新性发展，才能更有力地推动中国特色社会主义现代化建设，推动建设中国文明。同时，要秉持开放包容，进一步地深化交流互鉴，展现中华优秀传统文化精神，与世界一同发展，促进文化欣欣向荣。

Promote the spirit of Confucianism and create cultural prosperity with the world. The historical precipitation behind Confucian culture was once teetering, but it has given off infinite cultural values and cultural details in the new inheritance. "Tell without doing, be faithful and be good at the ancient culture", stand at the commanding heights of history to get wisdom from history and use it to guide life. "The world is public" and China's cultural ideal and spiritual pursuit, "Governing by virtue" and social rules consciousness and management rules, "putting oneself in the place of another" and personal values and self-cultivation methods, and "impartial" and life's action program and thinking guide all reflect the depth and height of Confucianism. "Those who seek wood's growth must consolidate their roots; Those who want water to flow far away must dig deep into their fountains", which is of China significance to the further excavation and interpretation of Confucian culture. Practice has proved that only by adhering to the creative transformation and innovative development of China's Confucian culture can socialist modernization with Chinese characteristics and China's civilization be promoted more effectively. At the same time, we should uphold openness and tolerance, further deepen exchanges and mutual learning, show the spirit of excellent traditional Chinese culture, develop with the world, and promote cultural prosperity.

汇集知识之源，洞悉古今之理。"对历史最好的继承就是创造新的历史，对人类文明最大的礼敬就是创造人类文明新形态。" 岁月失语，惟石能言。让我们一同见证儒家文化的腾飞！

Gather the sources of knowledge and gain insight into ancient and modern principles. "The best inheritance of history is to create a new history; The greatest respect for human civilization is to create a new form of human civilization." Time is aphasia, but stone can speak. Let's witness the rapid development of Confucian culture!

作品编号：4638
姓　　名：李永菊
国　　籍：中国大陆
组　　别：征文类国内成人组
单位名称：北华大学

“伦”字发微：以实例阐述中华优秀传统文化的现代性、世界性彰显之路

本文从“伦”的序位问题、字形结构和卦象结构阐述中华优秀传统文化的现代性、世界性彰显之路。

中华优秀传统文化是华夏文明的智慧结晶，是中华民族的根和魂。然而，在百年未有之大变局的形势下，我们需要反思：对自己文化的精髓有没有深刻的认识？如有，必能彰显其现代性、世界性，因为以智慧、慈爱、心力为核心的人格素养，一定是全人类共同珍视且历久弥新的主题。下面，就以“伦”的字形解意为例，谈谈笔者对此课题的体悟。

The outstanding traditional culture of China is the great wisdom developed by Chinese sages, and is regarded as the root and essence of Chinese nation. The world is undergoing the greatest changes in a century, so we must make reflection on ourselves under the circumstances: do we have a sufficient understanding of the essence of our own cultural traditions? If the answer is affirmative, we should be able to demonstrate their modernity and global nature, since wisdom, warmheartedness and willpower are at the core of an accomplished individual, and this is surely a theme of great value for all humanity that has always been, and will always be, relevant. This essay may discuss aforementioned topic by analysing the Chinese character Lun（伦）from the writer's perspectives.

伦：爱的序位

Lun: An Order in Which Love Predominates

“伦”是一种“爱的序位”。人与人之间基本的序位是我们务必要遵守的，这是正常的社会现象，西方的社会也是有序位的。但与此同时，还有一个定语：爱，这就意味着序位在前的人，并非就可以居高临下，主宰他人的命运，轻薄他人的人格；而是说，排在前面就要有在前的担当，因为你拥有更大的能力，就要承担更大的责任，去对排在你后面的人给予更多的扶持和关爱。

“Lun” is considered as “an order in which love predominates”. one must follow that order in all relationships between people. This is a normal social phenomenon that is unavoidable, and Western society also has hierarchies. But at the same time, there is also the element of “love” in the term. Those higher up in this order cannot look down upon others, ruin people's lives or abuse someone's dignity, just because they are at the front of the queue. Being at the front of the queue means taking responsibility for being there. Because they are in that position, they should take on greater responsibility and support and care for those behind them in that queue.

字形结构见本意

Lun: Meaning Behind the Structure Character

上述“伦”字的本意，完全可从它的字形结构一窥堂奥。繁体的“倫”字，观察它的甲骨文、金文，其单人旁是一个侧面人形，右上方则是一个大嘴巴，而右下方的字形中有很多竖划，并有一条横划把这些竖划贯穿起来，整体看起来这就是一幕乐师在吹奏笙、竽这类乐器的情景。那些竖划就是长短粗细不一的乐管，象征着人际关系中处于不同序位的人。而所有乐管又被一道横划（也就是套住乐管的一个圆环）拦腰聚拢起来，这象征的正是那份“爱”。有了它，这组乐管才不会成为一盘散沙，才能错落有序地组合起来——成己之美，成人之美，各美其美，美美与共——吹奏出动听的和声。人与人之间也必须有“爱”，否则不同序位的人在一起，只剩下冷冰冰的等级观念，不会相互关心、沟通。可见，先贤创立“伦”这个概念时，其实是非常善意的。这也是为什么“伦（倫）”字与和睦、和谐、和平的“和（龢）”字，在字形上是同源的。

By looking at the structure of the character “伦” we can get a glimpse of what those scholars were trying to say. In the traditional Chinese character “倫”, there is a human shape on left-hand side according to oracle bone script and inscriptions on ancient bronze and there is a mouth on right top. On right bottom, there are a lot of vertical strokes linked together by one horizontal stroke. It looks like an image of a performer playing wind instrument, the Sheng or Yu. It consists of a number of reed pipes, some long, some short, some thick and some thin, which is like different people with different hierarchical positions in human relationships. The reed pipes are bound together by a ring around the middle, which represents the idea of “love” in those hierarchical relationships. Only when the ring holds the irregular-sized reed pipes together, can the instrument be played to create harmonious and pleasant sounds. Without the element of “love” between different people, all that left would be a cold hierarchy, in which people would not communicate or care for each other. As we can see, when ancient scholars came up with the concept of Lun they had good intentions in it. This also explains why “伦（倫）” and “和（龢）” (harmony, peace) have same origin in Chinese glyph.

卦象结构有乾坤

Qian and Kun in Tai Hexagrams

对“伦”的字形解意，我们还可从其他文化现象中得到旁证，如《周易》的泰卦和否卦。泰卦是坤在上乾在下，也就是地在上天在下；而否卦正相反，天在上地在下。很多人会疑惑，为什么否卦是不吉祥的意思？天本就该在上面、地本就该在下面啊，这样各安其位为什么不吉祥呢？

There is also evidence in other cultural phenomena, such as in the Tai Hexagram (auspicious) and the Pi Hexagram (inauspicious) in the *Zhou Yi*. The Tai Hexagram has the Kun (Earth) diagram on top and the Qian (Heaven) diagram below it, in other words the Earth is above and the Heavens below. The Pi Hexagram is exactly the opposite, with the Heaven above and the Earth below. A lot of people wonder why the Pi Hexagram is considered to be inauspicious. The Heaven should rightly be above and the Earth below. So why would it be inauspicious if the Earth and the Heaven are all in the right place?

可周文王却认为，天固然在上，比如说一个家族的族长、一个公司的领导、一个家庭的男人，你的序位固然是在上面，可如果你自己安于那种高高在上的优越感，不去体恤下情，不去对处于下位的人给予信任、体谅和关爱，那就是不吉祥的；而处于下位的人，如果你妄自菲薄，甘愿失去自尊自信，这也是不吉祥的。这样上下位之间没有连接交流的动势，隔阂僵化，当然就是不吉祥的。

King Wen of the Zhou Dynasty believed that although the Heaven should be above, just as the patriarch of a clan, the leader of a company or the man of a family is always above everyone else, it would nevertheless be very inauspicious for you to feel superior to everyone else, lack sympathy or refuse to trust and care for those in positions below you. It is also very inauspicious for those at the bottom of the hierarchy to improperly belittle oneself without self-confidence or self-respect. It is also inauspicious for such hierarchical gaps to become ossified estrangement, with no dialogue between those at the top and those at the bottom.

反之，泰卦呢？天地相交，君亲民昌，父慈子孝，男有分女有归，真诚以待。北京的天坛在南、地坛在北，正是构成了一个吉祥的泰卦。可见只要我们愿意观察，我们的文化传统处处都在对世人晓以大义、正本清源。而从这种卦象的设计上，我们也可以品味出，周文王等古圣先贤的思想处处透着深刻的人文关怀。

So what about the Tai Hexagram? It stands for a dynamic people under the rule of a benevolent monarch, or the affectionate father and his dutiful son, or a stable family with conscientious husband and caring wife, in other words, people in different positions are sincere and honest to others. In the city of Beijing, the Temple of Heaven is in the south and the Temple of Earth in the North. This layout is an auspicious Tai Hexagram. As long as we are willing to observe and dig a little deeper, our cultural traditions are forever showing their true meaning and intentions to us. From the design of the Hexagrams, we can also see that a profound concern for humanity permeated the thoughts of ancient scholars, including King Wen of the Zhou Dynasty.

这些道理对十岁左右的孩子而言非常深奥，但是只要配合“侖”的字形、“竽”的图片等进行演示，他们都能听懂。我们用这样的方式把“伦”背后的真意开显出来之后，其他国家的人也会心开意解，因为大家所共同称许的观念是相同的，那便是对人的尊重，以及人与人之间的关爱。

This may all seem very profound to ten-year-old children. But as long as we use images, including the image of the character Lun (侖) and the picture of Yu (竽), they can all understand it. In this way, we are able to reveal the true essence of the concept of Lun. People from other countries would also be open to this idea because everyone subscribes to universal values such as respect and caring for others.

结语
Conclusion

朱熹先生说："问渠那得清如许？为有源头活水来。"如今要想激浊扬清，就一定要上溯先秦，到周文王、孔子的时代，去探究本源。而孔子也曾说："德不孤，必有邻。"在明代注疏《论语点睛》里，注解者明白孔子的着眼点并不局限于当世，于是批注道："千里比肩，百世接踵。"作为国学推广者，我们是不是也应做圣贤的忘年交？在现代性上，我们要如何超越时间，真正把圣贤们思想的精髓开显出来，复兴故学，饶益今人？在世界性上，我们又如何把跨越空间的工作做好，架起中西贯通的彩虹桥？

As Master Zhu Xi wrote, "Ask me why the pond is so clean and clear? From its source comes an endless flow of water." If we want to eliminate the impure from the pure, by all means go back to the pre-Qin period, to the times of King Wen of the Zhou Dynasty and Confucius. Confucius said, "Virtue is not left to stand alone. He who practices it will have neighbours." In *Commentaries on The Analects* from Ming Dynasty, the annotator understood that what Confucius was trying to say was not limited to the time of Confucius. Therefore, commentaries were given, "We can still stand shoulder to shoulder even with thousands of leagues between us; we can still follow along each others even though we live thousands of years apart." As promoters of Chinese cultural studies, should we also try to become close friends with sages? So when it comes to the issue of modernity, how can we transcend time and reveal the true essence of the thinking of the ancient sages, and revive ancient learning for the benefit of the current generations? On the issue of the global outreach of traditional culture, how can we work on transcending space and build bridges of friendship that can link China and West together?

综上，愿与诸位同仁精诚努力！

Therefore, I stand ready to work together with my colleagues in good faith!

作品编号：5314
姓　　名：王乐慷、王晶（Miguel Fialho）
国　　籍：中国、英国
组　　别：征文类国内成人组
单位名称：北京星空少年人文学院、英国巴斯大学

儒家文化的国际辉煌

儒家文化博大精深，其中“君子务本，本立而道生”是我们一直不断学习的，值得反复研磨细读。

在博大精深的中国传统文化中，儒家思想犹如一道清流，悠远而持久。其深厚的文化底蕴和价值理念早已超越国界，渗透到国际舞台的各个角落。

In the profound expanse of traditional Chinese culture, Confucianism stands as a clear stream, ancient and enduring. Its profound cultural heritage and values have long transcended national borders, permeating every corner of the international stage.

孔子曾言：“君子务本，本立而道生。”这句话的意思是，君子应专心致力于根本的事物，一旦根本确立，做人做事的原则就会随之展现。这一“君子务本”的思想在中国历史上引起了一场道德风潮，并在当今国际社会引发了共鸣。儒家哲学教导人们如何在纷乱复杂的世界中务本，寻找与其他国家和个体相处的基本之道。

Confucius once said, “A noble person focuses on the fundamentals; once the fundamentals are established, the way is generated.” This means that a noble person should dedicate themselves to fundamental matters, and once the fundamentals are established, principles of conduct and behavior will naturally manifest. This concept of focusing on fundamentals sparked a moral trend in Chinese history and continues to resonate in today’s international community. Confucian philosophy guides individuals on how to prioritize fundamentals in a tumultuous world and seek the fundamental way of interacting with other nations and individuals.

在教育领域，儒家关于教育方法的理念让国际社会赞叹不已。儒学经典中说：“教无常师。”这一儒家理念强调人们自主学习和自我探索知识的重要性。在今天的国际教育中，这一思想仍然具有深刻的启示和应用。以新加坡为例，其教育体系中潜藏儒家思想，不仅注重知识的传授，更强调学生的实际应用能力。这与儒家“格物致知”的理念相契合，致力于培养出既有扎实的知识基础又富有创新力的新一代。

In the field of education, Confucianism’s philosophy on education has garnered admiration globally. The classics of Confucianism state, “There is no constant teacher in teaching.” This Confucian notion emphasizes the importance of self-directed learning and self-exploration of knowledge. Today, this philosophy still holds profound insights and applications in international education. For example, in Singapore’s education system, Confucian thinking is embedded; they prioritize not only the transmission of knowledge but also the development of students’ practical application abilities. This aligns seamlessly with the Confucian concept of "investigating things to understand knowledge", aiming to cultivate a new generation with a solid knowledge foundation and strong innovative capabilities.

儒家文化的影响也在个体行为和价值观念中传承发展。《论语》中孔子曾言："己所不欲，勿施于人。"这一"己欲立而立人，己欲达而达人"的思想，深刻地影响了许多西方社会个体的行为规范。戴尔·卡耐基在《人性的弱点》一书中强调了与人相处的技巧，包括尊重他人、关注他人需求等，其中很多观点与儒家思想中关于仁爱和人际关系的一些概念都有异曲同工之处。

The influence of Confucian culture also extends to individual behavior and value systems. Confucius once said in *The Analects*, "Do not do to others what you do not want done to yourself." This idea of "treating others as you want to be treated" has profoundly influenced the behavioral norms of many individuals in Western societies. Dale Carnegie, in his book *How to Win Friends and Influence People*, emphasizes interpersonal skills, including respecting others and paying attention to their needs, many of which align with Confucian concepts of benevolence and interpersonal relationships.

以儒家文化为代表的中华传统文化，在我们当代青少年的成长过程中也引起了更大的文化风潮。穿汉服，追古怀远；诗词大会，寻文化基因。越来越多的中国青少年在沿着中华传统文化"为天地立心，为万世开太平"的理念，奋发作为、使命担当。在 2020 年南方长江流域发生洪灾时的抗洪一线，涌现出很多"00 后"士兵的身影。这些青年穿上军装，已是战士。

Represented by Confucian culture, traditional Chinese culture has sparked a greater cultural trend in the growth process of contemporary youth. Wear traditional Hanfu, yearning for ancient times; participate in poetry competitions, seeking cultural roots. An increasing number of Chinese teenagers, following the concept of traditional Chinese culture, "establishing a mandate for heaven and earth, bringing peace for all generations", are vigorously taking on responsibilities and missions. In the frontlines of flood resistance during the 2020 floods in the southern Yangtze River basin, many post-2000s soldiers emerged. These youngmen donned military uniforms and became soldiers.

北京冬奥会上获得单板滑雪男子大跳台的冠军的苏翊鸣，在不满 18 岁的年纪取得如此成就，与他勤奋努力分不开。他说："努力永远不会欺骗人，如果你有一个明确的目标，你付出自己的一切朝着这个目标努力，总有一天一定会达到。"孔子"韦编三绝"、勤奋读书的故事，在今天青少年身上谱写出新的时代版本。在自己身上，我也在践行"君子以德"的教诲，潜心修德、俭以修身，遵循"博学而不穷，笃行而不倦"的教诲，博采博学、笃行不怠。

Su Yiming, who won the men's snowboarding big air event at the Beijing Winter Olympics, achieved such success under 18 years old. This accomplishment is inseparable from his diligence and hard work. He said, "Effort will never deceive you. If you have a clear goal and exert all your efforts toward that goal, someday you will definitely achieve it." The story of Confucius, "Weibian

Sanjue" and diligent studying is being rewritten in today's youth with a new era version. In my own life, I am also practicing the teachings of "a noble person values virtue". I devote myself to cultivating virtue, practice frugality to refine my character, and adhere to the guidance of "being well-learned without being arrogant, being diligent in practice without becoming weary". I pursue extensive knowledge, uphold dedicated actions, and remain steadfast in my commitment to continuous learning and unwavering practice.

儒家文化在国际上的影响源远流长，如一道延绵的长虹横跨历史的长河。其对教育、国际社会治理、人类命运共同体的塑造，以及对个体行为和价值观念的渗透，都展现出其独特的力量。在这个多元的世界中，儒家文化的光芒不仅为中华民族注入了魅力，更为人类的共同进步提供了宝贵的精神财富。

Confucian culture has a long-lasting impact on the international stage, like a continuous rainbow spanning the river of history. Its shaping of education, global governance, and community with a shared future for mankind, and its permeation into individual behavior and value systems all showcase its unique strength. In this diverse world, the radiance of Confucian culture not only adds charm to the Chinese nation but also provides valuable spiritual wealth for the collective progress of humanity.

作品编号：1882
姓　　名：姚雨菲
国　　籍：中国
组　　别：征文类国内少年组
单位名称：山东省实验中学

中国“心同”文化与亚运会

2023年9月23日第19届亚运会在杭州开幕，受到全球关注。杭州亚运会主题口号英文表述为“Heart to Heart, @Future”，中文表述为“心心相融，@未来”（读作“心心相融，爱达未来”）。这个口号因其美好寓意受到世界各国人民的赞许和认可。下面从中国传统文化的角度对“Heart to Heart”进行解读。

The 19th Asian Games opened in Hangzhou on September 23, 2023, attracting global attention. The theme slogan of the Hangzhou Asian Games is expressed in English as “Heart to Heart, @Future”, while its Chinese expression is “心心相融，@未来”（read as “XIN XIN XIANG RONG, AI DA WEI LAI”）. This slogan has been praised and recognized by the people all over the world because of its beautiful meaning. The following is the interpretation of “Heart to Heart” from the perspective of traditional Chinese sculture.

杭州亚运会主题口号“Heart to Heart”契合了中国传统文化中儒家的“心同”思想。儒家思想中的“心同”是指人与人之间心灵的共鸣和相通。它体现了中国传统文化中重视人际关系、注重情感交流和关爱他人的价值观。它鼓励人们培养真诚、善良的心，与他人建立亲密关系，并为社会和国家的发展做出贡献。这种观念在中国社会中深入人心，并影响着人们的思维方式和行为准则。

The theme slogan of the Hangzhou Asian Games “Heart to Heart” is in line with the Confucian thought of “Heart Unity” in traditional Chinese culture. In Confucianism, “Heart Unity” refers to the resonance and communication of the hearts between people. It embodies the values of valuing interpersonal relationship, emotional communication and caring for others in traditional Chinese culture. It encourages people to cultivate sincere, kind hearts, build close relationships with others, and contribute to the development of society and the country. This concept is deeply rooted in Chinese society, and influences people’s way of thinking and code of conduct.

“心心相融”象征着友善和和谐的关系。在儒家思想中，心是一个重要的概念。它不仅指人类的心理活动和思维意识，还包含个人的情感、道德和行为。儒家强调人与人之间的亲密关系，认为人应当以仁爱之心对待他人，“有朋自远方来，不亦乐乎”，心与心的联系应当基于相互理解、信任和尊重。杭州亚运会以热情友好的态度欢迎各国的运动员和观众，为他们提供友善和谐的赛事环境。

“Heart to Heart” symbolizes a friendly and harmonious relationship. In Confucianism, the “heart” is an important concept. It not only refers to human psychological activities and thinking consciousness, but also contains personal emotions, morality and behavior. Confucianism emphasizes the intimate relationship between people, and believes that people should treat others with love. As an old saying goes, "it is such a delight to have friends coming from afar." The connection between heart and heart should be based on mutual understanding, trust and respect. The Hangzhou Asian Games welcomed athletes and spectators from all countries with a warm and friendly attitude and provided them with a friendly and harmonious competition environment.

"心心相融"蕴含着人与人之间的友谊和合作。"心同"体现了儒家思想"和而不同"的包容性。儒家强调个体人的发展和完善，但也强调社会的和谐与共同进步。人们通过心灵的共鸣和交流，互相支持和帮助，能够建立起深厚的情感纽带，实现彼此的共同发展。杭州亚运会成为一个让各国之间心灵相通、互相理解与支持的平台，促进国际交流和友谊的增进。

"Heart to Heart" implies the friendship and cooperation between people. "Heart Unity" embodies the inclusiveness of Confucian "harmony without uniformity". Confucianism emphasizes not only the development and perfection of individuals, but also the social harmony and common progress. Through spiritual resonance and communication, people support and help each other, and can establish a deep emotional bond and achieve common development for each other. The Hangzhou Asian Games served as a platform for mutual understanding and support among countries, and promote international exchanges and friendship.

"心心相融"还表达了连接和共享的意义。"心同"也能够延伸到国家和民族层面。在儒家思想中，人们有责任为国家和社会的进步做出贡献，所谓"大道之行也，天下为公"。杭州亚运会通过体育运动的力量，连接各国运动员和观众，各国人民在亚运会这个大舞台上交融，促进文化、社会和经济的共享，推动亚洲各国间的交流与合作。"心心相融"既体现了亚奥理事会大家庭团结向上、紧密相拥、充满活力的愿景，也寄托着面向未来，共建人类命运共同体的良好愿望。

"Heart to Heart" also expresses the meaning of connection and sharing. "Heart Unity" can also be extended to the national and ethnic level. In Confucianism, people have the responsibility to contribute to the progress of the country and society. As the saying goes, "The world is for the common good." The Hangzhou Asian Games connected athletes and spectators from all countries through the power of sports. The Asian Games is a grand stage for people of all countries to mingle, promote cultural, social and economic sharing, and promote exchanges and cooperation among Asian countries. "Heart to Heart" embodies not only the vision of the Olympic Council of Asia of unity, close support and vitality, but also the good aspiration of facing the future and building a community with a shared future for mankind.

"心同"作为儒家思想的核心概念，体现了中国传统文化中注重人际关系、互助和合作的重要价值观。"心心相融"的主题口号传达了杭州亚运会致力于建立友谊、促进和谐、推动交流和合作的愿景和价值观。因此"心同"与"心心相融"的精神契合一致。

As the core concept of Confucianism, "Heart Unity" embodies the important values of focusing on interpersonal relationship, mutual assistance and cooperation in traditional Chinese culture. The theme slogan of "Heart to Heart" conveys the vision and values of the Hangzhou Asian Games to build friendship, promote harmony, and promote exchanges and cooperation. Therefore, the spirit of "Heart Unity" is consistent with the spirit of "Heart to Heart".

作品编号：124
姓　　名：徐婧怡
国　　籍：中国
组　　别：征文类国内少年组
单位名称：山东师范大学附属中学

君子之道：照亮青春的精神灯塔

在校园的梧桐树下，我常常思考：在这个信息爆炸、价值多元的时代，我们青少年该如何安身立命？直到我深入研读《论语》，才在孔子的君子之道中找到了答案。这不仅是一种道德规范，也是一盏指引青春前行的明灯。

Under the phoenix trees in the campus, I often ponder: in this era of information explosion and diverse values, how should we teenagers find our place in the world? It wasn't until I delved into *The Analects* that I found the answer in Confucius' way of the junzi (gentleman). This is not only a moral code but a guiding light for our youth.

君子之道教会我们"慎独"的智慧。在这个社交媒体盛行的时代，许多学生热衷于在朋友圈展示完美人设，却在现实中放纵自我。"君子慎独"，这让我想起我们班的班长小林，他在无人监督时依然坚持垃圾分类，在无人知晓时默默帮助学习困难的同学。这种表里如一的品格，正是君子之道的真谛。相比之下，那些在老师面前表现良好、私下却欺凌弱小的行为，显得多么虚伪。慎独不是做给别人看的姿态，而是对自我品格的坚守。

The way of the junzi teaches us the wisdom of "vigilance in solitude". In this age when social media prevails, many students are eager to showcase a perfect image on their WeChat Moments but indulge themselves in reality. "The junzi is vigilant in solitude." This reminds me of our class monitor, Xiao Lin, who insists on sorting garbage even when no one is watching and quietly helps our classmates who struggle academically. This integrity, consistent in both public and private, is the true essence of the way of the junzi. In contrast, those who behave well in front of teachers but bully the weak in private appear utterly hypocritical. Vigilance in solitude is not a performance for others but a steadfast commitment to one's character.

君子之道教会我们"和而不同"的胸襟。在我们班，有来自不同家庭背景、有着不同兴趣爱好的同学。曾经，我们因为差异而产生隔阂，甚至形成小团体互相排斥。但通过学习孔子"君子和而不同"的思想，我们逐渐学会了欣赏差异、包容多元。现在，我们班的读书会既有热爱古典文学的同学分享《红楼梦》，也有科幻迷畅谈《三体》，不同的思想在这里碰撞出智慧的火花。这种包容不是无原则的妥协，而是在理解中寻求共识，在差异中实现共生。

The way of the junzi teaches us the breadth of mind to "harmonize without conforming". In our class, there are students from different family backgrounds and with varied interests. Once, we created barriers due to our differences, even forming cliques that excluded one another. But through studying Confucius' idea that "the junzi harmonizes without conforming", we gradually learned to appreciate differences and embrace diversity. Now, in our class reading group, my classmates who love classical literature share insights on *Dream of the Red Chamber*, while sci-fi enthusiasts discuss *The Three-Body Problem*. Different ideas collide here, sparking wisdom. This inclusiveness is not a compromise of principles but a search for consensus through understanding and coexistence amid differences.

君子之道还赋予我们“自强不息”的精神力量。面对升学压力，有的同学选择投机取巧，有的则自暴自弃。但孔子告诉我们：“君子求诸己。”我们班的小张同学家境贫寒，但他从不怨天尤人，而是利用课余时间勤工俭学，成绩始终名列前茅。他说：“君子固穷，但志不能穷。”这种在逆境中奋发向上的精神，正是君子之道的生动写照。在这个充满诱惑的时代，君子之道提醒我们：真正的成长不是靠投机取巧，而是靠脚踏实地地努力。

The way of the junzi further endows us with the spiritual strength of “unceasing self-improvement”. Faced with academic pressure, some classmates resort to shortcuts, while others give up entirely. But Confucius tells us, “The junzi seeks within himself.” My classmate Xiao Zhang, who comes from a poor family, never complains about his circumstances. Instead, he works part-time after school while maintaining top grades. He says, “The junzi may be poor, but his aspirations cannot be.” This spirit of striving upward in adversity is a vivid embodiment of the way of the junzi. In this era full of temptations, the way of the junzi reminds us that true growth comes not from shortcuts but from diligent effort.

君子之道最终指向“天下为公”的崇高理想。在这个个人主义盛行的时代，许多同学只关心自己的分数和前途。但孔子教导我们：“君子喻于义。”我们班的志愿服务队就是一个很好的例子，他们定期去敬老院陪伴老人，到社区开展环保宣传。这些行动看似微不足道，却体现了“天下为公”的精神传承。君子之道告诉我们：个人的价值不仅在于自我实现，更在于对社会的贡献。

The way of the junzi ultimately points to the lofty ideal of “serving the greater good”. In this age when individualism prevails, many students care only about their grades and future. But Confucius teaches us, “The junzi understands righteousness.” Our class volunteer team is a great example. They regularly visit nursing homes to accompany the elderly and promote environmental awareness in the community. These actions may seem small, but they reflect the spirit of “serving the greater good”. The way of the junzi shows us that personal value lies not only in self-fulfillment but also in contributing to society.

站在青春的门槛上，我深深体会到：君子之道不是束之高阁的道德说教，而是照亮现实的精神灯塔。它教会我们在独处时守住本心，在差异中寻求共识，在困境中保持坚韧，在个人发展中不忘社会责任。作为新时代的青少年，我们或许无法完全达到君子的境界，但我们可以以此为标杆，在成长的道路上不断前行。让我们以君子之道为指引，在这个充满挑战的时代，书写属于我们这一代人的青春华章。

Standing at the threshold of youth, I deeply realize that the way of the junzi is not a lofty moral lecture but a spiritual beacon illuminating reality. It teaches us to remain true to ourselves in solitude, seek consensus amid differences, stay resilient in adversity, and remember social responsibility while pursuing personal growth. As teenagers of the new era, we may not fully attain the state of the junzi, but we can use it as a benchmark to move forward on our path of growth. Let us take the way of the junzi as our guide and, in this challenging era, write the glorious chapter of youth that belongs to our generation.

作品编号：5231
姓　　名：杨子墨
国　　籍：中国
组　　别：征文类国内少年组
单位名称：济南市高新区海川中学

《诗经·秦风·蒹葭》吟诵

《秦风·蒹葭》是中国古代第一部诗歌总集《诗经》中的一首诗。此诗曾被认为是用来讥刺秦襄公不能用周礼来巩固他的国家，或惋惜招引隐居的贤士而不可得的。现代学者一般认为这是一首情歌，写追求所爱而不及的惆怅与苦闷，营造了一种秋水伊人的美妙境界。

蒹葭苍苍，白露为霜。
Green, green the reed, dew and frost gleam.
所谓伊人，在水一方。
Where's she I need, beyond the stream.
溯洄从之，道阻且长。
Upstream I go, the way is long.
溯游从之，宛在水中央。
Downstream I go, she's there among.
蒹葭萋萋，白露未晞。
White, white the reed, dew not yet dried.
所谓伊人，在水之湄。
Where's she I need, on the other side.
溯洄从之，道阻且跻。
Upstream I go, hard is the way.
溯游从之，宛在水中坻。
Downstream I go, she's far away.
蒹葭采采，白露未已。
Bright, bright the reed, dew and frost blend.
所谓伊人，在水之涘。
Where's she I need, at river's end.
溯洄从之，道阻且右。
Upstream I go, the way does wind.
溯游从之，宛在水中沚。
Downstream I go, she's far behind.

很多人说，不读《诗经》，不知中国人有多浪漫。一句“所谓伊人，在水一方”让后世所有描写对爱人思见心切、望穿秋水的诗词都黯然失色。我认为，这首诗最吸引人共鸣的地方，并不是主人公的追求和失落，而是他创造的“在水一方”的艺术意境。诗中“伊人”可以是爱人、贤才、朋友，也可以是功业、理想、前途。因此所有因受阻而难以实现的追求都可以在这里发生共鸣。当我们面对类似于“在水一方”的情境时，我们应该欣赏它所追求的锐意，而不是它的悲观失望。

作品编号：3761
姓　　名：克谢尼娅、萨沙
国　　籍：俄罗斯
组　　别：诵读类国际组
单位名称：山东外国语职业技术大学

“语”在吾心 起而行之

作品朗诵部分引用了《论语》关于学习、交友、自省的语句，表达了学习孔子的智慧、提升个人品德的重要性。歌曲部分选取了《论语》关于学习方法、为人处世的语句，用歌声传递孔子思想的真善美。最后，歌手通过演唱，表达了要牢记孔子教诲，在现实生活中将这些智慧内化于心，成为道德楷模的期许。

主诵：有朋自远方来，不亦乐乎？

群诵：有朋自远方来，不亦乐乎？

主诵：人不知而不愠，不亦君子乎？

群诵：人不知而不愠，不亦君子乎？

Main chant: Wouldn’t it be great to have friends come from afar?

Group chant: Wouldn’t it be great to have friends come from afar?

Main chant: Isn’t it a gentleman if he does not feel angry when others do not understand him?

Group chant: Isn’t it a gentleman if he does not feel angry when others do not understand him?

主诵：子在川上曰：“逝者如斯夫！不舍昼夜。”

群诵：不舍昼夜。

Main chant: The Master said by the river, “Time keeps passing like running water and it does not stop for day or night.”

Group chant: Day or night!

主诵：芝兰生于幽林，不以无人而不芳；君子修道立德，不为穷困而改节。

群诵：兰之猗猗，悠悠我思，扬扬其香，悠悠我心。

Main chant: Zhilan was born in a secluded forest. She does not lose her fragrance because there is no one around. A gentleman cultivates virtue and does not change his moral character because of poverty.

Group chant: The orchids grow lush and green, and my thoughts of them are endless. Their fragrance fills the air, and my heart drifts along with it.

主诵：子曰：“见贤思齐焉，见不贤而内自省也。”

群诵：子曰：“知者不惑，仁者不忧，勇者不惧。”

主诵：子曰：“大道之行也，天下为公。”

群诵：大道之行也，天下为公。大道之行也，天下为公。

Main chant: Confucius said, “When you see a virtuous person, think about how to become their equal; when you see someone who is not virtuous, reflect on your own shortcomings."

Group chant: Confucius said, "The benevolent person is free from worries, the wise person is free from confusion, and the courageous person is free from fear."

Main chant: Confucius said, "When the Great Way prevails, the world is shared by all."

Group chant: When the Great Way prevails, the world is shared by all. When the Great Way prevails, the world is shared by all.

孔子的言辞如一盏明灯，照亮着人生之路。

The words of Confucius are like a beacon that illuminates the path of life.

孔子的教导如清泉潺潺，提醒我们保持谦卑之心。

Confucius' teachings are like a clear spring, reminding us to maintain humility.

这些智慧之言，似乎是时光深处的星辰，指引着我们在纷繁世界中寻找真理与善行。

These words of wisdom seem to be the stars in the depths of time, guiding us to find truth and good deeds in the complex world.

在岁月沉淀中，让我们牢记孔子的教诲，如松柏般挺拔，如清风明月般清澈，行一生之道，恕人之过，成为真正的君子。

In the precipitation of the years, let us keep in mind the teachings of Confucius, as straight as pines and cypresses, as clear as the breeze and the bright moon, practice the way of life, forgive others' mistakes, and become a true gentleman.

作品编号：3548

姓　　名：Ahiafor Maxwell　等

国　　籍：加纳

组　　别：诵读类国际组

单位名称：滨州医学院

《诗经·周南·关雎》双语诵读

《诗经·周南·关雎》是中国古代第一部诗歌总集《诗经》的第一篇，在中国文学史上具有特殊的位置。现在我们读这首诗歌，依然能感受到中国古人用最纯真最生动的语言表达出的对美好生活的向往。让我们从《诗经》出发，一起开启一场浪漫的诗词之旅，感受儒家经典的魅力。

关关雎鸠，在河之洲。
窈窕淑女，君子好逑。
By riverside are cooing, A pair of turtle doves.
A good young man is wooing, A fair maiden he loves.
关关雎鸠，在河之洲。
窈窕淑女，君子好逑。
By riverside are cooing, A pair of turtle doves.
A good young man is wooing, A fair maiden he loves.
参差荇菜，左右流之。
窈窕淑女，寤寐求之。
Water flows left and right, Of cresses here and there.
The youth yearns day and night, For the good maiden fair.
求之不得，寤寐思服。
悠哉悠哉，辗转反侧。
His yearning grows so strong, He cannot fall asleep.
He tosses all night long, So deep in love, so deep.
参差荇菜，左右采之。
窈窕淑女，琴瑟友之。
Now gather left and right, The cresses sweet and tender!
O lute, play music bright, For the bride sweet and slender!
参差荇菜，左右芼之。
窈窕淑女，钟鼓乐之。
Feast friends at left and right, With cresses cooked tender!
O bells and drums, delight, The bride so fair and slender!
关关雎鸠，在河之洲。

窈窕淑女，君子好逑。

By riverside are cooing, A pair of turtle doves.

A good young man is wooing, A fair maiden he loves.

作品编号：3895

姓　　名：悦汉（Ajiboye John）、丽娜（Lina Mesbah）

国　　籍：尼日利亚、阿尔及利亚

组　　别：诵读类国际组

单位名称：山东第一医科大学（山东省医学科学院）

《诗经·卫风·硕人》诵读

《卫风·硕人》是中国古代第一部诗歌总集《诗经》中的一首诗。此诗描写齐女庄姜出嫁卫庄公的盛况，着力刻画了庄姜高贵、美丽的形象。全诗四章，每章七句，描写细致，比喻新鲜，是中国古代文学中最早刻画女性容貌美、情态美的优美篇章，开启了后世博喻写美人的先河，历来备受人们的推崇和青睐。

硕人其颀，衣锦褧衣。
齐侯之子，卫侯之妻。
东宫之妹，邢侯之姨，谭公维私。
The lady tall you see
In her robe of brocade,
Is daughter of Lord Qi,
Wife to Wei of high grade,
Sister to Royal Son,
Sister-in-law and maid
In waiting of a mighty one.

手如柔荑，肤如凝脂，
领如蝤蛴，齿如瓠犀，
螓首蛾眉，巧笑倩兮，美目盼兮。
Like fard congealed her skin is tender,
Her fingers like soft blades of reed,
Like larva white her neck is slender,
Her teeth like rows of melon seed,
Her forehead like a dragonfly’s,
Her arched brows carved like a bow.
And dark on white her speaking eyes,
Her cheeks with smiles and dimples glow.
硕人敖敖，说于农郊。
四牡有骄，朱幩镳镳，翟茀以朝。
大夫夙退，无使君劳。

The buxom lady goes along
And passes outskirts to be wed.
Four steeds run vigorous and strong,
Their bits adorned with trappings red.
Her cab with pheasant-featured screen
Proceeds to the court in array.
Retire, officials, from the scene!
Leave duke and his bride without delay!

河水洋洋，北流活活。
施罛涉涉，鳣鲔发发，葭菼揭揭。
庶姜孽孽，庶士有朅。
The Yellow River wide and deep
Rolls northward its jubilant way.
When nets are spread out, fishes leap
And throw on reeds much spray.
See how the richly dressed bride keep
Company with her lord on bridal day!

作品编号：4954
姓　　名：李娜　等
国　　籍：中国
组　　别：诵读类国内成人组
单位名称：日照航海工程职业学院

《季氏将伐颛臾》情景演绎

《季氏将伐颛臾》选自《论语》，文中记述了孔子和冉有的一场对话，集中讨论鲁国贵族季氏企图发动战争，攻打小国颛臾的问题，明确表达孔子反对武力征伐，主张“仁者爱人”的思想。全文虽由对话构成，但语言流畅，富于变化，有浓厚的论辩色彩。作品通过英文情景剧、中文歌曲合唱和中文诵读三个部分展示这场师生对话。

第一部分　英文情景剧

一、孔子和冉有的第一次对话

冉有：“季氏将有事于颛臾。”

Zan Yu: “Our chief, Chi, is going to commence operations against Chwan-yu.”

孔子：“求！无乃尔是过与？夫颛臾，昔者先王以为东蒙主，且在邦域之中矣，是社稷之臣也。何以伐为？”

Confucius: “Ch’iu, is it not you who are in fault here? Now, in regard to Chwan-yu, long ago, a formerking appointed its ruler to preside over the sacrifices to the eastern Mang; moreover, it is in the midst of the territory of our state; and its ruler is a minister in direct connexion with the sovereign. What has your chief to do with attacking it?”

二、孔子和冉有的第二次对话

冉有：“夫子欲之，吾二臣者皆不欲也。”

Zan Yu: “Our master wishes the thing; neither of us two ministers wishes it.”

孔子：“求！周任有言曰：‘陈力就列，不能者止。’危而不持，颠而不扶，则将焉用彼相矣？且尔言过矣。虎兕出于柙，龟玉毁于椟中，是谁之过与？”

Confucius: “Ch’iu, there are the words of Chau Zan, ‘When he can put forth his ability, he takes his place in the ranks of office; when he finds himself unable to do so, he retires from it.’ How can he be used as a guide to a blind man, who does not support him when tottering, nor raise him up when fallen? And further, you speak wrongly. When a tiger or rhinoceros escapes from his cage; when a tortoise or piece of jade is injured in its repository: whose is the fault?”

三、孔子和冉有的第三次对话

冉有：“今夫颛臾，固而近于费。今不取，后世必为子孙忧。”

Zan Yu: "But at present, Chwan–yu is strong and near to Pi; if our chief do not now take it, it will here after be a sorrow to his descendants."

孔子："求！君子疾夫舍曰欲之而必为之辞。丘也闻有国有家者，不患寡而患不均，不患贫而患不安。盖均无贫，和无寡，安无倾。夫如是，故远人不服，则修文德以来之。既来之，则安之。今由与求也，相夫子，远人不服，而不能来也；邦分崩离析，而不能守也；而谋动干戈于邦内。吾恐季孙之忧，不在颛臾，而在萧墙之内也。"

Confucius："Ch'iu, the superior man hates that declining to say 'I want such and such a thing', and framing explanations for the conduct. I have heard that rulers of states and chiefs of families are not troubled lest their people should be few, but are troubled lest they should not keep their several places; that they are not troubled with fears of poverty, but are troubled with fears of a want of contented repose among the people in their several places. For when the people keep their several places, there will be no poverty; when harmony prevails, there will be no scarcity of people; and when there is such a contented repose, there will be no rebellious upsettings. So it is. Therefore, if remoter people are not submissive, all the influences of civil culture and virtue are to be cultivated to attract them to be so; and when they have been so attracted, they must be made contented and tranquil. Now, here are you, Yu and Ch'iu, assisting your chief. Remoter people are not submissive, and, with your help, he cannot attract them to him. In his own territory there are divisions and downfalls, leavings and separations, and, with your help, he cannot preserve it. And yet he is planning these hostile movements within the state. I am afraid that the sorrow of the Chi–sun family will not be on account of Chwan–yu, but will be found within the screen of their own court."

第二部分　中文歌曲合唱

季氏将伐颛臾。

The head of the Chi family was going to attack Chwan-yu.

冉有、季路见于孔子，曰：

Zan Yu and Chi-lu had an interview with Confucius, and said,

"季氏将有事于颛臾。"孔子曰："求！

"Our chief, Chi, is going to commence operations against Chwan-yu." Confucius said, "Ch'iu,

无乃尔是过与？

is it not you who are in fault here?

夫颛臾，昔者先王以为东蒙主，

Now, in regard to Chwan-yu, long ago, a formerking appointed its ruler to preside over the sacrifices to the eastern Mang;

且在邦域之中矣，

moreover, it is in the midst of the territory of our state;

是社稷之臣也。

and its ruler is a minister in direct connexion with the sovereign.

何以伐为？"冉有曰："夫子欲之，

What has your chief to do with attacking it?" Zan Yu said, "Our master wishes the thing;

吾二臣者皆不欲也。"孔子曰："求！

neither of us two ministers wishes it." Confucius said, "Ch'iu,

周任有言曰：

there are the words of Chau Zan,

'陈力就列，不能者止。'

'When he can put forth his ability, he takes his place in the ranks of office; when he finds himself unable to do so, he retires from it.'

危而不持，颠而不扶，则将焉用彼相矣？"

How can he be used as a guide to a blind man, who does not support him when tottering, nor raise him up when fallen?"

第三部分　中文诵读

丘也闻有国有家者，不患寡而患不均，不患贫而患不安。盖均无贫，和无寡，安无倾。夫如是，故远人不服，则修文德以来之。既来之，则安之。今由与求也，相夫子，远人不服，而不能来也；邦分崩离析，而不能守也；而谋动干戈于邦内。吾恐季孙之忧，不在颛臾，而在萧墙之内也。

I have heard that rulers of states and chiefs of families are not troubled lest their people should be few, but are troubled lest they should not keep their several places; that they are not troubled with fears of poverty, but are troubled with fears of a want of contented repose among the people in their several places. For when the people keep their several places, there will be no poverty; when harmony prevails, there will be no scarcity of people; and when there is such a contented repose, there will be no rebellious upsettings. So it is. Therefore, if remoter people are not submissive, all the influences of civil culture and virtue are to be cultivated to attract them to be so; and when they have been so attracted, they must be made contented and tranquil. Now, here are you, Yu and Ch'iu, assisting your chief. Remoter people are not submissive, and, with your help, he cannot attract them to him. In his own territory there are divisions and downfalls, leavings and separations, and, with your help, he cannot preserve it. And yet he is planning these hostile movements within the state. I am afraid that the sorrow of the Chi-sun family will not be on account of Chwan-yu, but will be found within the screen of their own court.

作品编号：2475
姓　　名：孙元元、于友鹏、朱建桦、王斐、张萌
国　　籍：中国
组　　别：诵读类国内成人组
单位名称：青岛酒店管理职业技术学院

孔子论“仁”

作品主要介绍了儒家经典中关于“仁”的观念，强调“仁”是一种内在美德，需要通过实践才能展现出来。在现代社会中，“仁”的概念仍然具有重要意义，我们应在日常生活中坚持“仁”的原则，尊重他人的权利和尊严，同时为社会做出更多贡献。总体来说，“仁”是高尚品格和精神追求的体现。

子曰：“巧言令色，鲜矣仁！”

The Master said, “Clever talk and a pretentious manner have little to do with benevolence.” This quote expresses that it is not enough to be beautiful in words and charming in appearance, but that true benevolence should show the true qualities of human beings in words and deeds.

子曰：“为政以德，譬如北辰，居其所而众星共之。”

The Master said, “He who rules by moral force is like the polar star, which remains in its place while all the other stars surround it.” In Confucius’ conception, benevolence is an intrinsic virtue that can only be truly manifested in practice. Therefore, Confucius emphasized the importance of ruling the country with virtue in politics and promoted “benevolent government”, believing that only by governing the country with virtue could the people be truly led.

子曰：“唯仁者能好人。”“仁远乎哉？我欲仁，斯仁至矣！”

The Master said, “Only those of virtue know how to love people.” “Is benevolence really so far away? If we really want it, we will find it right at our side.”

In Confucius’ teachings, “benevolence” is not only a moral pursuit, but also an attitude toward life. He advocated for mutual respect and care to foster harmonious interpersonal relationships. Additionally, “benevolence” is a crucial pathway to personal growth. Through ongoing self-reflection and practice, one can gradually attain inner peace and kindness.

In modern society, the concept of “benevolence” is still of great significance. We should uphold the principle of “benevolence” in our daily lief, pay attention to the feelings and needs of others, and respect their rights and dignity. At the same time, we should also pursue the realm of “benevolence” in our work, treat others with kindness and fairness, and make more contributions to society.

In conclusion, “benevolence” is one of the core ideas of Confucius, which represents a noble character and spiritual pursuit. By constantly practising benevolence, we can not only improve our own moral quality and quality of life but also make contributions to the harmony and progress of society.

作品编号：3896
姓　　名：朱熙萌
国　　籍：中国
组　　别：诵读类国内成人组
单位名称：广东培正学院

千古太史公

作品以司马迁的《报任安书》为模本，以其创作《史记》的心路历程为主线，表现他从被处以宫刑后失魂落魄，到受到他崇拜的历史名人屈原、项羽、孔子的激励，最终找到生命价值，奋而著书，成一家之言的过程。诵读者深入挖掘人物特点，或哀伤或激昂，深情演绎主题。

【司马迁】陛下，陛下——

Sima Qian: Your Majesty! Your Majesty!

【司马迁】肠一日而九迴，居则忽忽若有所亡，出则不知其所往。每念斯耻，汗未尝不发背沾衣也！

Sima Qian: Like the intestines turning around in the stomach many times a day, I am in a trance at home, as if something has been lost. When I go out, I'm confused, not knowing where to go. Whenever thinking of this shameful failure, I have cold sweat on my back and it wet my clothes.

古者富贵而名摩灭，不可胜记，唯倜傥非常之人称焉。其如璀璨星斗，光耀后世，昭灼吾心。

In ancient times, there were numerous wealthy people whose names were not passed on. Only those who were extraordinary and unusual were famous in the world. They were like the bright stars, shining on the future generations, and serving as the guidance of my soul.

【屈原】长太息以掩涕兮，哀民生之多艰。亦余心之所善兮，虽九死其犹未悔。

Qu Yuan: Long did I sigh and wipe away my tears, to see my people bowed by griefs and fears. Since my heart did love such purity, I'd not regret a thousand deaths to die.

【李清照】生当作人杰，死亦为鬼雄。至今思项羽，不肯过江东。

Li Qingzhao: Be man of men while you're alive. Be soul of souls even if you're dead! Think of Xiang Yu who'd not survive. His men whose blood for him was shed!

【孔子】岁寒，然后知松柏之后调也。志不立，天下无可成之事。

Confucius: Only when the weather turns cold can we see that the leaves of pines and cypresses are the last to wither and fall. Without ambitions nothing can be achieved.

【司马迁】盖文王拘而演《周易》；仲尼厄而作《春秋》；屈原放逐，乃赋《离骚》；左丘失明，厥有《国语》；孙子膑脚，《兵法》修列；不韦迁蜀，世传《吕览》；韩非囚秦，《说难》《孤愤》；《诗》三百篇，大底圣贤发愤之所为作也。

Sima Qian: Xibo Jichang expanded *Zhou Yi* because of imprisonment. Confucius compiled *The Spring and Autumn Annals* because of plight. Qu Yuan created *Li Sao* because of exile. Zuo Qiuming wrote *Guo Yu* although he lost his vision. Sun Bin composed *The Art of War* even though his kneecaps were removed. Lv Buwei was relegated to Sichuan but *The Spring and Autumn of Lv Buwei* was passed on. Han Fei created *Shui Nan* and *Gu Fen* even if he was imprisoned in Qin state. *The Book of Songs* was created by the sages who expressed their indignation.

人固有一死，或重于泰山，或轻于鸿毛。

Though death befalls all men alike, it may be weightier than Mount Tai or lighter than a feather.

虽万被戮，岂有悔哉！哈哈哈——虽万被戮，岂有悔哉！

Even if being killed thousands of times, I have nothing to regret. Hahaha, even if I have been killed thousands of times, I have nothing to regret.

【合】刚正不阿，留得正气凌霄汉；幽而发愤，著成信使照尘寰！

作品编号：4390
姓　　名：于秀瑞、叶孜、盛业昌、韩兆凯
国　　籍：中国
组　　别：诵读类国内成人组
单位名称：东营职业学院

论相处之道

本经典诵读内容节选自《诗经》和《论语》，意在探究人际关系中的美好品德。我们以歌唱和诵读相结合的独特方式，宣扬与人交往应遵循的守望相助、严己宽人、推己及人、进德修业、言而有信等优良品质。通过此次诵读，我们学习并积极传播人与人和谐交往的相处之道。

相彼鸟矣，
Even though on the wing,
犹求友声。
It tries to seek a mate.
矧伊人矣，
We're more than what it is.
不求友生？
Can we not seek a friend?
神之听之，
If gods listen to this,
终和且平。
There is peace in the end.

子曰：“躬自厚而薄责于人，则远怨矣。”
The Master said, “If a man demands much from himself and little from others, he will certainly avoid resentments.”

子曰：“君子和而不同，小人同而不和。”
The Master said, “A true gentleman is conciliatory but not blind-accommodating. A petty man is blind-accommodating, but not conciliatory. ”

子贡问曰：“有一言而可以终身行之者乎？”子曰：“其‘恕’乎！己所不欲，勿施于人。”
Zi Gong asked, “Is there a single saying that one can act upon throughout his life?” The Master said, “Perhaps the word ‘forbearance’, which means ‘Never do to others what you would not like done to you’.”

孔子对曰：“有颜回者好学，不迁怒，不贰过。”
The Master answered him, saying, “There was Yan Hui. He had a great love of

learning. He never vented his wrath upon the innocent, nor did he make the same mistake twice."

子曰： "人不知而不愠，不亦君子乎？"

The Master said, "To feel no discontent when others do not know you, isn't that what is expected of a gentleman?"

子夏曰： "与朋友交，言而有信。虽曰未学，吾必谓之学矣。"

Zi Xia said, "If a man can speak sincerely in his intercourse with friends, though he is said to be uneducated, I would certainly say that he is."

皎皎白驹，
The pony white,
在彼空谷。
Feeds on fresh grass.
生刍一束，
My guest gem-bright.
其人如玉。
Leaves, me, alas!
毋金玉尔音，
O from you let me hear.
而有遐心。
So that to me you're near.

作品编号：2910
姓　　名：卢婉盈、邓晴、谢梦婷
国　　籍：中国
组　　别：诵读类国内成人组
单位名称：广东培正学院

《诗经》之美，妙不可言

《采薇》是一首守边将士思归诗。将士们在杨柳依依的季节阔别家乡，远赴边关，保家卫国，抵御猃狁之患，最终在一个雨雪霏霏的季节还家。《无衣》这首诗写在春秋初年周幽王末年，犬戎攻打镐京。大敌当前，团结就是力量，将士们意气风发，一起奋勇向前。

《诗经》是中国现存最古老的诗歌集，编纂于周朝（公元前 1046 年至公元前 256 年）。它总共包含 305 首诗歌，其中许多是民间歌曲，提供了中国古代的社会、文化和政治方面的见解。

The Book of Songs is the oldest existing collection of Chinese poetry, compiled during the Zhou dynasty. It consists of 305 poems in total, many of which are folk songs that provide insight into ancient China’s society, culture, and politics.

按照曲调的特点，这些诗歌可以划分为三类：风、雅、颂。《诗经》中的诗歌多以四言为主，就表现手法而言可分为赋、比、兴。作为中国文学的起点，《诗经》对于后代文学的影响非常深远。

In the light of their rhythms, the works can be divided into three sections: feng, ya, and song. The poems in *The Book of Songs* are mainly written in four-character lines. In terms of its writing technique, it can be classified into fu, bi, and xing. As the starting point of Chinese literature, *The Book of Songs* has great influence on the literary works of later generations.

今天带给大家的，是《诗经》中的千古佳作《采薇》和《无衣》。

Today, I bring you the masterpieces of *The Book of Songs*: *Caiwei* and *Wuyi*.

采薇（节选）

昔我往矣，杨柳依依。
When I left here, Willows shed tear.
今我来思，雨雪霏霏。
I come back now, Snow bends the bough.
行道迟迟，载饥载渴。
Long, long the way, Hard, hard the day.
我心伤悲，莫知我哀！
My grief o’erflows, Who knows? Who knows?

无衣

岂曰无衣？与子同袍。

Are you not battle-drest? Let's share the plate for breast!

王于兴师，修我戈矛。

We shall go up the line. Let's make our lances shine!

与子同仇！

Your foe is mine.

岂曰无衣？与子同泽。

Are you not battle-drest? Let's share the coat and vest!

王于兴师，修我矛戟。

We shall go up the line. Let's make our halberds shine!

与子偕作！

Your job is mine.

岂曰无衣？与子同裳。

Are you not battle-drest? Let's share the kilt and the rest!

王于兴师，修我甲兵。

We shall go up the line. Let's make our armour shine!

与子偕行！

We'll march your hand in mine.

作品编号：1579
姓　　名：董亚楠
国　　籍：中国
组　　别：诵读类国内成人组
单位名称：山东工程职业技术大学

三人行，必有我师焉

儒家思想已传承2,000余年，众多儒学学者随着孔夫子的脚步，保存了大量的历史经典。其代表作《论语》主张的“仁、义、礼、智、信、和”，早已深深刻在每一个中国人的骨子里。作为21世纪的青少年，我们有义务也必将全力以赴地传承中华优秀传统文化，持之以恒地学习儒家思想，做一个有内涵、有修养的新时代青少年。

子曰：“学而时习之，不亦说乎？有朋自远方来，不亦乐乎？人不知而不愠，不亦君子乎？”

The Master said: “Is it not a great pleasure to be able to practice frequently what you have learned? Is it not a real delight to have friends come to visit you from afar? Is it not the mark of a man of honor to not take offence when others fail to appreciate your worth?”

子曰：“学而不思则罔，思而不学则殆。”

The Master said, “Learning without thought is labor lost; thought without learning is perilous.”

子曰：“温故而知新，可以为师矣。”

The Master said, “If a man keeps cherishing his old knowledge, so as continually to be acquiring new, he may be a teacher of others.”

子曰：“由，诲女知之乎？知之为知之，不知为不知，是知也。”

The Master said, “You, shall I teach you what knowledge is? When you know a thing, to hold that you know it; and when you do not know a thing, to allow that you do not know it; this is knowledge.”

子曰：“三人行，必有我师焉！择其善者而从之，其不善者而改之。”

The Master said, “When I walk along with two others, they may serve me as my teachers. I will select their good qualities and follow them, their bad qualities and avoid them.”

作为21世纪的青少年，我们将全力以赴地传承中国传统文化，持之以恒地学习儒家思想，做一个有内涵、有修养的新时代青少年。

作品编号：2453
姓　　名：贾昀潼、姜智唯、张家铭
国　　籍：中国
组　　别：诵读类国内少年组
单位名称：山东省莱阳市大象教育培训学校

一勤班谈《论语》的故事

作品素材取自湖北经心·浦江学堂一勤班三年来学习《论语》《孟子》的经历，根据钱穆先生“自己读《论语》与劝人读《论语》”的理念，演绎了一段关于经典的中外对话。

故事中，两位分别来自美国和加拿大的外国小朋友来中国旅行。这一天，他们来到樱花园，走着走着，听到琅琅读书声，于是好奇地前去查探。这时，学堂小朋友正好下课了，于是热情接待远道而来的客人，为两位客人介绍孔子和《论语》，而且大家一起读了《论语·学而》。外国小朋友感受到中华传统经典的魅力，产生兴趣，表示要将《论语》带回自己的国家。

【第一幕：一组樱园外景】

【中文齐诵，诵声渐弱】

子曰：“学而时习之，不亦说乎？有朋自远方来，不亦乐乎？人不知而不愠，不亦君子乎？”

【Reading in unison , the sound fading out】

Confucius said, “Is it not pleasant to learn with a constant perseverance and application? Is it not delightful to have friends coming from distant quarters? Is he not a man of complete virtue, who feels no discomposure though men may take no note of him?”

【画外音，英文字幕】

【Off-screen narration, English subtitles】

Confucius said, “Is it not pleasant to learn with a constant perseverance and application? Is it not delightful to have friends coming from distant quarters? Is he not a man of complete virtue, who feels no discomposure though men may take no note of him?”

【第二幕：樱园内景。两位外国小朋友走在公园小路上】

【画外音】两个来自美国和加拿大的小朋友 Cherry 和 Max 到武汉旅行，来到樱花园中的经心书院外。

【Off-screen narration】Cherry from America and Max from Canada, they traveling in Wuhan. Now they arriving at Oriental Cherry Garden outside Jingxin Academy.

Max: Cherry, 听，什么声音？

Cherry, listen. What sound?

Cherry: 好像是读书的声音？

Like someone are reading.

Max: 是的。就在那儿。

Yes, right over there.

Cherry: 我们过去看看？

Shall we go and have a look?

Max: 好的，走。

Okay, let’s go.

【第三幕：学堂玄关，初相见】

Cherry: 你好！我是 Cherry, 我来自美国。

Hello! I’m Cherry from America.

Max: 嗨，我是 Max, 我从加拿大来。

Hi, this is Max from Canada.

Yilin: 你好，我是 Yilin。

Hi, I am Yilin.

Ethan: 我是 Ethan, 欢迎。

I am Ethan, welcome.

Cherry: 我们来武汉旅行。

We are traveling in Wuhan.

Max: 请问你们刚才读的是什么呀？

What were you just reading?

Yilin: 我们在读《论语》。

We were reading *The Analects*.

Max:《论语》?

The Analects?

Cherry: 孔子？他是什么人？

Confucius? What kind of person is Confucius?

Ethan: 孔子是中国古代的一位圣人。

Confucius was an ancient Chinese sage.

Yilin:《论语》是孔子和他弟子的对话集。

The Analects is a collection of dialogues between Confucius and his disciples.

Max: 圣人？

A sage?

Ivan:（带领 Max、Cherry 进课堂）我是 Ivan。Max、Cherry, 请跟我来。

I am Ivan. Max, Cherry, follow me please.

【第四幕：学堂内，孔子像前】

Ivan: 这就是我们中国古代的圣贤——孔子。

This is Confucius' portrait.

Coco: 他是中国历史上最伟大的思想家和教育家。

He is the greatest philosopher and educator in Chinese history.

Ethan: 因为对中国文化的巨大贡献，他被后人称为大成至圣先师。

Due to his immense contributions to Chinese culture, he is posthumously honored as the "Great Accomplished and Supreme Sage Teacher" by later generations.

Yilin: 他的思想到现在已经流传了 2,000 多年！

His philosophy has been transmitted for over 2,000 years until now.

Ethan: 他是享誉世界的文化名人！他的思想影响了亚洲很多国家。

He is a globally acclaimed cultural figure. His philosophy has influenced many countries in Asia.

Max: 哇！真了不起呀！

Wow! That's truly impressive!

Cherry: 那孔子都讲了些什么呢？

What did Confucius talk about?

【第五幕：书架前，介绍《论语》】

Tom: 孔子教导我们要孝敬父母。

Confucius teaches us to respect and be filial to our parents.

Yilin: 孔子说要"兄友弟恭"。

Confucius teaches that siblings should be friendly. The elders should care for the youngers, and the youngers should respect the elders.

Frank: 孔子说做人要"谨而信"。

Confucius says that one should be earnest and trustworthy.

Coco: 孔子说要"泛爱众"。

Confucius advises to have an overflow in love to all.

Ethan: 孔子教导我们要亲近仁人。

Confucius teaches to be close to those virtuous individuals.

Rachel: 孔子告诉我们如何交朋友。

Confucius tells how to make friends.

Frank: 孔子教导我们要做道德高尚的君子。

Confucius teaches us to be morally upright gentlemen.

Ivan: 孔子讲人要有"仁爱之心"。

Confucius teaches that people should have a heart full of compassion and benevolence.

Max: 孔子讲得太好了。

Confucius' teachings are truly excellent.

Cherry: 我们也可以学习《论语》吗？

Can we also learn *The Analects*?

众人：当然可以。

Of course, you can.

Yilin: 来，我们一起读《论语》吧！

Come on, let's read *The Analects* together.

【第六幕：教读《论语》】

Ethan: 这就是我们学习的《论语》。我们一起读。

This is *The Analects* we are reading. Let's read together.

Yilin: 请翻到第 2 页，跟着读。

Please turn to page 2 and read along with us.

领读：子曰："学而时习之，不亦说乎？"

Confucius said, "Is it not pleasant to learn with a constant perseverance and application?"

Cherry & Max: 子曰："学而时习之，不亦说乎？"

Confucius said, "Is it not pleasant to learn with a constant perseverance and application?"

众齐读：Confucius said, "Is it not pleasant to learn with a constant perseverance and application?"

Confucius said, "Is it not pleasant to learn with a constant perseverance and application?"

领读："有朋自远方来，不亦乐乎？"

"Is it not delightful to have friends coming from distant quarters?"

Cherry & Max: "有朋自远方来，不亦乐乎？"

"Is it not delightful to have friends coming from distant quarters?"

众齐读："Is it not delightful to have friends coming from distant quarters?"

"Is it not delightful to have friends coming from distant quarters?"

领读："人不知而不愠，不亦君子乎？"

"Is he not a man of complete virtue, who feels no discomposure though men may take no note of him?"

Cherry & Max: "人不知而不愠，不亦君子乎？"

"Is he not a man of complete virtue, who feels no discomposure though men may take no note of him?"

众齐读："Is he not a man of complete virtue, who feels no discomposure though men may take no note of him?"

"Is he not a man of complete virtue, who feels no discomposure though men may take no note of him?"

【第七幕：上课铃，四拜礼】

Yilin: 谢老师，今天来了两位外国小朋友。这位是 Cherry。这位是 Max。他们对《论语》很感兴趣。

Ms. Xie, two foreign children join us today. This is Cherry, and this is Max. They are interested in *The Analects.*

谢老师：欢迎你们！欢迎来到我们的《论语》课堂。

You are welcome! Welcome to *The Analects* class.

谢老师：上课前，我们要向孔子行礼，来表达我们对他的尊敬。

Before class, we will pay homage to Confucius.

谢老师：排班！班齐！诣大成至圣先师孔子之像前，行四拜礼！拜！兴！……

Assemble! Line up! Go to the statue of Confucius, the Great Accomplished and Supreme Sage Teacher, and perform four bows! Bow! Rise! ...

【第八幕：下课铃，介绍经典学习】

Ivan: 2020 年 12 月，我们来到经心书院开始学习国学。

We came here to start learning Chinese classics in December 2020.

Ethan: 我们花三年的时间，学习《论语》《孟子》《大学》《中庸》这四部书。

We spent three years learning the Four Books: *The Analects*, *Mencius*, *The Great Learning*, and *The Doctrine of the Mean*.

Max:《论语》课好玩吗?

Is *The Analects* class interesting?

Yilin: 老师会在课上讲很多有趣的故事。我们最喜欢听故事!

The teacher tells many fascinating stories during class. We enjoy listening to stories the most!

Tom: 学国学，让我明白了很多道理。

Learning Chinese classics has helped me understand a lot.

众人：学国学让我们自信、勇敢、仁爱!

Learning Chinese classics makes us confident, brave and kind!

Cherry: 我想学习《论语》哎!

I want to learn *The Analects*!

Max: 我也要学。

I also want to learn.

Yilin: 这是《论语》英文版，就送给你啦！喜欢就读一读吧。

Here is an English version of *The Analects*, it’s for you. Enjoy reading it.

Ethan: 这本送给你。

This book is for you.

【画外音】

经心·浦江学堂是鲍鹏山教授和湖北武汉经心书院合作的公益项目。2020年底，第一个班级——“一勤班”成立。这些孩子从二年级开始学习，至今已经完成《论语》《孟子》的诵读学习。在这里，孩子们学习做人做事的道理，培养思维能力与中正平和的气质。经过三年的熏陶，这些孩子对孔子和儒家文化发自内心地热爱。希望借由本次活动，让孩子们为传统文化的传播贡献一分力量。

Jingxin–Pujiang School is a public welfare project cooperated by Professor Bao Pengshan and Wuhan Jingxin Academy. At the end of 2020, the first class, named “Yiqin Class”, was established. These children began learning the Four Books at the age of eight. Up to now, they have completed the study of *The Analects* and *Mencius*. Here, they are learning the principles of being a person and handling matters, cultivating thinking abilities and a balanced and calm temperament. After three years of learning, these children have developed a genuine love for Confucius and Confucian culture from the bottom of their hearts. Hoping through this event, the children can contribute to the dissemination of traditional culture.

作品编号：5070
姓　　名：徐娅馨、胡铭佑　等
国　　籍：中国
组　　别：诵读类国内少年组
单位名称：湖北武汉经心书院

对话《论语》

日照以蓝天、碧海、金沙滩而闻名，不仅风景优美，而且文化底蕴深厚。一群来自这座美丽城市的孩子们热爱自己的家乡日照，热爱从小耳濡目染的儒家文化。机缘巧合之下，他们跨越时空，开启了和孔圣人的对话，用声音和舞蹈展现《论语》的别样之美。

学生：学而时习之，不亦说乎？有朋自远方来，不亦乐乎？人不知而不愠，不亦君子乎？先生，您好，请问您是何人？

孔子：我乃孔丘是也。此为何地？

学生：Master, this is Rizhao. It is the first city to get the sunshine. It's famous for its blue sky, jade sea and golden beach.

Look, this is Olympic Water Sports Park. And this is Lighthouse Scenic Area.

This is Dongyi Town.

孔子：观此景色，颇有心旷神怡之感。汝何如？

学生：我们正在读《论语》。

孔子：《论语》?

学生：《论语》是后人根据您和您的弟子们的言行及思想整理集合而成的一部典籍。我们从小就读。先生愿随我们一起领略《论语》的别样之美吗？

孔子：好！

To learn and at due times to review what one has learned, isn't that a pleasure?

学而时习之，不亦说乎？

To have friends come to you from afar, isn't that delightful?

有朋自远方来，不亦乐乎？

To feel no discontent when others do not know you, isn't that what is expected of a gentleman?

人不知而不愠，不亦君子乎？

If you can acquire new knowledge while reviewing the old, you may become a teacher of others.

温故而知新，可以为师矣。

He who learns but does not think is lost. He who thinks but does not learn still remains puzzled.

学而不思则罔，思而不学则殆。

When you know a thing, say that you know it; when you do not know a thing, admit that you do not know it. That is true wisdom.

知之为知之，不知为不知，是知也。

When several men are walking together, I am sure there is one I can learn from. I'd select his merits to follow, and his demerits for reference to correct my own.

三人行，必有我师焉！择其善者而从之，其不善者而改之。

We are walking on Qilu Avenue. We are studying Confucian culture. We love our school, and we love Confucius.

作品编号：3041
姓　　名：丁宝翠、赵金慧、申杰
国　　籍：中国
组　　别：诵读类国内少年组
单位名称：山东省日照市济南路小学

黄河礼赞

黄河——中国的第二大河，是中华文明最重要的发源地，中国人称其为中华民族的“母亲河”。我们勤劳勇敢的祖先在这块广阔的土地上劳作生息，创造了灿烂夺目的黄河文化。五千年历史绵延至今，我们仍在歌颂“黄河母亲”。

第一幕　源远流长

The history of the Yellow River

你，来自青藏高原，跨越万里，流经九省。

You, coming from the high mountains, flows through many places.

你是中华民族的母亲河，孕育了璀璨的华夏文明。

You are the mother of the Chinese nation, and you are the Yellow River.

涓涓细流汇聚，一路奔腾向海。

The trickling streams converge and rush to the sea all the way.

你流淌过的土地上，勤劳的中华民族繁衍生息，辛勤劳作。

On the land where you flow, the hard-working Chinese nation has survived and thrived for generations.

他们把岸边的石块磨成锋利的工具，叉鱼、围猎。

They grind stones on the riverbank into sharp tools to fish and hunt.

河里的泥土烧成质朴的陶器，取水，煮饭，储存食物。

The river mud is fired into simple earthenware to get water, cook rice, and store food.

人们临河而居、依河而生，那载歌载舞的祭祀是对黄河的依恋和敬畏。

People live by the river, rely on it for life, and revere and worship the Yellow River.

你是纽带，串联起悠久的华夏文明。

You are a bond that links the people of the Yellow River.

九曲连环，你蜿蜒出龙的模样。

You are like a dragon, flowing out of the Yellow River culture.

这是你，我们的黄河母亲。

This is you, our mother, the Yellow River.

第二幕　坚韧抗争

Heroic deeds of Yu the Great

你是慷慨的母亲，但你，也有狂怒的时候。

You are a generous mother, but you also have times of fury.

当平静的生活被汹涌的咆哮打断。

When the quiet life is interrupted by floods,

是大禹，那坚韧的身影，仿佛黎明的火炬，指引前进的方向。

It is Yu the Great, whose figure seems like a torch at dawn, guiding the way forward.

他带领人们开山脉、修堤坝、挖沟渠、疏河道。

He led the people to open up mountains, repair riverbanks, and control the floods.

终于，海晏河清，民生安然。

Finally, the floods receded and people returned to a better life.

第三幕　生生不息

Chinese nation who raised by the Yellow River

一声长音，响彻云霄，高亢嘹亮的号子在黄河的岸边回荡……

A long sound resonates through the sky, and the songs of the Yellow River echoes on the banks...

一条纤绳，拉起生活，劳动者的手，点燃历史的篝火。

A rope pulls up life, the hands of workers move forward, pushing the wheel of history.

粗犷、豪迈，是同舟共济、坚毅不屈的黄河人，顽强、坚忍，是团结协作、百折不挠的黄河魂。

The people of the Yellow River are brave, steadfast, united, and optimistic. This is the soul of the Yellow River.

开心的黄河娃也唱起了歌谣。

Happy children sing songs on the banks of the Yellow River.

黄河口，我的家，我是地道黄河娃。
甘甜河水润心田，伴着涛声我长大。
一桶河水半桶沙，淘来泥沙耍泥巴。
捏个爸爸长翅膀，捏个妈妈鱼尾巴。
泥水汗水满身沙，自己也成泥娃娃。
泥娃娃，赤脚丫，滔滔河水乐开花。

第四幕　归兮入海

The Yellow River flows into the sea in Dongying

黄河，你见证了五千年的荣光，也凝望过曾经的苦难。

Yellow River, you have witnessed the glory and suffering of the past five thousand years.

面对我们再次复兴的中国梦，你仍像我们慈爱的母亲一样，带着无尽的希冀与期盼奔涌前方。

In the face of our Chinese Dream, you still rush forward like a mother with endless hope.

黄河落天走东海。

The Yellow River falls from the sky and flows to the East China Sea.

这是母亲送给我们的最后一份礼物——中国最广阔、最年轻的黄河三角洲，我可爱的家乡，我可爱的东营。

This is the last gift you, the mother, have given us. The most extensive and youngest Yellow River delta in China, my lovely hometown, my lovely Dongying.

作品编号：3093
姓　　名：张广娟、成菲、李黎
国　　籍：中国
组　　别：诵读类国内少年组
单位名称：山东省东营市广饶县同和小学

共读《论语》 薪火相传

共读《论语》，薪火相传！Read *The Analects* and pass on the flame! 山东省烟台市蓬莱区郝斌中学的学生们诵读《论语》经典，展华夏风采！

最近，我们正在读孔子的《论语》，现在让我们一起分享我们最喜爱的名言。

These days, we are reading *The Analects* by Confucius. We have learned a lot from the book. Now let's share the sentences we like most.

弟子入则孝，出则悌，谨而信，泛爱众，而亲仁。行有余力，则以学文。

A youth, when at home, should be filial, and, abroad, respectful to his elders. He should be earnest and truthful. He should overflow in love to all, and cultivate the friendship of the good. When he has time and opportunity, after the performance of these things, he should employ them in polite studies.

学而时习之，不亦说乎？有朋自远方来，不亦乐乎？人不知而不愠，不亦君子乎？

Is it not pleasant to learn with a constant perseverance and application? Is it not delightful to have friends coming from distant quarters? Is he not a man of complete virtue, who feels no discomposure though men may take no note of him?

温故而知新，可以为师矣。学而不思则罔，思而不学则殆。敏而好学，不耻下问。

If a man keeps cherishing his old knowledge, so as continually to be acquiring new, he may be a teacher of others.

Learning without thought is labour lost; thought without learning is perilous. He was of an active nature and yet fond of learning, and he was not ashamed to ask and learn of his inferiors.

知之者不如好之者，好之者不如乐之者。我非生而知之者，好古，敏以求之者也。

They who know the truth are not equal to those who love it, and they who love it are not equal to those who delight in it.

I am not one who was born in the possession of knowledge; I am one who is fond of antiquity, and earnest in seeking it there.

三人行，必有我师焉！择其善者而从之，其不善者而改之。

When I walk along with two others, they may serve me as my teachers. I will select their good qualities and follow them, their bad qualities and avoid them.

默而识之，学而不厌，诲人不倦，何有于我哉？

The silent treasuring up of knowledge, learning without satiety, and instructing others without being wearied—which one of these things belongs to me?

吾日三省吾身：为人谋而不忠乎？与朋友交而不信乎？传不习乎？

I daily examine myself on three points:whether, in transacting business for others, I may have been not faithful; whether, in intercourse with friends, I may have been not sincere; whether I may have not mastered and practiced the instructions of my teacher?

读完《论语》后，我们受益匪浅。

After reading *The Analects*, we have learned a lot.

我懂得了要与人为善。

I have learned to be kind.

我学到了要知识渊博。

To be knowledgeable.

我明白了要勤奋努力。

To be hardworking.

我学会了谦虚待人。

To be modest.

我要学而不厌。

To keep learning.

我要诚实守信。

And to be honest.

所以，让我们知行合一吧！

So, let’s take action!

作品编号：1933

姓　　名：葛凯旋　等

国　　籍：中国

组　　别：诵读类国内少年组

单位名称：山东省烟台市蓬莱区郝斌中学

仁爱的光芒超越时空

翩翩少年眉眼含光，稚嫩女童书声琅琅。他们手执书卷，金声玉振，吟诵着千年流传的经典。在诵读中悟孝悌之道，植孝悌之根于骨髓，让中华传统美德如影随形、一生跟随。有了日复一日的经典诵读，相信传统文化在新时代的长空会蝶变共舞，仁爱的光芒能超越时空，穿越国度，照亮四方。

国家之魂，文以化之，文以铸之；人之魂，教以引之，德以固之。迎着朝阳，沐着晚霞，在师长的引导下，（女）我在传统文化的花园里尽情吸取芬芳，（男 1）我在雄伟而瑰丽的文化经典中徜徉，（男 2）我在中华传统美德中成长，（齐）我们，深深地沉醉在优秀文化的海洋中。

The soul of the country is shaped and cast by culture; the soul of the man is guided by teaching and strengthened by virtue. Facing the morning sun, bathing in the sunset, under the guidance of the teacher, (Female) I absorb the fragrance in the garden of traditional culture, (Male 1) I wander in the majestic and magnificent cultural classics, (Male 2) I grow up in traditional Chinese virtues. (Together) We are deeply intoxicated in the ocean of excellent culture.

（女）我翻开《孝经》，“孝悌之至，通于神明，光于四海，无所不通”。

(Female) I opened the *Classic of Filial Piety*. It says, “The perfect filial piety has access to the gods, brings glory to the whole world.”

（男 1）我打开《孟子》，“尧舜之道，孝悌而已矣”。

(Male 1) I opened *Mencius*. It says, “The way of Yao and Shun is just filial piety.”

（男 2）我翻开《朱子》，“善事父母为孝，善事兄长为弟”。

(Male 2) I opened *Zhu Zi*. It says, “Being a good son and a good brother is filial piety.”

（女）有子曰：“其为人也孝弟，而好犯上者，鲜矣；不好犯上，而好作乱者，未之有也。君子务本，本立而道生。孝弟也者，其为仁之本与！”

(Male 1) The philosopher You said, “They are few who, being filial and fraternal, are fond of offending against their superiors. There have been none, who, not liking to offend against their superiors, have been fond of stirring up confusion. The superior man bends his attention to what is radical. That being established, all practical courses naturally grow up. Filial piety and fraternal submission, are they not the root of all benevolent actions?”

（女）子夏曰：“贤贤易色，事父母，能竭其力；事君，能致其身；与朋友交，言而有信。虽曰未学，吾必谓之学矣。”

(Male 2) Zi Xia said, "If a man withdraws his mind from the love of beauty, and applies it sincerely to the love of the virtuous; if, in serving his parents, he can exert his utmost strength; if, in serving his prince, he can devote his life; if, in his intercourse with his friends, his words are sincere—although men say that he has not been educated, I will certainly say that he has."

（女）子曰："弟子入则孝，出则悌，谨而信，泛爱众，而亲仁。行有余力，则以学文。"

(Male 1) Confucius said, "A young man, when at home, should be a good son; when out in the world, a good citizen. He should be circumspect and truthful. He should be in sympathy with all men, but intimate with men of moral character. If he has time and opportunity to spare, after the performance of those duties, he should then employ them in literary pursuits."

国无德不兴，人无德不立。中国式现代化赋予优秀传统文化现代力量。孝悌之道，深入中国人的骨血，如影随形。让传统文化在新时代的长空蝶变共舞，让仁爱的光芒超越时空，穿越国度，照亮四方。

The country is not prosperous without virtue, and people are not established without virtue. Chinese modernization has given the modern power of excellent traditional culture. The way of filial piety and fraternal duty go deep into the bones and blood of the Chinese people. Let the traditional culture dance together in the sky in the new era, and let the light of benevolence transcend time and space, cross the country, and illuminate the whole world.

作品编号：3938
姓　　名：姜衍文、姜衍武、郭芯语
国　　籍：中国
组　　别：诵读类国内少年组
单位名称：山东省烟台市温泉东路66号

孔子的智慧

中国古代伟大的思想家、政治家、教育家孔子，被世人尊称为“圣人”。他创立的儒家思想至今依然闪烁着璀璨的光芒。他通过言传身教，培养了一大批学识渊博的“圣贤”。他充满智慧的经典著作，是浩瀚文明中的耀眼明珠。

孔子是中国著名的圣人。

Conscious is one of the most famous sage of China.

他的思想和名言在世界范围内广泛传播。

His ideas and sayings spread around the world.

但是你知道孔子到底是谁吗？为什么他如此重要？

But, do you really know who Confucius was? And why is he so important?

孔子名丘，字仲尼。

Confucius was surnamed Kong, forenamed Qiu, and honorarily titled Zhongni.

他是春秋战国时期的鲁国人。

He lived in the State of Lu during the Spring and Autumn Period.

孔子是伟大的教育家。

Confucius was a great educator.

孔子提倡“有教无类”。他的学生不论地位高低都一律获得平等的教育。

Confucius advocated “teaching everyone equally”. He taught his students without discrimination, no matter what their social status was.

他有 3,000 多名学生，其中 72 位成为贤人。

He had more than 3,000 students, of whom 72 became sages.

孔子主张“因材施教”，对不同的学生进行不同的教育。

Confucius proposed “teaching students according to their aptitude”.

他教育学生学习态度要诚恳。“知之为知之，不知为不知。”

He said one should be honest in learning, and not pretend to know what one did not know.

他告诉学生学习知识要经常复习，“温故而知新”。

He told his students to review what they had learned regularly during their study, because “new knowledge can be gained by reviewing old knowledge”.

他还要求学生把学习和思考结合起来。

And he also told his students to combine learning with thinking.

孔子也是中国古代伟大的哲学家。

Confucius was also a great philosopher in ancient China.

儒家思想的核心是“礼”和“仁”。

The core of the Confucian ideology is propriety and benevolence.

孔子有许多名言，富有哲理与智慧。

Confucius had many well-known sayings, which are full of philosophy and wisdoms.

例如：

For example:

有朋自远方来，不亦乐乎？

Is it not a delight to have friends coming from afar?

三人行，必有我师焉！

In the party of three, there must be one whom I can learn from.

儒家思想在中国历史上具有重大意义。

Confucianism has great significance in Chinese history.

2,000多年来，孔子的思想影响着中国乃至世界。

Over the last 2,000 years, his philosophy has continued to influence China and the rest of the world.

孔子名丘，字仲尼。春秋时期鲁国人，中国古代伟大的思想家、教育家，儒家学派创始人。他少年立志向学，青年游周适齐，壮年出仕谋政，周游列国，晚年归鲁兴学，纂订六经，垂范后世。

孔子还是伟大的教育家，有弟子三千，其中贤人七十二。他主张“有教无类”和“因材施教”。孔子有许多名言警句，比如“有朋自远方来，不亦乐乎？”“学而不思则罔，思而不学则殆”“三人行，必有我师焉”等。

孔子以“仁者爱人”的情怀，以“天下万民福祉”为己任，以“知其不可为而为之”的勇气，为理想而毕生奋斗。

孔子的思想和教育理念，对中国乃至整个世界都产生了深远的影响。

作品编号：4417

姓　　名：王腾

国　　籍：中国

组　　别：诵读类国内少年组

单位名称：山东省济宁市曲阜师范大学附属小学

中 韩 篇

儒家美学

笔者在中国留学期间，有感于根植于中国人日常生活中的儒家文化，通过旅行体验发现了其中蕴含的庄严肃穆、宁和平静的美学意味，希望这种东方美学也能成为自己的一抹人生底色。

中国儒家思想注重道德、家庭、社会秩序，是在人际关系中强调礼仪和相互尊重的最著名学问之一。它鼓励通过研修学问和加强自身修养，来引导和影响民众，使之具备君子的品德。中国儒家思想是一门追求社会整体稳定和和谐、通过个人道德成长实现共同繁荣的学问。

중국의 유교사상은 도덕 , 가족 , 사회 질서에 중정을 두며 인간관계에서 예의와 상호존중을 강조하는 가장 유명한 학문 중 하나이다 . 이 는 학문과 교육을 통해 스스로 깨달음을 얻기를 장려하며 , 지도자에게는 민중에 대한 성세한 관리와 군림의 덕목을 갖추도록 가르친다 . 중국의 유교는 전반적인 사회 안정과 조화를 추구하며 , 개인의 도덕적 성장을 통해 공동체의 번영을 이루고자 하는 학문이다 .

我在青岛中学留学期间，感受到儒家文化深深根植于中国人的日常生活中。它通过影响家庭、社会、教育来形成共同体意识，以人类的道德修养和社会行为为重点，提出了在日常生活中应该如何行动的意识规范和礼仪体系。

내가 중국 청도중학교에서 유학을 하고 있는 동안 , 유교 문화가 우리의 일상에 얼마나 깊이 자리잡았는지를 체감할 수 있었다 . 동양사회에서의 가정 , 교육 등에 미치는 영향을 통해 공동체 의식을 형성하며 , 인간의 도덕적 개발과 사회적 행동에 중점을 둠으로써 일상생활에서 어떻게 행동해야 하는지 결정하는 의식규범과 예절체계를 제시한다 .

中国儒家文化对海外的影响体现在各个方面，特别是在重视伦理和“以家庭为中心”方面，影响尤其深远。东方各国接受了儒家的教诲，重视社会稳定和家庭内的和谐，对我们韩国的家庭制度和教育体系也产生了很大的影响。此外，随着中国经济的增长和全球化，中国的儒家思想价值也在国际社会中不断增长。随着中国企业家在全球影响力的提升，中国儒家思维方式和重视团队精神的文化在全球商业环境中也备受关注。来自中国的儒家思想也在很大程度上影响了对全球伦理和可持续发展的关注，涉及环境保护、社会责任和社区的重要性等议题。在传统农耕社会产生的生态思维方式，更加关注对环境问题的责任，这些价值给国际社会带来了灵感，在中国参与的全球可持续性讨论中发挥着巨大作用。

중국의 유교 문화가 해외에 미치는 영향은 다양한 측면에서 나타난다. 윤리와 가족 중심의 가치를 중시하여 동양 국가들이 유교의 가르침을 수용하며 사회적 안정과 가족 간 조화를 중시하는 양상은 여전이다. 이는 한국의 가족 제도와 교육 체계에도 큰 영향을 미치고 있다. 또한, 중국의 경제적 성장과 세계화로 중국의 유교적 가치가 국제 사회에서 확대되고 있다. 중국의 기업가들이 세계적인 영향력을 키우면서 중국의 유교적 사고 방식과 팀워크 중시하는 문화는 글로벌 비즈니스 환경에서도 주목받고 있다. 마지막으로, 중국에서 나온 유교적 가치는 환경보호, 사회적 책임, 공동체의 중요성 등 글로벌한 윤리와 지속가능한 발전에 대한 관심에 큰 영향을 미치고 있다. 중국은 전통적인 농경사회에서 비롯된 생태학적인 사고방식을 통해 환경 문제에 대한 책임을 강조하고 있다. 이러한 가치는 국제사회에 영감을 주며, 중국이 세계적인 지속가능성 논의에 참여하는데 큰 역할을 하고 있다.

虽然学校是一个小社会，但只见学校内的人，总归是有局限，很难直接感受儒家思想的意义。因此，趁着今年十月的国庆节长假，我决定在中国国内旅行。在旅行地的选择上，从上海、西安、北京等众多候选城市中，我选择了能够亲眼看见中国悠久的历史、各类雄伟的文化遗产的北京。

하지만, 학교 특성상 학교 안의 사람들만 만나게 되었기 때문에 외출을 통해 중국의 본질적인 유교 사상의 뜻깊은 실천과 경험을 직접적으로 하는 것이 어려웠다. 이에, 올 10월 국경절을 맞아 학교 방학 동안 중국 내에서 여행하기를 결심하였다. 상하이, 시안, 베이징 등 다양한 후보들 중에서 중국의 유구한 역사, 기록, 웅장한 문화 유산을 직접 눈으로 볼 수 있는 베이징을 선택하였다.

到达北京后，我的第一站就是紫禁城，在它面前感叹其雄伟之美。这座中国的历史遗址，象征着儒家思想的独特价值和重要意义。在紫禁城和附近的天安门广场上，宁静肃穆的气氛似乎象征着儒家的平和教诲。之后，我参观了凤凰岭——中国古代国家体系的佛教寺庙风景区。凤凰岭分为北线、中线、南线，景点密集，我以著名寺庙龙泉寺为中心，游览了古代中国养生修行场。这里有黄普院、关帝庙、吕祖洞等，是佛教和儒家文化融为一体的场所。

베이징에 도착한 나는 가장 첫 일정으로 자금성을 찾아 그 웅장한 아름다움에 감탄했다. 이곳은 중국의 역사 유적지 중 하나로, 특히 유교적 가치와 중요성을 상징하는 곳 중 하나이다. 자금성과 그 옆의 천안문 광장에서 느껴지는 고요한 분위기는 유교의 평화로운 가르침을 상징하기도 했다. 그 다음 나는 봉황령(鳳凰嶺), 중국의 고대 국가 체계를 담은 불교 사찰에 방문하였다. 봉황령은 북선, 중선, 남선으로 나뉘어져 있으며, 다양한 명소가 밀집되어 있으며 유명한 사찰인 용천사를 중심으로 고대 중국 양생 수련장을 관광하였다. 여기에는 황보원, 관제묘, 여조동 등 있으며 불교와 유교의 문화가 한데 어우러져 있는 장소였다.

通过这次旅行，我体会到了中国的儒家思想在历史建筑、艺术作品以及当地文化中的体现。儒家思想本身就是一种宁静和平的教诲，通过这次旅行，我更是切身体验到了它构成中国文化基础的深厚影响力，是一种带着神秘色彩的东方美学。通过这次旅行，我感受到了儒家思想在现代中国也具有深厚的底蕴，但愿在这种底蕴的熏陶下，这种儒家的美学也能成为我生命中的一抹底色。

이번 여행을 통해 나는 중국의 유교적인 가치와 사상이 역사 건축물과 예술 작품，그리고 현지 문화에서 어떻게 실천되고 있는지 깨달았다. 유교는 그 자체로 고요하고 평화로운 가르침을 지니고 있으며，그것이 중국 문화의 근간을 이루고 있다는 것을 몸소 체험하였다. 이 여행을 통해 유교 사상이 현대 중국에서도 깊이 뿌리내려 있는 것을 체감하고，나의 삶에서도 이를 실천해 나가고자 다짐하였다.

作品编号：5259
姓　　名：文俊哲(Moon Juncheol)
国　　籍：韩国
组　　别：征文类国际组
单　　位：青岛中学

中华的人情味和智慧——理解儒家思想的深意

笔者通过来华留学期间对儒家文化的学习，游览孔府、孔林、孔庙的所见所感及传统茶文化的体验，探讨了理解的儒家思想的深意：一种根植于生活的人情味与人间智慧。

儒家思想是起源于东方的哲学思想，注重对社会关系和道德行为的教导。儒家重视人与人之间的关系，强调人在家庭、社会、政治中的作用和责任，又通过实践这些理念来实现社会的和谐稳定。儒家思想的核心理念可以说是“性”和“理”。“性”是指人的人格，“理”是指行事遵循的原则。儒家思想强调尊重和发展人性，并以此努力让人性与社会秩序相协调。另外，儒家思想讲究礼节。“礼”指的是遵循祖先的教诲和传统，意在通过礼来维护和传递社会规范和伦理。儒家思想起源于古代中国，但至今在东方社会仍具有很大的影响力，这是因为儒家的教诲具有维持社会秩序和追求个人和社会发展的价值。

유교 사상은 동양에서 기원한 철학적인 사상으로, 사회적 관계와 도덕적 행동에 대한 가르침을 제시합니다. 유교는 사람 간의 관계를 중시하며, 가족, 사회, 정치에서의 역할과 책임을 강조합니다. 이를 통해 사회적 조화와 안정을 추구하려는 목표가 있습니다. 유교 사상의 핵심 개념은 성리(성과 이리)라고 할 수 있습니다. 성은 사람의 도리와 인격을 의미하며, 이리는 이에 따라 행동하는 원칙을 의미합니다. 유교는 개인의 성을 존중하고 발전시키는 것을 강조하며, 이를 통해 사회적인 질서와 조화를 이루려는 노력을 다집니다. 또한, 유교 사상은 예를 중시합니다. 예는 선조들의 가르침과 전통을 따르는 것을 의미하며, 예를 통해 사회적인 규범과 윤리를 유지하고 전달하려는 의도가 있습니다. 이러한 예를 통해 사회 안에서의 역할과 책임을 다하는 것을 강조합니다. 유교 사상은 고대 중국에서 시작되었지만, 현재까지도 동양 사회에서 큰 영향력을 가지고 있습니다. 이는 유교의 가르침이 사회적인 질서와 조화를 유지하며, 개인과 사회의 발전을 추구하는 가치를 담고 있기 때문입니다.

儒家文化在海内外有着广泛的影响。首先，儒家思想在东方地区具有重要的文化影响力，中日韩等东方国家一直继承和发展儒家思想，在新的时代发展其新的价值。特别是注重和谐的社会秩序、以家庭为中心的人际关系、礼节和礼仪等对东方国家的文化产生了很大的影响。另外，我在中国留学时，也有过很多难忘的瞬间，在那些瞬间我直接感受到了儒家文化的影响。今年，我参加了学校去曲阜的研学，我参观了济宁曲阜代表性名胜孔府、孔庙、孔林，在那里参观了孔子和孔氏祖先们的墓地，这让我直观切实地感受到了儒家思想。墓地内明确划分了家族内的阶层与秩序，还有一些地方正在进行纪念祖先的仪式，可以感受到儒家的家庭观在社会中的巨大纽带作用，以及“敬重祖先”所具有的重要价值。

此外，墓园内部的设计和布局受儒家思想的影响，营造出和谐的氛围。不仅如此，中国传统建筑中也存在儒家思想的影响。宁静的中庭、池塘和红黄色屋顶，营造出一种和谐与具有秩序的美感，西方文明强调秩序，而儒家除了秩序，还带来了和谐。看着在这些景点里来来往往的人流，可以感受到儒家文化根植于中国社会的深厚文化土壤。

이러한 유교문화는 해외에서 또한 다양한 측면에서 나타납니다. 첫번째, 유교는 동양 지역에서 중요한 문화적 영향력을 지니고 있습니다. 특히 중국, 일본, 한국 등 동양 국가들은 유교 사상과 가치를 수용하고 발전시켜 왔습니다. 이를 통해 사회적인 조화와 질서, 가족 중심의 관계, 예절과 예의 등이 동양 국가들의 문화에 큰 영향을 미쳤습니다. 또한 저는 중국에서 유학을 하면서 유교 문화의 영향을 직접 느낄 수 있는 순간이 있었습니다. 저는 학교를 통해 산동 곡부에 체험 학습을 갈 기회가 있었습니다. 저는 곡부의 대표적인 명소인 공부, 공묘와 공림을 방문하고 그곳에서 선조들의 묘역을 둘러보면서 중국의 유교적인 관념이 뚜렷하게 드러난다는 것을 깨달았습니다. 묘역 안에는 가족 간의 계층이 명확하게 나뉘어져 있었고, 조상을 예배하고 기리는 의식이 행해지고 있었습니다. 가족의 연대성과 조상에 대한 존경이 중요한 가치로 여겨지는 것을 느낄 수 있었습니다. 또한, 묘역 내부의 설계와 배치는 유교의 영향을 받아 조화롭고 순수한 분위기를 자아내고 있었습니다. 뿐만 아니라, 중국의 전통적인 건축물에서도 유교적인 영향을 발견할 수 있었습니다. 고즈넉한 중정과 연못, 그리고 홍황색 지붕은 균형과 조화의 원리를 강조하는 유교적 가치를 반영하고 있었습니다. 이러한 경험들은 중국에서 유교가 여전히 깊이 뿌리내린 문화적 토양을 형성하고 있다는 것을 명확히 보여주었습니다.

其次，在许多国家，包括欧美等国，都直接或间接地接受和应用了儒家的教育体系与价值观。儒家的教育哲学和重要教诲都强调了学问的重要性、道德的不可或缺、个人成长和社会贡献的相辅相成等，这些深刻地影响了世界的教育体系。例如，儒家思想强调学问和知识的重要性。这种影响体现在欧美大学体系中。大学里对于学术态度、教育目的、学术氛围的重视与儒家思想如出一辙。此外，儒家思想也重视“士”的精神和对礼法的教导。美国和欧洲的一些教育体系也倾向于追求学科以外的价值，尤其是注重礼节和相互尊重的教育。

두번째, 유럽과 미국을 포함한 많은 국가들은 유교의 교육 체계와 학문적인 가치를 수용하고 적용하고 있습니다. 유교의 교육 철학과 중요한 가르침은 학문의 중요성, 도덕적 가치의 강조, 개인의 성장과 사회 기여 등에 영향을 미쳤습니다. 예시로 유교에서는 학문과 지식의 중요성이 강조됩니다. 이 영향은 유럽과 미국의 대학체계에서 나타납니다. 대학에서의 학문적인 태도, 교육의 목적에 대한 존경, 그리고 학문적 열정을 중시하는 분위기는 유교적인 가치와 유사한 면이 있습니다. 또한 유교에서는 선비 정신과 예법에 대한 가르침이 중요하게 여겨집니다. 미국과 유럽의 일부 교육 시스템에서는 학문뿐만 아니라 학문 외의 가치, 특히 예절과 상호존중에 중점을 둔 교육을 추구하는 경향이 있습니다.

再次，随着儒家重要著作被翻译并传播到海外，儒家思想和价值被全世界所熟知。《论语》《大学》等被翻译成多种语言，在欧洲、美国、亚洲等地均被广泛地阅读和研究。 经典是儒教思想的重要载体之一，其中，《大学》和《中庸》非常有名。《大学》是一部涉及教育目的和教育方法的著作，说明了做学问的原理，教个人按照道理正确生活、学习知识、履行职责。另外，《大学》为了实现社会和谐和有序，还强调了个人成长和教育的重要性。

《中庸》是一部围绕个人道德，涉及社会关系与行为的著作。《中庸》以个人道德和社会伦理为基础，阐述家庭、国家、社会的原理和原则。《中庸》追求社会和谐稳定，强调个人和社会发展的正确路径和责任。在欧美大学，中国文学、儒家哲学、中国历史等学科围绕这些内容进行教学研究。欧洲几所高校通过中国学术交流，探索中国儒家传统，将其整合为教学和研究的一部分。此外，这些儒教文献被翻译成多种语言，成为国际学术期刊或学会研究论文的主题。其特点是：通过一点深入考察世界各地对儒家思想和思想价值的理解。

세번째, 유교의 중요한 저작물들이 번역되고 해외로 전파되면서, 유교 사상과 가치가 전 세계로 알려지고 있습니다. 예를 들어,《논어》,《대학》등은 다양한 언어로 번역되어 유럽, 미국, 아시아 등에서 읽히고 연구되고 있습니다. 중화 경전은 유교 사상의 중요한 매개체 중 하나이며, 그 중《대학》과《중용》이 아주 유명합니다.《대학》은 교육의 목적과 방법을 다루는 글로, 개인의 성장과 사회 질서의 유지를 강조합니다. 이 글은 대학(大學)의 원리를 설명하며, 개인이 도리에 따라 올바른 생활을 하고 지식을 습득하여 지도자로서의 역할을 수행할 수 있도록 가르칩니다. 또한,《대학》은 사회적인 조화와 질서를 이루기 위해 개인의 성장과 교육의 중요성도 강조하고 있습니다.《중용》은 개인의 도리를 중심으로 사회적인 관계와 행동에 대해 다루는 글입니다.《중용》은 개인의 도리와 사회적인 윤리를 바탕으로 한 가정, 국가, 사회의 원리와 원칙을 설명합니다.《중용》은 사회적인 조화와 안정을 추구하며, 개인의 성과 사회의 발전을 위해 올바른 행동과 책임을 강조합니다. 유럽과 미국의 대학에서는 중국 문학, 유교 철학, 중국 역사 등을 전공하는 학과에서 이러한 텍스트들을 중심으로 교육 및 연구가 이루어지고 있습니다. 유럽의 몇몇 대학은 중국 학술 교류를 통해 중국의 유교적 전통을 탐구하고, 이를 교육과 연구의 일환으로 통합하고 있습니다. 또한, 이러한 유교적인 문헌들은 다양한 언어로 번역되어 국제 학술지나 학회에서 연구 논문의 주제로 다뤄지고 있습니다. 이를 통해 세계 각지에서 유교적인 가치 및 사상에 대한 이해를 깊이 있게 고찰하고 있는 것이 특징입니다.

最后，儒家思想包含社会关系和礼仪的教导，在商业和社会活动中也具有影响力。特别是在东方国家，商业上的相互尊重、合同履行、合作等方面往往体现出儒家思想的价值。例如，儒家思想重视相互尊重和礼貌，这在商业环境中也会产生影响。表达对对方的敬意和礼貌很重要，这在商业谈判或会议上也有所体现。 对话时保持郑重有礼貌的态度，尊重对方的立场很重要。此外，儒家思想的价值之一是信任的重要性。在东方国家的商业环境中，履行合同很重要，以信任为基础进行交易。为了建立与对方的信任，在发生意想不到的事情时，也会强调相互合作和妥协。而且儒家思想比起个人更强调共同体，在商业上也会促进团队合作和协作。在经营决策中，倾向于听取集体意见，优先考虑集体利益。因此，儒家思想文化在海外的影响体现在各个领域，对社会和谐有序、教育体系、商业文化等产生积极影响。

네번째, 유교는 사회적인 관계와 예절에 대한 가르침이 포함되어 있어, 비즈니스와 사회적인 활동에도 영향력을 미칩니다. 특히 동양 국가에서는 비즈니스에서의 상호 존중, 계약 이행, 협업에 있어 유교적 가치가 반영되는 경우가 많습니다. 예를 들어 유교는 상호존중과 예의를 중요시하며, 이는 비즈니스 환경에서도 영향을 미칩니다. 상대방에 대한 경의와 예의를 표현하는 것이 중요하며, 이는 비즈니스 협상이나 회의에서도 나타납니다. 대화 시에는 정중하고 예의 바른 태도를 유지하며 상대방의 입장을 존중하는 것이 중요하게 여겨집니다. 또한 유교적 가치 중 하나는 신뢰의 중요성입니다. 동양 국가의 비즈니스 환경에서는 계약 이행이 중요하며, 신뢰를 토대로 거래가 이루어집니다. 상대방과의 신뢰를 구축하기 위해서는 예상치 못한 일이 발생했을 때도 상호 협력과 타협이 강조됩니다. 그리고 유교는 개인보다는 공동체를 강조하며, 비즈니스에서도 이는 팀워크와 협업을 촉진합니다. 비즈니스 결정에서는 집단의 의견을 수렴하고 공동체의 이익을 최우선으로 고려하는 경향이 있습니다. 그러므로 해외에서의 유교문화의 영향은 다양한 영역에서 나타나며, 사회적인 조화와 질서, 교육 체계, 비즈니스 문화 등에 긍정적인 영향을 미치고 있습니다.

在中国旅行时，我亲身经历和感悟了中华传统文化的惊人实践。其中印象最深刻的瞬间之一就是与中国传统茶文化相关的经历。我参观了中国历史名城西安的一家茶馆。在那里，茶馆老板热情地谈论了茶的制造过程和服务方法。不仅如此，他还强调，喝茶不能单纯地享受饮料，而更应该作为一种礼节和一段精神休息的时间。茶馆老板介绍说，泡茶过程中，静下心来，边喝茶边与大自然沟通、沉思，这是中华茶文化的传统和价值。这个经历让我看到了中华传统文化多么深刻地融入了生活中。

중국 여행 중에 저는 중화의 전통문화의 놀라운 실천과 깨달음을 직접 경험하게 되었습니다. 그 중에서 가장 인상 깊은 순간 중 하나는 중국의 전통적인 차문화와 연관된 경험이었습니다. 저는 중국의 역사적인 도시인 시안의 한 찻집을 방문했습니다. 그곳에서 찻사장은 차의 제조 과정과 서빙 방법에 대해 열정적으로 이야기했습니다. 그뿐만 아니라, 그는 차를 마시는 것은 단순히 음료를 즐기는 것이 아니라 예절과 정신적인 휴식의 시간으로 삼아야 한다고 강조했습니다. 찻사장은 차를 우려내는 과정에서 마음을 진정시키고, 차를 마시면서 자연과 소통하며 생각에 잠기는 것이 중화의 전통이자 가치라고 설명했습니다. 그 이야기는 나에게 중화의 전통문화가 얼마나 생활 속에 깊이 녹아들어 있는지를 보여주었습니다.

另外，在参观中国的寺院和宫殿的过程中，我对中华的美学和艺术有了深刻的了解，在寂静的寺院里感受到了静寂的能量。美丽的美术作品也证明了中华的艺术是与自然和谐相融而形成的。通过这些经历，我明白了中国不是单纯的旅游胜地，而是自豪地守护自己的传统文化并将其融入日常生活的国家。中华传统文化已经成为中国人生活的一部分，也是我人生体悟的重要来源。

또한, 중국의 사원과 궁전을 방문하면서 중화의 미학과 예술에 대한 깊은 이해를 얻었습니다. 고요한 사원 안에서 느껴지는 정적인 에너지와 아름다운 미술 작품들은 중화의 예술이 자연과 조화롭게 어우러져 만들어진 것임을 명확하게 보여주었습니다. 이런 경험들을 통해 중국은 단순히 관광지가 아닌, 자신들의 전통과 문화를 자랑스럽게 지키고 이를 일상생활에 녹여내는 나라임을 깨닫게 되었습니다. 중화의 전통문화는 그들의 삶의 한 부분으로 자리 잡아 있으며, 그 실천과 깨달음은 저에게도 큰 영감을 주었습니다.

作品编号: 5309

姓　　名: 崔多赟(Choi Dayun)

国　　籍: 韩国

组　　别: 征文类国际组

单　　位: 青岛中学

智慧融创：儒家与人工智能的文明交响

打破时空维度，拉开历史纵深，与儒家先贤对话，带来全新文化体验。学先哲故事解学习之难，“正人先正己，律己方律人”解生活之惑，“君子和而不同”是人生感悟，亦含中国态度。AI赋能中华传统文化，以科技助力儒家经典在当代社会的传播与接受，促进优秀儒家思想的世代弘扬与传承。

在打破时空维度的奇妙舞台上，我们得以与儒家先贤展开深刻的对话，共同构筑一场跨越历史纵深的全新文化体验。这次与儒家智者的碰撞让我们深刻感悟到“正人先正己，律己方律人”这一处世智慧的博大精深，以及“君子和而不同”所蕴含的宽广世界观。

시공간 차원을 뚫고 펼쳐지는 놀라운 무대에서, 우리는 유가 선견 지명한 유학자들과 심도 있는 대화를 나누며, 역사적인 심오함을 뛰어넘는 새로운 문화 체험을 만들어내고 있습니다. 이번 유학자와의 충돌은 “정인 선 정기, 율기 방 율인” 이라는 삶의 지혜와 “군자 화이부동” 이 함축하는 넓은 세계관에 대한 깊은 깨달음을 안겨주었다.

当下，科技全球化的浪潮下，人工智能如一股强大的推动力量，助力人类社会的进步与发展。然而，这股力量也伴随着一系列伦理问题，引发了我们对AI发展规范的深刻思考。在这个背景下，汲取儒家智慧，以儒家义礼为AI道德规范，成为引领人工智能技术良性发展的关键所在。

현재, 기술 국제화의 흐름 속에서 인공지능은 강력한 추진력으로 우리 인류 사회의 진보와 발전을 촉진하고 있다. 그러나 이 추진력은 동시에 일련의 윤리적 문제들을 동반하며, 우리에게 AI 개발의 규범에 대한 심사숙고를 일으키고 있다. 이러한 맥락에서 유가 선견 지명한 유학자들로부터 영감을 받아, 유학의 예, 의례를 AI 도덕의 규범으로 삼음으로써, 인공지능 기술의 건전한 발전을 주도하는 것이 중요한 역할을 하고 있다.

“正人先正己，律己方律人”蕴含着深刻的人生哲理。倘若我们能将这一原则融入人工智能的开发和运用过程中，不仅能够规范技术的应用，更能为AI赋予人性光辉。在理解并尊重人类价值观的前提下，通过对机器进行良好的“律己”，我们将更好地保障人工智能服务的公正性和道德性。

“정인 선 정기, 율기 방 율인” 은 깊은 삶의 철학을 내포하고 있다. 만약 우리가 이 원칙을 인공 지능의 개발과 활용 과정에 통합할 수 있다면, 기술의 적용을 규범화하는 데에 그치지 않고, AI 에 인간성의 빛을 불어넣을 수 있을 것이다. 인간의 가치관을 이해하고 존중하는 전제하에 기계에 대한 양질의 “율기” 를 행함으로써, 우리는인공지능 서비스의 공정성과 도덕성을 더욱 확실히 보장할 것이다.

同时，儒家思想所倡导的“君子和而不同”也为我们提供了独特的视角。在当今社会，多元文化的交流日益频繁，不同国家、不同文明间的碰撞愈发频繁。通过将“君子和而不同”的理念融入人工智能的设计中，我们能够打破文化障碍，让AI更好地适应多元世界的需求。这种开放、包容的态度不仅有助于技术的创新，更能够加强全球科技合作，推动世界朝着更为和谐的方向发展。

동시에, 유가 선견 지명한 유학자들의 “군자 화이부동” 은 우리에게 독특한 시각을 제공한다. 현대 사회에서는 다문화 교류가 점점 더 증가하며, 다양한 국가 및 문명 간의 충돌이 더욱 빈번해지고 있다. “군자 화이부동” 의 이념을 인공지능의 디자인에 융합시킴으로써, 우리는 문화적 장벽을 허물고 AI 가 다양한 세계의 요구에 더욱 잘 적응하도록 할 수 있다. 이러한 개방적이고 포용적인 태도는 기술혁신에 도움이 되는 것뿐만 아니라, 세계적인 기술 협력을 강화하고 세계가 더욱 조화로운 방향으로 나아갈 수 있도록 도와줄 것이다.

儒家义礼的内核是人际关系的和谐，而在人工智能的领域里，正是通过弘扬这一理念，我们能够在技术创新中实现社会和谐。将儒家思想融入AI的伦理规范中，就是要用传统智慧引导现代技术，使之更好地服务于人类社会。

유학의 도덕과 예술의 핵심은 대인 관계의 조화에 있다. 그리고 인공지능 분야에서는 이러한 개념을 널리 퍼뜨려 기술혁신을 통해 사회적 조화를 실현할 수 있습니다. 유학 사상을 AI 의 윤리 규범에 융합시킴으로써 우리는 전통 지식을 활용하여 현대 기술을 이끌어, 이를 통해 인류사회에 더 나은 서비스를 제공할 수 있게 된다.

儒家文化与人工智能技术的相辅相成体现在相互传承与发展上。借助先进的科技手段，我们能够更好地传播儒家思想，使之在当代社会焕发新的生机。同时，通过人工智能为儒家文化注入现代元素，实现儒家传统与科技的完美融合。

또한, 유학문화와 인공지능기술은 상호 보완적인 관계에서 나타난다. 선진기술 수단을 활용하여 우리는 유학 사상보다 효과적으로 전파할 수 있으며, 그것이 현대사회에서 새로운 생명력을 얻도록 할 수 있다. 동시에, 인공 지능이 유학문화에 현대적인 요소를 주입함으로써, 유학 전통과 기술의 완벽한 융합을 실현할 수 있다.

在这场人工智能与儒家智慧的交汇中，我们不仅看到了技术的辉煌，更感受到了思想的深沉。儒家智慧为AI的伦理建设提供了源源不断的动力，而AI的发展则为儒家文化的传承注入了全新的活力。这两者之间的默契配合，让我们走向了一个技术与文明相互融合的崭新时代。

인공지능과 유학 지혜가 교차하는 이 시점에서, 우리는 기술의 뛰어난 면뿐만 아니라 사상의 깊이도 느낄 수 있다. 유학 지혜는 AI 의 윤리적 건설에 꾸준한 원동력을 제공하며, AI 의 발전은 유학 문화에 새로운 활력을 불어넣는다. 이 두 가지 요소 간의 조화로움은 우리를 기술과 문명이 상호 융합하는 새로운 시대로 이끈다.

总体而言，打破时空的限制，将儒家文化与人工智能技术有机结合，既能够规范AI的发展，又能够推动儒家思想在现代社会的传承与发展。这不仅是对传统文化的尊重，更是对未来社会的责任担当。在这场思想的盛宴中，我们期待儒家文化与人工智能携手共进，为构建更为美好的世界贡献力量。

전반적으로 말하면, 시공간의 제약을 깨고 유학문화를 인공지능 기술과 유기적으로 결합함으로써, 우리는 AI 의 발전을 규제하는 데 도움을 주는 동시에 유학사상이 현대 사회에서 계승되고 발전되도록 장려할 수 있다. 이것은 전통문화에 대한 존경뿐만 아니라 미래 사회에 대한 책임을 진다. 이 아이디어 축제에서 우리는 유학문화와 인공지능이 손을 잡고 더 나은 세계를 만들기 위해 기여할 것을 기대한다.

作品编号: 4009
姓　　名: 张慧敏
国　　籍: 中国
组　　别: 征文类国内成人组
单位名称: 烟台大学外国语学院

《论语》智慧

《论语》中蕴含着深刻的智慧和价值，孔子强调学习的重要性，认为它是个人修养和社会进步的基石。在今天信息爆炸的时代，持续学习和提升是应对挑战的关键。孔子对诚信的强调也深深触动了我们。他认为诚信是人格的核心，失去信用就失去了一切。在现代社会，诚信不仅关乎个人声誉，也影响社会稳定和发展。

张宏洁：老师您在写毛笔字啊?

장홍재: 선생님 , 붓글씨를 쓰시나요 ?

宋龙圭: 上次你不是说想看我写毛笔字吗?

송용규: 지난번 내 붓글씨를 보고 싶다고 했잖아요 ?

张宏洁：哇，老师，您还记得啊，真守信用!

장홍재: 와 ! 선생님 아직도 기억하시네요 ! 정말 믿음직하신 분이 세요 !

宋龙圭: 子曰:“人而无信，不知其可也。大车无輗，小车无軏，其何以行之哉?”

송용규: 공자께서 말씀하시기를 , “사람으로서 신의가 없으면 , 그 가한 줄을 알지 못하겠다 . 큰 수레에 멍에채가 없고 , 작은 수레에 멍에걸이 없으면 , 어떻게 길을 갈 수 있겠는가 ?” 하셨다 .

张宏洁：宋老师，您又在学习啊?

장홍재: 선생님 , 아직도 공부 중이신 가요 ?

宋龙圭：对啊，子曰：“学而不思则罔，思而不学则殆。”而且，子曰：“温故而知新，可以为师矣。”

송용규: 네 . 공자께서 말씀하시기를 , “배우기만 하고 생각하지 않으면 소득이 없고 , 생각만 하고 배우지 아니하면 위태롭다 .” 하셨다 .

张宏洁：宋老师，你们在聊什么呢?

장홍재: 송선생님 , 무슨 이야기를 하고 계세요 ?

宋龙圭: 我在向他们请教问题呢。

송용규: 나는 그들에게 뭔가 물어보고 있어요 .

张宏洁：您的汉语比他们的都好，还需要向他们请教吗?

장홍재: 선생님의 중국어실력은 남들보다 훨씬 좋은데 남들에게도 가르침을 청해야 돼요 ?

宋龙圭：当然，子曰：“三人行，必有我师焉！择其善者而从之，其不善者而改之。”

송용규: 당연해요 . 공자께서 말씀하시기를 , “옛 것을 되새겨 잊지 않고 새로운 것을 알 면 스승이 될 수 있다 .” 하셨다 .

作为韩国人，学习中国儒家文化让我深受启发。学习儒家经典《论语》，不仅帮助我加深了对中韩两国传统文化的理解，还为我在现代社会中的行为提供了有益的指导。例如，儒家强调的仁爱、礼仪和孝道，提醒我在与他人交往时要相互理解和尊重，在家庭和社会生活中要恪守自己的角色和责任，尊重长辈和尊长，等等。这些价值观与韩国的家庭观念和社会结构有着显著的共通性。此外，儒家强调修身齐家治国平天下的理念，也激励我在日常生活中追求个人的道德修养和自我提升。总之，儒家文化不仅是东亚文化的重要组成部分，也是我个人成长道路上的重要导师 。

한국인으로서 중국 유교 문화를 공부하며 깊은 영감을 받았다. 유교 경전인《논어》를 공부함으로써 중국과 한국의 전통문화에 대한 이해를 넓히는 데 도움이 되었을 뿐만 아니라 현대 사회를 살아가는 나에게 큰 가르침을 제공했다. 예를 들어, 유교에서 강조하는 인(仁), 예의범절, 효(孝)는 다른 사람과 교류할 때 서로를 이해하고 존중해야 하며, 가족과 사회 생활에서 나의 역할과 책임을 준수하고, 어른들을 존경해야 한다는 점 등을 일깨워준다. 이러한 가치는 한국의 가족 가치 및 사회 구조와 상당한 유사성을 가지고 있다. 또한 유교는 자신을 수양하고, 가족을 보살피고, 나라를 다스리고, 세계에 평화의 개념을 강조하며 일상생활에서 개인적인 도덕 수양과 자기계발을 추구하도록 영감을 준다. 유교문화는 동아시아 문화의 중요한 부분일 뿐만 아니라, 나의 개인적 성장 경로에 있어서 중요한 멘토이기도 한다.

作品编号：3581
姓　　名：张宏洁、宋龙圭
国　　籍：中国、韩国
组　　别：诵读类国际组
单位名称：韩国国立安东大学孔子学院

《论语》的仁爱思想

子曰："富与贵，是人之所欲也；不以其道得之，不处也。贫与贱，是人之所恶也；不以其道得之，不去也。君子去仁，恶乎成名？君子无终食之间违仁，造次必于是，颠沛必于是。"今天我们对《论语》中的这一章内容进行讲解，得其之道理。

一部《论语》，千古流传；一位老师，万世师表。中国人的仁德智慧，两千年的风骨性格，都蕴藏在这位老师和他学生的对话里。

한 편의《논어》, 천년의 전승 ; 한 분의 선생님 , 만세의 모범 . 중국인의 인덕지혜 , 2 천 년의 풍격 성격 , 모두 이 선생님과 그의 학생들 사이의 대화 속에 숨겨져 있습니다 .

那么今天我们就来欣赏《论语》中"里仁"篇的内容。

그러면 오늘 우리는《논어》중 '이인편' 을 감상해 보겠습니다 .

子曰："富与贵，是人之所欲也；不以其道得之，不处也。贫与贱，是人之所恶也；不以其道得之，不去也。君子去仁，恶乎成名？君子无终食之间违仁，造次必于是，颠沛必于是。"

공자께서 "부유함과 존귀함은 사람들이 욕구하는 바이나 그 도리에 합당하게 얻은 것이 아니면 처하지 않으며 , 가난함과 천함은 사람들이 싫어하는 것이나 그 도리에 합당하게 얻어진 것이 아니더라도 버리지 말라 . 군자가 인을 버리면 어찌 이름을 이룰 수 있겠는가 ? 군자는 밥 먹을 사이에도 인을 떠남이 없으니 . 급박하고 구차한 사이에서도 반드시 인을 한다 . 엎어지고 넘어지는 상황에서도 반드시 인을 한다 ." 라고 말씀하셨습니다 .

这一章反映了孔子的理欲观。以往的孔子研究中往往忽略了这一段内容，似乎孔子主张人们只要仁、义，不要利、欲。事实上并非如此。任何人都不会甘愿过贫穷困顿、流离失所的生活，都希望得到富贵。但这必须通过正当的手段和途径去获取，否则宁守清贫而不去享受富贵。这种观念在今天仍有其不可低估的价值。这一章值得研究者们仔细推敲。

이 장은 공자의 이욕관을 반영하였습니다 . 과거 공자 연구에서는 이 단락을 간과하는 경우가 많았는데 , 공자는 사람들이 인자하고 의로우면 이익과 욕망을 갖지 말아야 한다고 주장한 것 같습니다 . 사실은 그렇지 않습니다 . 누구도 가난하고 떠도는 삶을 달가워하지 않고 부귀안삶을 원합니다 . 그러나 이는 정당한 수단과 경로를 통해 획득되어야 합니다 . 그렇지 않다면 부귀를 누리지 않고 청빈을 지켜야 할 것입니다 . 이런 관념은 오늘날에도 여전히 과소평가할 수 없는 가치가 담겼습니다 . 이 장은 연구자들이 자세히 퇴고할 가치가 있습니다 .

这章内容，让我们懂得了我们应当"坚守信念，不违于仁"。

이 논어를 읽은 후 우리는 "신념을 굳건히 지키고, 인애에 어긋나지 말아야 한다" 는 것을 알게 되었습니다.

在孔子看来，每个人都想过上富裕的生活，摆脱贫困的局面，这是好事。但是即便贫困的生活再不好，想要去之也应有道，这才是君子所为。而这个道，就是仁义之道，它是君子安身立命的基础。无论是富贵还是贫贱，都不能违背这个原则。

공자에게 따르면, 모든 사람이 부유한 삶을 살고 빈곤한 상황에서 벗어나고자 하는 것은 좋은 일입니다. 그러나 빈곤한 삶이 아무리 좋지 않더라도, 그를 떠나는 데도 도덕적인 방법을 취해야 하며, 이것이 바로 군자의 행동입니다. 그리고 그 도덕적인 방법은 바로 인의의 길이며, 이것은 군자가 자신의 삶을 세우는 기초입니다. 부유하든 가난하든, 이 원칙을 어기지 말아야 합니다.

有些人认为，人生充满苦难，人总是在痛苦中挣扎。这个观点有些道理，但是我们再想一下，人们为何会这样呢？造成他们痛苦的根源是什么？有没有一种人能摆脱这种痛苦，让生命充实而又快乐？从某个角度看，造成人痛苦的根源在于思想的矛盾。比如，有人看重财富，可等他拥有了财富，面对子孙对自己的财富觊觎和争夺的现实，他心里充满苦恼。这是因为他脑子里有强烈的伦理思想，财富观念与伦理的冲突，导致了他的痛苦。倘若坚守一个信念，他就不会痛苦了。譬如有的人看重家庭，在他的努力下，子孝妻贤，也许他们很贫穷，也许他们的生活充满磨难，但只要亲情还在，他们就能生活得很充实，很美好。

어떤 사람들은 인생이 고난으로 가득 차 있고 우리는 항상 고통 속에서 힘써 버티고 있다고 생각합니다. 이 관점은 일리가 있지만, 다시 생각해 보면 사람들은 왜 그럴까요? 그들의 고통의 근원은 무엇입니까? 이 고통에서 벗어나 삶을 기쁨으로 가득 채울 수 있는 사람이 있을까요? 다른 각도에서 보면 고통의 근원은 우리 사상의 갈등에 있습니다. 예컨대, 어떤 사람들은 부유를 갖게 되면 후손들이 자신의 부유를 빼앗아 갈까봐 걱정하여 마음은 고통과 고민으로 가득차게 될 것입니다. 이러한 현상을 초래한 원인은 그의 머릿속에는 부유와 윤리의 충돌로 고통받는 윤리적인 생각이 강했기 때문입니다. 만약 다만 한 신념을 견지한다면, 그는 고통받지 않을 것입니다. 예를 들어 가족을 소중히 여긴다면 그들의 삶은 힘들 수도 있겠지만 가족애만 있다면 그들은 매우 충실하고 아름다운 삶을 살 수 있습니다.

"仁"就是有积极意义的观念。如果坚守仁德，其实是不会在乎贫困还是富贵的，不会去谋求不义之财，也不会为改变处境而出卖良知。

'인' 은 긍정적인 의미를 갖는 관념입니다. 어진 덕을 지키면 가난이나 부귀에 신경 쓰지 않고, 부정한 재물을 추구하지도 않고, 처지를 바꾸기 위해 양심을 팔지도 않습니다. 그러나 그 신념을 버리면 사람은 처지의 노예가 되어 타인의 포폄에 휘둘려 괴로워하게 됩니다.

《论语》是记录孔子及其弟子对话的书，是"四书"之一。作者虽然没有明确地告知，但据推测是孔子的弟子们及再传弟子共同编纂的。

《논어》는 공자와 그 제자들의 대화를 기록한 책으로 사서의 하나입니다. 저자는 명확히 알려져 있지 않으나, 공자의 제자들과 그 문인들이 공동 편찬한 것으로 추정되고 있습니다.

《论语》不是以一个人的生平为基础叙述的，而是集中了孔子整个生平的言行，因此与其他经典不同，具有收集格言的性质。孔子回答弟子及众人的提问并讨论的是"论"，对弟子们的教诲叫“语”。

한 사람의 저자가 일관적인 구성을 바탕으로 서술한 것이 아니라 , 공자의 생애 전체에 걸친 언행을 모아 놓은 것이기 때문에 여타의 경전들과는 달리 격언이나 금언을 모아놓은 성격을 띱니다 . 공자가 제자 및 여러 사람들의 질문에 대답하고 토론한 것이 “논” . 제자들에게 전해준 가르침을 “어” 라고 부릅니다 .

孔子时代以后，《论语》对中国哲学家和价值观产生了深远的影响，此后对东亚其他地区也产生了影响。《论语》与儒教经典的其他三本书一起被称为“四书”，教授儒教的基本价值观“礼、义、忠、仁”。

공자 시대 이후로《논어》는 중국의 철학자들과 가치관에 깊은 영향을 끼쳤고 , 이후 동아시아에도 영향을 미쳤습니다 .《논어》는 유교 경전의 다른 세 책과 함께 사서라고 불리며 유교의 기본 가치관인 “예 , 의 , 충 , 인” 이라는 유교적 인본주의를 가르쳐왔습니다 .

作品编号：1718
姓　　名：程冉
国　　籍：中国
组　　别：诵读类国内成人组
单位名称：曲阜师范大学

《论语》之孝道

《论语》是中国古代文化宝库中的经典之作，也是儒家学派的重要经典之一。其中《论语》的“孝”思想对中国朝鲜族的影响深远。例如，朝鲜族特别注重父慈子孝，人们非常鄙视不孝不敬的人和事。并且在与人交往时，特别注意用语。朝鲜语有三种阶称，即“尊敬阶”“对等阶”“谦卑阶”，以不同的语法格式，表达不同的感情色彩。延边朝鲜族自治州地区从1984年起，将每年的8月15日定为老人节。我们一直非常重视这个节日，以此铭记长辈的养育之恩。

子夏问孝，子曰：“色难。有事，弟子服其劳；有酒食，先生馔，曾是以为孝乎？”

자하가 효도에 대하여 물으니, 공자께서 말씀하시기를, “얼굴빛을 온화하게 하는 것이 어려우니, 일이 있으면 자녀가 그 부모의 수고로움을 대신하고, 술과 밥이 있으면 부형에게 먼저 대접하는 것을 효라고 할 수 있겠는 가?” 하셨다.

子游问孝。子曰：“今之孝者，是谓能养。至于犬马，皆能有养；不敬，何以别乎？”

자유가 효도에 대하여 물으니, 공자께서 말씀하시기를, “오늘날 효도란 잘 봉양함을 이르나니, 개나 말에 이르러서도 모두 길러줌이 있으니 공경하지 않으면 무엇으로 구별할 수 있겠는가?” 하셨다.

孟懿子问孝。子曰：“无违。”樊迟御，子告之曰：“孟孙问孝于我，我对曰，‘无违’。”樊迟曰：“何谓也？”子曰：“生，事之以礼；死，葬之以礼，祭之以礼。”

맹의자가 효도에 대하여 물으니, 공자께서 말씀하시기를, “어김이 없어야 한다.” 하셨다. 번지가 수레를 몰고 있었는데, 공자께서 말씀하시기를, “맹손이 나에게 효도에 대하여 묻기에 나는 ‘어김이 없어야 한다.’ 고 대답을 하였다.” 번지가 말하기를, “무엇을 이르신 것입니까?” 하고 물으니, 공자께서 말씀하시기를, “살아계실 때에는 예로써 섬기고, 돌아가시면 예로써 장사지내고, 예로써 제사를 지내는 것이다.” 하셨다.

子曰：“父在，观其志；父没，观其行；三年无改于父之道，可谓孝矣。”

공자께서 말씀하시기를, “아버지가 살아계실 때에는 그 자식의 뜻을 보고 아버지가 돌아가셨을 때에는 그 행동을 볼 것이나, 삼년동안 아버지의 도를 고치지 말아야 효라 이를 수 있을 것이다.” 하셨다.

子曰：“事父母几谏。见志不从，又敬不违，劳而不怨。”

공자께서 말씀하시기를, “부모를 섬기는데 은미하게 간할 것이니, 부모의 뜻이 내 말을 따르지 않을 것을 보더라도 더욱 공경하고 부모의 뜻을 어기지 말며, 수고로워도 원망

하지 말아야 한다.” 하셨다.

作品编号：4036
姓　　名：李炫颖
国　　籍：中国
组　　别：诵读类国内成人组
单位名称：大连民族大学

遇见孔子·天下大同

舞台剧《遇见孔子·天下大同》以舞蹈、诵读、讲故事等形式阐述了《论语》颜渊篇“子贡问政”的内容。故事主线为小金同学在诵读“子贡问政”这一节时感到晦涩难懂，通过孔子及弟子演绎的小故事，理解了这一段的含义，并总结出孔子提出的“天下大同”的思想的含义。

子贡问政。子曰：“足食，足兵，民信之矣。”子贡曰：“必不得已而去，于斯三者何先？”曰：“去兵。”子贡曰：“必不得已而去，于斯二者何先？”曰：“去食。自古皆有死，民无信不立。”

자공이 정사에 대하여 물으니 , 공자께서 말씀하시기를 , “양식을 풍족하게 하고 , 국방을 튼튼히 하고 백성들이 믿게 하는 것이다 .” 하셨다 . 자공이 말하기를 , “부득이 해서 반드시 버린다면 이 세 가지 중에서 무엇을 먼저 버려야 합니까 ?” 하니 , 공자께서 말씀하시기를 , “군병을 버려야 한다 .” 하셨다 . 자공이 말하기를 , “부득이 해서 반드시 버린다면 이 두 가지 중에 무엇을 먼저 버려야 합니까 ?” 하니 , 공자께서 말씀하시기를 , “양식을 버려야 한다 . 예로부터 사람은 누구나 다 죽음이 있으나 , 사람은 신의가 없으면 설 수 없는 것이다 .” 하셨다 .

子贡问政。子曰：“足食，足兵，民信之矣。”子贡曰：“必不得已而去，于斯三者何先？”曰：“去兵。”子贡曰：“必不得已而去，于斯二者何先？”曰：“去食。自古皆有死，民无信不立。”

자공문정 . 자왈 ：“족식 족병 민신지의 .” 자공왈：“필부득이이거 , 어사삼자 하선 ?” 왈：“거병 .” 자공왈：“필부득이이거 , 어사이자 하선 ?” 왈 ：“거식 . 자고개유사 , 민무신 불립 .”

子贡：夫子，子贡有个问题想请教一下。
孔子：请说吧。
子贡：颜回想问政。治理国家最重要的措施是什么呢？
孔子：足食，足兵，民信之矣。
子贡：老师的意思是说，粮食充足，军备充足，老百姓对当政者的信任度，一共三项。
孔子：对，这三点都非常重要。
子贡：必不得已而去，于斯三者何先？
颜回：哎，你的意思是不是说，如果不得已要去掉一项，那么三项中先去掉哪一项呢？

子贡：对。

孔子：去兵。

子贡：必不得已而去，于斯二者何先？如果不得不再去掉一项，这两项中去掉哪一项呢？

孔子：去食。自古皆有死，民无信不立。

子贡：老师，您的意思是说，去掉粮食，吃饭尽管重要，但是自古以来人总是要死的，如果老百姓对当权者信任，那么没有粮食也能生产出粮食来，如果老百姓对当权者不信任，那么国家就不能存在了，是吗？

孔子：对。

颜回：老师，您的见解真是太深刻了。对于当权者来说，最重要的是要实行仁政，言而有信，取信于民，因为只有这样才能得到老百姓的拥护和爱戴，只有这样国家才能够长治久安，否则国家就会失去了存在的基础。

자공: 선생님, 정치는 어떻게 하는 것이 좋겠습니까?

공자: 양식을 풍족하게 하고, 국방을 튼튼히 하고 백성들이 믿을 수 있게 해야 한다.

자공: 그 세 가지 중에 어쩔 수 없이 하나를 포기해야 한다면 무엇을 포기하시겠습니까?

공자: 군사를 포기하겠다.

자공: 나머지 둘 가운데 하나를 포기해야 한다면 무엇을 포기하시겠습니까?

공자: 양식을 버려라. 예로부터 사람은 누구나 죽는 법이지만 백성들의 신뢰를 얻지 못하면 나라는 설 수 없다.

看完这个故事，我终于知道政治的核心在于赢得人民的信任。孔子所说的“大同社会”是指所有人都能共同富裕的理想社会。大同社会是实现人伦的社会，任何人都可以保障基本的生活，充分发挥自己的能力，相互信任和帮助。让我们一起来诵读吧。共同体会《论语》的魅力！

이 이야기를 듣고 정치의 핵심은 국민의 신뢰를 얻는 것이다는 것을 깨달았습니다. 공자가 말한 “대동사회” 는 모든 사람이 더불어 잘 살 수 있는 이상 사회를 말합니다. 대동사회는 인륜이 실현된 사회로 누구에게나 기본적인 삶이 보장되고 자신의 능력을 충분히 발휘할 수 있으며 서로가 신뢰하고 도와주기 때문에 범죄가 발생하지 않는 사회입니다. 그럼, 우리 다같이 중국어로 한번 읽어볼까요? 《논어》의 매력을 함께 느껴 봅시다!

子贡问政。子曰：“足食，足兵，民信之矣。”子贡曰：“必不得已而去，于斯三者何先？”曰：“去兵。”子贡曰：“必不得已而去，于斯二者何先？”曰：“去食。自古皆有死，民无信不立。”

자공이 정사에 대하여 물으니, 공자께서 말씀하시기를, “양식을 풍족하게 하고, 국방을 튼튼히 하고 백성들이 믿게 하는 것이다.” 하셨다. 자공이 말하기를, “부득이 해서 반드시 버린다면 이 세 가지 중에서 무엇을 먼저 버려야 합니까?” 하니, 공자께서 말씀하시기를, “군병을 버려야 한다.” 하셨다. 자공이 말하기를, “부득이 해서 반드시 버린다면 이 두 가지 중에 무엇을 먼저 버려야 합니까?” 하니, 공자께서 말씀하시기를, “양식을 버려야 한다. 예로부터 사람은 누구나 다 죽음이 있으나, 사람은 신의가 없으면 설 수 없는 것이다.” 하셨다.

作品编号：2397
姓　　名：张楠　等
国　　籍：中国
组　　别：诵读类国内成人组
单位名称：山东省烟台艺术学校

中 俄 篇

孔子名句与当今世界

文章选取孔子的名句“不患人之不己知，患不知人也”，以俄罗斯人的角度分析了体现其中的和谐平衡思想以及对当今世界的启示。认为“知己”固然重要，但“知人”更可以因为了解别人的需求给予善意与帮助，更有利于形成和谐共生的氛围。中国迄今一直遵循和践行这一点，不断地为建设和谐温暖的世界而努力。

中国文化博大精深，有很多思想家，他们的名句直到今天都令人动容。孔子是西方国家人们心目中最著名的东方思想家，他为后代留下了无数令人印象深刻的精神遗产。

Китайская культура богата мыслителями, идеи которых не оставляют нас равнодушными и по сей день. Наибольшую известность среди восточных мыслителей в умах людей западных стран имеет именно Конфуций, который оставил впечатляющее наследие для будущих поколений.

子曰：“不患人之不己知，患不知人也。”

Не беспокойся о том, что люди тебя не знают, а беспокойся о том, что ты не знаешь людей.

孔子说：“不要担心别人不了解自己，而要担心自己不了解别人。”这是在外国传播不广的一句孔子的话，这句话与孙子的“不知彼不知己，每战必殆”异曲同工，但是后者在国外流传更广。孙子的话可以概括为“了解你的敌人”。虽然两句名言都有“了解别人”的关键思想，但我个人对孔子的立场印象更深刻，因为我觉得孔子将和平、和谐和平衡放在首位。

Это недооцененное высказывание Конфуция, которое также находит отражение в получившем более широкое распространение высказывании Сунь — Цзы, сократившемся до крылатого: «Познай врага своего». Несмотря на то, что главная мысль о важности познания других людей присутствует в обоих высказываниях, лично мне больше импонирует позиция Конфуция, ставящего во главу угла мир, гармонию и баланс.

人的生活是螺旋循环的，这既可以在各国的历史上看到，也可以在时尚、文学和其他文化现象中看到。我们的思维也具有相同的循环性。对纷杂多变的人类来说，最令人惊奇的是人类变异的稳定性，就像循环性一样，这正如隐藏在不完美中的完美。这就是为什么几千年后孔子的思想还不会失去其相关性，仍然适用于今天。

Человеческая жизнь спирально циклична, это можно заметить как в истории каждого государства, так и в моде, в литературе и других культурных явлениях. Такой же цикличностью отличается и наше мышление. Самое удивительное в человеческой изменчивости — это ее стабильность, как у той самой цикличности. То самое совершенство в его несовершенстве. Именно поэтому идеи Конфуция не теряют свою актуальность и тысячи лет спустя, оставаясь применимы и по сегодняшний день.

有人会说，世界已经改变了这么多、改变得这么快，现在不可能按这样的语句进行自己的生活。 他们说的不是全无道理。是的，世界正在发生变化，但我们是否已经不珍惜善良、毅力、礼貌等品质了呢？你的努力成果是否不愿意与亲人或一个愉快的路人沟通了呢？答案当然是否定的。我们仍然像以前一样，本能地追寻着我们的理想、我们的道路和我们的幸福。

Кто-то может сказать, что мир изменился так сильно и стремительно, что невозможно строить свою жизнь, опираясь лишь на подобные высказывания. Они будут правы и неправы одновременно. Да, мир меняется, но разве мы перестали ценить такие человеческие качества, как доброта, упорство, вежливость? Ты больше не хочешь поделиться плодами своего труда с родными или просто с приятным незнакомцем? Конечно, нет. Мы все так же, как и раньше, по наитию ищем себя, свой путь и свое счастье.

我们这个时代，当任何人都有可能出现在网络或者媒体上，许多人已经将名声和幸福等同起来，这并不完全正确。名声是一个沉重的负担，不是每个人都能承受的，它本身不应该带有目的指向，不应该为了名声而成名，它应该是为社会服务的最高目标实现的伴随因素。

В наш век, когда любой человек может вещать с экрана, многие поставили знак равенства между известностью и счастьем, что не совсем правильно. Известность — тяжелая ноша, которую не каждый сможет вынести, она не должна быть самоцелью, известность ради известности, а лишь сопутствующим фактором при достижении высшей цели служения обществу.

不了解、不理解别人，很容易伤人。我们可以在新闻中看到大量的例子，社会对一个人的行为误解，三人成虎、众口铄金是如何毁掉了他的生活。不了解却去评价、去批评甚至去诋毁，可以说恶莫大焉。从这个角度来看，我觉得两千年前孔子的话最是恰切：不知人应该不予揣测，不予置评。

Своим незнанием, непониманием других очень легко причинить людям боль. Мы можем увидеть огромное число примеров в новостях, когда ошибочное понимание обществом поступка человека ломало жизнь последнему, ведь ложь, повторенная тысячу раз, становится правдой. Ничего не зная, они берутся судить, лишь скрывая за своей ложной правдой истину. Именно с этой точки зрения я вижу наилучшее применение данного высказывания.

我们不要只从功利的态度来看待这句话，就是了解了他人就会更容易控制操纵这些人。了解别人有助于在各种各样的场合建立健康的人际关系，包括家庭和团队以及社会、国际舞台。毕竟，如果每个人因为了解别人，而去根据他的需要进行帮助与支持，那么世界上就不会有人感到孤单无助。这有助于和谐和平的社会的形成。在当今世界，我清晰地看到孔子的国家——中国，作为一个大国，长期以来，不仅在中国社会的框架内，而且在国际舞台上，都在努力遵循这一点，一直在为建设和谐文明的世界而努力！

Не стоит смотреть на него только с прагматичной точки зрения, когда понимание поведения других облегчит манипулирование этими людьми. Понимание других помогает при построении здоровых межличностных отношений в семье и коллективе в частности, и в обществе, на международной сцене в целом. Ведь если каждый человек будет заботиться о другом, помогать и поддерживать именно так, как нужно другому, а не ему самому, то в мире не останется людей, которые чувствовали бы себя одинокими и беспомощными, ненужными. Сейчас мы можем наблюдать, как родина Конфуция, Китай, будучи великой державой, старается следовать этому не только в рамках китайского общества, но и на международной арене в надежде построить гармоничный цивилизованный мир.

当然，了解自己也很重要。了解自己的长处和短处、爱自己的优点与缺点，对于每个人都是必要的。但我们的“我”是由我们周围的一个个个体构成的。我们千万不要忘记，一个人在社会中也扮演着“镜子”的角色。我们会反映出其他人的行为和品行，也会被反映给其他人。而互相之间反映的影像将永远留在我们的认识里。通过“镜子”我们可以知人，通过“镜子”，别人也可以知我。

Важно знать себя, свои сильные и слабые стороны, любить себя, но наше «я» складывается из нашего окружения. Не стоит забывать, что человек также играет роль зеркала в обществе. Мы отражаем поступки и поведение других людей, и тени этих отражений остаются с нами навсегда. Но и мы отражаемся в чужих зеркалах. Отражая других, словно зеркало, не только мы познаем их, но и они получают возможность познать нас.

请问亲爱的读者，你想在“镜子”中反映什么呢？

Так что же хочешь отражать ты, мой дорогой читатель?

作品编号：4862
姓　　名：班薇莉
国　　籍：俄罗斯
组　　别：征文类国际组
单位名称：鲁东大学国际教育学院

儒家经典的智慧之光照亮世界文明之路

本文深入挖掘儒家经典文化的智慧与道德标准，通过精炼的篇章与名句解读，展示了儒家文化的独特魅力。文中不仅阐述了儒家“仁爱”与“礼义”的核心价值，还从个人修养和国际关系等多个角度剖析了儒家经典的智慧，并通过实际案例展示其现代意义。

在中华文化的璀璨星河中，儒家经典以其深厚的底蕴和普世的价值，犹如璀璨的明珠，熠熠生辉。它们不仅塑造了我们民族的品格，更是人类文明宝库中不可或缺的瑰宝。在这个全球化的时代，我们更应借助儒家经典，向世界传递中华文化的智慧与道德之光。

В сияющей звездной ровнине китайской культуры, конфуцианские классические труды, обладая глубокими традициями и универсальной ценностью, сияют как ярчайшие звезды. Они не только сформировали характер нашей нации, но и являются неотъемлемым элементом в сокровищнице человеческой цивилизации. В эпоху глобализации мы должны еще более активно использовать конфуцианские классические труды, чтобы передать мудрость и нравственность китайской культуры всему миру.

儒家经典的核心价值——“仁爱”与“礼义”，是构建和谐社会的基石。孔子曾言：“己所不欲，勿施于人。”这一简单而深刻的道理，不仅体现了对他人的尊重与关怀，更是指引我们如何与他人和谐相处的黄金法则。当我们跨越语言和文化的隔阂，向世界传递这一理念时，我们实际上在传递对人性深刻的洞见与尊重。

Основные ценности конфуцианства—«благородная любовь» или «доброта» и «церемония и праведность»—являются основой для построения гармоничного общества. Конфуций сказал: «Не делай другим того, чего не желаешь, чтобы другие сделали тебе». Эта простая, но глубокая истина отражает уважение и заботу о других, и является золотым правилом, который направляет нас к гармонии в отношениях с другими. Когда мы, преодолевая языковые и культурные барьеры, передаем этот идеал миру, мы фактически передаем глубочайшее понимание и уважение к человеческой сущности.

儒家经典强调“学而时习之，不亦说乎？”这句话道出了学习的乐趣与重要性。在全球化的浪潮中，持续学习、不断进步成为个体与国家发展的必由之路。让我们将这一理念传递给世界，点燃人们追求知识、提升自我、实现梦想的热情。

Конфуцианские классики подчёркивают: «Учиться и постоянно практиковать—разве это не радостно?» Это выражение передаёт радость и значимость обучения. В волне глобализации непрерывное обучение и постоянный прогресс становятся необходимым путём для индивидуального и национального развития. Позвольте нам передать эту концепцию миру, чтобы разжечь страсть в людях к погоне за знаниями, самосовершенствованию и реализации мечт.

儒家经典中的“修身齐家治国平天下”，为我们描绘了一个从个人修养到国家治理的宏伟蓝图。在全球化的背景下，这一理念同样具有深远的现实意义。每个人都应通过提升道德修养，为家庭、社会乃至国家作出贡献。让我们将这一理念推向世界，倡导人们注重个人修养，积极参与社会事务，共同构建一个更加美好的世界。

В конфуцианской классике «Совершенствование личности, гармония в семье, управление государством, мир под небом» представлен грандиозный план от личностного совершенствования до управления государством. В условиях глобализации этот идеал также имеет глубокий практический смысл. Каждый человек должен развивать свои моральные ценности и вносить вклад в семью, общество и государство. Давайте продвигать этот идеал в мире, призывая к личностному совершенствованию, активному участию в общественных делах и к совместному строительству более прекрасного мира.

儒家经典倡导的“和为贵”思想，是全球文化交流的基石。在多元文化交流中，我们应以开放包容的心态，尊重不同文化的差异，寻求共同发展的道路。让我们携手传递儒家经典的和谐理念，增进不同文化间的理解与信任，共同构建人类命运共同体。

Идея «мир как высшая ценность», провозглашаемая в конфуцианских классических трудов, является фундаментом глобального культурного обмена. В процессе взаимодействия разнообразных культурных традиций мы должны демонстрировать толерантность, уважать различия культур и активно стремиться к обоюдному развитию. Давайте вместе продвигать идею гармонии, отраженную в конфуцианских классических трудах, укреплять взаимопонимание и доверие между различными культурными традициями, стремясь к построению сообщества единой судьбы человечества.

以儒家经典为桥梁，加强国际传播能力建设，促进文明交流互鉴。愿中华文化的智慧与道德之光，如同温暖的春风，拂过世界各地的心灵，为世界文化的繁荣与发展贡献力量。正如《大学》所言：“大学之道，在明明德，在亲民，在止于至善。”让我们携手共进，追求至善之境，共创人类美好未来！

Используя конфуцианские классические труды в качестве моста, мы укрепляем международные коммуникационные способности и способствуем обмену и взаимопониманию между цивилизациями. Мы надеемся, что мудрость и нравственное сияние китайской культуры, подобно теплому весеннему ветеру, коснутся сердец людей по всему миру, внося вклад в процветание и развитие культуры мира. Как говорится в “Великое Учение”: «Путь Великого Учения заключается в раскрытии светлой добродетели, породненим с народом, остановке на совершенном добре». Давайте вместе стремимся к высшей доброте и создаем прекрасное будущее для человечества в целом!

作品编号：1293
姓　　名：武云健
国　　籍：中国
组　　别：征文类国内成人组
单位名称：北华大学

儒家仁义传千古，传承发展共飞扬

儒家思想是中国传统文化的核心之一，儒家经典则是儒家思想的集中体现。随着国际交流的不断深入，儒家文化在海外也产生了广泛的影响。作为新时代的高中生，我深知自己肩负着传承和弘扬中华优秀传统文化的责任。让我们共同努力，传承和弘扬中华优秀传统文化，为实现中华民族伟大复兴的中国梦贡献自己的力量！

自古以来，中华民族就有着悠久的历史和灿烂的文化。其中，儒家思想作为中华民族的主流文化之一，对中国古代社会的政治、经济、文化等方面产生了深远的影响。作为一名高中学生，我深感自己肩负着传承和弘扬中华优秀传统文化的责任。在此，我将阐述儒家思想的内涵，解读中华经典，介绍儒家文化在海外的影响，并畅谈我对中华优秀传统文化的践行与感悟。

С древних времен китайский народ имеет долгую историю и великолепную культуру. Среди них конфуцианство, как одна из основных культур китайской нации, оказало глубокое влияние на политику, экономику и культуру древнего китайского общества. Будучи старшеклассником, я глубоко осознаю свою ответственность за наследование и продвижение великой традиционной китайской культуры. Здесь я подробно расскажу о сути конфуцианства, интерпретирую китайскую классику, познакомлю вас с влиянием конфуцианской культуры за рубежом а также поделюсь своим опытом воплощения и восприятия выдающейся традиционной китайской культуры.

儒家思想的内涵丰富多样，主要包括仁、义、礼、智、信等五个方面。仁是指关爱他人，尊重生命，追求和谐共处的品质；义是指遵循道义，明辨是非，坚守正义的行为准则；礼是指规范人际关系，维护社会秩序，体现文明礼仪的制度和规范；智是指具备判断力、洞察力和创新精神的智慧；信是指诚实守信，言行一致，树立良好信誉的品质。这五个方面共同构成了儒家思想的基本原则，为中华民族的道德伦理和行为规范提供了指导。

Конфуцианство богато и разнообразно, в основном включает в себя пять аспектов: человеколюбие, справедливость, вежливость, мудрость и доверие.Человеколюбие относится к качеству заботы о других, уважения к жизни и стремления к гармоничному сосуществованию; вежливость относится к системе и нормам, которые регулируют межличностные отношения, поддерживают социальный порядок и воплощают цивилизованный этикет; мудрость относится к мудрости с рассудительностью, относится к рассудительности, проницательности и новаторскому духу. а доверие относится к качеству честности и надежности, постоянству между словами и делами и созданию хорошей репутации. Вместе эти пять аспектов составляют основные принципы конфуцианства и служат ориентиром для морали, этики и поведенческих норм китайской нации.

儒家经典是儒家思想的集中体现，包括《论语》《孟子》《大学》《中庸》等著作。《论语》是孔子及其弟子的言行录，主要阐述了仁、义、礼、智、信等儒家思想的核心观念；《孟子》是孟子的思想体系，强调人性本善，主张通过修身、齐家、治国、平天下来实现社会和谐；《大学》和《中庸》分别是孔子的弟子曾参和子思的著作，分别阐述了修身、齐家、治国、平天下的道理和方法。这些经典著作为我们提供了丰富的儒家思想资源，有助于我们更好地理解和传承中华优秀传统文化。

Конфуцианская классика является концентрированным воплощением конфуцианства, включая такие работы, как “Лунь Юй”, “Мэн-цзы”, “Да сюэ” и “Чжун юн”. “Лунь Юй” — это запись слов и поступков Конфуция и его учеников, в основном излагающая основные понятия конфуцианства, такие как доброжелательность, праведность, вежливость, мудрость и вера; “Мэн-цзы” — это идеологическая система Мэн-цзы, подчеркивающая неотъемлемую доброту человеческой природы и выступающая за достижение социальной гармонии через самосовершенствование, семейную гармонию, управление страной и выравнивание мира; а “Да сюэ” и “Чжун юн” — это работы учеников Конфуция Цзэн Шэня и Цзы Си соответственно, в которых излагаются принципы и методы «добиваться самосовершенствования, в порятке содержать семью, управлять государством и нести Поднебесной мир». Эти классические труды дают нам богатые ресурсы конфуцианства, которые помогают нам лучше понять и унаследовать прекрасную традиционную китайскую культуру.

儒家文化在海外也产生了广泛的影响。随着中国的改革开放和国际交流的不断深入，越来越多的外国人开始关注和学习儒家文化。在世界各地，孔子学院、孔子课堂等教育机构如雨后春笋般涌现，为世界各地的人们提供了学习汉语和了解中华文化的平台。此外，儒家思想中的仁爱、和谐、礼仪等理念也受到了国际社会的认同和尊重，有力地推动了中外文化交流和人类文明的共同进步。

Конфуцианская культура также оказала большое влияние за рубежом. С углублением реформ и открытости Китая, а также международных обменов, все больше и больше иностранцев начали обращать внимание на конфуцианскую культуру и изучать её. По всему миру появились Институты Конфуция, Классы Конфуция и другие учебные заведения, предоставляющие людям со всего мира платформы для изучения китайского языка и понимания китайской культуры. Кроме того, понятия человеколюбия, справедливости, вежливости в конфуцианстве также были признаны и уважаемы международным сообществом, что эффективно способствовало культурному обмену между Китаем и другими странами и общему развитию человеческой цивилизации.

我深知自己肩负着传承和弘扬中华优秀传统文化的责任。在学习儒家经典的过程中，我逐渐明白了仁爱、诚信、礼仪等品质的重要性。在日常生活中，我努力践行儒家思想，关爱他人，尊重师长，遵守纪律，诚实守信。同时，我也积极参加各种文化活动，如朗诵比赛、演讲比赛等，以提高自己的文化素养和综合素质。通过这些实践，我深刻体会到了中华优秀传统文化的魅力和价值。儒家思想是中华民族的宝贵财富，对于我们今天的成长和发展具有重要的指导意义。

Я прекрасно осознаю, что на мне лежит ответственность за то, чтобы унаследовать и продолжить прекрасную традиционную китайскую культуру. В процессе изучения конфуцианской классики, я постепенно понимала важность таких качеств, как человеколюбие, справедливость, вежливость. В своей повседневной жизни я стараюсь практиковать конфуцианство, заботиться о других, уважать учителей, соблюдать дисциплину, быть честным и заслуживающим доверия. В то же время я также активно участвую в различных культурных мероприятиях, таких как конкурсы декламации, конкурсы речи и т. д., чтобы повысить свою культурную грамотность и всестороннее качество. Благодаря этим практикам я глубоко осознала очарование и ценность превосходной традиционной китайской культуры.Конфуцианство является драгоценным богатством китайской нации и имеет большое направляющее значение для нашего роста и развития сегодня.

让我们共同努力，传承和弘扬中华优秀传统文化，为实现中华民族伟大复兴的中国梦贡献自己的力量！

Давайте работать вместе, чтобы унаследовать и развивать прекрасную традиционную китайскую культуру и внести свой вклад в реализацию китайской мечты о великом возрождении китайской нации!

作品编号：2728
姓　　名：王昭涵
国　　籍：中国
组　　别：征文类国内少年组
单位名称：山东省济南市莱芜区第十七中学

诵读《中庸》，品中庸之道

《中庸》是一部重要的儒家经典著作，其中蕴含了丰富的哲理智慧。此作品中五位留学生用中文和俄语诵读《中庸》第二十章的内容，并构建交流场景，结合茶艺表演进行展现，表达自身对《中庸》的理解。

诚者，天之道也；诚之者，人之道也。诚者，不勉而中，不思而得，从容中道，圣人也。诚之者，择善而固执之者也。

Искренность — это путь неба, стремление стать искренним — это путь человека. Искренний человек без усилий добивается своих целей, спокойно, без размышлений сливается с путем середины, таков мудрый человек, стремящийся стать по нему искренним, это тот кто выбирает добро и крепко держится его.

博学之，审问之，慎思之，明辨之，笃行之。

Широко изучайте свой путь, старайтесь добраться до своей цели, тщательно продумывайте его, добивайтесь четких суждений о нем, не покладая рук — воплощайте.

有弗学，学之弗能弗措也；有弗问，问之弗知弗措也；有弗思，思之弗得弗措也；

Если чего-то не доучил — изучай, не осилил — не останавливайся. Если в чем–то не добрался до сути — допытывайся, не познал — не отступай. Если что–то не додумал до конца — думай, не добился — не сдавайся.

有弗辨，辨之弗明弗措也；有弗行，行之弗笃弗措也。

Если о чем-то не добился четкого суждения — рассуждай, не прояснил — не отчаивайся. Если что-то не осуществил — добейся, не постарался — не бросай.

人一能之，己百之；人十能之，己千之。

Там, где другой прилагает одно усилие, ты прилагай сто. Там, где другой прилагает десять усилий, ты прилагай тысячу.

果能此道矣，虽愚必明，虽柔必强。

В движении будь, трудись, тогда постигнешь свой путь. Коль глупым был, то станешь умным, дальновидным. Коль слабым был и уязвимым, станешь сильным.

作品编号：3550

姓　　名：金诚（Kubanychbekov Akimbai）、刘备（Azizov Ramil）
心悦（Ryndina Alina）、安娜（Davydova Anna）
陆思达（Shukurov Rustam）

国　　籍：俄罗斯、吉尔吉斯斯坦、乌兹别克斯坦

组　　别：诵读类国际组

单位名称：潍坊职业学院

《论语》——“礼之用，和为贵”

“礼之用，和为贵”是《论语》中的一句名言，它深刻地揭示了礼仪在人际交往中的重要性。自古以来，中国以其独特的礼仪文化闻名于世，被誉为“礼仪之邦”。礼仪不仅是一种传统，更是一种深入人心的价值观。来自俄罗斯的留学生美丽希望通过这句话，向大家传递注重和谐、尊重和包容的理念。

大家好！我是 Liza, 来自俄罗斯。我的中文名字是美丽。我学习中文两年了，现在我在山东外国语职业技术大学交换学习。我很喜欢中国和中国文化。我在学习中国文化的时候，了解到孔子是中国最早的老师，也学习了他的很多名言名句。今天，我想和大家分享一下我最喜欢的句子。

Привет всем! Меня зовут Лиза, я из России. Мое китайское имя — 美丽 . Я изучаю китайский язык уже два года и сейчас нахожусь на программе обмена в Шаньдунском профессионально — техническом университете иностранных языков. Мне очень нравится Китай и китайская культура. Когда я изучала китайскую культуру, я узнала, что Конфуций был самым ранним учителем в Китае, а также выучила много его знаменитых цитат и высказываний. Сегодня я хочу поделиться с вами своими любимыми фразами.

有子曰：“礼之用，和为贵。先王之道，斯为美，小大由之。有所不行，知和而和，不以礼节之，亦不可行也。”

Ю – цзы сказал: — Использование ритуала ценно потому, что оно приводит людей к согласию. Путь древних правителей был прекрасен. Свои большие и малые дела они совершали в соответствии с ритуалом. Совершать то, что нельзя делать, и при этом в интересах согласия стремиться к нему, не прибегая к ритуалу для ограничения этого поступка, — так поступать нельзя.

这句话出自《论语》“学而”篇。《论语》是记录孔子及其弟子言行的一本书，我喜欢的这句是孔子的弟子有若说的。这句话的意思是，礼的运用，以做到和谐最为可贵。古代帝王治理天下的方法中，这是最美好的。不论大事小事，都要遵从这个道理。但也有行不通的时候，知道和谐为贵而一味求和，却不用礼法来节制，也是不可行的。

Эта цитата взята из «Лунь Юй», в которой записаны слова и поступки Конфуция и его учеников, а моя любимая цитата принадлежит ученику Конфуция, Ю Жо . Смысл этой фразы таков: использование ритулов для достижения гармонии — самое ценное. Это лучшая часть древнего императорского метода управления миром. Его следовало придерживаться во всех делах, независимо от того, насколько они велики или малы. Однако бывали случаи, когда это не срабатывало, и было невозможно понять, что гармония — это самое ценное, и стремиться к ней, не используя ритулы и законы для ее контроля.

来到中国之后，我听到、学到了很多与“和”有关的成语：心平气和、和气生财、和和美美等。但是，当我学习了这句话之后，我明白了，我们做任何事情都要重视“礼”与“和”的协调。“和”不是你好我好大家好，而是各自有各自的价值观和目标，大家走到一起后，仍然能团结合作。小到我们的家庭，大到国家与国家之间、人与自然之间，都应遵守礼节、规则，和谐、和睦相处。所以，礼与和，缺一不可。我也希望，所有的国家都能像中国与俄罗斯一样，和谐共处，共同发展。谢谢大家！

С тех пор как я приехала в Китай, я услышала и выучила множество идиом, связанных с «和», таких как 心平气和、和气生财、和和美美 и т. д. Однако, когда я выучила эту фразу, я поняла, что мы должны обращать внимание на «вежливости» и «гармонии» во всем, что мы делаем. Гармония заключается не в том, чтобы быть хорошим для тебя, хорошим для меня и хорошим для всех, а в том, чтобы быть единым и сотрудничать, даже если у нас есть свои ценности и цели. От самой маленькой семьи до самой большой нации, между людьми и природой мы должны соблюдать этикет и правила и жить в гармонии. Поэтому этикет и гармония незаменимы. Я также надеюсь, что все страны смогут жить в гармонии и развиваться вместе, как это делают Китай и Россия. Спасибо всем!

作品编号：3676
姓　　名：美丽（Batishcheva Elizaveta）
国　　籍：俄罗斯
组　　别：诵读类国际组
单位名称：山东外国语职业技术大学

中 法 篇

儒家思想与今日布隆迪

布隆迪，这片非洲心脏地带的文化瑰宝，正经历着与儒家思想的奇妙交融。尽管距离遥远，文化迥异，但儒家智慧却在这片土地上生根发芽，为布隆迪注入了新的活力。通过当地媒体等机构的积极推动，《布隆迪之魅》与《来杂志》等主流媒体将孔子的智慧名言翻译成当地语言，巧妙地融入布隆迪的社会文化背景中。儒家思想中的仁爱、和谐与乌班图思想中的人与自然和谐共处的理念不谋而合，共同描绘出了一幅中非文化和谐共存的美丽画卷。在布隆迪，每周媒体都会推送不同的孔子名言，用以指导人们的生活，丰富他们的精神世界。这种跨越时空和地域的文化交融，不仅增进了中布两国人民的友谊，也为世界文化的多元发展增添了新的篇章。

布隆迪，一个位于非洲心脏地带的国家，拥有丰富的文化底蕴和独特的社会风貌。作为班图文化的传承者，布隆迪人民的生活方式和价值观似乎与远在东方的中国并无太多直接联系。然而，随着近年来中非合作的加深，中国古老的儒家思想，特别是孔子那些充满智慧的名言，开始在布隆迪的土地上悄然绽放，融入人们的日常生活。

Le Burundi, un pays situé au cœur de l’Afrique, est riche en culture et présente une société unique. En tant que gardien de la culture Bantou, la façon de vivre et les valeurs des Burundais semblent ne pas avoir grandement de choses en commun avec la Chine, située à l’autre extrémité de l’Est. Cependant, avec le renforcement des relations sino-africaines ces dernières années, la sagesse de la pensée confucéenne, vieilles de plusieurs siècles en Chine, et en particulier les maximes pleines de sagesse de Confucius, commencent à s’épanouir discrètement sur le sol burundais, devenant une partie intégrante de la vie des gens.

您可能会问，儒家思想为何能在布隆迪这片遥远的非洲大陆生根发芽呢？答案其实很简单：儒家思想与布隆迪的传统价值观——乌班图思想，有着惊人的相似之处。无论是儒家倡导的仁爱、和谐，还是乌班图思想强调的人与自然的和谐共处，都体现了对美好社会的共同追求。这种跨越时空的共鸣，使得儒家思想在布隆迪得以迅速传播。

Vous pourriez vous demander pourquoi la pensée confucéenne a pu s’implanter dans ce continent africain lointain jusqu’au Burundi. La réponse est en fait très simple: la pensée confucéenne et les valeurs traditionnelles burundaises, l’ubuntu, ont de nombreux points communs.

Que ce soit l'amour et l'harmonie prônés par le confucianisme ou l'accent mis sur l'harmonie entre l'homme et la nature dans l'ubuntu, ils expriment tous deux un désir commun pour une société meilleure. Ce résonance qui transcende l'espace et le temps a permis à la pensée confucéenne de se propager rapidement au Burundi.

那么，儒家思想是如何在布隆迪传播开来的呢？这背后离不开布隆迪当地媒体与机构的积极努力与推动。《布隆迪之魅》与《来杂志》这两大主流媒体，以及布隆迪商业银行，都成了儒家思想在布隆迪传播的重要推手。它们不仅将孔子的智慧名言，如“躬自厚而薄责于人，则远怨矣”与“工欲善其事，必先利其器”等，精心翻译成当地语言，以便布隆迪人民更好地理解和接受，还结合布隆迪独特的社会文化背景，对儒家思想中的名言进行了巧妙的本土化解读与运用。例如，“不积跬步，无以至千里；不积小流，无以成江海”以及“知错能改，善莫大焉”等，都成了指导布隆迪人民生活的智慧箴言。

Alors, comment la pensée confucéenne s'est-elle répandue au Burundi? Il faut reconnaître l'effort actif et la promotion des médias et institutions locales au Burundi. Les deux principaux médias, *Akeza.net* et *IngoMag*, ainsi que la Banque Commerciale du Burundi (Bancobu), ont joué un rôle important dans la diffusion de la pensée confucéenne. Non seulement ils ont traduit soigneusement les sages dictons de Confucius en langues comprises localement, tels que « Exige beaucoup de toi-même et attends peu des autres. Ainsi, beaucoup d'ennuis te seront épargnés » et « L'ouvrier qui veut bien faire son travail doit commencer par aiguiser ses outils » , pour que les Burundais puissent mieux les comprendre et les accepter, mais ils ont également interprété et appliqué de manière astucieuse les dictons confucéens en fonction du contexte social et culturel unique du Burundi. Par exemple, « Ne pas progresser pas à pas, et l'on ne peut pas parcourir mille lieues » et « Qui reconnaît ses erreurs et les corrige est meilleur que celui qui ne fait pas d'erreur » sont devenus des maximes de sagesse qui guident la vie quotidienne des Burundais.

在布隆迪，儒家思想与乌班图思想的和谐共舞，构成了一道独特的文化风景线。媒体在每周的不同时间推送不同的孔子名言，以此指导人们的生活。比如，在周初，他们会推送“工欲善其事，必先利其器”，提醒人们要做好工作准备；在周二和周三，他们会推送“躬自厚而薄责于人，则远怨矣”，教导人们要严于律己、宽以待人；而在周五，他们会推送“乐山乐水，智者乐也”，鼓励人们在忙碌的工作之余，也要享受生活的乐趣。

Au Burundi, la cohabitation harmonieuse entre la pensée confucéenne et l'ubuntu crée une scène culturelle unique. Les médias diffusent des citations de Confucius à différents moments de la semaine pour orienter la vie des gens. Par exemple, au début de la semaine, ils diffusent « L'ouvrier qui veut bien faire son travail doit commencer par aiguiser ses outils », pour rappeler aux gens de se préparer bien à leur travail; les mardi et mercredi, ils diffusent « Exige beaucoup de toi-même et attends peu des autres. Ainsi, beaucoup d'ennuis te seront épargnés », pour enseigner aux gens à être stricts avec eux-mêmes et tolérants envers les autres; et le vendredi, ils diffusent « La joie est en tout : il faut savoir l'extraire », pour encourager les gens à profiter des plaisirs de la vie en dehors de leur travail occupé.

这些儒家名言在布隆迪的使用，已经与当地的文化习惯完美融合。它们不仅仅是文字，也是传递智慧和哲理的载体。儒家思想与乌班图思想相互辉映，共同展现了中非文化和谐共存的美丽画卷。这种跨越时空和地域的文化交融，不仅丰富了布隆迪人民的精神世界，也为中布友谊搭建了一座坚实的桥梁。

L'utilisation de ces maximes confucéennes au Burundi est parfaitement intégrée à la culture locale. Ce ne sont pas seulement des mots, mais des porteurs de sagesse et de philosophie. La pensée confucéenne et l'ubuntu s'illuminent mutuellement, créant une toile de la coexistence harmonieuse des cultures sino-africaines. Cette fusion culturelle qui transcende le temps et l'espace ne se borne pas à enrichir l'esprit des Burundais, mais également à établir une passerelle solide pour l'amitié sino-burundaise.

作品编号：2087
姓　　名：班超（Bankuwiha Etienne）
国　　籍：布隆迪
组　　别：征文类国际组
单位名称：南京大学

《诗经》选篇双语诵读

许苎黎同学通过中文诵读、传统调吟诵及法语译作诵读的方式演绎《诗经·国风》中的两篇《桃夭》及《匪风》。其中《桃夭》采用唐调吟诵，《匪风》采用王更生先生的河南吟诵调吟诵。法语版采用许渊冲先生译作。

桃夭
La Fleur De Pecher

桃之夭夭，灼灼其华。
La fleur de pêcher sourit; Son charme nous éblouit.
之子于归，宜其室家。
La jeune fille se marie, Comme une fileur épanouie.
桃之夭夭，有蕡其实。
La fleur de pêcher sourit; Sa douceur nous éblouit.
之子于归，宜其家室。
La jeune fille se marie, Sa douceur évanouie.
桃之夭夭，其叶蓁蓁。
La fleur de pêcher sourit; Sa verdure nous éblouit.
之子于归，宜其家人。
On se marie, jeune homme et fille. Qu’elle est bonne à la famille !

匪风
La Nostalgie

匪风发兮，匪车偈兮。
Le vent chasse en hurlant, la voiture en roulant.
顾瞻周道，中心怛兮。
Voyant derrière la piste, comme mon cœur s’attriste !
匪风飘兮，匪车嘌兮。
Le vent chasse d’arrière, la voiture légère.
顾瞻周道，中心吊兮。

En chemin allongé, mon cœur est désolé.

谁能亨鱼？溉之釜鬵。

Qui sait cuire des poissons ? J'ai chaudière et chaudron.

谁将西归？怀之好音。

Qui va à l'ouest en retour ? Dites aux miens bonjour.

作品编号：2953

姓　　名：许苧黎

国　　籍：中国

组　　别：诵读类国内少年组

单位名称：山东省泗水县尼山孔子博雅学校

双语诵读《氓》

《氓》是一首弃妇自诉婚姻悲剧的长诗，音调铿锵自然，富有真情实感。该诗最初广泛流传于民间，经过无数劳动人民的反复歌唱、不断修改，才形成现在这样完整的诗篇。主人公叙述的悲惨遭遇，反映了当时的社会现实，正如孔子所说："《诗》，可以兴，可以观，可以群，可以怨。"

氓之蚩蚩，抱布贸丝。
匪来贸丝，来即我谋。
送子涉淇，至于顿丘。
匪我愆期，子无良媒。
将子无怒，秋以为期。
Un homme vient souriant , acheter du fil fin.
Il n'est pas marchand mais demande ma main.
Nous passons le ruisseau jusqu'au pied du coteau.
Je ne veux nul délai, il faut nous arranger.
Si l'entremetteur vient, en automne tout va bien.
乘彼垝垣，以望复关。
不见复关，泣涕涟涟。
既见复关，载笑载言。
尔卜尔筮，体无咎言。
以尔车来，以我贿迁。
Je monte sur le mur, l'attendre, le coeur pur.
Quand je le vois pas, mes yeux de pleurs ondoient.
Enfin quand je le vois, je ris à haute voix.
La tortue consultée, on sait la destinée.
Il est venu avec son chariot, et m'a menée avec ma dot.
桑之未落，其叶沃若。
于嗟鸠兮，无食桑葚！
于嗟女兮，无与士耽！
士之耽兮，犹可说也。
女之耽兮，不可说也！

Les feuilles du mûrier ne sont guère tombées.
Tourterelle, sois sûre de ne pas manger mûre.
Que la femme à loisir ne cherche nul plaisir.
L'homme fait ce qu'il veut et jouit de ce qu'il peut.
Mais voulant le chercher, la femme est reprochée.

桑之落矣，其黄而陨。
自我徂尔，三岁食贫。
淇水汤汤，渐车帷裳。
女也不爽，士贰其行。
士也罔极，二三其德。

Les feuilles du mûrier, jaunissant vont tomber.
J'ai vécu trois années chez lui en pauvreté.
Je passe le ruisseau ondoyant de nouveau.
Mon homme est inconstant, son coeur toujours changeant.
Puisqu'il veut me chasser, il me faut retourner.

三岁为妇，靡室劳矣。
夙兴夜寐，靡有朝矣。
言既遂矣，至于暴矣。
兄弟不知，咥其笑矣。
静言思之，躬自悼矣。

Sa femme durant trois années, j'ai toujours travaillé.
Couchée tard, levée tôt, j'avais peu de repos.
J'ai fait ce qu'il m'a dit, c'est un violent mari.
Je rentre chez mes frères, quelle mauvaise affaire.
Ils en rient par méprise, tant je suis incomprise.

及尔偕老，老使我怨。
淇则有岸，隰则有泮。
总角之宴，言笑晏晏。
信誓旦旦，不思其反。
反是不思，亦已焉哉！

La vieillesse est à Craindre. Vieille, je n'ai qu'à plaindre.
La rivière a ses bords, vieilli, on n'est plus fort.
Jeune, on jouit de loisir et rit avec plaisir.
Mais que fait-on vieilli ? Il ne fait pas ce qu'il a dit.
A quoi bon repentir ? Vivre est mieux que mourir !

作品编号：4618
姓　　名：姚艳平、严玉洁
国　　籍：中国
组　　别：诵读类国内成人组
单位名称：三峡大学

舞雩咏归 志远达行

在现代社会背景下，中国特色社会主义继承并发扬了孔子的治国理念，为实现国家长治久安和繁荣发展提供了坚实的理论指导和实践支持。

子路、曾皙、冉有、公西华侍坐。子曰："以吾一日长乎尔，毋吾以也。居则曰：'不吾知也。'如或知尔，则何以哉？"

Le Maître dit à Tzeu Lou, à Tseng Si, à Jen Jou et Koungsi Hua, qui étaient assis à ses côtés : «Parlez-moi : franchement, sans considérer que je suis un peu plus âgé que vous. Laissés dans la vie privée, vous vous dites : "Les hommes ne reconnaissent pas mes mérites." Si les hommes les reconnaissaient, que feriez-vous ? »

子路率尔而对曰："千乘之国，摄乎大国之间，加之以师旅，因之以饥馑；由也为之，比及三年，可使有勇，且知方也。"

Tzeu Lou se hâta de répondre : « Supposons qu'une principauté, possédant mille chariots de guerre, soit tenue en servitude entre deux principautés voisines très puissantes, que, de plus, elle soit envahie par une armée nombreuse; qu'ensuite les grains et les légumes viennent à lui manquer, si j'étais chargé de la gouverner, en trois ans, je pourrais inspirer du courage au peuple; et leur faire connaître l'orientation à prendre. »

夫子哂之。

Le Maître sourit.

"求，尔何如？"

« Et toi, K'iou, que ferais-tu ? »

对曰："方六七十，如五六十，求也为之，比及三年，可使足民。如其礼乐，以俟君子。"

Jen Jou répondit : « Si j'avais à gouverner un petit pays de soixante-dix stades, ou de cinquante à soixante, en trois ans, je pourrais mettre le peuple dans l'aisance. Pour ce qui concerne les rites et la musique, j'attendrais la venue d'un homme honorable. »

"赤，尔何如？"

Confucius dit : « Toi, Tch'eu, que ferais- tu ? »

对曰："非曰能之，愿学焉。宗庙之事，如会同，端章甫，愿为小相焉。"

Koungsi Hua répondit : « Je ne dis pas que j'en sois capable, mais je désirerais l'apprendre. Je désirerais, portant la tunique noirâtre et le bonnet noir, remplir l'office de petite aide dans les cérémonies en l'honneur des ancêtres, et, dans les réunions des vassaux. »

"点，尔何如？"

Confucius dit : « Toi, Tien, que ferais-tu ? »

鼓瑟希，铿尔，舍瑟而作，对曰："异乎三子者之撰。"

Tseng Si cesse de jouer de la cithare dont les cordes vibrent encore. Il la dépose, se lève, et répond : « Je ne partage pas les aspirations des trois autres disciples. »

子曰："何伤乎？亦各言其志也！"

Le Maître dit : « Quel mal y a-t-il ? Chacun peut exprimer ses intentions. »

曰："莫春者，春服既成，冠者五六人，童子六七人，浴乎沂，风乎舞雩，咏而归。"

Tseng Si reprit : « À la fin du printemps, quand les vêtements des saisons sont achevés, aller cinq ou six jeunes gens en âge de porter le bonnet viril, avec six ou sept jeunes garçons, me baigner dans la rivière I, respirer l'air frais sur la terrasse des Danses pour la Pluie, puis revenir en chantant des vers, voilà ce que j'aimerais. »

夫子喟然叹曰："吾与点也。"

Le Maître dit en souriant : « J'approuve le sentiment de Tien. »

孔子认为，前三个人的治国方法都没有谈到根本上。他之所以只赞赏曾点的主张，是因为曾点用形象的方法描绘了礼乐之治下的景象，体现了"仁"和"礼"的治国原则，这就谈到了根本点上。

Confucius ne croyait qu'aucune des trois premières méthodes de gouvernement du pays ne traitait des fondamentaux. La raison pour laquelle il n'appréciait que la proposition de Zeng Dian est que ce dernier a utilisé une méthode figurative pour dépeindre la scène sous la règle de l'étiquette et de la musique, incarnant ainsi les principes directeurs de la « bienveillance » et de la « Politesse », ce qui aborde le point fondamental.

孔子的治国理念是"仁政"和"礼治"。他认为，国家的治理应该基于道德和礼节，而不仅仅是法律和权力。他提倡的"仁"，是指以爱人、恻隐之心为核心的人伦道德，强调人与人之间的和谐相处。而"礼"则是维护社会秩序的一种行为规范，包括政治、社会、家庭等各个层面的礼节和仪式。

La philosophie de gouvernance de Confucius est celle d'un « gouvernement bienveillant » et d'une « règle d'étiquette ». Il croyait que la gouvernance de l'État devait être basée sur la moralité et l'étiquette, et pas seulement sur la loi et le pouvoir. La « bienveillance » qu'il prônait se réfère à la morale humaniste, avec l'amour et la compassion, mettant l'accent sur la coexistence harmonieuse entre les individus. Le « Politesse » est un code de conduite pour maintenir l'ordre et l'harmonie sociale, qui englobe l'étiquette et les rituels à tous les niveaux, tels que la politique, la société et la famille.

中国特色社会主义强调以人民为中心，这与孔子提倡的"仁"的理念相符。在现代社会治理中，这体现为关注人民的需求，保障人民权益，促进人的全面发展，以及推动全体人民共同富裕。

Le socialisme à la chinoise met l'accent sur l'être humain, ce qui est conforme au concept de « bienveillance » prôné par Confucius. Dans la gouvernance sociale moderne, cela se traduit par une attention particulière aux besoins de la population, la protection des droits et des intérêts du peuple, la promotion du développement global des individus, et la recherche de la prospérité commune pour tous.

在现代社会中，孔子所强调的“礼”在法治中找到了体现。全面依法治国是中国特色社会主义的基本战略之一，通过构建社会主义法治体系，确保国家治理的规范性和公正性。

Dans le contexte de la société moderne, l'accent mis par Confucius sur la « Politesse » se manifeste dans la primauté du droit. Gouverner le pays de manière globale selon la loi est l'une des stratégies fondamentales du socialisme à la chinoise, et la normalisation ainsi que l'équité de la gouvernance nationale sont assurées par la construction d'un système socialiste d'État de droit.

在现代社会背景下，中国特色社会主义治理继承并发扬了孔子的治国理念，为实现国家长治久安和繁荣发展提供了坚实的理论指导和实践支持。

Dans le contexte de la société moderne, la gouvernance socialiste aux caractéristiques chinoises hérite et perpétue le concept de gouvernance de Confucius, et fournit une orientation théorique solide et un soutien pratique pour la stabilité et la prospéritéé à long terme du pays.

作品编号：4339
姓　　名：王雅琦
国　　籍：中国
组　　别：诵读类国内成人组
单位名称：山东大学

穿越千年，致敬儒家先贤

本作品聚焦儒家经典代表人物，追寻他们的人生轨迹，走进他们的精神世界，与有趣的灵魂相互探讨，一起领略从古至今的日异月殊！

领队：同学们，今天我们面前的雕塑是圣人孔子。

Chers étudiants, aujourd'hui, la statue que nous voyons est celle de Confucius.

他是中国古代伟大的思想家、教育家、政治家，儒家学派创始人。

Il était un grand penseur, éducateur, homme d'État et fondateur du confucianisme dans la Chine antique.

领队：孔夫子。

Maître Confucius.

孔子：（起身相迎）你们是？

Qui êtes vous ?

领队：我们是来自两千年以后的读书人。

Nous venons de 2023, 2 000 ans plus tard. Et nous savons lire et écrire.

孔子：两千年以后？有朋自远方来，不亦乐乎？

Deux mille ans plus tard ? Il y a des amis qui viennent de loin chez toi, n'est-ce pas un délice ?

徒弟 1：请问两千年以后的世界是什么样的？

À quoi ressemblera le monde 2 000 ans plus tard ?

学生 1：那是一个人人都可以读书的时代。每个人都拥有受教育的权利，无论男女。老师会根据学习的人的不同志趣、资质来进行不同的教育。

C'est une époque où tout le monde peut apprendre à lire et à écrire. Tout le monde a droit à l'éducation, hommes et femmes. L'enseignant donnera une direction différente en fonction des différentes idées et aptitudes de ceux qui étudient.

徒弟 1：这便是"有教无类、因材施教"啊！

C'est un enseignement sans distinction pour tout le monde, tout en respectant le principe d'individualisation et de différentiation.

徒弟 2：那你们这个时代的人是如何学习的呢？

Eh bien, comment les gens de votre temps apprennent-ils ?

学生 2：我们这个时代的人博览群书，精益求精。

Les gens de notre époque lisent des livres de toutes sortes et s'améliorent constamment.

见贤思齐焉，见不贤而内自省也。

Quand tu rencontres un sage, efforce-toi de l'égaler; Quand tu rencontres un homme dépourvu de vertu,fais bien ton examen de conscience.

学生 1：我们爱好读书，常读常新，常思常悟。

Nous aimons lire, nous lisons et nous y pensons.

徒弟 1：温故而知新，可以为师矣。

Qui peut acquérir de nouvelles connaissances en repassant ce qu'on a appris peut devenir professeur.

孔　子：那你们这个时代一定培养出了很多人才。

Vous devez certes avoir beaucoup de talents à votre époque.

君子务本，本立而道生。

Un homme de bien s'applique à l'essentiel du travail. Quand la fondation a été fermement établie , les règles et les vertus y sont nées.

学生 2：我们不只会读书，还会孝敬父母，诚实守信，尊敬他人。

Non seulement nous faisons nos études assidûment, mais aussi nous sommes pieux et soumis à nos parents, honnêtes et dignes de confiance, et nous avons du respct pour les autres.

徒弟 2：这便是：弟子入则孝，出则悌，谨而信，泛爱众，而亲仁。

Le jeune homme doit se conduire respectueusement, chez lui envers ses parents, en société envers ses aînés. Il doit être précautionneux et de bonne foi, fraterniser avec les masses populaires, ne vivre dans l'intimité qu'avec les hommes vertueux.

孔　子：那你们的国家一定是繁荣而昌盛的。

Votre pays doit être prospère et puissant. C'est évident...

学生 1：是的，"道千乘之国……"

Oui. « Pour diriger un pays de mille chars de combat... »

儒家思想博大精深，影响深远，"修身齐家治国平天下"应该被我们后人传承下去。

Le confucianisme est vaste et profond, et son influence est d'une grande portée, « la culture de soi, la bonne gestion familiale, la gouvernance successive du pays et du monde » devraient être transmises par nos descendants de générations en générations...

作品编号：4040

姓　　名：张悦　等

国　　籍：中国

组　　别：诵读类国内成人组

单位名称：山东航空学院

中　德　篇

青矜之志，履践致远

本作品取自《论语》“学而”篇，阐释了儒家思想中为人处世的哲学，强调了君子应有的自律、节俭、勤奋、谨慎和好学的品质，以及不断追求道德完善和自我提升的重要性。

第一部分：君子食无求饱

甲：太好吃了，我已经吃饱了，但我想吃更多。

A: So lecker! Ich bin schon satt, aber ich möchte mehr essen.

乙：仅此足矣。

B: So viel reicht es schon!

孔子：我们应该适量饮食，过节俭的生活。这样才能称得上真正的君子。

Konfuzius: Wir sollten in Maßen essen und trinken und versuchen ein enthaltsames Leben zu führen. So kann man als rechtschaffener Mensch bezeichnet werden.

第二部分：居无求安

甲：这个床可真舒服。我现在真的很想拥有它。

A: Das Bett ist so bequem. Ich möchte es jetzt unbedingt haben.

孔子：我们不应该追求奢华的住所，这样才能称得上真正的君子。

Konfuzius: Wir sollten nicht nach einer luxuriösen Residenz streben. So kann man als Gentleman bezeichnet werden.

第三部分：敏于事而慎于言

甲：我的鹅不见了。你知道是谁偷的吗?

A: Meine Gans ist weg. Weißt du, wer sie gestohlen hat?

乙：我不知道，不是我!

B: Keine Ahnung, nicht ich!

丙：快看，两只鹅！也许她偷了你的鹅。

C: Schau mal, zwei Gänse! Vielleicht hat sie deine Gans gestohlen.

丁：不！不！不！不是我！我没偷！它们是我的！

D: Nein! Nein! Nein! Nicht ich! Ich habe es nicht gestohlen! Die sind meine!

乙、丙：我们不相信！

B und C: Wir glauben nicht!

甲：没有证据还是不要乱下结论。谣言会毁掉一个人。

A: Ziehen Sie keine voreiligen Schlusse ohne Beweise. Gerüchte können einen Menschen zerstören!

孔子：做事要谨言慎行，工作要严谨认真。这样才能称得上真正的君子。

Konfuzius: Wir müssen vorsichtig sein in unseren Worten und Taten, und sich in unserer Arbeit gewissenhaft und ernsthaft verhalten. So kann man als Gentleman bezeichnet werden.

子曰："君子食无求饱，居无求安，敏于事而慎于言，就有道而正焉，可谓好学也已。"

Der Meister sprach: „Ein Ehrbarer ist der, der beim Essen nicht nach Sättigung und beim Wohnen nicht nach Bequemlichkeit trachtet, eifrig und flink handelt, aber mit Bedacht redet. Er orientiert sich an jenen, die den rechten Weg gehen. So kann er als jemand gelten, der das Lernen liebt."

作品编号：3732
姓　　名：刘凡晶　等
国　　籍：中国
组　　别：诵读类国内成人组
单位名称：齐鲁工业大学（山东省科学院）

中 日 篇

形神虽散 吾仁存之
——儒学生死观含义及其影响

本文以孔孟有关生死哲学之言论为切入口，介绍儒学积极的生死观，并以儒学核心“仁”为脉络，针对质疑儒教生死抉择的观点解惑。同时参考儒学生死思想为日本带来的深厚影响及其哲学延伸，向日本友人介绍儒学乃至中华民族的生命理念。最后放眼未来，弘扬中华民族热爱生命、不懈奋斗于当下的优良品质。

古往今来，中华民族无时无刻不在对生死这一命题进行求索。古人唏嘘道：“譬如朝露，去日苦多。”昔人渴求长生以成大业却难以得志的忧愤满刻历史长河的悠悠书卷。在这般众人长叹生命易逝的时代，在这因短生之苦而滋生出所谓及时行乐、苟且偷生主义的时代，伟大的儒学思想家孟子以“鱼与熊掌”一喻，猛然敲醒沉浮于贪生幻梦中的众生世人，拨开生死一问上方的浮云。孟子曾云：“生，亦我所欲也；义，亦我所欲也。二者不可得兼，舍生而取义者也。”舍生取义，凛然面对死亡，这便是儒家先人立于人类生死这一终极命题前所给出的答案。

中華民族は古来より、常に死生という問いへの答えを求め続けている。「譬えば朝露の如し、去る日は苦だ多し」人生の短さを、古人は嘆いた。出世のために長生きを望んでおり、多数の場合も思うように行かずじまいだったのである。そのような憂いに満ちた物語も、長い歴史を持つ中国の大地に数え切れないほどあったという。人々が世を儚み、命の脆さと弱さによって人生を虚しく思う時代には、刹那主義や自分の命を中心とするエゴイズムなどの消極的な思想も絶えずに出現した。ひたすら生に執着する夢幻泡影に彷徨う人々を強く覚まし、死生の問いに漂う霞を散らしてくれたのは、正に偉大な儒学思想家—孟子である。彼は「魚」と「クマの掌」を例えに、「もがするなり。も亦我が欲する所なり。ねることをべからずんば、をてて義を取る者なり」と、力強く語ったのである。命を捨て義を取り、堂々と死亡に立ち向かう—それこそ儒学の聖賢が残された、死生という人類に与えられた究極の問題に対する鮮明な解き方である。

如此一来，质疑之声便不绝于耳：相较于舍生取义，一心顽强生存，遍历磨难而永不屈服的品性更加难能可贵。所谓质疑其存在合理性的诸多批判层出不穷。试问古人当真不懂生命可贵，不惜寻死以换取名利吗？实际上，通过深入了解贯穿儒家学说始终，且占据诸多儒学经典内容的核心的“仁”，我们便能大有所悟，上述众多言论也就不攻自破了。

その後、批判の声も絶えずに上がってきた。正義のために死を選ぶより、生きる希望を失わず、世間のあらゆる苦難をなめつくすという根性がもっと大切なのではあるまいか、と。つまり、儒学の死生観が存在する合理性はほぼないと疑われている。ところが、先人たちは果たしてそのとおりに、命を惜しまず、世間の名誉だけを勝ち得るのだろうか。実際のところ、儒教の教えを貫き通し、多くの儒教経典に宿っている「仁」という理念を深く掘り下げることで、つまりこの一文字を捉えれば、批判の意見が自然になくなり、儒学が死を選んだ理由に対しても納得できるだろう。

仁之道，亦是人之道。所谓“仁”，拆字而看便是“两人”，即自我与他人。对于生死抉择前的“仁”，圣贤孔子如此阐述道：“志士仁人，无求生以害仁，有杀身以成仁。”由此可见孔子高度重视仁爱之道。教唆他人以轻生换取名誉，便是害仁，便是与仁之道背向而行。孔子所倡导的，并非以生命为代价来攫取所谓名利的“仁”，而是珍惜生命、热忱追求生命的每分每刻、渴求生命真谛的“仁”。“仁”中所蕴含的自我与他人，无不体现出“自爱”，即修身养性，关爱自我；“尊他”，即尊重他人、爱人如己的品质。此等仁道，亦寄宿于中华民族和平年代友待善邦、国难当头以命阻敌的家国情怀之中。

仁の道、即ち人たる道である。「子曰わく、は、生を求めてて仁を害すること無し。身を殺して以て仁を成すこと有り」から、仁という一文字を分けて見れば「二人」であり、自分と他人を象徴している。こうして見ると、孔子の思想に仁愛の心が大いに重んじられる。人々に命の代わりにひたすら名誉を追求するのを唱えることは仁の精神を害し、その道とは真逆である。孔子が呼びかけているのは、生命を元本に行われた取り引きではなく、命の重さを惜しみ、生きていることを絶えずに実感することで、命の真諦をつかむ「仁の道」である。その一文字に含まれている「自身」と「他人」の理念も、自分のからだと精神を大切にする「自愛」と自分を愛するような他人への「尊重」を表している。先まで述べていた「仁の道」も当然、平和の時代に他国の友好関係を深め、国難に臨む時に死の覚悟で祖国を守るという中華民族の愛国心に宿っている。

如此柔性而又坚韧的儒学生死观生生不息、万代流转。在中华民族如岳飞、屈原等仁人志士辈出之时，儒家的生死哲学亦漂洋过海，传入邻国日本。日本《古事记》记载道，《论语》于五世纪前后经由百济古国学者王仁之手传入日本。随后江户时代朱子学广泛传播，作为幕府文治天下的精神支柱而存续；身负拼杀宿命的武士阶级，亦从儒学生死观中受教。正如《叶隐》一书所言：“武士之道，洞彻生死者也。”儒学生死观影响日本民族之深，由此便可窥见一斑。

このような柔らかみのあるたくましい死生観は生々流転し、万代に受け継がれて行く。中華民族の中で、武将のや政治家などの英霊が終わりなく出てくるうちに、儒学における死生の哲学も海を越え、隣国である日本に輸入された。『古事記』によると、『論語』は五世紀前後に百済から日本に渡来してきたことによって伝来されたという。後の江戸時代に朱子学が隆盛し、『論語』にある死生の教えも幕府が教化で世を治める精神の柱として保たれた。生まれながら殺し合いの宿命を背負う侍たちも、その死生の教養に教わっている。「武士道と云ふは死ぬ事と見付けたり」と、『葉隠』に書かれているこの一説から、日本民族にもたらした大きな影響が見られる。

在和平与发展为时代主题的当下，我们自不必效仿古人走向极端。孔夫子“未知生，焉知死”的教诲警醒世人需活好当下每分每刻。但唯有怀抱孟子为后人所留下的这份向死而生的觉悟，人性才能焕发光辉。儒家生死观以仁彰显中华民族之血性，笔者为此深感自豪。

私達は現在、「平和と発展」の時代に暮らしており、先人のように極端な道を歩むに及ばない。「未だ生を知らず、焉んぞ死を知らん」という言葉のように、孔子は今をしっかり生きようと人々に忠告しており、その上で、孟子が授けてくれた決死の覚悟で断固と進めてはじめて、人間性の輝きが現れてくる。儒学の死生観は「仁」という教えを以って、中華民族の血脈に流れている決意と情熱を示すことを、誇らしく思う。

作品编号：1721
姓　　名：陈杰
国　　籍：中国
组　　别：征文类国内成人组
单位名称：山西大学外国语学院

儒家的人生态度

“知者不惑，仁者不忧，勇者不惧”是孔子对君子应有三德的阐述，这三者相辅相成，共同构成了君子的品格和境界。我们面对人生中各色各样的经历，应该抱着什么样的人生态度去面对？孔子文化历经千年检验，于现在依旧具有重要的启示意义。智者通过不断学习和积累知识，形成自己独特的人生观和价值观；仁者通过宽容待人和真诚待己，保持良好的心理和精神状态；勇者则通过坚守道义和勇敢面对挑战，展现了无畏无惧的精神风貌。我们要在自己的人生道路上不断地磨炼自己，使自己成为一个拥有智慧、道德、勇气的君子，活出自己的价值。

当今时代，在各种困难、挑战、诱惑的影响下，一个人想要保持初心并向着理想坚持奋斗并不是一件容易的事情。我们不仅面临着体力、智力层面的挑战，更面临着精神层面的挑战。那么，我们应该成为什么样的人？我们如何成为那样的人？上述问题，孔子早在两千多年前就给出了答案：“知者不惑，仁者不忧，勇者不惧。”

今の時代においては、様々な難事、挑戦や誘惑などがあり、初心を忘れず理想に向かって努力するのは容易なことではない。私たちは体力と知力の面だけでなく、精神の面においても挑戦に直面している。では、私たちはどんな人になるべきであろうか。そして、どのようにしてそのような人になれるのか。二千年以上も前に、孔子がその答えを教えてくださった。それは「知者は惑わず、仁者は憂えず、勇者は懼れず」ということである。

孔老夫子的答案非常明确：我们只要不断地求取知识，就不会感到困惑；只要真诚地对待他人，就不会感到忧愁；只要勇敢地迈出前行的脚步，就不会畏惧挑战。

孔子の答えははっきりしている。知識を求め続ければ、疑問を感じることはない。正直に付き合えば、悲しむことはない。勇敢に実行すれば、挑戦を恐れることもない。

“知者不惑”对应儒家思想中的“智”，代表一种聪慧、理性、求问的人生态度。“书山有路勤为径，学海无涯苦作舟。”当我们找不到问题的答案的时候，应该努力去尝试、去思考、去积累、去学习。北宋时期著名诗人苏轼，虽三次被贬，但他不颓废、不怨天尤人。在贬谪期间，他一心为百姓的幸福生活而努力，同时创作出了许多千古佳作。从逆境中汲取力量，从容理性地面对困境，正是“才子苏轼”的故事。

「知者不惑」(知者は惑わず）というのは儒家思想の「智」を指しており、それは頭がよく、理性的で、真理を尋ねる人生の態度である。漢詩の中には「書山有路勤為径、学海無涯苦作舟」という名句がよく知られている。回答が見つからない際、試したり、考えたり、積み重ねたり、勉強したりするようにしてください。北宋時期の有名な詩人蘇軾は、三度も左遷されたが、退廃を感じなく、文句も言わない。その期間中、一心不乱に民衆の幸せな生活のために努力し続けると同時に、千古の名言を多く作り出していた。逆境の中から力を吸い取り、悠然かつ冷静に困難に向き合うというのは、まさに「才子蘇軾」という物語である。

“仁者不忧”是指儒家思想中的“仁”，是一种善良、无私、友爱的人生态度。品德高尚的人应该如同宋代的范仲淹那般，“先天下之忧而忧，后天下之乐而乐”；如同南宋诗人陆游那样，“位卑未敢忘忧国，事定犹须待阖棺”；更如同唐朝诗人杜甫那样，“安得广厦千万间，大庇天下寒士俱欢颜”。当我们跳出自私自利的牢笼时，许多的烦恼忧愁也就随之消散了。

「仁者不憂」(仁者は憂えず）というのは儒家思想の中の「仁」であり、善良、無私、友愛の人生の態度である。このような品格を持っている人は、宋の範仲淹のように「先天下之憂而憂、后天下之楽而楽」、南宋の詩人陸游のように「位卑不敢忘憂国、事定犹须待阖棺」、さらに唐の詩人の杜甫のように「安得広厦千万間、大庇天下寒士俱歓顔」。このように、我々は利己的な檻から抜け出せば、様々な悩みや憂さはすっかり取り除かれる。

“勇者不惧”对应儒家思想中的“勇”，代表一种勇敢、践行的人生态度。这里的“勇”有两层含义。一是勇气，指我们面对困难时，要不惧怕、不退缩。三国时期，诸葛亮草船借箭，迎难而上，是计谋，更是胆识。二是勇于，指我们要敢于前行。正所谓“万事开头难”，很多人一生碌碌无为，正是缺少敢于开始的勇气。

「勇者不懼」(勇者は懼れず）という言葉は儒家思想の「勇」と対応し、勇気と実行の人生態度を表している。ここで、「勇」には二つの意味がある。一つ目は勇気であり、困難に直面する時は、恐れず縮退しないこと。三国時代、諸葛亮が草船で矢を拝借することは、知恵というより、むしろ勇気があると言えよう。二つ目は勇敢であり、大胆に前進すること。「初めが大事だ」という諺の通り、多くの人が何の為すところなく一生を送っているのは、仕事を始める勇気が足りないからであろう。

“知者不惑，仁者不忧，勇者不惧”是孔子对理想人生态度的刻画，更是他对于人生内涵的理解与感悟。成长的道路漫长而曲折，我们只有明确目标、坚定梦想、鼓足勇气，才能成为孔子所言的“知者、仁者、勇者”。

「知者不惑、仁者不憂、勇者不懼」というのは、孔子による理想的な人生態度への描写であり、人生の内包への理解と悟りでもある。成長とは延々と続くいばらの道であり、我々は目標を立て、夢を堅持し、勇気を出してこそ、孔子のおっしゃった「知者、仁者、勇者」のような人になることができるのである。

儒家思想从春秋战国时期到现在，历经数千年的演变与发展，对我国社会发展、治国理政和为人处世等方面都具有重要的指导意义。儒家思想是中华文明不可或缺的文化瑰宝，也在世界舞台上自信地展示着其独有的文化魅力。

儒家思想は春秋戦国時代から現在まで、数千年にわたる成り行きと発展を経て、我が国の社会発展、国政運営および個人の処世などの面においては指導的な役割を果たしている。儒家思想は中華文明に欠かせない文化の珠玉であり、自信をもって世界の舞台に独特な文化魅力を展示している。

作品编号：4025
姓　　名：刘小莉、刘小菡
国　　籍：中国
组　　别：征文类国内成人组
单位名称：山东青年政治学院

弘扬儒家思想，感悟传统文化

儒家思想是中华文明的瑰宝，其深刻的内涵在海外得到了广泛传播。通过解读儒家经典，我们更好地理解了中华文化的丰富内涵。儒家文化在海外的影响不仅丰富了国际社会的文明交流，也为我们提供了在当代社会中践行中华优秀传统文化的有益借鉴。

儒家思想是中国古代传统文化的重要组成部分，其内涵深厚，贯穿于中华文明的方方面面。通过解读中华经典，我们能够更加深刻地理解儒家思想的精髓，并且使其在海外发挥积极的影响。同时，对中华优秀传统文化的践行与感悟也是我们对这一宝贵遗产的珍视和传承。

儒家思想は中国古代の伝統文化の重要な構成部分であり、その内包は深く、中華文明の各方面を貫いている。中華経典を解読することで、儒家思想の真髄をより深く理解し、海外で積極的な影響を発揮することができる。同時に、中華の優れた伝統文化の実践と悟りは私たちがこの貴重な遺産を大切にし、伝承することでもある。

儒家思想的内涵可以追溯到《论语》《大学》等经典著作。其中，孔子被尊奉为儒家学派的创立者，他强调的“仁”“义”“礼”“智”等观念构成了儒家核心价值观的基石。仁者爱人，义者正己，礼者治身，智者治国。这一系列理念在儒家经典中得以深刻体现，构筑起一幅关于人伦道义的宏伟画卷。

儒家思想の内包は『論語』、『大学』などの古典著作にさかのぼることができる。その中で、孔子は儒家学派の創立者として尊崇され、彼が強調した「仁」、「義」、「礼」、「智」などの観念は儒家の核心的価値観の礎を構成した。仁者は人を愛し、義者は己を正し、礼者は身を治め、智者は国を治める。この一連の理念は儒家の経典の中で深く体現され、人倫道義に関する壮大な絵巻を構築した。

首先，仁者爱人是儒家思想的基石之一。在《论语》中，孔子曰：“己所不欲，勿施于人。”这句话直截了当地表达了仁爱之道。儒家认为，一个人应该以慈悲之心对待他人，设身处地地为他人着想。这种仁爱的理念贯穿于儒家文化的方方面面，塑造了中华民族勤劳、宽容、友善的传统形象。

まず、「仁者爱人」（仁者は人を愛し）は儒家思想の礎の一つである。『論語』の中で、孔子が言われた、「己の欲せざるところは、人に施すなかれ」という言葉は、ずばり仁愛の道を表している。儒家は、一人は慈悲の心で他人に接し、自分の身になって他人のために考えるべきだと考えている。このような仁愛の理念は儒家文化の各方面を貫き、中華民族の勤勉、寛容、友好の伝統的なイメージを形作った。

其次，义者正己是儒家思想的又一支柱。儒家注重个体的道德修养，要求每个人在面对困境时能够坚守正义，不为私利而屈从于邪恶。《大学》中提到“修身齐家治国平天下”，正己被赋予了更加广泛的社会责任。这种正义的理念，为社会奠定了稳固的伦理基础，推动了社会的和谐发展。

次に、「義者正己」（義者は己を正し）は儒家思想のもう一つの柱である。儒家は個人の道徳修養を重視し、苦境に直面した時に正義を守り、私利のために悪に屈しないことを求めた。『大学』では、「身を修めて国を治めて天下を平定する」と述べ、正己はより広範な社会的責任を与えられた。この正義の理念は、社会のために確固とした倫理的基礎を築き、社会の調和のとれた発展を推進した。

再者，礼者治身是儒家思想的独特之处。儒家强调个体的行为应该符合礼法之道，从而维护社会的稳定和秩序。孔子在《论语》中指出：“有朋自远方来，不亦乐乎？人不知而不愠，不亦君子乎？”这种注重礼仪的观念，不仅体现了对人际关系的重视，也为社会交往提供了一种规范。

また、「礼者治身」（礼者が身を治める）は儒家思想の独特な点である。儒家は個人の行為が礼法の道に合致し、それによって社会の安定と秩序を守るべきだと強調した。孔子は『論語』の中で、「朋ありて遠方から来て、亦楽乎ではないか？人は知らずして正しからず、亦君子ではないか？」という礼儀を重視する観念は、人間関係に対する重視を体現しているだけでなく、社会交流にも規範を提供している。

最后，智者治国是儒家思想的集大成者。儒家强调统治者应该具备高度的智慧和卓越的领导能力，以便有效地治理国家。《大学》中提到格物致知、诚意正心、修身齐家治国平天下。这种强调学识和道德修养的理念，对于培养一代又一代的领导者具有深远的影响。

最後に、「智者治国」（賢者による国家統治）は儒家思想の集大成者である。儒家は統治者が国家を効果的に統治するために高度な知恵と卓越した指導力を備えなければならないと強調した。『大学』では、「格物致知、誠意正心、修身斉家治国平天下」という学識と道徳修養を強調する理念は、一代また一代の指導者の育成に深い影響を与えている。

通过对儒家经典的解读，我们更加深刻地理解了中华文明的独特之处。儒家思想在中国几千年的历史中一直发挥着深远的影响，但其影响不仅仅局限于中国境内。随着全球化的推进，儒家思想逐渐渗透到海外，为世界文明的交流与融合提供了有益的借鉴。

儒家の経典の解読を通じて、私たちは中華文明の独特な点をより深く理解した。儒家思想は中国の数千年の歴史の中でずっと深遠な影響を発揮しているが、その影響は中国国内に限らない。グローバル化の推進に伴い、儒家思想は次第に海外に浸透し、世界文明の交流と融合に有益な参考を提供した。

在海外，儒家文化逐渐成为中华优秀传统文化的重要代表。许多国家的学者和智者深入研究儒家经典，试图从中汲取智慧，为各自国家的社会发展提供借鉴。儒家思想的关注人伦道义、注重和谐共处的理念，为国际社会的发展提供了积极的参考。

海外では儒家文化が中華の優れた伝統文化の重要な代表になりつつある。多くの国の学者や知者は儒家の経典を深く研究し、そこから知恵をくみ取り、それぞれの国の社会発展のために参考を提供しようとしている。儒家思想の人倫道義に関心を持ち、調和共存を重視する理念は、国際社会の発展に積極的な参考を提供した。

儒家文化在海外的影响不仅体现在学术领域，还表现在文化交流和人际关系上。许多国家的人们学习儒家经典，认同其中的理念，并将其融入自己的生活中。儒家思想所倡导的仁爱、正义、礼仪等观念，为人际交往提供了一种积极的指导原则，促进了不同文化之间的理解与尊重。

儒家文化は海外での影響が学術分野だけでなく、文化交流や人間関係にも表れている。多くの国の人々は儒教の経典を学ぶことで、その理念を認め、それを自分の生活に溶け込んでいる。儒家思想が提唱した仁愛・正義・礼儀などの観念は、人間関係に積極的な指導原則を提供し、異なる文化間の理解と尊重を促進した。

对于中华优秀传统文化的践行与感悟，我们应该深刻领会儒家思想中的智慧，并在实际生活中融入其中。在现代社会，儒家思想所强调的道德修养、社会责任等观念仍然具有现实意义。通过学习儒家经典，我们可以汲取古代智慧，指导自己的行为，培养良好的品德和道德风范。

中華の優れた伝統文化の実践と悟りに対して、私たちは儒家思想の知恵を深く理解し、実際の生活の中で溶け込まなければならない。現代社会では、儒家思想が強調する道徳修養、社会的責任などの観念は依然として現実的な意義を持っている。儒家の経典を学ぶことによって、私たちは古代の知恵をくみ取り、自分の行為を指導し、良好な品格と道徳風格を育成することができる。

在个人层面，儒家思想教导我们要修身齐家治国平天下。通过不断提升自己的学识和道德修养，我们能够更好地为社会做出贡献。在家庭中，我们应该尊重父母，关心亲人，建立和谐的家庭关系。在社会中，我们应该履行公民责任，为社会的发展贡献自己的力量。

個人的なレベルでは、儒家思想は私たちに斉家治国平天下を修めるように教えてくれた。自分の学識と道徳修養を絶えず向上させることによって、私たちはよりよく社会に貢献することができます。家庭の中で、私たちは両親を尊重し、家族に関心を持ち、調和のとれた家庭関係を築くべきだ。社会の中で、私たちは公民の責任を履行し、社会の発展に自分の力を貢献しなければならない。

总体而言，儒家思想是中华文明的瑰宝，其深刻的内涵和积极的影响在海外得到了广泛传播。通过解读儒家经典，我们更好地理解了中华文化的丰富内涵。儒家文化在海外的影响不仅丰富了国际社会的文明交流，也为我们提供了在当代社会中践行中华优秀传统文化的有益借鉴。在传承中华优秀传统文化的过程中，我们要不断弘扬儒家思想的核心价值观，让其在当代社会中焕发新的光彩。

全体的に言えば、儒家思想は中華文明の至宝であり、その深い内包と積極的な影響は海外で広く伝播されている。儒家の経典を解読することによって、私たちは中華文化の豊富な内包をよりよく理解した。海外における儒家文化の影響は国際社会の文明交流を豊かにするだけでなく、現代社会における中華の優れた伝統文化の実践のための有益な参考を提供してくれた。中華の優れた伝統文化を伝承する過程で、儒家思想の核心的価値観を絶えず発揚し、現代社会の中で新たな輝きを放つようにしなければならない。

作品编号：1023
姓　　名：周子佳
国　　籍：中国
组　　别：征文类国内成人组
单位名称：临沂大学

经典越千年，立身天地间

中国历史上下五千年，文化博大精深、源远流长。其中《论语》是宝贵的文化遗产之一，多次研读其中关于学习的篇幅让我感触颇深。

中国历史上下五千年，文化博大精深、源远流长。在这传承千年的中华文化中，儒学是中华民族传统文化的宝贵文化遗产，《论语》是儒家经典之一。孔子在《论语》中多次强调了学习的必要性，并提出了一系列关于学习的理念，这些思想对于我们当代大学生同样具有启发意义。

五千年くらいの歴史を持つ中国には、深遠で広範な文化がある。こうした数千年にわたり受け継がれてきた中華文化の中では、儒教は中華民族の伝統文化を伝える貴重な文化遺産であり、『論語』は経典の一つである。孔子は『論語』の中で何度も学習の必要性を強調し、学習に関する一連の理念を提唱していた。これらの思想は現代の大学生にとっても啓発的な意義を持っている。

子曰："学而时习之，不亦说乎？有朋自远方来，不亦乐乎？人不知而不愠，不亦君子乎？"这句话强调了持续不断地学习和反复练习以及与他人交流学习的重要性，以及要保持谦逊的态度。这样的学习道理不仅有助于提高我们的学习效果，还有利于发展健康的人际关系和积极的人生态度。

子曰く、「学びて時に之を習ふ、亦説ばしからずや。朋有り遠方より来る、亦楽しからずや。人知らずして慍らず、亦君子ならずや」という言葉は、謙虚さを保ちつつも、継続的な学習と反復練習、そして他者とのコミュニケーションの重要性を強調している。このような学習観は、私たちの学習効果を高めるだけでなく、健全な人間関係や人生に対する前向きな態度の育成にも役立つ。

子曰："笃信好学，守死善道。"作为新时代的大学生，我们要怀有真诚的信念，并持续不断地追求知识和智慧。同时，也要坚守良好的人生道德，走在一条正义、真善美的道路上。这样的学习不仅有助于个人的成长和成功，还能为社会的进步和和谐做出贡献。

子曰く、「篤く信じて学を好み、死を守りて道を善くす」新時代の大学生として、私たちは誠実な信念を持ち、知識と知恵を追求し続けなければならない。同時に、人生におけるモラルを守り、正義的・真実的・善的・美的な道を歩むべきである。このような学習は、個人の成長と成功に役立つだけでなく、社会の進歩と調和にも貢献できる。

子曰："十室之邑，必有忠信如丘者焉，不如丘之好学也。"即使在一个小城镇中，也必然会有像丘那样忠诚可靠的好学之人。作为当代大学生，我们需要对知识和学习怀有真诚的信念，并以诚信的态度对待学业和研究。只有保持永不满足的好学之心，不断追求知识和智慧，才能在人生道路上不断进步、不断超越。

子日く、「十室の邑、必ず忠信丘の如き者有らん。丘の学を好むに如かさるなり」小さな町にも、丘のような忠実で信頼できて学習好きの人がいるに違いない。現代の大学生である私たちは、知識と学習に対する真摯な信念を持ち、誠実に勉学や研究に取り組む必要がある。また、飽くなき向学心を持ち、常に知識と知恵を追い求め、人生の道を進歩し、超えていくことができる。

子曰："吾尝终日不食，终夜不寝，以思，无益，不如学也。"即使终日不食、终夜不寝，所从事的思考也没有学习的效果好，说明了单纯思考而不实际学习的局限性，以及学习的重要性。在学习的道路上，我们不仅需要进行深刻的思考，也需要勤奋努力，刻苦钻研，真实地去获取知识，这样才能不断地提升自己的学识水平和综合素养。

子曰く、「吾嘗て終日食らはず、終夜寝ず、以て思ふ。益無し。学ぶに如かさるなり」一日中食べなくても、寝なくても、考えることは学ぶことに劣り、学ぶことの重要性と単純に思考して実際に学習しない限界を説明した。学習の道では、深く考えるだけでなく、勤勉に努力し、勉学に励み、真摯に知識を身につけることで、学問や専門リテラシーを絶えず向上させていく必要がある。

学习儒家经典，读儒家经典之《论语》，不断提升自己的学识和品德修养，培养仁爱之心，树立正确的人生观和价值观，从个人做起，从小事做起，为中华民族的复兴伟业做出自己的贡献。

私たちは儒教の知識を学び、『論語』を読み、自分の知識と道徳心を絶えず向上させ、仁と愛の心を育み、正しい人生観と価値観を立つ。個人から始め、小さなことから始め、中華民族の偉大な復興を実現するために貢献することができるだろう。

作品编号：3499
姓　　名：李丽婷
国　　籍：中国
组　　别：征文类国内成人组
单位名称：山东省青岛市莱西市山东文化产业职业学院

浅析儒家思想的内涵与传播

儒家思想跨越了时空限制，承载了华夏文明的精髓，被誉为东方文化的瑰宝，现已成为一种世界性的哲学体系。随着世界文化向着多元化深入发展，我国也在积极探索儒家思想传播发展的新出路，使儒家思想的真理性为世界各民族所接受，从而为构建和谐世界做出积极贡献。

中华文化源远流长，贯穿于中华民族的发展过程之中，其中儒家思想跨越了时空的限制，承载了华夏文明的精髓，以其深厚的内涵和博大的胸怀，影响了无数炎黄子孙，被誉为东方文化的瑰宝。

中華文化は歴史が長く、中華民族の発展過程の中を貫いており、その中で儒家思想は時空の制限を越え、華夏文明の精髄を担い、その深い内包と博大な心で、無数の炎黄子孫に影響を与え、東方文化の至宝と誉められている。

儒家思想是一种“德性”文化，强调发展人的道德品行，其核心可以概括为“仁、义、礼、智、信”五个字，构成了一个完整而深刻的伦理道德体系，涵盖了个人的道德、家庭关系、朋友关系、社会责任等多个方面，形成了一系列道德原则、行为准则和发展规则。“仁、义、礼、智、信”被称为儒家“五常”，这“五常”贯穿于中华伦理的发展中，成为中国价值体系中最核心的因素。其中，“仁”是儒家思想的核心，也是儒家伦理道德的基本原则；“义”是指做人的原则和道理，强调了公正、公平、合理；“礼”是指礼仪、规矩和秩序，是人际关系的调节器；“智”是指智慧和知识，强调了学习和思考的重要性；“信”是指诚信和信任，强调了人格和道德的重要性。儒家“五常”相互联系、相互依存。

儒家思想は「德性」文化であり、人の道徳品行を発展させることを強調する。その核心は「仁・義・礼・智・信」の5つの字に概括でき、完全で深い倫理道徳体系を構成し、個人の道徳、家庭関係、友人関係、社会責任などの多方面をカバーし、一連の道徳原則、行為準則と発展規則を形成している。「仁・義・礼・智・信」は儒家の「五常」と呼ばれ、この「五常」は中華倫理の発展に貫かれ、中国の価値体系の中の最も核心的な要素となっている。その中で「仁］は儒家思想の核心であり、儒家倫理道徳の基本原則でもある。「義」は人間としての原則と道理を指し、公正、公平、合理を強調する。「礼」は礼儀、規則、秩序を指し、人間関係の調節器である。「智」は知恵と知識を指し、学習と思考の重要性を強調する。「信」とは誠実さと信頼を指し、人格と道徳の重要性を強調する。儒家の「五常」の間に相互につながり、相互に依存している。

总的来说，儒家思想凝聚了我国古代优秀思想家的智慧，备受中国历代统治者的推崇，形成了许多至今仍在发挥价值的传统文化，例如，“中而不同”“允执其中”“克己慎独”“仁者爱人”等传统文化为我国社会的发展提供了源源不断的精神动力，是我国现代化建设重要的文化支撑。同时，儒家思想经过几千年的发展和演变，已经成为一种世界性的哲学体系，对世界的政治、伦理、道德、文化等领域也产生了深远影响。

総じて言えば、儒家思想は我が国の古代の優れた思想家の知恵を凝集し、中国の歴代統治者に推賞され、今でも有益な価値を発揮している多くの伝統文化を形成している。例えば、「中で異なっている」「その中に従う」「克己的で慎重」「仁者愛人」などの伝統文化は我が国の社会の発展に絶えず精神的原動力を提供して我が国の現代化建設の重要な文化の支えである。同時に儒家思想は数千年の発展と進化を経て、それはすでに世界的な哲学体系になり、世界の政治、倫理、道徳、文化などの分野にも深い影響を与えている。

随着信息时代的来临，世界文化向着多元化深入发展，我国也在积极探索儒家思想传播发展的新出路。自2004年开始，孔子学院便在全球范围内设立，秉承孔子“和为贵”“和而不同”的理念，以建设一个持久和平、共同繁荣的和谐世界为宗旨，致力于加强中国与外国教育文化交流合作，成为世界认识中国的一个重要平台。在未来我们也要持续扎实推进儒家思想对外传播战略，使以儒家思想为核心的中国传统文化屹立于世界优秀文化之林，使儒家思想的真理性为世界各民族所接受，从而为构建和谐世界做出积极贡献。

情報時代の到来に伴い、世界文化は多元化に向かって深く発展し、我が国も儒家思想の伝播発展の新たな活路を積極的に模索しており、2004年から孔子学院は世界範囲内に設立され、孔子の「和を貴とする」「和を以って異なる」という理念を受け継ぎ、恒久的で平和で共同で繁栄する調和のとれた世界を建設することを宗旨として、中国と外国の教育文化交流協力の強化に力を入れている。世界が中国を認識する重要なプラットフオームとなっている。今後も儒家思想の対外宣伝を着実に推進し続けなければならない。儒家思想を核心とする中国の伝統文化を世界の優れた文化の森にそびえ立たせ、儒家思想の真理性を世界の各民族に受け入れ、調和のとれた世界を構築しに積極的に貢献する。

作品编号：1608
姓　　名：李聪
国　　籍：中国
组　　别：征文类国内成人组
单位名称：山东化工职业学院

双语诵读《诗经》选篇

《诗经》是中国最古老的诗集，也是儒家文学经典著作，不仅在中国，在东亚汉文化圈亦影响深远。山川异域，风月同天，中日文化交流源远流长。《诗经》传入日本后，丰富了日本的文化表达，成了日本国民表达美好希冀的语言宝藏，已经深深浸润到日本文化之中。本文撷取《诗经》中的经典篇目《桃夭》《关雎》，以中日文对照的方式，请大家一嗅开在扶桑的儒家文化之花的芬芳。

《诗经》是中国最古老的诗集。该书收录了公元前 11 世纪至公元前 6 世纪约 600 年间的 305 首诗歌，据说是孔子整理归纳的，分为风、雅、颂三个部分。《诗经》的格律基本是四字一句，被称为“四言诗”。四字一句多采用 2 字 +2 字的形式。

『詩経』とは中国最古の詩集です。BC11 世紀から BC6 世紀まで、約 600 年間の詩が 305 編を集められています。孔子が整理してまとめたと言われ、風・雅・頌の三つに分かれています。詩経のリズムは基本的に 4 文字 1 句で「四言詩」と呼ばれています。4 文字の中身は 2 文字 +2 文字の構造になっているものが多いです。

桃夭

桃夭

桃之夭夭，灼灼其华。
桃の夭夭たる 灼灼たり其の華
之子于归，宜其室家。
之の子于き帰ぐ 其の室家に宜しからん
桃之夭夭，有蕡其实。
桃の夭夭たる 蕡たる其の実有り
之子于归，宜其家室。
之の子于き帰ぐ 其の家室に宜しからん
桃之夭夭，其叶蓁蓁。
桃の夭夭たる 其の葉蓁蓁たり
之子于归，宜其家人。
之の子于き帰ぐ 其の家人に宜しからん

关雎

関雎

关关雎鸠，在河之洲。
関関たる雎鳩は 河の洲に在り
窈窕淑女，君子好逑。
窈窕たる淑女は 君子の好逑
参差荇菜，左右流之。
参差たる荇菜は 左右に之を流む
窈窕淑女，寤寐求之。
窈窕たる淑女は 寤寐之を求む
求之不得，寤寐思服。
之を求めて得ざれば 寤寐思服す
悠哉悠哉，辗转反侧。
悠なる哉 悠なる哉 輾転反側す
参差荇菜，左右采之。
参差たる荇菜は 左右に之を采る
窈窕淑女，琴瑟友之。
窈窕たる淑女は 琴瑟もて之を友とす
参差荇菜，左右芼之。
参差たる荇菜は 左右に之を芼る
窈窕淑女，钟鼓乐之。
窈窕たる淑女は 鍾鼓もて之を楽しましむ

传承中华优秀传统文化，让世界聆听中国声音。和而不同，美美与共。

中華の優れた伝統文化を伝承し、中国の声を世界に届けよう。和して同ぜず、自他の美をともにする。

作品编号：4534
姓　　名：徐向安、鲍传亮
国　　籍：中国
组　　别：诵读类国内成人组
单位名称：济宁医学院

中葡篇

《论语》：儒家经典之作

本文通过分析《论语》原文原句，介绍了《论语》中的四个重要儒家观点：仁爱、道德、家庭以及教育。最后表达希望海外友人阅读《论语》的期待。

当提到儒家思想，《论语》就不得不被提及。这本儒家经典记录了中国古代思想家孔子及其弟子的言行和教导，其中蕴含了丰富的儒家思想，对于世界多国都具有重要的借鉴意义。

Sempre que se faz uma referência ao confucionismi também tem que ser mencionado *Os Analectos*. Este clássico do confucionismo registra as palavras, ações e ensinamentos do antigo pensador chinês Confúcio e dos seus discípulos. Tem em si mesmo a riqueza do confucionismo e é uma importante referência para muitos países em todo o mundo.

第一，仁爱之道。子曰："不仁者不可以久处约，不可以长处乐。仁者安仁，知者利仁。"意思是：没有仁德的人不能够长久地安于穷困，也不能够长久地处于安乐之中；有仁德的人长期安心于推行慈爱精神，聪明的人认识到仁对他有长远的利益而实行仁。儒家思想的核心价值观之一是仁，即仁爱、仁慈、同情和善意。孔子认为，仁爱是人际关系的基础；通过培养仁爱之心，人们可以建立和谐的社会。以仁为本，以仁爱他人来实现高尚的道德。

Primeiro, o Caminho da caridade. Confúcio afirmou: "Quem não tiver benevolência não conseguirá permanecer, por um longo período, nas condições de pobreza e sofrimento, nem nas condições favoráveis. O homem benevolente sente-se em paz na benevolência; o sábio aproveita os benefícios da benevolência." Um dos valores fundamentais do confucionismo é o "Ren", isto é, benevolência, compaixão e boa vontade. Confúcio acreditava que a benevolência é a base das relações humanas e que, cultivando a benevolência, as pessoas podem construir uma sociedade harmoniosa. Ser benevolente com os outros para alcançar a nobreza moral.

第二，道德品性。"君子周而不比，小人比而不周。"这句话的意思是德行高尚的人以正道广泛交友但不互相勾结，品格卑下的人互相勾结却不顾道义。可见，孔子对于个人的道德水平要求极高。儒家强调个人修养和道德品质的培养。这包括自律、自我反省、谨慎和诚实等。在儒家思想中，有德行的人才能为家庭和社会做出有益的贡献。

Segundo, moral e caráter. Confúcio afirmou: "O cavalheiro associa-se com outras pessoas mas não toma partido; o homem vulgar toma partido mas não se associa com ninguém." Como se vê, Confúcio era extremamente exigente em relação ao nível moral do indivíduo. O confucionismo enfatiza o cultivo pessoal e o cultivo de qualidades morais. Isso inclui autodisciplina, auto-reflexão, discrição e honestidade, entre outros. No confucionismo, apenas uma pessoa virtuosa pode dar um contributo útil para a família e para a sociedade.

第三，家庭伦理。孔子曰："父母在，不远游，游必有方。"意思是说，父母在世的时候，不出远门去求学、做官，万一要出远门，必须有一定的去处。孔子强调家庭的重要性，认为家庭是社会的基本单位。他提倡孝道，即对父母的尊重和孝顺，对父母负责。不出远门，一是可以方便照顾父母，二是可以避免父母过于思念孩子。中国有句俗话："家是最小国，国是千万家。"这与儒家思想不谋而合。善待好自己的父母，才有可能善待全天下的老人。孝道是每个人都应具备的美好品德。

Terceiro, a ética familiar. Confúcio afirmou: "Enquanto os pais estão vivos, o filho não pode viajar para longe. Se ele viajar para longe, deve ter um local fixo para os pais saberem onde ele está." Ele promoveu o desenvolvimento de um sistema de controle de natalidade. Em primeiro lugar, é conveniente cuidar dos pais e, em segundo lugar, evita que os pais sintam muita falta dos filhos. Há um ditado chinês que diz: "a casa é o menor país e o estado é dez milhões." Isso coincide com o confucionismo. Tratar bem dos pais é tornar possível tratar bem dos idosos de todo o mundo. A piedade filial é o bom caráter que todos possuem.

第四，教育观点。子曰："由，诲女知之乎？知之为知之，不知为不知，是知也。"这句话的意思是，孔子说："由，我教给你的，你懂了吗？知道就是知道，不知道就是不知道，这才是真正的智慧！"从这句话可以看出，孔子非常重视教育。教育应该包括道德和品德的培养，而不仅仅是知识的传授。就比如这句话中，孔子教育弟子不要不懂装懂，做人要诚实。教育应该培养学生成为有道德和智慧的人。

Quarto, a perspetiva da educação. Confúcio afirmou: "You! Devo ensiná-lo o que é conhecimento? Quando se sabe uma coisa, afirmamos que a conhecemos; e quando você não sabe uma coisa, afirma que você não a conhece—isto é conhecimento." Como pode ser visto nesta afirmação, Confúcio deu grande importância à educação. A educação deve incluir o cultivo da moralidade e do caráter, e não apenas a transmissão do conhecimento. Neste caso, Confúcio ensinou os seus discípulos a não fingirem saber aquilo que não compreendem, e a serem honestos no seu comportamento. A educação deve preparar os alunos para se tornarem pessoas morais e inteligentes.

儒家思想强调了仁爱、道德、家庭、教育等多个方面，不仅在中国历史上具有深远的影响，现如今，也在其他国家和地区产生了重要的文化和道德影响。儒家思想博大精深，一篇短小的文章难以阐明。海外的朋友们可以亲自阅读《论语》，一定会大有收获。

O confucionismo enfatizou vários aspetos, incluindo moral, benevolência, família e educação.

O confucionismo teve uma profunda influência não só na história da China, mas também hoje em dia, tem uma influência cultural e moral importante noutros países e regiões do mundo. O confucionismo é tão vasto e profundo que se torna difícil explicar através de um pequeno ensaio. Esperamos também que os nossos amigos no exterior possam ler o livro, o que será muito proveitoso.

作品编号：960
姓　　名：郭丰博
国　　籍：中国
组　　别：征文类国内成人组
单位名称：中国传媒大学

《论语·为政》节选诵读

在战国时期，百家争鸣，天下该如何治理成了各家门派热衷于探讨的问题。该篇节选自《论语·为政》，开篇讲述了孔夫子对于为政的看法。孔子认为治国理政当以道德为根基，这一思想为无数后人的言行带来启示。

同时，"为政"篇还谈论了学习与何为孝道的问题，可将其归为修身的重要部分。《礼记·大学》中有"修身齐家治国平天下"这一观点，可见古人常将修身置于治国之前。因此，人们只有端正自身态度、提高道德修养，才能做成大事，成为可用之才。

子曰："为政以德，譬如星辰，居其所而众星共之。"

Confúcio afirmou: "Aquele que governa pela virtude pode ser comparado à estrela, que mantém sua posição enquanto todas as estrelas se dispõem à volta dela."

子曰："《诗》三百，一言以蔽之，曰：'思无邪'。"

Confúcio afirmou: "Em *Livro de Odes* há trezentas peças, mas todas podem ser resumidas a uma única frase 'Não há pensamentos depravados'."

子曰："道之以政，齐之以刑，民免而无耻；道之以德，齐之以礼，有耻且格。"

Confúcio afirmou: "Se o povo for regulado por leis e restringido através de punições, as pessoas tentarão evitar o castigo, mas não terão a capacidade de sentir vergonha. Se for regulado pela virtude e restrito pelas regras de decoro, as pessoas desenvolverão o sentimento de vergonha e, além disso, tornar-se-ão bons."

子曰："吾十有五而志于学，三十而立，四十而不惑，五十而知天命，六十而耳顺，七十而从心所欲，不逾矩。"

Confúcio afirmou: "Aos quinze anos, eu estava decidido a dedicar-me à aprendizagem. Aos trintas, construí a minha personalidade. Aos quarenta, sem mais incertezas. Aos cinquenta, conhecia os decretos do Céu. Aos sessenta, fiquei obediente para ouvir as verdades. Aos setenta, eu podia seguir o meu coração sem transgredir o que era certo."

孟懿子问孝。子曰："无违。"樊迟御，子告之曰："孟孙问孝于我，我对曰，'无违'。"樊迟曰："何谓也？"子曰："生，事之以礼；死，葬之以礼，祭之以礼。"

Meng Yizi perguntou o que era piedade filial. Confúcio respondeu: "Não seja desobediente." Logo depois, enquanto Fan Chi conduzia a carruagem de Confúcio, e este disse-lhe: "Meng Sun perguntou-me o que era piedade filial, e eu lhe respondi: 'não seja desobediente.'" Fan Chi disse: "O que quis dizer com isso?" Confúcio respondeu: "Que os pais, quando vivos, sejam servidos de acordo com respeito e cortesia; que, quando mortos, sejam enterrados com os devidos ritos e sejam honrados com as cerimónias adequadas."

孟武伯问孝。子曰："父母唯其疾之忧。"

Meng Wubo perguntou o que era piedade filial. Confúcio respondeu: "Agir de forma a que os pais só sintam ansiedade quando os filhos ficam doentes."

子游问孝。子曰："今之孝者，是谓能养。至于犬马，皆能有养；不敬，何以别乎？"

Zi You perguntou-lhe sobre o que é a piedade filial. Confúcio respondeu: "Hoje em dia, a piedade filial é tida apenas como a capacidade de sustentar os pais. Mas até cães e cavalos também são alimentados; sem respeito, em que se distinguirá o homem?"

子夏问孝。子曰："色难。有事，弟子服其劳；有酒食，先生馔，曾是以为孝乎？"

Zi Xia perguntou o que era piedade filial. Confúcio respondeu: "A dificuldade está em manter uma boa atitude. Se, quando os mais velhos tiverem problemas, os jovens fizerem o trabalho deles, e se, quando os jovens tiverem vinho e comida, eles os colocarem diante dos mais velhos, isso já pode ser considerado como piedade filial?"

作品编号：1617
姓　　名：林毓琳
国　　籍：中国
组　　别：诵读类国内成人组
单位名称：华东交通大学

“贤哉，回也”释读

一天，正在吃午饭的颜回遇到了朋友，朋友看到颜回简单的饭菜大为震惊，颜回却乐在其中。接下来颜回说出的话让朋友明白，即使外在的物质条件恶劣，也不会影响内心世界充实的人。正如孔子说的那样：“贤哉，回也！”

朋友：颜回，晚上好。你最近怎么样啊？

Amiga: Oh, Hui. Boa tarde! Como estás?

颜回：哦，我的朋友，我最近一切都好。我正在吃午饭……

Yan Hui: Oh, minha amiga. Tudo bem. Estou a almoçar e ...

朋友：天哪！你吃的都是什么啊？只有米饭和冷水？你应该来和我吃一次饭，我吃的可都是烤鸡、蒸鱼和各种各样的饮品。那才是一顿美餐啊！

Amiga: Meu Deus! O que é que estás a comer? Só arroz com água? Devias vir jantar comigo um dia. Costumo comer frango assado, peixe cozido por vapor e todo o tipo de bebida. Que celebração!

颜回：一顿美味的饭食对我来说什么都算不上。对我来说比食物更珍贵的东西还有很多。我认为那些在现在以及将来的生活中，能帮助我们开阔视野、增长见识的事情才更加重要。

Yan Hui: Uma refeição saborosa não é nada para mim. Há muitas outras coisas mais valiosas para mim do que comida. Acho que o mais importante são as coisas que, no presente e no futuro, nos ajudam a alargar os horizontes e a enriquecer os conhecimentos.

朋友：你总是对的。我不和你争论这些。如果那些食物只是为了填饱肚子，那么你的房子呢？如果没有房子的话，你就不能舒适地生活了。房子不仅仅是我们在一天劳累工作后休息的地方，它也是家庭的象征。

Amiga: És sempre correto! Não vou discutir isto contigo. Apesar de as comidas serem para encher o estômago. E como é a tua casa? Não tens uma casa, não podes viver confortavelmente. A casa não é só um lugar para descansar depois de um dia cansativo de trabalho, mas é também um símbolo de família.

颜回：事实上，我并不在乎我住什么样的房子，也不介意住在什么地方。仅仅是手臂弯曲做枕头躺在那里就足以让我愉悦了。这是因为我的老师孔子曾经教育我说我们不应该在意外部环境怎么样，而是应该追求内心的平和。

Yan Hui: De fato, eu não me importo que tipo de casa seja ou onde fique. Posso divertir-me mesmo deitado numa casa simples e tendo um braço como almofada. Isso porque meu professor Confúcio certa vez me ensinou que não nos devemos preocupar com o ambiente externo. Desde que estejamos calmos no interior.

朋友：确实如此。抱歉我之前误解了你。你真的称得上是一个很谦虚的人，我应该向你学习！

Amiga: Exato. Desculpa ter-te interpretado mal. És realmente uma pessoa nobre e deveria aprender contigo.

子曰："贤哉，回也！一箪食，一瓢饮，在陋巷，人不堪其忧，回也不改其乐。贤哉，回也！"

Confúcio afirmou: "Que admirável é a virtude de Hui! Mora numa casa simples e tosca, por dia, tem apenas uma tigela de arroz para comer e uma cabaça de água para beber por dia. Os outros não poderiam suportar esta condição miserável, mas ele não permite que a sua alegria seja afetada por isto. Que admirável é a virtude de Hui!"

作品编号：1728
姓　　名：贾品端、夏闻秋
国　　籍：中国
组　　别：诵读类国内成人组
单位名称：上海外国语大学

中 西 篇

《论语》的世界 世界的《论语》

孔子是中国乃至世界影响力最大的人物之一。《论语》是一部记录孔子言行和儒家思想的经典，对世界文化也有着深远的影响。华曜济南实验学校7年级学生尤贞吉用自己的亲身经历，向大家讲述了一个《论语》在遥远的阿根廷传播的故事。我们相信，随着传承发展中华优秀传统文化上升为国家战略，儒学也将在世界范围内产生更大的影响。

孔子是中国乃至世界影响力最大的人物之一。《论语》是一部记录孔子言行和儒家思想的经典，自然也是世界闻名。离中国万里之遥的阿根廷友人们，也同样受到孔子和儒家思想的影响。

Confucio es una de las figuras más influyentes en China y en el mundo. El *Lunyu* es un clásico que registra las palabras y acciones de Confucio y el confucianismo, y es naturalmente conocido en todo el mundo. La Argentina, a miles de kilómetros de China, también puede ser influenciada por confucio y confucianismo.

几年前，我曾经跟爸爸妈妈一起在阿根廷生活了一段时间。有一次，我们跟随导游的脚步，踏入了伊瓜苏瀑布国家公园这片神奇、美丽的仙境。蝴蝶在漫不经心地游荡着，浣熊悠闲地寻觅着食物，一切都是如此宁静。

Hace unos años viví un tiempo en Argentina con mis padres. Una vez en el parque nacional de las cataratas del Iguazú, seguimos los pasos de nuestro guía y entramos en este lugar de belleza mágica. Las mariposas vagan despreocupadamente, los mapache en busca de comida, todo es tan tranquilo.

"你好！你们是中国人对吗？"导游热情地向我们打招呼。"欢迎欢迎！'有朋自远方来，不亦乐乎？'这是我非常尊敬的中国哲学家孔子说过的名言，今天我终于能跟真正的中国朋友说这句话了！"

"¡Hola! ¿Son chinos?" —nos saludó el guía con entusiasmo—. "¡Bienvenidos, bienvenidos! '¿No es un placer tener amigos que vienen de lejos? Es una famosa frase de Confucio, un filósofo chino a quien respeto mucho. ¡Hoy por fin puedo decirles esto a mis verdaderos amigos chinos!"

经过一番交流，我们得知导游曾经学过一点中文，也十分了解中国文化，热爱儒家文化。不知不觉地，我们就走到了伊瓜苏瀑布的边上。

Después de algunos intercambios, nos enteramos de que el guía había aprendido un poco de chino, también conocía muy bien la cultura China y amaba la cultura confuciana. Sin saberlo, llegamos al borde de las cataratas del Iguazú.

“逝者如斯夫！不舍昼夜。”我对导游说：“您知道吗？这是孔子在看到滔滔的黄河水时，留下的对时光流逝的感叹。”

“El tiempo transcurre como este río, que fluye día y noche.” Le dije al guía: “¿Sabe qué usted? Es una exclamación sobre el paso del tiempo que Confucio dejó al ver las aguas del río Huanghe.”

“这句话简直妙极了！我要马上记下来。”导游听到后立刻拿纸和笔写了下来。

“¡Eso es maravilloso! Voy a tomar nota inmediatamente.” Al oír esto, el guía tomó papel y bolígrafo para escribir.

记完后，导游一脸真诚地看着我们：“亲爱的中国朋友们，你们还知道《论语》中的哪些名言，可以告诉我吗？我很崇拜孔子，我一直想把孔子的思想和名言教给我的孩子们。”

“Queridos amigos chinos, ¿Saben alguna otra cita de *Lunyu* para decirme? Admiro a Confucio y siempre he querido enseñarle a mis hijos sus pensamientos y algunas de sus citas.” Después de recordar, el guía nos miró con una cara sincera y dijo.

爸爸在一旁高兴地对他说：“这真是一件好事。我们非常欣赏您的这种行为。‘博学而笃志，切问而近思，仁在其中矣。’您可以告诉您的孩子这句话。它的意思是：广泛学习，刻苦钻研，坚定自己的志向，恳切地提出问题，并且联系实际去思考，那么你就会找到‘仁’的含义。”

Mi padre le dijo alegremente desde un lado: “Es realmente una buena cosa. Apreciamos mucho este comportamiento de su parte. ‘博学而笃志，切问而近思，仁在其中矣 .’ Usted puede decírselo a tus hijos. Esto significa que: Cuando uno lee mucho, mantiene su aspiracion, plantea preguntas y reflexiona asuntos de actualidad, sepuedc dccir que sus actos contienen la benevolencia.”

看过了壮丽的瀑布景观，天色渐晚，我们也该回去了。

Después de haber visto el magnífico paisaje de cascadas, se hace tarde, también es hora de volver.

“这次与真正的中国朋友交流中国文化，让我很高兴。希望下次有机会我们能好好坐下来，喝着马黛茶，一起谈谈我们中国和阿根廷的趣事！”导游说。

“Estoy muy feliz de poder compartir la cultura china con verdaderos amigos chinos esta vez. ¡Espero que la próxima vez tengamos la oportunidad de sentarnos, tomar mate y conversar sobre cosas interesantes de China y Argentina!”, dijo el guía.

“好啊，四海之内皆兄弟嘛！”我们高兴地笑了起来。

“¡Bueno! ¡Todos los hombres del mundo son hermanos!” Nos pusimos a reír de alegría.

如果每个国家都能实现孔子所说的“己所不欲，勿施于人”，和平共处，共同发展，那么全人类应该能像一个大家庭。

Confucio dijo: “No hagas a los demás lo que no quieres que te hagan a ti.” Si cada país puede realizar el ideal de confucio de coexistencia pacífica y desarrollo común, entonces toda la humanidad debe ser como una gran familia.

英国18世纪诗人蒲伯曾说过，孔夫子超凡入圣，教我们如何做人。《论语》是全世界的财富，《论语》的世界属于全人类。

El poeta inglés del siglo XVIII, Alexander Pope, dijo una vez que Confucio es tan santo que nos enseña a ser humanos. *Lunyu* es la riqueza del mundo. El mundo en Lunyu pertenece a toda la humanidad.

作品编号：4369
姓　　名：尤贞吉
国　　籍：中国
组　　别：征文类国内少年组
单位名称：华曜济南实验学校

我爱中国话

来自俄罗斯、西班牙、韩国的三名国际学生因中国话汇聚在山东外国语职业技术大学。他们用汉语诵读孔子经典语录，用自己国家的语言阐述对孔子语录的理解，努力讲好中国故事，传播好中国声音，让中国话更加国际化。

有一种语言，它很神秘，它蕴含着一个民族上下几千年悲喜交加的情感。

Существует один язык, который очень загадочный. Он содержит в себе и печальные, и радостные эмоции одной нации.

有一种语言，它很古老，古老到那刻在骨头上的文字里都找不到它的起源。

Hay un lenguaje tan antiguo que su origen no se puede encontrar en las palabras grabadas en los huesos.

有一种语言，它很丰富，阴阳上去中回荡着慷慨激昂，倾诉着温婉缠绵。

오르고 내리는 억양에서 격앙된 감정과 온유함을 호소하는 풍부한 언어가 있습니다.

中国话，是如诗如画的表达。

中国话，是中国人心灵深处的吐纳。

中国话，是孔子的谆谆教诲。

己所不欲，勿施于人。

Не навязывай другим людям то, чего сам не хотел бы делать.

学而不思则罔，思而不学则殆。

Aprender sin pensar lleva a la perplejidad. Pensar sin aprender lleva a problemas.

知之为知之，不知为不知。

아는 것을 안다하고 모르는 것을 모른다고 하는 것이 참으로 현명한 것이다.

温故而知新，可以为师矣。

Сначала повторите старые знания, а потом выделите из них новые. Только на этой основе вы сможете стать учителем.

士不可以不弘毅，任重而道远。

Los eruditos deben tener amplias ambiciones y tenaz perseverancia, porque sus responsabilidades son pesadas y el camino por delante es largo y lejano.

工欲善其事，必先利其器。

장인이 일을 잘하려면, 반드시 그 연장을 날카롭게 해야 한다. 즉 어떤 일을 잘하려면 그 준비 과정이 매우 중요하다는 말입니다.

三人行，必有我师焉！
我们因中国话相聚在此，互相学习，共同成长。
未来，我们散作满天星，让中国话更加国际化！

作品编号 3664
姓　　名：Kondrateva Iuliia、Mascarena Benitez Carlos、Moon Chaewon
国　　籍：俄罗斯、西班牙、韩国
组　　别：诵读类国际组
单位名称：山东外国语职业技术大学

双语演绎《孟子·尽心上》第九节

本作品采用表演和诵读的方式，结合“一带一路”具体案例，对篇章中“穷则独善其身，达则兼善天下”做出了详细阐释。本作品展现了孟子“以天下为己任”的情怀和理想，弘扬了中华传统文化从“天下一家”到“以和为贵”“兼济天下”等价值观念。其中，“全球共建人类命运共同体”思想，就源于中华民族始终不变的“天下”情怀。

第一幕

主持人：下面有请第六组参赛选手。

Aquí está el sexto grupo de concursantes.

《孟子·尽心上》第九节。

Leer la novena sección de *Mencio · Jin Xin I*.

学生 1：到我们了。走吧。

Es nuestro turno. Vamos.

学生 2：好！

Vale.

学生 1：孟子谓宋勾践曰：“子好游乎？吾语子游。”

Mencio le dijo a Song Goujian, “¿Te gusta presionar a los monarcas de varios países? Yo te diré cómo hacerlo.”

学生 2：Mencio le dijo a Song Goujian, “¿Te...te gusta...te...”

第二幕

老师：娜娜，你来说一下对“穷则独善其身，达则兼善天下”的理解。

Nana, dinos qué te parece esta frase de la pizarra “Cuando seas pobre, cultiva tu propio carácter moral; cuando tengas éxito, ayuda a los demás”.

学生：好，老师。一个人过得不好的时候要让自己变优秀，一个人……老师，我不知道“达”的意思。

De acuerdo, profesora. Cuando no te va bien, tienes que arreglártelas tú solo. Cuando… Profesor, no sé lo que significa “da”.

老师：“达”是显贵的意思，当人得志显达时就要造福天下百姓。

“Da” significa noble. Cuando un hombre ha alcanzado la grandeza, debe beneficiar a los pueblos del mundo.

学生：可是老师，我还是不明白为什么人过得好了，就要主动帮助别人呢？我一个人过得很好，不可以吗？

Pero, profesora, todavía no lo entiendo por qué la gente se ofrece a ayudar a los demás cuando ellos están mejor. ¿no puedo que lo estoy haciendo bien por mi cuenta?

老师：只关注个人是远远不够的。当一个人拥有了财富和权力的时候应当去关心他人，造福社会。

Centrarse en el individuo no es suficiente. Cuando un hombre tiene riqueza y poder, debe destinarse a cuidar de los demás y beneficiar a la sociedad.

学生：老师，我明白了。但是在中国，真的有人这么做吗？

Profesora, lo entiendo. Pero, ¿realmente alguien hace eso en China?

老师：是的。“一带一路”就是典型的案例。

Sí. La Iniciativa de la Franja y la Ruta es un buen ejemplo.

学生：我听说过“一带一路”。我记得，有一列中国的火车经过西班牙能够把西班牙的火腿带到中国。

He oído hablar de la Franja y la Ruta. Recuerdo que hay un tren chino que pasaba por España. Fue capaz de llevar el jamón español a China.

老师：“一带一路”倡议的提出就是希望世界各国能够共同发展，共同繁荣。今年是该倡议提出的第十个周年。今年八月，中国援助印尼建设了第一条海外高铁，雅万高铁。这也是印尼与东南亚的第一条海外高铁。

La Iniciativa de la Franja y la Ruta se presentó con la esperanza de que los países del mundo pudieran desarrollarse y prosperar juntos. Este año se cumple el décimo aniversario de esa iniciativa. En agosto de este año, China ayudó a Indonesia a construir su primer ferrocarril de alta velocidad, el Ferrocarril de Alta Velocidad Yakarta-Bandung. Este es también el primer ferrocarril de alta velocidad en Indonesia y el Sudeste Asiático.

第三幕

学生 1：孟子谓宋勾践曰：子好游乎？吾语子游。

学生 2：Mencio le dijo a Song Goujian, ¿Te gusta presionar a los monarcas de varios países? Yo te diré cómo hacerlo.

学生 1：人知之，亦嚣嚣；人不知，亦嚣嚣。

学生 2：Cuando los demás me entienden, estoy tranquilo; cuando los demás no me entienden, estoy tranquilo.

学生 1：曰：何如斯可以嚣嚣矣？

学生 2：Song Goujian dijo: “¿Qué debo hacer para estar tranquilo?”

学生 1：曰：尊德乐义，则可以嚣嚣矣。

学生 2：Él respondió: “Si veneras la virtud y estás obsesionado con la rectitud, estarás tranquilo.”

学生 1：故士穷不失义，达不离道。

学生 2：Por lo tanto, las personas no pierden sus valores morales cuando son pobres, ni abandonan sus principios cuando prosperan.

学生 1：穷不失义，故士得己焉；

学生 2：No pierde su rectitud cuando no tiene ambiciones, por lo que puede conservar su naturaleza;

学生 1：达不离道，故民不失望焉。

学生 2：No abandona la Vía cuando tiene ambiciones, por lo que la gente no se sentirá decepcionada.

学生 1：古之人，得志，泽加于民；

学生 2：Cuando los hombres de la antigüedad lograban su ambición, beneficiaban al pueblo;

学生 1：不得志，修身见于世。

学生 2：si no lograban sus ambiciones, cultivaban su carácter personal y dejaban que sus grandes virtudes se desplegaran ante el mundo.

学生 1：穷则独善其身，达则兼善天下。

学生 2：Cuando no se tenía voluntad, se era bueno sólo consigo mismo; cuando se tenía voluntad, se era bueno con el mundo.

作品编号：3400

姓　　名：胥元喆、王欣冉、董禹希

国　　籍：中国

组　　别：诵读类国内成人组

单位名称：大连外国语大学新闻与传播学院

《论语》诵读

《论语》是经典中的经典，古人云“半部论语治天下”，学了《论语》，修身齐家治国平天下便有了很好的文化根基。作为新时代的小学生，我们要继承这些中华传统文化，并将其发扬光大，让中华文化向世界发声，让孔子的精神光泽、文化精华浸润到中华大地乃至世界的每一寸土壤。

大家好，我是于佳禾，东营市实验小学一名 9 岁的三年级小学生。

Hola, todos, soy Jiahe Yu, un estudiante de tercer grado de nueve años en la escuela primaria Shiyan de Dongying.

《论语》是一部中国古代作品，是由孔子及其同时代人的言论和思想组成的哲学作品。传统上《论语》被认为是由孔子的追随者编撰的，其中蕴含着无穷的智慧。接下来我想诵读《论语》中我最喜欢的一些句子。

Las Analectas son una antigua obra filosófica china que contiene los dichos y pensamientos de Confucio y sus contemporáneos. Tradicionalmente, se cree que fueron compiladas por los seguidores de Confucio y que contienen una gran sabiduría. Me gustaría recitar algunas de mis frases favoritas de *Las Analectas*.

子曰：“学而时习之，不亦说乎？有朋自远方来，不亦乐乎？人不知而不愠，不亦君子乎？”

Confucio dijo: “Aprendes, luego repasas y practicas, ¿no te sientes contento? Si un amigo de lejos, ¿no te sientes complacido? Cuando no te entienden, no te enfadas, por lo tanto ¿no serías una persona de carácter noble?”

子曰：“巧言令色，鲜矣仁！”

Confucio dijo: “¡Los que tienden a usar palabras zalameras y fingen ser agradables no suelen ser personas piadosas!”

曾子曰：“吾日三省吾身：为人谋而不忠乎？与朋友交而不信乎？传不习乎？”

Zengzi dijo: “Cada día reflexiono repetidas veces, ¿para saber que ayudo a otros con toda mi fuerza? ¿Soy honrado con mis amigos? ¿Repaso todo lo que me enseñan mis profesores?”

子曰：“君子食无求饱，居无求安，敏于事而慎于言，就有道而正焉，可谓好学也已。”

Confucio dijo: “No comas para estar lleno, no vivas deseando comodidad. Trabaja mucho y habla con cautela. Codéate con personas de carácter noble. Si haces todo esto podrás llamarte estudioso.”

子曰：“吾十有五而志于学，三十而立，四十而不惑，五十而知天命，六十而耳顺，七十而从心所欲，不逾矩。”

Confucio dijo: “Yo decidí aprender cuando tenía quince años, y pude mantenerme a mí mismo cuando tenía treinta. Cuando tenía cuarenta, no había nada que pudiera confundirme. Y aprendí lo que significaba el destino cuando tenía cincuenta. Y podía tratar todas las ideas correctamente cuando tenía sesenta. Y cuando tenía setenta podía hacer todo lo que quería dentro del marco justificado.”

子夏问孝，子曰：“色难。有事，弟子服其劳；有酒食，先生撰，曾是以为孝乎？”

Zixia preguntó sobre la piedad filial a Confucio, y él le dijo: “Lo más difícil es ser amable con los padres. Si sólo los ayudas en la vida o sólo les das comida, no tienes piedad real.”

子曰：“温故而知新，可以为师矣。”

Confucio dijo: “Si puedes sacar inspiración repasando lo estudiado, podrás ser maestro.”

子曰：“学而不思则罔，思而不学则殆。”

Confucio dijo: “Si sólo aprendes pero no reflexionas, te quedas perplejo. Y si sólo piensas pero no aprendes, te quedas perplejo.”

子曰：“由，诲女知之乎？知之为知之，不知为不知，是知也。”

Confucio dijo: “¡You! ¿entiendes lo que he dicho? Nunca finjas saber algo que no sepas. Eso es sabiduría.”

子曰：“士志于道，而耻恶衣恶食者，未足与议也。”

Confucio dijo: “Si la clase noble quiere aprender y practicar la moralidad, pero creen que es una vergunza no tener ropas preciosas o comidad abundante, entonces no vale nada tratar sobre la moralidad con ellos.”

子曰：“不患无位，患所以立；不患莫己知，求为可知也。”

Confucio dijo: “Uno no debe preocuparse por no tener cargo, lo preocupante es la carencia de la capacidad. No se preocupa por ser desconocido, lo importante es esforzarse por conseguir la fama.”

子曰：“见贤思齐焉，见不贤而内自省也。”

Confucio dijo: “Aprende de los morales y talentos, y al ver a los indignos, debe examinarse a sí mismo.”

子曰：“德不孤，必有邻。”

Confucio dijo: “Un moral no se siente aislado, siempre tiene allegados.”

这里有更多我们可以一起读的有意思的句子。我们一起来读《论语》吧！

Aquí hay más frases interesantes que podemos leer juntos. Vamos a leer *Las Analectas* juntos.

作品编号：3213
姓　　名：于佳禾
国　　籍：中国
组　　别：诵读类国内少年组
单位名称：东营市实验小学

《论语》节选诵读

一部《论语》千古流传，一位老师，万世师表。中国人的仁德智慧，两千年的风骨性格，都蕴藏在这位老师和他学生的对话里。做人的道理，处世的智慧，这些都是中华民族精神和智慧的源泉，值得每一个中国人诵读，也值得世界上每个人诵读。

大家好，我是济南新航实验外国语学校初一四班的杨丛荣，今天为大家朗读中西语《论语》节选内容。

¡Hola a todos! Me llamo Yang Congrong. Estudio en la Escuela Experimental de Idiomas Extranjeros de Jinan Xinhang, de la clase 4, el grado 7. Hoy voy a recitar *Las Analectas de Confucio* escogidas en chino y español.

子曰："君子求诸己，小人求诸人。"

El Maestro dijo: "El caballero se exige a sí mismo, el hombre vulgar exige a los demás."

子曰："君子坦荡荡，小人长戚戚。"

El Maestro dijo: "El caballero es generoso y tolerante, pero el hombre vulgar está lleno de preocupaciones mezquinas."

子曰："知者不惑，仁者不忧，勇者不惧。"

El Maestro dijo: "Los sabios están libres de dudas, los benevolentes carecen de desasosiego, y los valientes no tienen miedo."

子曰："有教无类。"

El Maestro dijo: "Para mis enseñanzas no existe discriminación alguna de clases sociales."

子在川上曰："逝者如斯夫！不舍昼夜。"

El Maestro dijo contemplando un río: "Todo fluye como estas aguas, ininterrumpidamente, durante día y noche."

子曰："岁寒，然后知松柏之后凋也。"

El Maestro dijo: "Cuando llega el frío del invierno, nos damos cuenta de que el pino y el ciprés no pierden hojas ."

谢谢大家！

¡Gracias por su atención!

作品编号：2342

姓　　名：杨丛荣

国　　籍：中国

组　　别：诵读类国内少年组

单位名称：山东省济南新航实验外国语学校

中 阿 篇

我的《论语》故事

《论语》是一部记录了中国古代伟大思想家孔子及其弟子的言论和行为的经典著作，全书共20篇。《论语》以言论简短而精炼闻名，包含了丰富的道德、政治、教育等方面的思想，对中国古代和现代社会都有重要的影响。

中文被认为是世界上最难的语言之一。当我开始学习中文的时候，我才真正意识到这有多难，但我从来没想过放弃，而是继续努力。正所谓“知者不惑，仁者不忧，勇者不惧”，只有不断学习，才能获得智慧，不会感到困惑。我知道这很难，但我想通过自己的努力达成这个目标，我也相信自己可以实现这个目标。

在约旦时，我经常和中国友人聊天，还向老师请教关于中文学习的问题，和同学们一起交流讨论，就算在假期我也没有松懈，而是一直在学习。同时，我也知道在学习的过程中也要不断思考，因为如果只学习而不思考，所学的一切都只停留在书本上，没有实际作用，无法解决实际问题；如果只思考而不学习，那么知识迟早会因为没有补充或启发新知识而停滞不前，即“学而不思则罔，思而不学则殆”。

通过我的不断努力，我的中文水平提高了很多。我不仅可以听懂中文，也可以流利地用中文交流。我深刻地体会到了中国文化的魅力。我不会停止学习中文的步伐，而是一直保持“学如不及，犹恐失之”的心态，因为学习是没有止境的。我会做一位追赶者，向着追求至高至深的学问的目标前进！

作品编号：13138
姓　　名：马小力(Ahmad Tahseen Ahmad Alzubaidi)
国　　籍：约旦
组　　别：征文类国际组
单位名称：聊城大学

中国古人之论学

中国文化博大精深，古代先贤给我们留下许多珍贵的文化遗产，其中包括许多关于学习的真知灼见。他们强调学习中提问、思考、实践的重要性，启迪后世千百年，也给我们留下许多弥足珍贵的文献资料。本文讨论中国古代先贤之论学，论述其对学习的看法，充分展现“古人学问无余力”。

子曰：“学而时习之，不亦说乎？”学习并常常复习，不是件很快乐的事情吗？中国传统文化对学习这件乐事十分重视，《论语·学而》甚至以之开篇。仔细研究古人关于学习的名言，就能发现，这些名言已经说透了学习的各个方面。

يقول كونفوشيوس: "أليست الدراسة والمراجعة المستمرة تجعلان المرء سعيدًا؟"، اهتم القدماء الصينيون غاية الاهتمام بهذا النوع من السعادة، حتى أن كتاب الحوار لكونفوشيوس بدأ بفصل سُمي "الدراسة". والمتأمل في أقوال القدماء الصينيين حول الدراسة نجد أنهم قد غطوا جوانبها كافة.

中国古代非常重视学习。《礼记·学记》有言，“人不学，不知道”，将学习看作了解生活的方式。《诫子书》中指出“非学无以广才”，将学习视为人增长才干的唯一途径。“万般皆下品，唯有读书高”，充分体现出读书在古人心中的崇高地位——读书入仕是最高尚、最能够出人头地的事业。

اهتم القدماء اهتمامًا جمًا بالدراسة، وقد ذكر "كتاب الأخلاق -- باب الدراسة": "لا مجال للمعرفة بدون دراسة"، أي أن الدراسة هي السبيل الوحيد لمعرفة الحياة، كما ذكر أيضًا جو قلاينغ في كتابه "الوصايا": "لا يُبتغى تطوير المهارات بدون التعلم"، فهي الطريقة الوحيدة لتنمية مهارات الإنسان، كما أنها أسمى المجالات، فيقول أحد القدماء: "الدراسة هي المبتغى الأسمى بين المجالات كافة"، الأمر الذي يعكس مكانة التعليم لدى القدماء، فهي الرسالة الأسمى وسبيل التفوق.

对于何时学习、学到何时以及如何学习，古人均已论及。关于何时学习，古人认为早上是读书最好的时辰，如“一天之计在于晨”，且从幼年就要开始学习，因为“人生百年，立于幼学”。那么学到什么时候呢？“活到老，学到老”是家喻户晓的谚语；“学无止境”，学习没有终点。但是要注意，学习的脚步不能停歇，因为“学如逆水行舟，不进则退”，“君子之学必日新。日新者，日进也。不日新者必日退”（《二程集》）。学习上没有不进而不退者！中国古人也教我们勤奋学习，“三更灯火五更鸡，正是男儿读书时”，要夜以继日、发愤忘食地学。要知道，“黑发不知勤学早，白首方悔读书迟”，黑发青春时耗费光阴，白发年衰时便徒有后悔了！

فمتى علينا أن نبدأ الدراسة إذن؟ ومتى نتوقف؟ لم يغفل القدماء عن ذلك، فَيَرَونَ أن البكور هو الميعاد الأفضل لبدء الدراسة، فتقول الحكمة "يبدأ الإعداد لليوم بدءًا من البكور"، كما علينا أن نبدأ الدراسة منذ نعومة أظافرنا، كما تقول الحكمة

الصينية "تتشكل حياة الإنسان وفقًا لدراسته في طفولته"، وندرس إلى متى؟ تقول المقولة الصينية المشهورة "ادرس ما دمت حيًا"، كما يقول المثل الصيني أيضًا "لا نهاية للدراسة"، لكن يجب أن ننتبه، الدراسة لا يمكن أن تتوقف أبدًا، فقد ذكر "ديوان تشن وتشن" أن "الدراسة كالمركب إن لم يسر إلى الأمام، فسيرجع إلى الخلف". وذكر أيضًا "كريم الأخلاق يجدد دراسته يوميًا، فيتطور يوميًا، وإن لم يفعل فحتمًا سيتأخر يومًا بعد يوم!" كما يعلمنا الصينيون القدماء الاجتهاد في الدراسة، فيقول بيت الشعر "أضئ شعلتك حتى منتصف الليل، واستيقظ عند سماع صياح الديكة، فهذان هما وقت دراسة الرجال"، فيدعونا إلى إضاءة الليل ووصله بالنهار وقضاء الوقت كله في الدراسة، كما يقول البيت الآخر "إن لم تجتهد في الدراسة وأنت في ريعان شبابك، لن ينفعك الندم على ما ضيعته عندما يشيب شعرك".

此外，古人还认为，不应独自一人闷头学习而不交朋友，因为“独学而无友，则孤陋而寡闻”，要营造适合学习环境的“芝兰之室”，不然就要像孟母一样为环境而“三迁”。

بالإضافة إلى ذلك، لا يمكنك الانغماس في الدراسة وعدم عقد الصداقات، مصداقًا للبيت القائل: "الدراسة دون عقد صداقات، تجعلك سطحي المعرفة"، كما ينبغي تكوين بيئة مناسبة للدراسة، لتكون كما وصفها كونفوشيوس "غرفة مليئة بالزهور العطرية" تساعد على الدراسة، وإلا ستضطر إلى الهجرة "ثلاث مرات" كما فعلت "والدة مو" لتبحث عن بيئة مناسبة.

那么，学习过程该当如何？《礼记・中庸》中说：“博学之，审问之，慎思之，明辨之，笃行之。”广泛学习的同时，也要常常请教他人。“古之学者必有师”（《师说》），学习的时候要有老师，但“学无常师”，老师不是固定的一个人，“三人行，必有我师焉”（《论语》），哪怕是一起行走的三个人中，也必定有可以向之学习的人。

فكيف هي مراحل الدراسة؟ يقول "كتاب الطقوس -- باب الوسطية": "تَبَحَّر في العلم، واسأل بحرص، وفكّر بعمق، واحكم بوضوح، وطبّق بجد"، فبالإضافة إلى الدراسة الواسعة، يجب أن نسأل دومًا الآخرين، وكما ذكرت مقالة "التدريس والدراسة": "التزم الدارسون القدامى دومًا بالتتلمذ على يد معلم"، كما أن المعلّم لا يجب أن يكون ثابتًا، كما يقول كونفوشيوس "لا معلّمًا ثابتًا في الدراسة"، كما أنه أكد على هذه الفكرة في موضع آخر قائلًا: "حتى وإن كنا ثلاثة نمشي سويًا، يجب أن يكون منهم من أتعلم منه".

“切问而近思”（《论语・子张》），请教询问以后，就要认真思考，即“慎思”，因为，“学而不思则罔”，只学习而不思考，就会迷惑而无所得。

وذكر كونفوشيوس أيضًا مفهوم "طرح الأسئلة بدقة والتفكير بجد في الأوضاع الحالية"، فبعد "السؤال بحرص"، يجب التفكير بدقة وجد، فالدراسة بدون تفكير، كما يقول كونفوشيوس "لن تفيدك وستجعلك مرتبكًا".

学习、思考之后，应当实践，即“笃行”。“纸上得来终觉浅，绝知此事要躬行”（《冬夜读书示子聿》），从书上学到的知识总会不够完善，要深入理解其中的道理必须亲自实践。王守仁的“知行合一”，朱熹的“论轻重，行为重”，均是此理。

بعد الدراسة والتفكير، عليك الانتقال إلى التطبيق، وأن "تطبق بجد"، كما يقول بيت الشعر الصيني "العلوم في الورق سطحية، وإن أردت لبها فعليك بالتطبيق"، كما ذكر وانغ شو رن مفهوم "الجمع بين المعرفة والتطبيق"، وقال جوشي: "التطبيق أهم من المعرفة".

总之，“古人学问无遗力”，中国古人的论学之理透彻深奥，谈论学习的意义、地位、环境、启蒙、态度方方面面，强调学习中提问、思考、实践的重要性。

ختامًا، صدق الشاعر في قوله "لم يدخر القدماء الصينيون جهدًا في الدراسة"، فقد تناولوا الدراسة بعمق وتفصيل، وتحدثوا عن أهميتها ومكانتها ومتى تبدأ ومتى تنتهي وبيئتها وغيرها، وأكدوا على أهمية طرح الأسئلة والتفكير والتطبيق.

作品编号：4608
姓　　名：马坚(Mohamed Ahmed Saad Ahmed Obied)
国　　籍：埃及
组　　别：征文类国际组
单位名称：上海外国语大学高级翻译学院

有朋自远方来 学在孔孟之乡

“岁寒，然后知松柏之后凋也。”这是儒学经典《论语》中的一句话。来自约旦的国际学生柏霖用中阿双语生动地阐释了他所学到的《论语》知识，并结合他在聊城大学就读期间的学习、生活经历，用“有朋自远方来，学在孔孟之乡”为题，讲述了自己学习汉语的故事，表达了对中国的深切情感和对中华文化的热爱。

我叫柏霖，来自约旦，现在在聊城大学学习汉语。山东是孔孟之乡，我想以儒家经典《论语》中的话为引，为大家讲讲我的中国故事。

我在约旦的乡村长大，小时候，我的父亲从事农业和贸易工作时经常带着我。父亲的言传身教让我早早明白了做人要诚信，人与人之间的信任是相互的，你希望别人善待你，你就要先善待别人。在我学习中文后，我在《论语》中找到了心灵的共鸣。

曾子曰：“吾日三省吾身：为人谋而不忠乎？与朋友交而不信乎？传不习乎？”我每天多次问自己：“替别人做事有没有尽心竭力？和朋友交往有没有诚信？老师传授的知识有没有按时温习？”

《论语·雍也》中子贡曰：“如有博施于民而能济众，何如？可谓仁乎？”子曰：“何事于仁，必也圣乎！尧、舜其犹病诸！夫仁者，己欲立而立人，己欲达而达人。能近取譬，可谓仁之方也已。”自己想成功首先要让别人成功，自己想被人理解首先要理解别人。它与“己所不欲，勿施于人”共同组成儒家的道德准则，是儒家道德修养中用于处理人际关系的重要原则，这也和我们约旦的至理名言非常相似。

遥远的中国和约旦，古老的过去和今天，在我的心中相遇了。

两年前，我一边工作一边学习中文，虽然时间有限，有时候也会遇到困难，但我从没有想过放弃。我的老师给我起了一个很好听的名字“柏霖”。子曰：“岁寒，然后知松柏之后凋也。”只有经历了严寒的考验，才能真正认识到坚韧的松柏在凋零后的坚强。这个名字支撑着我，陪伴着我，鼓励我永不放弃。

子曰：“学而不思则罔，思而不学则殆。”在学习汉语的过程中，我也锻炼了深度思考的能力。中国明代的王阳明曾经说要“知行合一”。我想，学习、思考和实践是相辅相成的，只有将学习和深刻思考相结合，立足实践，才能使知识具备实际价值。读万卷书，行万里路，是时候来中国走一走、看一看了。

“德不孤，必有邻。”中国是礼仪之邦，是君子之国，有君子之道。中国在国际上重信守诺，体现了古老的中华文明的智慧和中国作为一个负责任大国的历史担当。今年是中国和约旦建交46周年，也是我来到中国的第一年，我想对中国说："我爱你，中国。"

作品编号：13127
姓　　名：柏霖（Malkawi Abdel Rahman Ayoub Hussein）
国　　籍：约旦
组　　别：诵读类国际组
单位名称：聊城大学

双语诵读《采薇》

《采薇》出自《诗经·小雅》，该诗主要描绘了将士戍边征战和生活的艰苦、强烈的思乡情绪以及久久未能回家的原因，体现了士兵对和平的渴望。通过留学生的朗诵，传达全世界人民对和平生活的期盼。

采薇采薇，薇亦作止。
نجمع السرخس ،نجمع السرخس ،السرخس الآن طري.
曰归曰归，岁亦莫止。
نقول إننا عائدون إلى الوطن ،نقول إننا عائدون إلى الوطن ،لكن السنة قد انتهت.
靡室靡家，猃狁之故。
ليس لدينا منزل ولا أسرة ،بسبب عدوان الغزاة.
不遑启居，猃狁之故。
ليس لدينا وقت للراحة ،بسبب عدوان الغزاة.
采薇采薇，薇亦柔止。
نجمع السرخس ،نجمع السرخس ،السرخس الآن طري.
曰归曰归，心亦忧止。
نقول إننا عائدون إلى الوطن ،نقول إننا عائدون إلى الوطن ،لكن القلب مليء بالهم.
忧心烈烈，载饥载渴。
القلوب مضطربة ،نعيش بالجوع والعطش.
我戍未定，靡使归聘。
خدمتي لم تنتهِ بعد ،وليس هناك من يساعدني على العودة.
采薇采薇，薇亦刚止。
نجمع السرخس ،نجمع السرخس ،السرخس الآن قاسي.
曰归曰归，岁亦阳止。
نقول إننا عائدون إلى الوطن ،نقول إننا عائدون إلى الوطن ،لكن السنة قد انتهت.
王事靡盬，不遑启处。
مهام الملك لا تنتهي ،وليس لدينا وقت للراحة.
忧心孔疚，我行不来！
القلوب مليئة بالقلق ،ولا أستطيع العودة.
彼尔维何？维常之华。
ما هذا الذي اراه؟ إنه زهرة البرسيم.

彼路斯何？君子之车。

ما هذا الطريق؟ إنه عربة النبيل.

戎车既驾，四牡业业。

العربة الحربية مجهزة ،والأحصنة الأربعة جاهزة.

岂敢定居？一月三捷。

كيف يمكنني البقاء؟ لقد انتصرنا ثلاث مرات في شهر واحد.

驾彼四牡，四牡骙骙。

العربة تجرها أربعة أحصنة ،والأحصنة الأربعة قوية.

君子所依，小人所腓。

النبلاء يعتمدون عليها ،والعامة يحتمون بها.

四牡翼翼，象弭鱼服。

الأحصنة الأربعة مطيعة ،والأقواس مغطاة بجلود السمك.

岂不日戒？猃狁孔棘！

ألا نكون حذرين كل يوم؟ إن الغزاة يشكلون خطراً كبيراً.

昔我往矣，杨柳依依。

عندما ذهبت في الماضي ،كانت أشجار الصفصاف تتمايل برفق.

今我来思，雨雪霏霏。

الآن عندما أعود ،تتساقط الثلوج بغزارة.

行道迟迟，载饥载渴。

الطريق طويل وبطيء ،ونحن نعاني من العطش والجوع.

我心伤悲，莫知我哀！

قلبي حزين جداً ،ولا أحد يعرف معاناتي.

作品编号：3645

姓　　名：苏悦、伊荻、伊琪、韩勇为

国　　籍：摩洛哥

组　　别：诵读类国际组

单位名称：滨州职业学院

中约情 携手行

来自约旦的国际学生柔兰同学，选用《论语·学而》《论语·为政》《论语·里仁》中的句子阐述了她心中的“仁”。她结合自己的亲身经历，对如何践行“仁”、成为君子进行了阐述。“大美华夏，雅乐儒家”，优美的葫芦丝演奏表达了她对儒家文化的崇敬之情，也表达了她对中国和约旦友谊长存、并肩携手前行的美好祝愿。

我叫柔兰，我想分享三句来自孔子的经典语录，并阐述我自己的理解。这些语录虽然来自古代，但依然具有深远的含义，对我们的人生和学习有着重要的启示。

第一句出自《论语·学而》，“学而时习之，不亦说乎？有朋自远方来，不亦乐乎？人不知而不愠，不亦君子乎？”对于这句话，我的理解是，学习知识并不断实践和巩固，是一件非常快乐的事情；有志同道合的朋友从远方来，也是一种幸福的体验；而当别人对我们不了解或误解时，作为一个君子，我们不会因此生气或不悦。

第二句出自《论语·为政》，“学而不思则罔，思而不学则殆”。我对这句话的理解是，只学习而不思考，就会感到迷茫和不知所措；只思考而不学习，就会陷入虚无和困惑之中。学习和思考是互相依存的，只有二者结合才能取得真正的进步。

第三句出自《论语·里仁》，“德不孤，必有邻”。我的理解是，有道德的人是不会孤单的，他们必定会找到志同道合、与之相伴的人。就像光芒无法独自存在，德行也需要通过与他人交流和分享，形成较大的影响力。

因此，我鼓励大家在学习的道路上，不断思考，不断结交志同道合的朋友；保持虚怀若谷、宠辱不惊的心态，就算“人不知”，也要坦然面对；在追求德行的过程中，寻找志同道合的伙伴，携手前进。

在我们的人生和学习中，我们应该时刻铭记孔子的智慧教导。只有学以致用，不断思考与实践，与好友共同前行，我们才能不断进步，实现自己的价值，并影响他人。

作品编号：13128
姓　　名：柔兰（Sa'ad Aldin Raghad Sa'di Mahmoud）
国　　籍：约旦
组　　别：诵读类国际组
单位名称：聊城大学

国之大美，美美与共

《仲弓问仁》是孔子与其弟子仲弓的一段对话，讲述了仁德的内涵和实践。《樊迟问仁》描绘的是樊迟对孔子“何为仁”的疑问，以及孔子的回答，强调了仁的本质是对他人的关爱和尊重。在中阿双语的情景剧中，这一场景被生动再现，孔子的教诲穿越时空，使得中东地区的观众能够理解和感受儒家思想的核心理念——仁爱、公正和自我修养。这种跨文化的交流，不仅提升了人们对儒家文化的认知，也促进了不同文明之间的对话与理解。国之大美，今人共守，意味着我们要尊重和保护这些文化遗产，同时要让经典在时间的流转中熠熠生辉，成为连接过去与未来的纽带，守护好传统的根脉。这是一份历史的使命，也是一份时代的召唤。

今天我们用中阿双语分享《论语》中的章节。

اليوم، دعونا نتبادل بعض الفصول في «كتاب الحوار» باللغة العربية والصينية.

仲弓问仁。子曰：“出门如见大宾，使民如承大祭。己所不欲，勿施于人。在邦无怨，在家无怨。”仲弓曰：“雍虽不敏，请事斯语矣！”

سأل (جونغ كونغ) عن المروءة، فقال الأستاذ: "إذا خرجت من بيتك، فعامل الناس كأنك تقابل كبار الضيوف احتراما، وإذا استخدمت رعيتك، فاستخدمهم كأنك تقدم القرابين في الاحترام، ولا تعامل الناس بما لا ترضى أن تعامل به، ليكن التذمر منك غير موجود في بلادك وفى بيتك." قال (جونغ كونغ): "إني ولو كنت غبيا، لأبذل وسعى في العمل بهذا الكلام."

樊迟问仁，子曰：“爱人。”问知，子曰：“知人。”樊迟未达。子曰：“举直错诸枉，能使枉者直。”樊迟退，见子夏，曰：“乡也吾见于夫子而问知，子曰：‘举直错诸枉，能使枉者直’，何谓也？”子夏曰：“富哉言乎！舜有天下，选于众，举皋陶，不仁者远矣。汤有天下，选于众，举伊尹，不仁者远矣。”

سأل (فان جيه) عن المروءة، فقال الأستاذ: "حب الناس." ثم سأل عن المعرفة، فقال الأستاذ: "معرفة الناس." ولم يدرك (فان جيه) معنى الجواب، فقال الأستاذ: "إن رفعت مستقيم السلوك، فمن الممكن أن تقوم سلوك المعوجين." لما تولّى (فان جيه)، رأى (تسه شيا)، فقال له: "قد قابلت الأستاذ آنفا وسألته عن المعرفة." فقال: "إن رفعت مستقيم السلوك، فمن الممكن أن تقوم سلوك المعوجين. ماذا كان يعني بهذا القول؟" فقال (تسه شيا):"هناك أقوال كثيرة، أي أن شونغ كان يختار نجيباً من العامة أثناء حكمه، واختار قاو ياو من الجميع، فابتعد شخص غير مستقيم. وكان (تانغ) يحكم العالم بسبب أنه كان يختار شخصاً متميزاً مستقيم السلوك، وغيره، فتركه."

下面请看中文演绎。

仲弓曰：“夫子，何为仁？”

子曰：“出门如见大宾，使民如承大祭。己所不欲，勿施于人。在邦无怨，在家无怨。”

仲弓曰：“雍虽不敏，请事斯语矣！”

樊迟曰："夫子，何为仁？"

子曰："爱人。"

樊迟曰："夫子，何为知？"

子曰："知人。"

樊迟未达。

子曰："举直错诸枉，能使枉者直。"

樊迟退，见子夏，曰："乡也吾见于夫子而问知，子曰：'举直错诸枉，能使枉者直'，何谓也？"

子夏曰："富哉言乎！舜有天下，选于众，举皋陶，不仁者远矣。汤有天下，选于众，举伊尹，不仁者远矣。"

这是《论语》中非常有名的章节，孔子认为，"礼"就是为人的本分和守则。

هذا فصل مشهور جدا في المختارات، ويعتقد كونفوشيوس أن "التأدّب" هو واجب وقواعد للسلوك البشري.

"仁"的伦理信条，出发点在个人，每个人必须实行于他的家人，进而才是家人的亲戚、亲戚的亲戚。

المبادئ الاخلاقية عن مفهوم "التراحم"، الهدف الأول هو الناس، يجب على كل واحد أن يطبقها مع أفراد الأسرة، ثم أقارب الاسرة وأقارب الأقارب.

孔子是一位被称为"万世师表"的伟大教育家，孔子的教学内容非常广泛。

كونفوشيوس عالم تربويّ عظيم يحمل لقب المعلّم الخالد، كانت مناهج التدريس لكونفوشيوس وافرة المضمون.

他把整理的文化典籍传给门人，这些典籍成为儒家的经典，也成了中华文化的元典。

وكان يعلم تلاميذه الكتب القديمة والسجلات التي جمعها ورتبها، وأصبحت هذه الكتب القديمة والسجلات أمهات الكتب للمدرسة الكونفوشيوسية في الفكر، وصارت من كلا سيرياس الثقافة الصينية.

如今，许多国家都将孔子的《论语》奉为经典。

وفي الوقت الحاضر، تعتبر كثير من الدول «كتاب الحوار» من أهم الأعمال الكلاسيكية.

在世界各地，有 100 多个国家设立了 300 多所"孔子学院"。

أكثر من مائة دولة يستحدث أكثر من ثلاثمائة "معاهد كونفوشيوسية" في أنحاء العالم.

《论语》与博大精深的孔子思想不仅影响了中国文明史，而且在国际上流传广泛，成为全世界人类文明的共同财富。

لم يؤثر «كتاب الحوار» وروح كونفوشيوسية العظيمة في تاريخ الحضارة الصينية فقط، بل ينتشر في دول العالم انتشارا واسعا، حتى يصير ثروة مشتركة لحضارة البشرية بالعالم.

作品编号：5315

姓　　名：李子寒、陆红宇、随鑫阳、李文玉、王雪婷

国　　籍：中国

组　　别：诵读类国内成人组

单位名称：山东青年政治学院

中 意 篇

儒家思想与中华优秀传统文化

作为一名来自意大利的华侨，我认为中华文化是博大精深的。儒家思想是中国传统文化的重要组成部分，它强调仁爱、孝道等价值观念。儒家思想文化在海外的传播推动了跨文化的交流和影响。讲好中国故事，有助于提高我国的综合实力！

儒家思想是中华民族悠久文化传统的重要组成部分，被誉为东方智慧的瑰宝。它以人为本，追求和谐、仁爱和理性的境界，影响了中国社会数千年的发展。作为儒家文化的传承者和倡导者，我们有责任将这一优秀传统文化内涵解读给海外友人，以期促进不同文化之间的交流与融合。

Il pensiero confuciano è una parte importante della lunga tradizione culturale della nazione cinese, considerato un gioiello di saggezza orientale. Si basa sul principiodi mettere l'uomo al centro, perseguendo l'armonia, benevolenza e il ragionamento, ha influenzato lo sviluppo della società cinese per migliaia di anni. Come eredi e sostenitori della cultura confuciana, abbiamo la responsabilità di interpretare il significato della cultura tradizionale cinese agli amici d'oltremare, al fine di promuovere la comunicazione e l'integrazione tra le diverse culture.

儒家思想的核心价值在于"仁"。仁是指人与人之间的亲和力和关怀之情，强调理解、包容和宽容。这种观念与意大利文化中的"家庭中心主义"有着相似之处。在意大利，人们也非常重视家庭关系，强调共同体的利益，并追求相互支持和团结。

Il valore fondamentale del pensiero confuciano è il "Ren" (benevolenza). Ren si riferisce all'affetto e alla cura tra le persone, accentuando la comprensione, la tolleranza e l'accettazione degli altri. Questo concetto è simile alla cultura italiana che enfatizza il punto di vista dell'"italianità" e la relazione tra i membri della famiglia, valorizzando il l'interesse della comunità e il sostegno reciproco.

当我们谈到中华经典时，《论语》无疑是最具有代表性的作品之一。这部作品以语录的形式记述了孔子及其弟子们的言行，体现了儒家思想的核心理念和道德规范。正如庞大的中华文化遗产一样，《论语》的思想精华远播海外，深深地影响着世界各地的思想家、学者和文化爱好者。

Quando si parla dei classici cinesi, "Lunyu" ("i dialoghi di Confucio") è senza dubbio una delle opere più rappresentative. Quest'opera, scritta come registro delle parole e delle azioni di

Confucio e dei suoi discepoli, rappresenta le idee fondamentali e le norme etiche del pensiero confuciano. Come un grande patrimonio culturale cinese, "Lunyu" ha influenzato profondamente i pensatori, gli studiosi e gli amanti della cultura in tutto il mondo.

儒家文化在海外的影响力也是不可忽视的。作为具有包容性和传播力的文化传统，儒家思想在各国学术界、文化界崛起的同时，也为国际社会所关注。世界各地的大学开设了儒家文化研究课程，翻译出版了大量的儒家经典著作，为世界人民了解中华优秀传统文化提供了渠道。

L'influenza della cultura confuciana all'estero non può essere sottovalutata, dal momento che i suoi valori di inclusività e capacità di diffusione hanno attirato l'attenzione della comunità accademica e culturale globale. Le università di tutto il mondo offrono corsi di studio sulla cultura confuciana e traducono e pubblicano in grande quantità i classici confuciani per offrire un'opportunità ai popoli del mondo di comprendere la cultura cinese.

在当代社会中，践行中华优秀传统文化已成为一种现代价值的追求。这不仅是对历史文化的传承与弘扬，更是对和谐共处、全球文明发展的一种贡献。儒家文化所倡导的中庸之道、诚信、尊重、礼仪等观念，都值得全球社会共同践行与感悟。

Nella società contemporanea, la pratica della cultura tradizionale cinese è diventata una ricerca di vaolori moderni. Questa è non solo una trasmissione e promozione della cultura storica, ma anche una contribuzione alla convivenza armoniosa e progresso della civiltà globale. Concetti come la via di mezzo, l'integrità, il rispetto, la cortesia, suggeriti dalla cultura confuciana, meritano di essere praticati e apprezziati nella società globale.

换言之，儒家思想和中华优秀传统文化并非僵化的概念，而是一个活生生的文化传统。它在海外的影响力不断扩大，为人类社会的发展带来了新的思考，并对全球文化的多样性与交流做出了积极的贡献。

In altre parole, il pensiero confuciano e la cultura tradizionale cinese non sono concetti cristallizzati, ma piuttosto una tradizione culturale viva. La loro influenza all'estero continuerà a crescere, contribuendo ai progressi della civiltà mondiale e alla sua sviluppo armonioso attraverso il promuovimento del dialogo e dello scambio tra diverse culture.

我们应当以中华优秀传统文化为荣，展示其在海外的影响与感召力。通过推动跨文化对话和交流，儒家思想和中华优秀传统文化将继续为世界文明的进步和和谐发展做出贡献。

In sintesi, dovremmo nutrire grande orgoglio per la nostra pregiata cultura tradizionale cinese, e mostrare la sua influenza e capacità di ispirazione ai popoli all'estero. Attraverso la promozione del dialogo interculturale e lo scambio culturale, il pensiero confuciano e la cultura tradizionale cinese continuerà a offrire contributi positivi al progresso della civiltà mondiale e alla sua armoniosa evoluzione.

作品编号：1089
姓　　名：夏冰雪
国　　籍：中国
组　　别：征文类国内成人组
单位名称：华侨大学（厦门校区）

中 越 篇

双语诵读《诗经·小雅·鹿鸣》

《鹿鸣》出自《诗经·小雅》，描绘的是周天子宴请群臣时的场景。从东汉曹操的《短歌行》到唐宋时代的宴会，人们不断地吟唱着《鹿鸣》的诗章，这就是它的魅力。诗中不仅有情感，有欢乐，更有礼乐，有教化，这才是真正的中华大美境界。

呦呦鹿鸣，食野之苹。
Con hươu hoà dịu tiếng kêu, gọi nhau ăn cỏ đồng nội xanh tươi.
我有嘉宾，鼓瑟吹笙。
Ta nay khách quý đến đông, đánh đàn thổi sáo tiệc vui tưng bừng.
吹笙鼓簧，承筐是将。
Sáo kèn rộn rã đông vui, bưng lên rổ lụa trao tặng tân khách.
人之好我，示我周行。
Những người yêu mến ta ơi, xin hãy chỉ ta nẻo đường ta đi.
呦呦鹿鸣，食野之蒿。
Con hươu hoà dịu tiếng kêu, cùng nhau gặm cỏ hao ngoài đồng.
我有嘉宾，德音孔昭。
Ta nay khách quý đến đông, vui tươi rạng rỡ tiếng lừng gần xa.
视民不恌，君子是则是效。
Dạy dân bỏ thói gian tà, lấy quân tử làm gương noi theo.
我有旨酒，嘉宾式燕以敖。
Ta đây có rượu quỳnh tương, khách cùng nâng chén lên đường dạo chơi.
呦呦鹿鸣，食野之芩。
Con hươu hoà dịu tiếng kêu, cùng nhau gặm cỏ cầm cao ngoài đồng.
我有嘉宾，鼓瑟鼓琴。
Ta nay khách quý đến đông, đàn cầm đàn sắt tiếng ca vang lừng.
鼓瑟鼓琴，和乐且湛。
Đàn cầm đàn sắt tiếng ca vang lừng, vui mừng hòa nhịp cùng nhảy tình tang.
我有旨酒，以燕乐嘉宾之心。

Ta đây có rượu quỳnh tương, để cho khách quý vui say thoả lòng.

在中国学习中文是一段充满挑战和成长的经历。刚开始时，面对生疏的语言和文化，我感到有些不知所措。然而，随着时间的推移，我逐渐适应了这种新的语言环境，也开始理解和欣赏中国文化的深厚底蕴。学习中文不仅仅是学习了一门语言，还深入了解了中国人的思维方式和生活方式。每天的语言课程不仅提升了我的听说读写能力，也让我更加敏感地感受到语言背后的文化内涵。例如，中国的成语、俗语和诗歌不仅仅是语言表达，更蕴含着历史典故和智慧。与此同时，我还有机会通过参观历史古迹、体验传统节日和品尝地道美食来直接感受和了解中国文化。这些经历不仅开阔了我的眼界，也让我更加珍惜并尊重不同文化间的差异和共通之处。在这个过程中，我虽然遇到了许多困难和挑战，但正是这些困难和挑战使我更加坚定地学习和进步。总的来说，学习中文让我不断成长，不仅在语言能力上有所提高，更在跨文化交流方面有了深刻的体会。这段宝贵的经历将成为我人生中不可或缺的一部分，激励着我继续探索和学习。

作品编号：4985
姓　　名：杜兰英（Do Lan Anh）
国　　籍：越南
组　　别：诵读类国际组
单位名称：大连外国语大学